FLORENCE NIGHTINGALE

FLORENCE NIGHTINGALE

Reputation and Power

F. B. SMITH

ST. MARTIN'S PRESS NEW YORK

© 1982 F.B. Smith
All rights reserved. For information write:
St. Martin's Press, Inc., 175 Fifth Avenue, New York, N.Y. 10010
Printed in Great Britain
First published in the United States of America in 1982

Library of Congress Cataloging in Publication Data

Smith, F.B.
    Florence Nightingale: reputation and power.
    1. Nightingale, Florence, 1820-1910. 2. Nurses
– England – Biography. I. Title.
RT37.N5S57 1982   610.73'092'4   81-21332

ISBN 0-312-29649-5   AACR2

CONTENTS

Preface

1. Character and Public Life   11

2. Miss Nightingale at Scutari   25

3. The Campaign for Army Sanitary Reform   72

4. India   114

5. Nursing   155

6. Reputation and Power   183

Select Bibliography   205

Index   212

To my daughters, Deborah and Laura

PREFACE

This is a study of some of Florence Nightingale's thoughts in action. It is not an attempt to retell the story of her life. There are already dozens of biographies and hagiographies of the Lady with the Lamp, beginning with the great biography by Sir Edward Cook. His two volumes form a monument worthy of their subject: they show his marvellous industry in combing through a huge archive which must have been largely unsorted when he began; he is accurate and has a keen sense of personality and period; his tact and fairness never falter when narrating the conflicts involving his redoubtable heroine; above all, he conveys the nature and force of Miss Nightingale's superb intelligence. These qualities together set his work on that rare plane with Morley on Gladstone, Maitland on Leslie Stephen and Forster on Dickens.

All subsequent works on Florence Nightingale, including Lytton Strachey's essay and the liveliest and perhaps least known study, that by Margaret Goldsmith, are recensions of Cook. The most pretentious and popular of them, the book by Cecil Woodham-Smith, is careless, often misleading, and ungrateful to Cook, from whom her work is closely derived. Instead of writing another biography, I have tried to discover from a fresh, close examination of the Nightingale Papers, and the manuscripts of some of her allies which were not available to Cook or Goldsmith, and not used by Woodham-Smith, why and how Miss Nightingale assumed the career of reformer, why and how she chose particular strategies and fought particular battles, and how she fared with them. I hope my accounts of these episodes will give the reader a clearer idea of Miss Nightingale's ambitions and beliefs than existing studies provide. I have tried, too, to place her in her context as a social improver and thereby to illuminate more widely the unofficial mind of reform in High Victorian England.

I am deeply grateful to my colleagues in the Research School of Social Sciences for their generous, expert and varied help with this book: Janice Aldridge shepherded my tangled drafts through the new technology; Cameron Hazlehurst supplied me with unlikely but profitable sources; Ken Inglis, Oliver McDonagh and Allan Martin criticised my drafts with marvellous acuity and forbearance; Pauline

Barratt, Jeanette Horrocks and Christine Woodland unearthed crucial facts.

Notes

I would like to clarify one or two points relating to the text. Parentheses within quotes are Miss Nightingale's own and square brackets contain my additions. I have also used square brackets within the notes to indicate my suggested names and dates for letters and memoranda where these are absent or uncertain in the original.

CHARACTER AND PUBLIC LIFE

Florence Nightingale's first chance to deploy her talent for manipulation came in August 1853. She then became resident lady superintendent of the Invalid Gentlewomen's Institution at 1, Upper Harley Street. This charity provided refuge for distressed ladies who paid for single rooms or 'compartments' at the subsidised but still formidable rates of 10/6 or one guinea a week. The Institution was a few years old; it was run down, and ill-managed by separate committees of ladies and gentlemen led by a half-hearted council; it had newly removed to the Upper Harley Street premises. The post was Miss Nightingale's first (though unsalaried) job, her first exercise of independent control. Her father made her an allowance of £500 a year. Her aunt Mai Smith secured her a flat in Pall Mall so that Florence could as she put it, 'clear off . . . at my *own* time' from the Institution.[1] The new superintendent had about five months' practical observation of hospital nursing. She was 33 years old.

Even while she was negotiating for the appointment, Miss Nightingale was insisting upon changes in the nursing arrangements and upon the installation of mechanical improvements at Upper Harley Street. Henceforth each nurse was to sleep next to her ward, and 'the bells of the patients should all ring in the passage outside the nurse's own door *on that story*, and should have a valve which flies open when its bell rings, and *remains* open in order that the nurse may see who has rung'. A piped hot water system and a 'windlass', a kind of tray hoist, were also to be built, to save the nurses' legs when serving meals, and their time in carrying water. The alterations were made. The superintendent-elect supervised the work by letter from Paris, simultaneously with mobilising biddable supporters in Lady Canning, Lady Inglis and Mrs Sidney Herbert to become more active on the committee.[2]

Within a week of her arrival at the Institution Miss Nightingale challenged the governing bodies with her decision to admit Catholics and even Jews. She let it be said that she would resign on the question. The governing bodies capitulated, in writing. There is no evidence that any Catholic or Jew ever sought admission or was admitted; but among the high-minded High Church aristocratic would-be tolerant membership of the committees, it was an inspired choice of issue. The new superintendent also dismissed the incumbent matron, an act which did not technically lie completely within her province, and introduced her own housekeeper, paid from her own pocket.[3] Within weeks of Miss Nightingale's installation the house surgeon resigned and she took a leading part in selecting his successor and defining his duties, once more exceeding her authority. She insisted, yet again upon threat of resignation, on accompanying the doctors on their rounds in order to ensure that orders were executed and that what she called the patients' 'legerdemain of Hysteria' should not prevail with the medical men. The young, zealous and personable Puseyite chaplain was forced out and, against the inclinations of the ladies' committee, the lady superintendent replaced him, with 'good, harmless Mr Garnier', older, physically and theologically nondescript, and tame.

These early victories confirmed Florence Nightingale in a strategy which she followed to the end of her career. She had discovered two great strengths in herself, necessary strengths in all reformers. She fed on an unyielding, unremitting drive to dominate her associates and opponents and to this end she defined issues and goals, distinct from theirs, in the pursuit of which she never faltered, regardless of the worth of her rivals' goals, the cogency of their arguments or the solidity of their facts. She had also an extraordinarily rich and firm imaginative grasp of the relations between individuals and the siting and working of things and of human beings' relations to them. This sense, which we might best describe as Balzacian —uncanny insight into both human obsessions, ambitions and delusions and the concreteness of 'things' — was to enable her to become a successful, indefatigable politician and disposer of persons and objects. Like a novelist drawing upon a month's visit to Bath or a few months as a governess, Florence Nightingale absorbed during her brief visits to hospitals sufficient ideas to sustain a lifetime of admonition, exposition and rule-making.

After three months at the Institution Florence Nightingale reported her successes in a long letter to her father:

> When I entered into service here, I determined that, happen what would, I never would intrigue among the Comtee. Now I perceive that I do all my business by intrigue. I propose in private to A, B, or C the resolution. I think A, B, or C most capable of carrying in Committee, and then leave it to them — and I always win.
>
> I am now in the hey-day of my power. At the last General Committee they proposed and carried (without my knowing

anything about it) a Resolution that I should have £50 per month to spend for the House, and wrote to the Treasurer to advance it me — whereupon I wrote to the Treasurer to refuse it me. Ly Cranworth, who was my greatest enemy, is now, I understand, trumpeting my fame thru' London. And all because I have reduced their expenditure from 1/10 per head per day to 1/-. The opinions of others concerning you depend, not at all, or very little, upon what <u>you</u> are, but upon what <u>they</u> are. Praise and blame are alike indifferent to me, as constituting an indication of what myself is, though very precious as the indication of the other's feeling . . .

Last General Meeting I executed a series of resolutions on five subjects, and presented them as coming from the Medical Men.

The new rules included in-house dispensing of drugs to save druggists' bills, new rules to enforce old provisions limiting each patient's stay to two months, new reduced diets, fixed by the superintendent, and a public advertisement for the Institution, also composed by Miss Nightingale.

All these I proposed and carried in Committee without telling them that they came from <u>me</u> and not from the Medical men — and then, and not till then, I showed them to the Medical Men, without telling <u>them</u> that they were already passed <u>in committee.</u>

It was a bold stroke, but success is said to make an insurrection into a revolution. The Medical Men have had two meetings upon them, approved them all nem-con — and thought they were their own — and I came off in flying colours, no one suspecting of my intrigue, which, of course, would ruin me, were it known.

Intriguers are often torn, as Florence Nightingale usually was, between savouring their triumphs in private and boasting of their victories to intimates. Florence was close to her father, her weak but indispensable ally against her mother, Fanny, and sister, Parthenope. Her revelation of her new powers seems to have been designed to fortify the faith William Nightingale showed in her when he backed her venture into pursuing a life independent of the family circle. The striking thing about Miss Nightingale's intrigues is their elaborateness, often amounting to elaboration for art's sake. At Upper Harley Street her reforms were easily accepted. No group, except the patients and servants, who were voiceless, was threatened by them. Patients and servants could only vote with their feet. Her rules on diet and restricting the sojourns of patients appeared to the doctors and some committee members to be rational and parsimonious, and not inhumane; her public measures promised to enhance the reputation of the Institution and its governors, and to improve the doctors' standing within it. Miss Nightingale chafed at the committee's dilatoriness and slack indulgence to patients rather than their indecisive opposition; by October 1853 she had overcome the 'treasurer who dealt with inexpedient principles and my Committee who dealt with unprincipled expedients . . . My Committee are such children in administration', she informed her father. This is a severe characterisation of men and women and medical men who most of them possessed many more years' experience of the charity arena than their lady superintendent. But none of them matched the force and ingenuity she brought to intrigue.

Miss Nightingale's urge to boast served yet another purpose which she seems not to have recognised. Her setbacks were numerous and glaring but she none the less recorded them, glossed them and laid the blame elsewhere. In November 1853, unprompted, she inaugurated a series of quarterly reports to the ladies' committee. The reports chronicle, jauntily and unaware, the decline of the Institution. During the three months after her arrival, she dismissed or lost one complete set of servants and nurses, with the exception of the cook and one nurse, and there are indications that she subsequently lost a second set. She also changed most of the tradespeople. Typically, she forsook the local grocer for Fortnum and Mason's. Within seven months she apparently was compelled to change several of the tradespeople again. She also started a frenetic bout of home-jam making, producing, on my estimate, many more pots than the patients could possibly consume. The charwoman had disappeared; this had permitted a great saving in money but 'the house has not now the advantage of efficient cleaning − the housemaids being two inexperienced girls, who, though willing and anxious to do all in their power, are unequal to the work without constant superintendence'. Miss Nightingale purchased and begged a great deal of new kitchen utensils, new linen and new furniture. Thereby she raised the capacity of the Institution to 27 beds, but from about March 1854 the average number of inmates was only nine. At this level the Institution's income from paying patients and subscriptions was falling £500 short of the running expenses which had jumped, under the new superintendent, from under £1,000 to £1,500 a year. The dismissals continued: 'I have changed one housemaid, on account of her love of dirt and inexperience, & one nurse, on account of her love of Opium & intimidation'[4]. The superintendent and her matron do not appear to have excelled in picking and training staff.

The shortcomings of the Institution were not, apparently, the lady superintendent's responsibility. She warned the ladies' committee that 'The fact of the deficiency of Patients calls for immediate attention. Otherwise, this Institution will degenerate into a luxurious piece of charity, not worth burthening the public with.' Meanwhile the furiously busy sewing, mending and jam making continued. By May 1854 the bedroom arm-chairs received spare covers made from the former curtains which Miss Nightingale disliked and discarded. The five bedroom sofas were all provided with spare covers, specially lined with calico. In addition, there were one dozen more dusters, two table-cloths, eight toilet-covers, four sand-bags, made out of 'old green baize', and two anti-macassars, together with extra dusters, old towels doubled into cloths (bringing the total to over 50 in six months – there is no indication of what they were used for, or if they were used), carpets repaired, counterpanes, pillow cases and towels mended. By August there were more sofa-covers, two more hassocks, more repairs to the linen, together with 30 more pots of red currant jam and six of jelly, at a cost of twopence per pot. The superintendent reported, in a single sentence apparently as an afterthought, that there was only one nurse left at the Institution. This development had saved £9 in wages for the quarter.

Miss Nightingale blandly concluded that the August report would be her last. She informed the Committee that she considered her work to be done, 'as far as it can be done' and that the Institution had 'been brought into as good a state as its capabilities admit'. 'Good order, good nursing, moral influence & economy' had all been satisfactorily implemented. She had not, she admitted, been able to effect her promised scheme of nurse training, but this was the committee's fault because they had allowed her too few patients. Moreover, the few they had introduced included too many of the wrong kind. Florence Nightingale always took a cool view of patients, and never wavered from her opinion, announced in the February report, that only the 'seriously ill' deserved hospital care. This classification excluded all 'trifling, hysterical or incurable cases'.[5] Such patients tended to press their individual needs and were difficult to control. The results of the superintendent's sharp way with patients shows in the final report. After less than a year of her ministrations only ten patients remained in the Institution, that is, only one-third of the beds were occupied:

five of the ten were dying, another was a child, and yet another was an apparently immovable 'spine case'. (The remaining three, who presumably were open to being discharged or to discharging themselves, included, in Florence Nightingale's judgement, '2 fancy-Patients' and a 'moral case'). About two years before the Harley Street episode Parthe, who was no fool, had confided to her and Florence's special friend, Madame Mohl, that Florence had 'little or none of what is called charity . . . she is ambitious – very, and would like to regenerate the world with a grand *coup de main*. . . I wish she could see that it is the intellectual part that interests her, not the manual. She has no *esprit de conduite* . . . she was a shocking nurse.'[6]

In her August report Miss Nightingale had given notice of three months, though adding that she might stay on for six; but she was already privately negotiating to transfer to King's College Hospital. But before the month was out she had moved without warning her committee to the Middlesex Hospital, she claimed, to supervise the admission of female cholera victims. Our knowledge of this episode comes from the vivid account Miss Nightingale gave Mrs Gaskell, the novelist, later in August while both were on holiday at one of the Nightingale country houses, Lea Hurst. Mrs Gaskell reported to Catherine Winkworth that Florence told her

> The prostitutes come in perpetually – poor creatures staggering off their beat! It took worse hold of them than of any. One poor girl, loathsomely filthy, came in, and was dead in four hours. I held her in my arms and I heard her saying something. I bent down to hear. 'Pray God, that you may never be in the despair I am in at this time.' I said, 'Oh, my girl, are you not now more merciful than the God you think you are going to?' . . . Then, again, I never heard such capital mimicry as she gave of a poor woman, who was brought in one night, when F.N. and a porter were the only people up – every other nurse worn out for the time. . . F.N. undressed the woman, who was half tipsy but kept saying, 'You would not think it ma'am, but a week ago I was in silk and satins; in silk and satins dancing at Woolwich' . . . She got better.

This story is not supported by the Middlesex Hospital archives. Miss Nightingale is not mentioned in the medical superintendent's detailed record of the Hospital's work during the cholera outbreak in late August and the first three weeks of September. He named many devoted workers, from senior physicians to general servants; it is inconceivable that he would have overlooked an exotic lady volunteer. There is no evidence that any of the female patients were prostitutes and the notably proper behaviour of both male and female inmates [the men were mostly 'respectable artisans' from a neighbouring piano factory] suggests that it is unlikely that the females were prostitutes or indeed that they would have been admitted had they been known as such. Moreover, the first female case diagnosed as suffering from 'undoubted [Asian] cholera' was not admitted until 5 September.[7] Miss Nightingale's account of her good works at the Middlesex Hospital constitute a memorable example of her powers as titillating fabulist.

By early October 1854 she was back at Upper Harley Street, preparing to leave for the Crimea. After Miss Nightingale's departure the Institution became moribund, presumably burdened with the debts she had incurred. It seems to have revived somewhat in the 1860s and to have lingered on, beset by financial troubles, into the present century. There is no evidence that Miss Nightingale ever revisited Harley Street or took any further interest in it.

Biographers from Cook to Woodham-Smith, even Strachey and the editor of the quarterly reports I have quoted, are unanimous in representing Miss Nightingale's sojourn at Harley Street as her first great triumph. Yet the evidence they quote is mostly from people like Mrs Gaskell, who never saw the Institution and knew of it only from hearsay from Mr Nightingale, Parthe and Fanny, whose acquaintance with it was equally remote and whose information derived from Florence's own self-justifying letters. Each was gradually enfolded in Florence's great plans. 'Our vocation is a difficult one', she confided in January 1854 to her cousin, Marianne Galton, who had no vocation, 'as you, I am sure, know; and though there are many consolations, and very high ones, the disappointments are so numerous that we require all our faith and trust. But that is enough. I have never repented nor looked back.'[8] The sheer oddity of her enterprise beguiled her relations, as it beguiled the ladies and gentlemen of the committees, underpinned as it was by her insouciant explanations of her failures with staff, patients, tradesmen and accounts and her generalising of the blame; and biographers have been beguiled ever since. Her superbly assured epigrammatic Byronic prose by a process of stylistic legerdemain turns small gains with linen and jellies into mighty personal feats and big set-backs into everybody's moral shortcomings. By style and instinct she was a consummate politician.

The ladies and gentlemen of the committees were the more easily beguiled by Florence Nightingale because she was one of them. Her name represented enormous wealth, expressed in two large country estates and easy membership of the best circles – yet with a difference, quite apart from her superb intelligence. Miss Nightingale came of a politically radical Unitarian dynasty which had become in her parents' generation wealthier, probably, than many of the titled families whose members graced the committees. As her reports reveal, she stood a little apart, unresponsive to the claims of birth.

There is no need for the purposes of this revaluation to recount her childhood and early adulthood. What can be assumed and indeed rather more than can be proved has been delicately told by Cook and splendidly over-dramatised by Strachey and Woodham-Smith. Nearly all of the evidence about Florence Nightingale's conflicts with her mother and Parthe derives from Florence herself, as does her largely retrospective account of her religious travails as an adolescent and young woman. As I shall show later, Florence Nightingale's uncorroborated accounts of her troubles cannot be trusted. The only points that are clear are that William, her father, Fanny and Parthe realised very early that they had a very brilliant obstinate being to cope with and that at every crisis, whether in Florence's foreign travels, her impulsive ventures into local village nursing and other charitable works, her interest in Egyptology, music and natural history, or Monckton Milnes's proposal of marriage, they were supportive. Typically, it was Parthe who took over caring for the owl Florence brought back from Athens. Occasionally Fanny's and Parthe's sympathy wore thin, as when the latter diagnosed Florence as 'a poseur', but in general they appear to have been discerning about Florence's moody egotism and extraordinarily patient in coping with it.[9]

Her father, a clever, amiable dilettante, taught Florence and Parthe fluent Italian, French, Latin and Greek and mathematics. He also required his daughters to write essays on philosophical and historical themes. Both he and Fanny wrote easily and aphoristically and Florence probably acquired her style from them. Parthe's prose is more novelettish and wordy but it is still effective. Florence, unlike Parthe, was blessed with a prodigious memory for anecdotes and quotations from a huge range of reading, from Aristotle, Shakespeare and Milton to Spanish mystics such as St Teresa. It is a measure of the family's intellectual and fashionable standing, and their confidence in their conversational resources, that they knew not only the best of the English intelligentsia but also cultivated such foreign luminaries as

Sismondi, de Tocqueville, Thiers and Élie de Beaumont.

The family's sceptical intellectualism and wealth made them the less ready to give in to Florence's threats to express her capabilities in hospital work or superintending a religious sisterhood. Yet outside conducting a London salon or presiding over charities, controlling a sisterhood was the one avenue to power open to ambitious single women of the upper classes.

Florence's private estimates of her parents and sister did not reciprocate their tolerance. Her father she unsparingly yet accurately characterised as wanting in the strenuousness she found in herself. He was 'a man who has never known what struggle is . . . & having never by circumstances been forced to look into anything, to carry it out'. Had he succeeded in entering Parliament in 1835 he might have found a focus for his abilities but he lost the election because he refused to bribe the voters, and never tried again. On hearing of his death in 1874 Florence noted privately that he was a weak, inexpressive man: 'It was his utter indifference to me – he never cared what I was or what I might become.' A little later on a second slip of paper she added that 'he never had a[n]. . . office of his own'. But she kept up appearances. On about the same day she told at least one close friend, probably Benjamin Jowett, the master of Balliol College Oxford, that her one consolation was that 'my Father cared for my work'.[10] 'Parthe', she privately assured herself in 1851, 'was a child'. Child or not, Parthe was a formidable rival who, as Florence knew, often saw through her, but who nonetheless exemplified a feminity which Florence sought to dismiss as trivial. 'Parthe says I blow a trumpet – that it gives her indigestion – that is alas true – Struggle must make a noise – & every thing that I have to do that concerns my real being must be done with struggle.' Parthe's interests in music, art and dress, and her attempts to reform her sister's dowdiness, Florence rejected as petty and womanish.[11] Parthe had a sharp literary intelligence, too, as her subsequent five novels, essays on agricultural and landholding questions and invaluable *Memoirs of the Verney Family during the Civil War* [vols. I and II] were to prove. Rather than the nonentity depicted by Florence's biographers, she was a considerable competitor. Florence reserved her sharpest comment and keenest resentment for her mother. Fanny was intelligent and formidable. Florence noted that her mother had a 'genius for doing all she wants to do & has never felt the absence of power'. She had 'organized the best society' for her daughter, who did not want it. 'I felt insane at her disappointment.'[12] Her family's ready acknowledgement of Florence's talents made her revolt the harder to sustain. About 1851-2 she wrote, 'There is scarcely anyone who cannot, within his [sic] own experience, remember some instance where some amiable person has been slowly put to death at home — aye, and at an estimable & virtuous home.' Only when Fanny's health broke in the mid-1860s did Florence accept her: 'I don't think my dear mother was ever more touching or interesting to me than she is now in her state of dilapidation', Florence told Madame Mohl in 1866. By 1869 Fanny's memory was 'almost gone', but Florence confided to Dr Sutherland that she found her 'far more respect=able than ever she was before'. Even so, after her mother became completely senile and blind Florence visited her rarely and then only under protest at being, as she told herself in 1872 during her first visit for about six years, 'turned back into this petty, stagnant stifling life'. Florence kept to her room at Embley; her mother was wheeled in to her each day at 12.30 for a brief meeting. Two years later, at the time of her father's death even this meeting with the helpless old woman stopped, 'on account of my [Florence's] weakness'.[13]

Occasionally, as in the preceding note from 1851-2, Miss Nightingale referred to herself in the male gender. She apparently believed, reasonably enough, that her parents would have preferred her, their second and last child, to have been a male, in order to inherit the estate and continue the new family name, changed from Shore with a fresh accession of wealth in 1815. Her father liked to praise his daughter as the possessor of 'quite a man's mind', while Florence in one of her imaginary conversations with her mother in 1851-2 informed her that 'with my "talents" & my "European reputation"' she was not 'going to stay dangling about my mother's drawing-room . . . I shall go out and look for work . . . You must look upon me as your son . . . You must consider me married or a son.'[14]

Her parents had encouraged her to marry Richard Monckton Milnes, the rising Liberal social reformer and literary man, during his nine-year-long courtship during the 1840s. But their hopes that Florence would thereby realise her talents for conversation and philanthropy in becoming a great London hostess foundered on her resolve not to marry and perforce subordinate her career. As she remarked in her anonymously published *Suggestions for Thought* (first drafted 1851-2) 'Marriage is the most selfish of all ties . . . as Milton put "He thy God, thou mine".' 'Can one man or woman', she added, 'be more interesting to us than mankind? I know that I could not bear his life — that to be nailed to a continuation & exaggeration of my present life without hope of another would be intolerable to me.' John Stuart Mill, whom she subsequently bullied into reading her manuscript, noted that her Milton quotation was incorrect: 'Milton says worse than this: he says He thy God, I his.'[15] Mill, theoretically a more thoroughgoing egalitarian feminist whose correction was even more egregiously inaccurate, prudently did not draw the implications of Miss Nightingale's slip. Her emotional attachments were directed to her own sex and from adolescence onwards she engaged occasionally in sentimentally effusive protestations of love for various female relatives and acquaintances. These sudden outbursts, during which Florence lost her usual steeliness and even her curt prose-style, were to continue into her old age.

Miss Nightingale's struggles to reconcile her egotism with her unfixed, non-Biblical, non-sacerdotal religiosity were equally explosive. When she reached her early twenties she had learned to exist with her dilemma by imagining herself a victim of special persecution and as destined endlessly to re-live Christ's crucifixion. Thereby she mortified her narcissism. Whilst travelling in Egypt in 1849 she experienced a severe crisis of suffocated ambition. She recorded in her diary that Christ appeared to her on five occasions, two of them on successive days. At each apparition she heard Him ask her the same general question: 'Would I do good for Him, for Him alone without the reputation?' (7 March 1849). A week later, at Thebes, 'as I sat in the large dull room waiting for the letters, God told me what a privilege he had reserved for me . . . & how I had been blind to it. If I were never thinking of the reputation how I should be better able to see what God intends for me.'[16]

Soon after this visitation Florence Nightingale accepted an instruction she heard from God to proceed, against the wishes of the family, to Kaiserswerth, to sample the communal nursing and reformative duties of the Lutheran evangelical deaconesses gathered there by Pastor Fliedner. Her visit may have satisfied her urge to defy the family but she found Kaiserswerth nursing grubby and ineffectual and the devotions of the community profoundly anti-intellectual; although she never ceased subsequently to praise Kaiserswerth and Fliedner in public. Indeed Kaiserswerth was a valuable experience for her: it provided a living lesson in what to avoid both in the shape of high-minded, affected spirituality and in stupid nursing routines which ignored common cleanliness, rational comfort, and punctuality.[17] Miss Nightingale determined that nurses should serve their Creator by helping patients physically and morally and not by worshipping while their charges died in their own filth. Still, the dedication and obedience of the deaconesses impressed her. They were 'consecrated' by the pastor after probation, but did not take religious vows. Florence Nightingale approved this compromise. She distrusted Catholic and High-Church sisterhood vows because they enjoined obedience to a supernatural regime which deflected commands issued by rational mundane authority and provided an excuse for non-compliance. Nurses should nurse to meet God's purposes and to advance their personal quest for selflessness, but under human direction – as it turned out – Nightingale direction. Moreover, vows entailed a self-abased striving for the humblest office, whereas, Miss Nightingale wrote in 1851-2, 'we should strive for that we can best do and what is most attractive & thereby find our duty'.[18] She formed this view of nursing, like her other beliefs, early in her career when she knew little of their results in practice, but she never wavered from her formulas. Her approach was *a priori* all her life.

There is another element, rather less obvious, which must be added: the narcissistic quality of her personality. Throughout her career there is abundant evidence to attest to this strand in her behaviour. Florence Nightingale's diaries and hundreds of letters and private memoranda show her to have been an untiring watcher of herself. She observed every play of her intelligence and weighed it, fluctuating between self-admiration and self-contempt. Her self-regard was never stable. In public she was gracious and ingratiating, immensely productive and politically effective. In private she indulged in bouts of self-depreciation, scorn of others, and guilt for her passion for fame and her destructive use of her allies. Within the family her father, her mother and Parthe were too easy and yielding, and emotionally inaccessible, to supply the tensions and gratifications that Florence craved. Her mother's retrospective accounts of Florence's essays on keeping pets, sick nursing in the village and management of her dolls all indicate, however falsified and toned down they were in memory, that from childhood Florence was alternately unpredictably wilful and petulant, and a docile seeker of adult approval. Her mother's remarks also indicate that neither she nor her husband was very interested in Florence's enthusiasms. As Florence reminded herself in the *Suggestions* of 1851-2,

'God makes the family' . . . Perhaps it is just the contrary. God makes attractions – & the principle of the family is <u>not</u> to go by attractions . . . In an amiable family, the common cause of things is for everyone to give up just enough to prevent such a 'row' as would make it intolerable.

— Good for us to practise self-denial & forebearance — But if God wants us to do what we like — we overturn the family. Man is born into the world — woman into a family. Woman must be born into world to find joy — to exercise their powers. People are 'robbed & murdered' by their families & no one notices — their time to do original thought is murdered.[19]

Outside the family Miss Nightingale used auxiliaries to obey her orders and reinforce her self-esteem; she dropped them when they rebelled or lost their ability to service that esteem. She yearned for intimacy, to fuse herself with idealised others, yet she retained a profound sense of her psychological distance from other human beings, a contradiction, as I shall outline later, that permeated her dealings with such confidants as Sidney Herbert and Mary Jones, the superintendent of a High Church nursing sisterhood. Florence Nightingale's sexual relationships remained infantile. She never permitted herself to become unguardedly close or unreservedly dependent upon anyone. Throughout her career she made public emotional investments in others, in shared great plans and objects, and when the others' commitment wavered or their contribution disappointed her, as invariably they did, she ostentatiously withdrew the outlay and reinvested it in herself. In all her ventures she played by turns the role of trusting acolyte and the only begetter who was always let down. Ultimately she had made a mystic marriage with God's work: 'real mothers & fathers of the human race', she told her soul mate Jowett about 1865, 'are not the males and females, according to the flesh'.[20] They were instead spiritual heroines and heroes consecrated to spirituality. In this scheme of things there was little place for earthly competitors, as the Crimean adventure was to show.

Notes

1. Sir Harry Verney (ed.) *Florence Nightingale At Harley Street*, (London, 1970), p.viii.
2. F.N. to Madame Mohl, 8 April 1853, Sir Edward Cook, *The Life Of Florence Nightingale* (2 vols., London, 1913), vol. I, p.130.
3. F.N. to Lady Canning, 29 April [1853], BL Add.Mss 45796 ff.17-28.
4. F.N. to William Edward Nightingale (her father), 3 December 1853, BL Add.Mss 45790, ff.152-6.
5. Verney, *Harley Street*, p.28.
6. Quoted in Margaret Leland Goldsmith, *Florence Nightingale. The Woman and the Legend*, (London, 1937), p.97.
7. Mrs Gaskell to Emily Shaen, 27 October 1854, in J.A.V. Chapple and Arthur Pollard (eds.), *The Letters of Mrs Gaskell* (Manchester, 1966), p.318;

'Report on the recent outbreak of Cholera near the Hospital; and the means adopted to meet the influx of patients, 23 September 1854', Admission Books for 1854, Middlesex Hospital Archives. I am indebted to Mr W.R. Winterton, FRCS, FRCOG, for help with these sources.

8. Cook, *Nightingale*, vol. I, pp.137-8.

9. Goldsmith, *Nightingale*, p.112.

10. F.N. memoranda, BL Add.Mss 43402 f.79 [1851?]; 'My Father', BL Add.Mss 45845 ff.136, 139 [January 1874?]; F.N. to [Benjamin Jowett?] draft with first page missing [January 1874?], Nightingale Collection, Greater London Record Office, SU 214.

11. F.N. memoranda, Whit Monday, 8 June 1851, 15 June [1851?], BL Add.Mss 43404 ff.72-6.

12. F.N. Memorandum [1851?] BL Add.Mss 43402, f.80.

13. F.N. Draft for 'Stuff' (later partly incorporated into 'Suggestions for thought') [1851-2?], BL Add.Mss 45843 f.18; Goldsmith, *Nightingale*, p.259; F.N. to Sutherland [1869?], BL Add.Mss 45754 f.61; Memorandum, Embley, 7 August 1872, BL Add.Mss 45844 f.18; F.N. to Lizzie Herbert (copy), 8 January 1874, BL Add.Mss 43396 f.220.

14. 7 December 1851 quoted in Goldsmith, *Nightingale*, p.99.

15. F.N. draft for 'Suggestions, vol. II', BL Add.Mss 45840 f.126.

16. F.N. Diary 7, 16 March 1850, BL Add.Mss 45846 ff.23-5.

17. F.N. to Sutherland [December 1864?] BL Add.Mss 45751 ff.250-1.

18. F.N. 'Suggestions', draft [1851-52?] BL Add.Mss 45838 ff.220.

19. F.N. 'Suggestions', draft [1851-2?] BL Add.Mss 45838 f.171.

20. F.N. to Jowett, draft [1865?] BL Add.Mss 45783 f.68.

2 MISS NIGHTINGALE AT SCUTARI

Miss Nightingale's expedition to the Crimean War had no British precedent. She was free to make her own rules. When she decided to go, her first steps were to oust competitors and secure sole authority.

The idea that women should help nurse the British wounded, as the Sisters of Charity helped nurse the French, was first propounded by W.H. Russell, *The Times* special correspondent at the front. It had not occurred to anyone at home. Russell's despatches from Constantinople at the end of September 1854, after the casualties from the Battle of the Alma had arrived, were published in London on 9 October. He passionately described the collapse of the army nursing system and the agonies of the common soldiers. Such collapses and neglect had accompanied the army through centuries, but for the first time the mismanagement and suffering were recounted at middle- and upper-class breakfast tables. Russell's reports aroused two early volunteer leaders of nurses: the Rev. Mr Hume, a former chaplain at the Birmingham General Hospital with seven years' experience of the army, undertook to bring his two daughters and twelve paid nurses; Lady Maria Forester, a philanthropic widow of Evangelical persusasion, offered herself to lead nurses from the Low Church Fitzroy Square training institution. Miss Nightingale apparently decided to head an expedition on 11 October, after she learned of Lady Maria's move.[1]

Unlike Hume and Lady Maria, who applied only to the War Office and to Dr Andrew Smith, the head of the Army Medical Department, Miss Nightingale sought personal backing at the highest level. The Home Secretary, Lord Palmerston, a neighbour in Hampshire, agreed to ask the Foreign Secretary, Lord Clarendon, to write on her behalf to the ambassador at Constantinople, Lord Stratford de Redcliffe. She also saw Dr Smith and secured an introduction to the Chief Medical Officer at Scutari establishing her right to nurse in his hospitals. By 14 October she had, according to Parthe, persuaded Lady Maria Forester that she would 'not have been of the slightest use' at the Crimea, and Miss Nightingale had accepted the £200 Lady Maria had raised for her venture.[2] All these transactions were concluded before Miss Nightingale received any official invitation to lead a party at Scutari. Only on 14 October did she charge Mrs Herbert with obtaining her severance from the Harley Street Institution, of which she was still nominally head, and with securing specific authorisation for the expedition from Sidney Herbert and the War Secretary, the Duke of Newcastle. In an artful postscript she put the onus on to Lizzie Herbert and tightened the web of personal allegiances: 'Perhaps it is better to keep it quite a private thing, and not apply to Govt qua Govt.' On the morning of that same Saturday 14th, before she announced her intentions to the Herberts, Miss Nightingale sent her uncle Sam Smith to her parents to obtain their consent.[3]

Then follows one of the dramatic set-pieces of Victorian history. Miss Nightingale's biographers, even sceptical Strachey, agree that her announcement of her readiness to go to the Crimea and Sidney Herbert's invitation, written on Sunday 15 October, crossed in the mail. Thereby a charming coincidence is revealed and two great minds and hearts are shown as one. The story was popularised by Lord Stanmore's *Sidney Herbert* (compiled from about 1890 and published in 1906), using letters selected by Miss Nightingale. The episode is worth scrutiny because it exhibits Miss Nightingale's *modus operandi* and the hagiographical temptations of even the best biographers. The first oddity is that Miss Nightingale's letter was not addressed to Sidney Herbert, but to his wife. Moreover, Miss Nightingale asked specifically about applying for official sanction for her venture to the Duke of Newcastle, the Secretary for War, within whose province the issue lay. Sidney Herbert had no proper standing in the matter and no authority to invite anyone to help nurse the army. His remark about the Bracebridges — old friends of the Herberts and Nightingales with whom they had travelled in Rome in 1847 and whom Florence had accompanied to Egypt — that he was certain they would go with her; his assurance that Lizzie was writing to Mrs Bracebridge about the mission and the need to have the consent of the Nightingale family, together with the shelving of Lady Maria Forester and the other early volunteer, Mr Hume — 'the difficulty of finding nurses who are at all versed in their business is probably not known to Mr Hume' — despite his seven years experience — imply an appreciation of the situation that came from coaching by Mrs Herbert, coached in turn by Miss Nightingale. The unusual briskness of Herbert's letter and its remarkable confidence that Miss Nightingale would accept such an extraordinary commission from the War Office and place herself instantly at its disposal allow us to infer that Herbert's letter was the formal product of a prior understanding. This inference is strengthened by Parthe's private account of the affair, written on Monday 16 October, to Richard Monckton Milnes, whom she had no reason to deceive. Parthe explained that all was resolved on Friday 13 October, that is, before Miss Nightingale wrote to Mrs Herbert. On that day the Bracebridges, indomitable travellers both, decided to go and the Nightingale family then immediately adopted the venture.

The underlying purpose of Miss Nightingale's formal approach to the Herberts also emerges in Parthe's letter to Monckton Milnes:

> There has been but one feeling tho' in all the Institutions, they have given up their rules, the 10 Sisters of Mercy wished to take a head, Miss Sellon wished to go herself with her 8, St John's Home wanted to send a chief with their 6, but all gave way & Florence is sole leader.[4]

Sole leadership was a *sine qua non* with Miss Nightingale. The War Office and Sidney Herbert found it easiest to allow this imperious, unstoppable woman to lead. Within the pertinent areas of hospital experience and proven ability to select and manage nurses her claims were insubstantial. She did not emphasise them in her letters to Mrs Herbert; instead, she begged Mrs Herbert 'or some one of my Committee [to] write to Lady Stratford [the Constantinople ambassador's wife] to say, "This is not a lady but a real Hospital Nurse", . . . "And she has experience"'.[5] Quite apart from Rev. Mr. Hume, the superioress of the Sisters of Mercy had much more nursing experience and knowledge of handling women, while Miss Sellon was a proven charismatic, creative, dominating person with six years' experience of directing nurses. The chaplain of St John's House was also used to commanding women whose vocation was nursing. But their Catholic, Puseyite and High Church affiliations, amidst the febrile bigotry of the early 1850s, put them all beyond consideration. Miss Nightingale had the advantage in the government's view of being safely Protestant but otherwise religiously neuter.

Miss Sellon, who had offered herself and eight of her followers, without telling them, acquiesced with uncharacteristic meekness when Miss Nightingale took over her followers but rejected her. Miss Sellon enforced austerities on her communities which she never observed herself.[6] The Crimea promised a hard life. The St John's House chaplain, Rev. C.P. Shepherd, proved more obdurate. He had applied on 13 October to his bishop, Blomfield, for permission to head a party of seven nurses. A letter in *The Times* of that day, opening a Crimea fund with £200, 'removed', as one of Shepherd's female coadjutors observed, 'all hesitation on the score of Funds'. Miss Nightingale had to use Sidney Herbert to direct the Bishop of London to squash him.

On 17 October Herbert informed the Bishop that:

> Miss Nightingale has consented to go out to Scutari to undertake the
> whole management of the female nursing — Her great hospital
> experience & skill & courage in surgical treatment together with her
> administrative capacity peculiarly fit her for the undertaking and in
> a military hospital where subordination is everything, without some
> recognized head with ample authority, there [?] will be no chance
> of success. She is in communication with the nurses of St John's
> House & I have no doubt will take them with her.

Blomfield, who had already on 14 October told Shepherd that he 'quite
approve[d]' of his proposal and had commended it to Herbert, now
apparently accepted Shepherd's exclusion, for we hear no more of him.[7]
The Evangelical Protestant communities at Fitzroy Square and
Devonshire Square, suspicious of the Puseyite-Papist ambience of the
Nightingale contingent and, probably, piqued by the rejection of Lady
Maria Forester, refused to surrender control of their nurses to Miss
Nightingale who thereupon refused to have them. None went to the
Crimea.

   This rebuff was the more damaging to Miss Nightingale because she
had been forestalled in the race to Scutari by a group of Catholic nuns.
Bishop Thomas Grant of Southwark had seized the opportunity to
counter anti-Roman feeling by making his nuns into conspicuous
patriots. He unhesitatingly made his nuns subject to Miss Nightingale's
general superintendence and got ten of his contingent, Sisters of Mercy
from Bermondsey, to France within 24 hours of informing them that
they were going. Thereby they took a four day lead on the official
party, but Miss Nightingale ensured that Grant ordered them to wait
in Paris until she caught up.[8] Their rushed travel arrangements were so
incomplete that they would hardly have been able to proceed without
her anyway. The Bermondsey sisters were experienced nurses. Grant
had rashly promised ten nuns: Bermondsey refused to supply more
than five. He finally unearthed five others at the Convent of the
Daughters of the Faithful Virgin at Norwood, where they conducted
an orphanage. They were members of a high caste French order, with
no tradition of nursing. Bishop Grant signed on their behalf Miss
Nightingale's tightly worded agreement subjecting them to her
authority. Miss Nightingale had composed the agreement and had it
lithographed within four days of deciding on the expedition. Like the
Anglicans, the Catholic nuns went without a chaplain.[9]

   Bishop Grant had also sought nuns from Ireland but was brusquely rejected by the Irish bishops. Now the despatch of the Bermondsey sisters, chaplainless and subject to a Protestant superintendent, provoked a reaction. Father Henry Edward Manning, Miss Nightingale's and the Herberts' erstwhile religious mentor in Rome in 1847, now a Catholic and as always an astute, compulsive politician, moved to ensure that the Catholics contingent retained its identity. The expedient way of doing this was to gather a party of Irish nuns reinforced by their own chaplains. Manning wanted to drive the point home: he envisaged at least 20 Catholic nurses, all religious – 'we shall not do well to take any seculars'.[10] Sister Evelyn Bolster gives the details of his negotiations to obtain an offer of Irish nuns and there is no need to recount their devious course here. The salient moves in the challenge were, first, the offer to the War Office on 18 October by the Vicar-General of Dublin, Dr Youl, of twenty Irish Sisters of Mercy, to be accompanied by a chaplain, all to be paid for by the government. The first move nearly misfired because the Irish bishops still proved obstructive (many of them were in Rome for the promulgation of the doctrine of the Immaculate Conception and found it easy to hinder the Manning initiative by dilatory letter-writing). In the event only eleven Sisters of Mercy came from convents in Ireland and the final total of fifteen was made up with nuns from Liverpool and Chelsea. Meanwhile, despite Manning's desperate pressure, Herbert and the War Office had still not agreed to the chaplain.[11]

The second part of the challenge was the selection of Rev. Mother Mary Francis Bridgeman to head the Irish contingent. She was less senior than Rev. Mother Mary Clare of the Bermondsey sisters and she had less experience in dealing with the sick and with English authorities, but Rev. Mother Clare was mild and Rev. Mother Francis was the opposite. Indeed she was the analogue in beefier form of Florence Nightingale. Mother Francis was born in 1813 into an ancient Irish gentry family, with a rakehelly father. Her mother died when she was five and she was brought up by a maiden aunt who devoted herself to rescuing prostitutes and visiting the sick in Limerick. They nursed together during the cholera epidemic of 1832. Miss Bridgeman joined the new and rapidly growing Sisters of Mercy in 1838, and soon emerged as a forceful organiser and administrator, used to being heard and obeyed. Father Manning found her 'ardent, high-tempered and . . . somewhat difficult . . . but truly good'.[12]

Rev. Mother Francis collected her nuns together in Dublin while Manning worked to win the chaplaincy issue. Led by Mother Francis, the nuns acceded to a written code. This code assumed the presence of a chaplain; it subtly transgressed the War Office ruling against proselytism; it ignored the existence of the other nurses in the Nightingale contingent, even the London nuns; it set aside Miss Nightingale's authority by not mentioning her and instead interposed Rev. Mother Francis as sole head of the nurses and intermediary with the hospital authorities. The relevant clauses run:

> They shall not discuss religious topics with those outside the Catholic Church. If a desire for knowledge of Catholic doctrine is evinced, they shall inform the chaplain ... Any notable difficulties which the Sisters may experience in the discharge of their hospital duties, are to be mentioned to the Superior, who if she deems it expedient, shall refer the matter to the administrator of the hospital.[13]

By 30 October Manning had still not prevailed with the War Office. Afraid that the Irish nuns would disband and return to their convents, he wrote to John Henry Newman to tell them that the War Office had agreed to the nuns having a chaplain attached at the hospital, chosen from among the six or seven Catholic chaplains already with the army, and that the party would be permitted to form a separate community under their own superior in distinct quarters. Manning presented this as a major concession from the War Office but it was only what had already been promised to the Bermondsey and Norwood nuns. It is even uncertain whether it was a specific concession: I have been unable to find it in the War Office papers. (I did not obtain access to the Manning Papers.) Concession or not, Manning was resolved that the Irish party should go: 'I do not know', he warned Newman, 'what would do us more harm or injustice than to be backward at this moment.' Newman did nothing: he kept clear of the intrigue.[14]

Rev. Mother Francis finally sought to force matters by journeying to London and confronting Manning and Herbert on 3 November. Herbert gave ground. He agreed that the Bridgeman party might be accompanied by a chaplain of their choice, but the priest was to be unofficial and not their 'chaplain'. He also acknowledged Rev. Mother Francis's standing as superior of her group, although there is no evidence that Herbert saw this arrangement as more than the equivalent recognition accorded the heads of the Bermondsey and Norwood contingents with respect to their duties as religious. This point gained, Rev. Mother Francis spent the next fortnight visiting London convents and hospitals in a new move to increase her contingent by 20. Effectively, she was enlarging the outsiders' challenge into an insiders' take-over bid.

This transformation was furthered by Rev. Mother Francis's new-found disciple, Mary Stanley. They were introduced to one another by Manning, who had been Miss Stanley's spiritual director since at least 1847, when she had been yet another of the Nightingale party of pilgrims in Rome. She was the daughter of the Anglican Bishop of Norwich and sister to A.P. Stanley, the future Dean of Westminster, with whom she appears to have had an unusually close relationship. Mary Stanley was a gawky, short-sighted woman, plodding through life aspiring to parish visiting and other good works, successively attaching herself to more powerful personalities. In 1852 she had exhibited a short devotion to Florence Nightingale. Now, after her attachment to Manning, she immediately came under the thumb of Rev. Mother Francis. Miss Stanley was to announce her conversion to Catholicism at the Crimea. In the three weeks to 1 December Mary Stanley's High Anglican contacts and Rev. Mother Francis's drive through the London convents (she finally had to go as far as Liverpool) yielded 15 Catholic nuns, 22 nurses and nine 'ladies', a contingent more than double the size of Manning's original offer.

Sidney Herbert and the War Office took fright and ordered absolutely that no priest should travel with the nuns. With what must have been deliberate provocation, midst the anti-Catholic furor of the early 1850s, Rev. Mother Francis had already equipped herself with a Jesuit, made available by the Vicar General of Westminster.[15] It seems that the Irish hierarchy refused to release any secular Irish priests. The Jesuit, Father William Ronan, justified his selection: he emerged in the Crimea as an unrelenting bigot who fostered Rev. Mother Bridgeman's worst tendencies.

The news of Father Ronan's appointment and Herbert's new-found resistance put Manning in a fresh dilemma. Using Mary Stanley as go-between, he tried to placate Herbert and compel Rev. Mother Bridgeman to shed Father Ronan:

I have from first to last understood that the chaplain is not to travel with the Sisters. I have said so and written ten times. If power of mine can hinder it, it shall not be. Say this to Sidney Herbert in my name, and tell him I have borne many censures on this point, and will do so to the end for his sake.[16]

Father Ronan promised Manning not to travel with the nuns.

Rev. Mother Bridgeman completed her challenge by refusing on her own behalf and forbidding her sisters to sign the agreement, endorsed by the British cabinet, acknowledging Miss Nightingale's headship of the mission. She took her stand on the document agreed among the Irish nuns establishing her own headship of her nuns which was a private agreement among the volunteered nuns; it had no standing with the War Office or the Nightingale contingent. Sidney Herbert gave way and Rev. Mother Bridgeman signed a copy of the sisters' agreement for his benefit. The final irony of Manning's offer and the Irish challenge was the admission that the sisters could not afford the outfitting and incidental expenses of the journey to Scutari. Manning scraped £200 together:[17] at over £14 a head they cost the equivalent of a common nurse's wages for five months.

Miss Nightingale, after the rebuff from the Evangelical institutions and the contretemps with Rev. Mr Shepherd, had made the confirmation of her authority a cabinet matter. On 19 October she secured from Sidney Herbert official notification of her headship. The nature of the authority conveyed in the letter bespeaks Miss Nightingale's instigation, but the loose drafting suggests that Herbert composed it:

Having consented at the pressing instance of the Government to accept the office of Superintendent of the Female Nursing establishment in the English General Military Hospitals in Turkey, you will, on your arrival there, place yourself at once in communication with the Chief Medical Officer of the Hospital at Scutari, under whose orders and direction you will carry on the duties of your appointment.

Everything relating to the distribution of the nurses ... their allotment to particular duties, is placed in your hands, subject, of course, to the sanction and approval of the Chief Medical Officer ...

I feel confident that ... you will impress upon those acting under your orders the necessity of the strictest attention to the regulations of the Hospital, and the preservation of that subordination which is indispensable in every Military Establishment.

And I rely on your ... vigilance carefully to guard against any attempt being made among those under your authority, selected as they are with a view to fitness and without any reference to religious creed, to make use of their position in the Hospitals to tamper with ... the religious opinions of the patients ... and at once to check any such tendency and to take, if necessary, severe measures to prevent its repetition.[18]

The reference to Turkey, rather than to the seat of war in the Crimea, shows that the Nightingale mission was conceived, sensibly, as a minor ancillary aid in the general base hospitals away from the front. Herbert and possibly Miss Nightingale at this stage did not envisage the whole war area as a field to be subjected to her ministrations. Miss Nightingale, as head of her nurses, was made responsible to the Chief Medical Officer at Scutari, Dr Duncan Menzies; implicitly, this made her subject to the Chief Medical Officer at the Crimea, Dr John Hall, but apparently Herbert and Nightingale saw no need to define this relationship. It might be thought that omission of the Crimea reveals a careful limitation on Miss Nightingale's ambitions: but that entails a prevision on Herbert's part which he does not otherwise display. In the result both omissions were to cause trouble.

While preparing the mission Miss Nightingale concentrated upon establishing her authority with government and heads of religious houses. She left the recruitment of nurses to loyal busybodies like Mrs Herbert, Lady Canning and Mrs Bracebridge. Nurses proved as scarce as nuns: there was no rush to the colours. Their wages had to be raised to about double the going rate: 12 shillings to 14 shillings a week plus keep and uniform, rising to 18 shillings to 20 shillings a week after a year's good conduct. Selina Bracebridge, Florence Nightingale's dearest 'E' during the Egyptian tour, was especially haughty to the candidates she inspected. During the preparation week she travelled to Oxford to look over the potential recruits assembled by Miss Felicia Skene, another High Anglican lady active in the prison visiting and prostitute rescue business. Miss Skene, who seems to have resented her supercession by Mrs Bracebridge as recruiting agent, recalled the lady as acting like the Duchess (recte — Queen of Hearts?) in *Alice in Wonderland*. She lined the postulants along a wall and fired 'sudden questions' at them. If the questions were not answered immediately and to her satisfaction she barked, 'She won't do; send her out.'[19] No 'ladies' were accepted for the mission, apparently by Miss Nightingale's decision. The exertions of Lady Canning, Mrs Herbert and Mrs Bracebridge, after the impossibly old and blatantly dissolute had been excluded, yielded 38 nurses, only 14 of whom were 'seculars'; the rest comprised six St Johnites and eight Sellonites and the ten Catholic nuns.[20]

Mr Bracebridge, a veteran of the Greek War of Independence, also secured his role in the drama. He assumed the management of the accounts for the trip and attempted to take charge of protecting the nuns' and nurses' virtue. Once in Turkey he also set up as a propagandist for the mission, with bad results for the standing of the party. Irrepressible, on his return from the war he adopted the cause of Shakespeare's innocence of deer-stealing, and of protecting the Bard's house at Stratford. He also promoted reformatories, and garotting as tidier than hanging, especially for female and other subjects deficient in weight.[21]

Miss Nightingale and her party had a wretched journey. Their ship, the *Vectis*, was ill-found and they ran into heavy storms, which continued almost throughout the eight days of the voyage. Like most of the group, Miss Nightingale suffered badly from prolonged sea-sickness. Her cabin and the Bracebridges' room were separate from the rest who were huddled in the airless fo'castle, awash with vomit. Even so, she arrived exhausted. The terrible journey weakened her, as it weakened others in the party, even before they reached their work. The delicate Norwood nuns proved feeble at Scutari and Miss Nightingale sent them home within the month. Sister Ethelreda, one of the Sellonites, also never recovered from the journey and could not eat the coarse Scutari food. She went home shortly after the Norwood sisters, together with four of the nurses from St John's Home who rejected the discipline and privations of Scutari life.[22]

The poor, skimpy food and the sordid living conditions were army routine. The new element, unique in the history of war, was that some of the human beings involved could choose to leave the shambles and report them, unpunished. Miss Nightingale quickly diagnosed the weaknesses in the army hospital system and their consequent limitations upon her ambitions. From hindsight the weaknesses are glaring, but no military man or minister for war had done anything about them; melioration meant money. The fundamental difficulty was the subordination of the medical officers to their military colleagues. Medical officers were inhibited from taking decisions and implementing plans to ensure optimal sanitary safety and hospital comfort for their charges. Decisions about the siting and management of camps, the ordering of the soldiers' food and dress and the organisation of regimental and base hospitals were the side results of military officers' choices of ground and disposition for tactical and display purposes. The men drafted as orderlies in the hospitals were ne'er-do-wells or the walking sick: the military officers retained the ablest men for the fighting and as camp servants; there was no separate trained orderly corps. Soldiers' wives sho had traditionally done some nursing and washing around the hospitals had been eased out in 1832. There had been a move to revive female nursing when the army left for the East, but it had been rejected because, as the Duke of Newcastle explained, 'it was not liked by the military authorities'.[23]   Within the hospitals authority over medicines, food and furniture for the sick was divided between the medical officers who ordered the items and the purveyors who were supposed to supply them, and the ill-supervised orderlies who were supposed to administer them to the patients. The outside transport of wounded and supplies was yet another distinct authority; the men in the corps were notorious, even in the army, for their slovenliness. At best, in times of peace and in benign weather, the routine was inefficient and callous. The death rate from disease and gangrenous wounds was heavy and steady. Disasters — typhus and dysentery outbreaks, severe battles, lost supply ships — all of which occurred immediately before and after the Nightingale party assumed their posts in the two Scutari hospitals, overwhelmed the system and men died in their hundreds. Two thousand wounded and sick men were unloaded into the Scutari hospitals in the month after the battles of Balaclava (25 October) and Inkerman (5 November). During that same month about 330 men died in the hospitals from scurvy, dysentry, typhoid and other diseases. During the worst of the winter the death rate was to climb to about 46 per cent of all admissions.[24]

Under the direction of the surgeons, Miss Nightingale's sisters and nurses were set to prepare the prescribed diets and extras such as beef tea and wine for the patients, dress their wounds, make up palliasses — these were almost non-existent when the Nightingale party arrived — cajole the orderlies into caring for their patients, and write letters for the illiterate, the dying and the dead. They also distributed fresh clothes and bedding from Miss Nightingale's stock, supplied by *The Times* and other patriotic relief funds.

Miss Nightingale believed that only the 'really sick', those unable to help themselves, and the dying required nursing. Nursing comprised watching, giving medication under doctors' orders, feeding under doctors' orders, and washing patients and bed linen. Her belief prevented her from using the nurses of both contingents to the best advantage. The 43 nurses who were to help nurse a projected 500 patients at Koulali in May 1855 she regarded as dangerously numerous. 'The greater the number the harder they are to manage.' Ultimately they endangered the army too; unsupervised nurses 'over indulged' soldiers who were unused to cosseting and thereby had their discipline 'spoilt'.[25] As at Harley Street, Miss Nightingale failed to win the allegiance of subordinates or to allocate tasks efficiently. The nuns and nurses engaged in the kitchens and the administration of the extra

comforts were overworked, while the nurses detailed to wash, feed and
solace patients were underemployed, especially as they were forbidden
to speak with their charges and prevented from attending convalescents
who, the Lady Superintendent believed — perhaps rightly — should help
themselves. Moreover, such attendance led to intimacies which were
'obviously objectionable'.[26] The male orderlies, dressers and soldiers
continued to do the bulk of the work in the hospitals. The nuns' and ladies'
delicacy, reinforced by the men's modesty, generally inhibited them from
dealing with the men's evacuations and with wounds to their abdominal
regions. Emma Fagg, an experienced St John's nurse, complained from
'Scrutaria' Barracks Hospital in early January 1855 that she and her
colleagues found it a 'great *disappointment* . . . we are not fatigued with
our duties'.[27]

The slackness of the orderlies, apothecaries and purveyors, the filth
and muddle, the general unfitness of affairs, affronted Miss Nightingale.
Her resource was her independent store of medicines, food and
clothing and her headship of her nurses. Her lever on the doctors and
the military authorities was her link with Sidney Herbert reinforced by
her role as the lady of mercy. She placed her housekeeper, Mrs Clarke,
in charge of her kitchen stores, the superioress of the Bermondsey
nuns, Mother Mary Clare Moore, was appointed to direct the
kitchen cooking at the Barracks Hospital and other Bermondsey nuns
were set over the stores. They drudged devotedly throughout the war.
Miss Nightingale's response to her powerlessness to influence lazily
inflexible purveyors like Mr Ward and tough old army doctors like Dr
Menzies was to inveigle Sidney Herbert into acting on her behalf. She
essayed this in a flow of nagging, half resentful, half conspiratorial
letters that ran throughout her time in the East. The first that survives
dates from 25 November 1854, within three weeks of her arrival. The
purveyors held up soap and bathing utensils because, Miss Nightingale
explained, they considered the washing of the men and the linen 'a
minor detail . . . though our remonstrances have been treated with
perfect civility, yet no washing whatever has been performed . . . except
by ourselves & a few wives of the Wounded . . . we are organizing a
Washing Establishment of our own'. This she did, and she ended by
developing the specifications of washing and drying machines specially
devised for the Crimea, paid for from *The Times* fund.

> Your name, [she told Herbert], is also continually used as a bug-
> bear — they make a deity of cheapness here . . . The cheese-paring
> system, which sounds unmusical in British ears, is here identified
> by the officers who carry it out with you.

The requirements are, unity of action [that is, ending the division between doctors' requisitions and purveyors' supplying them] & personal responsibility . . .

All the above is written in obedience to your <u>private</u> instructions. Do not let me appear as a Govt. spy here.'[28]

This was consummate web-spinning. Florence Nightingale gradually entangled Herbert in her concerns. He was to act, as inferentially instructed in this letter, to realise Miss Nightingale's designs but never to betray his leading strings. Herbert seems to have tamely accepted his subjection. Beginning with his mother, a strong-willed Russian aristocrat, then Caroline Norton, the much-wronged blue stocking, and then the devout Lizzie O'Brien, Sidney Herbert was habituated to acquiescing in the plans of handsome, determined women.

This letter also signals a new development in Miss Nightingale's statecraft. A woman in a man's world, she was adopting a secretarial mode of gaining her ends. Secretive, purposeful, she was to satisfy herself with manipulating persons having executive powers whilst she remained unseen and unsung, savouring the private knowledge of the process. Occasionally, as the boasting episode at Harley Street revealed, she could not resist the craving for reputation and published her secrets, but for the remainder of her life she was to relish supplying ideas, data, schemes for others to propagate and carry forward. Long before H.G. Wells's piercing evocation of the Webbs, she personified the new Machiavelli.

As part of the programme of capturing Sidney Herbert, Miss Nightingale essayed to neutralise the influence of the local British ambassador and his wife, Sir Stratford and Lady de Redcliffe. He was a pompous, lazy aristocrat who patronised Miss Nightingale; his lady was a gushing, High Anglican snob who had begun to interfere with Miss Nightingale's relief stores. Lady Stratford was doubly dangerous because she was an intimate of Lizzie Herbert's. The ambassador's wife was an incompetent 'impediment', Florence Nightingale warned Herbert; ten days after this, on 5 December, she protested to Herbert that Lady Stratford had wrecked her plans for rebuilding unusable parts of the Barrack Hospital. Indeed, Lady Stratford had had the impertinence to place herself 'as my correspondent . . . [but] I don't want her'. Yet Miss Nightingale had used Lady Stratford to persuade her husband, whose authorisation was necessary, to allow the expenditure for the work. Initially 125 Turkish workmen were engaged. They struck for higher pay. Miss Nightingale had them dismissed and recruited 200 Greeks. Lord Stratford disclaimed responsibility. Miss Nightingale claimed that she had paid for the rebuilding out of her own pocket, assisted by *The Times* fund, although her report is very unclear. In fact, although the War Office never published it, the government paid all the bills. Miss Nightingale had only guaranteed 70 sovereigns from *The Times* fund. None of her own money was guaranteed or spent. The 70 sovereigns were never needed and presumably remained in the fund. Long after the War Miss Nightingale continued to let it be known that she had paid for the hospital and had never been reimbursed by a pinch-penny government.[29] It is equally unclear that Lady Stratford was to blame: she had helped when asked and seems not to have meddled too deeply. If anything she too easily allowed her mean-spirited husband to wash his hands of the job. But then neither she nor her husband could before have encountered a young woman who expected deference and who independently possessed funds for public purposes.

In the midst of coping with 715 sick and wounded in the Barrack Hospital and 650 wounded in the General Hospital, her building operations and her clash with Lady Stratford, Miss Nightingale was faced with a mutiny among the St John's nurses. Several of them were Irish and some others were about to go over to Rome. One who did convert was Mrs Lawfield who protested in mid November against having to wear her thick ungainly nurse's cap. Miss Nightingale quashed Mrs Lawfield, temporarily at least, and she became, Miss Nightingale reported, 'quite a different person, and she is now, though not skilful (she does not know a fractured limb when she sees it) one of the most valuable nurses I have from her great propriety of conduct & kindness'.[30] On 4 December a St John's nurse — she forgot to sign her indignant note — informed a superior in London, probably Miss Jones, that at 'Scutariar Baricks . . . We are treated With the greates disrepect and unkindness by Miss nightingale and her housekeeper [Mrs Clarke from Harley Street] she all but starves us an it is very hurtfull to our feelings . . . she picks out all the wirst side Sortes(?) of meate and We Cannot get our teeth through and the Magets get out on our plats'.[31] Miss Nightingale, the Bracebridges, and the nuns and sisters got better fare, although meat, eggs and milk were always short. This must have been a special privation to Florence Nightingale who, in later life at least, took a keen interest in good meat and bread. But at Scutari sisterhood in service did not mean equality. Miss Nightingale and her entourage, the Bermondsey nuns, Sellonites and St John's nurses all dined separately. Miss Nightingale was too little interested in other people to discover in herself the art by which she might unite and lead.

Moreover, she made no effective allocations of authority. Mother Mary Clare ruled her nuns, but the anomalous roles of Mrs Bracebridge, and Mrs Clarke her housekeeper and personal servant, were never defined and each was allowed to play the tyrant. There was a second complaint from a St Johnite, Mary Ann Coyle, on the day following the first letter:

> wee are all so very unappey Miss Nightingale have sum spite against us but for wat cawse wee know not: and Mrs Brasebridg has treated us with Contempt ever since the day Mr. Sheperd left us: I woold not mind minde wat harde ships wee had to incaunenter with if they woold be kinde to us: thay treate us worse than the Coman low wimon thay brate oute. I was never so unappey in My life, and wee are truley sorey that wee ever came oute withoute some one to care for us: wee do the thing that is rite and if good be for us wee nead not feer ... Mrs Clarke the housekeeper Is A Compleate tirant she insults us every time she sees us Maryann in particular.[32]

Mary Ann Coyle went on to allege that she and her colléagues were kept in ignorance of the progress of the war. Newspapers were, she said, sent out for the nurses 'but they will not lett us see them'. But the St Johnites had their pride too. Mrs Bracebridge and Mrs Clarke might domineer over them, but they would 'not Mix with those Low womin Miss Nightingale braught out [Mrs Bracebridge's chosen nurses?] and for that reason they are so invitered against us'.[33] It was the first time in British history that women of diverse classes, regional origins and religions were brought to work together for a common secular cause in a foreign land. Rather than notice that the mission was fragmenting, we should marvel that it achieved anything at all, let alone its eventual successes in deaths eased and lives saved.

The mission survived partly because Miss Nightingale must have intercepted these two letters. They remain among her papers. The likelihood of seizure — rather than their having been duly posted and received and then entering the Nightingale collection later — is increased by the existence of a draft of a letter from Miss Nightingale to Miss Gipps, a lady superior at St John's House in London, dated the following day, 5 December, denouncing four St Johnites as 'flibberty-gibbet'. 'They do not command the respect imperatively necessary where forty women are turned loose among three thousand men. They do not keep the rules which I have made to ensure female decorum.' They visited the wards at nights, they fed patients without first obtaining medical orders. They dressed wounds carelessly. They would 'not take a hint except from me — I have consequently employed them less in nursing & more in making Stump pillows . . . with the view of protecting them — And they said, which is very true, that they did not come out for needlework — They have consequently done little or nothing.' Miss Nightingale never learned how to deploy and handle nurses. Sewing, as at Harley Street, was a safe diversion. Miss Nightingale concluded by asking, indirectly, that Miss Gipps recall the errant four, 'because you want them, rather than because I don't.[34] They sailed by the first available ship, before a recall could have been received at Scutari. By Christmas 1854, Miss Nightingale had dismissed — on my estimate, because the evidence is ambiguous — 13 of her original contingent, leaving her with 25 nuns and nurses to help about 11,000 men admitted to the hospitals rotten with disease — only about 100 had war wounds. The total was to rise to its peak in January 1855.

Miss Nightingale's narrow but effective notion of nursing was adjusted to these constraints. It consisted of caring for the seriously ill with unremitting attention to the patient's comfort, cleanliness, quiet and mental solace, and the administering of medicines and plasters under medical direction. She herself did little actual nursing at the hospitals. By day she negotiated with doctors, drove orderlies, and inspected stores, the nurses' work and hospital maintenance. She was like the new owner of a run down great estate. The Bracebridges, Aunt Mai and Sister Mary Clare were her agents, Mrs Clarke her housekeeper, the nurses and orderlies were her labourers, the patients her tenantry. The evidence is contradictory about her manner. One Catholic nun recalled years later that she was never heard to raise her voice — she had a peculiarly soft, clear intonation. (Even in old age the Edison recording of her voice displays a precise enunciation and an effortlessly resonant actressy voice.) But nearer the time, that is on 20 November 1854, Mr Bracebridge boasted to the family that 'She scolds sergeants and orderlies all day long; You would be astonished to see how fierce she is grown.' One old transport orderly recalled that she asked him sharply whether he carried his patients gently, admonished him to do so even after he averred that he did, and gave him a plug of tobacco as a reminder. Thereafter, he said, he revered Miss Nightingale and tried especially to be gentle.[35] By night she broke her own rule about walking the wards alone and glided in her peculiarly beautiful floating walk, her tallish slight figure erect, carrying her Turkish lantern, inspecting the patients and the wards, noting the dying. Then she returned to her room in the corner tower of the hospital to write: letters of condolence, answers to enquiries about the missing and above all orders, insinuations and recriminations in 10-30 page repetitive private letters to Sidney Herbert. She and her ladies constituted a proto-army welfare branch, long before the Army established a system of its own:

I grieve to be obliged to inform you, [she wrote to Mrs Maria Hunt in a letter typical of many others, dated September 1855 from the General Hospital, Scutari] that your son died in this Hospital on Sunday last... His complaint was Chronic Dysentery — he sank gradually from weakness, without much suffering. Everything was done that was possible to keep up his strength. He was fed every half hour with the most nourishing things he could take, & when there was anything he had a fancy for, it was taken to him immediately... He spoke much of his mother, & gave us the direction to you in his last moments... His great anxiety was that his Mother should receive the pay due to him, & should know that he had not received any since he had been Out... You may have the satisfaction of knowing that he had the most constant & careful care from the Doctors and the Nurses... The Chaplain and myself saw him every day ...

From 'Catforth near Swillbrook near Preston' Elizabeth Kellett wrote in a struggling copperplate to Miss Nightingale, the soldiers' friend, one of a dozen similar letters which survive among the Nightingale Papers:

Dear madam

it is with reagret that inow persume to adress these few lines to you Beging won kind favour from you will you pleas dear madam to wright and let me no if hever my son Robert kellet has Been in this hospital they last account I herd of in he had Been Brought to they ospital iashure you that I have rote several times But has recived no answer from im dear madam they acount that iherd was that he was Brought to scutarion ospital in they later end of genuary and idoo ashure you that ifeel verry unapy about im and if he Bee dead pleas to let mee know what was is complaint I will now give you they discriptions of im he his a streight nice clean looking light complexioned young youth near twenty so now imust conclude with hevery kind regards towards you and Belive mee to Be yours affectionetley frend John and ElisaBeth kellet...

> privat Robert kellet
> No 3510 34th Rigiment
> Light Division[36]

No wonder the common people regarded Miss Nightingale as a saint. She depended on their gratitude. They, for the first time in war, had a great person who made it her business to console them in their deepest distresses.

Her letters to Sidney Herbert were her safety-valve. She rarely wrote to her family. That task she left to the Bracebridges and to Aunt Mai Smith after she replaced them at Scutari in August 1855. Throughout her time at the Crimea, apart from the period of her illness, Miss Nightingale allowed herself but a few hours sleep in the early hours of the morning. Had she been prepared to delegate authority and create a chain of command she might have been able to cope with more than 25 women and enjoy more rest. But there is no evidence she ever entertained that choice.

She first learned that more women were on their way to Scutari on 9 or 10 December, a week after the second party had left London. Fearing her reaction, Sidney Herbert had not used the telegraph to warn her, nor did he write. After his ordeal with Manning and Rev. Mother Bridgeman and his knowledge of Miss Nightingale's temperament, his evasion is understandable. His more ingenuous wife finally conveyed the news by writing to Mrs Bracebridge on 23 November, leaving it to the latter to inform Miss Nightingale.[37]

Immediately upon reading the letter Miss Nightingale enrolled the deputy Inspector-General of hospitals, Dr Menzies, 'under whose order I am', in her 'private' remonstrance to Sidney Herbert. The pliant, cautious Menzies, who secretly disliked having women in his hospitals, 'considers', Miss Nightingale reported, that as large a number are now

> employed . . . as can be usefully appropriated & as can be made consistent with morality and discipline − [Privately, she had warned Herbert that Menzies was weak on discipline] And the discipline of 40 women, collected together for the first time, is not trifling matter − under these new and strange circumstances.
>
> He considers that, if we were swamped with a number increased to 60 or 70, good order would become impossible and in all these views [and here Miss Nightingale finally emerges in her own persona, having nowhere earlier indicated that Menzies had authorized her to report his views, if indeed they were his views] I so fully concur that I should resign my situation as impossible, were such circumstances forced upon me.
>
> For our quarters are already inadequate to preserving one tenth

our number. More quarters cannot be assured us . . . With regard to taking a house in Scutari the Medical Officers considered it as simply impossible. Regularity could not be preserved, where the Sisters & Nurses were living from under our eye.

Miss Nightingale went on to argue that 40 nurses for 3,000 sick were 'sufficient'. Indeed, she added that the party would have done better with 20: 'The work has really been done by 10 — the rest "get under our feet".' The letter continues over 19 pages.[38]

The threat of resignation presumably was meant to compel Herbert to recall the Stanley-Bridgeman party by telegraph at their next land fall. This Herbert could have done, because their ship, the *Egyptus*, called in for repairs at Navarino and Athens before arriving at the Dardanelles; but Herbert did not take the hint. Miss Nightingale's threat also gave her the option of sending the new party packing the moment they arrived at Scutari. Certainly the hospital quarters were extremely crowded and certainly the sisters, at once delicate ladies and religious zealots, could not be trusted unsupervised as the Norwood nuns and Sellonites had proved, while the nurses, as their sorry tale of drunkenness and insubordination showed, could not be trusted either. But there was no great difficulty in securing houses in Scutari if money was available for the exorbitant rentals, as the venturesome Lady Alicia Blackwood had demonstrated. She had arrived at Scutari ready to join in the nursing, but Miss Nightingale had adroitly steered her outside to nurse soldiers' wives and camp followers in two dwellings Lady Alicia privately rented.[39] The notion that 40 nurses could cope with 3,000 patients, especially cholera and dysentery victims, and that ten — in another letter at this time Miss Nightingale put the number at eighteen and five in successive sentences — would really suffice, throws a startling light on her views on management. It also highlights the fact, which Miss Nightingale — followed by her biographers — managed to obscure, that the greater part of the nursing was done, as it always had been done, by male medical orderlies. She commandeered about 300 more of them than the army normally allowed, most of them near able-bodied. She and her ladies supplied essential norms of gentleness and concern and harried the orderlies into doing their duty; they also raised standards of cleanliness, cookery and promptitude — although meals were often six hours late even near the end of the war — and, perhaps most vital of all, Miss Nightingale was the agent who supplied large quantities of food and clothing to debilitated men.[40] In this last aspect of her work, as in the rest, nursing was for Miss Nightingale merely a form of applied housekeeping — a view she retained all her life.

Without waiting for Herbert's reply or news that the second party had been stopped, Miss Nightingale wrote again on 15 December, eleven pages of harangue, not counting the repetitive postscripts. Some of her remonstrances were dubiously grounded. She claimed that she undertook the mission only on

> the distinct undertaking (expressed both in your hand-writing and in the printed announcement . . .) that nurses were to be sent out at my requisition only, made with the approbation of the Medical Officers here.
>
> You came to me in your distress, and told me that you were unable for the moment to find any other person for the office, and that, if I failed you, the scheme would fail. I sacrificed my own judgment and went out with 40 females.

The first paragraph refers to the original agreement, which I suggested had been generally inspired at least by Miss Nightingale. The agreement refers to the allocation of nurses in Turkey and does not mention any further party, which was apparently not envisaged at the time. But implicitly, the document does confirm Miss Nightingale's supremacy in all matters relating to female nurses, subject only to the medical officers. Similarly, the second paragraph is a rearrangement of the truth. I have suggested that Miss Nightingale set up the approach from Sidney Herbert, but even if that interpretation is false, it is at least indisputable that his written invitation and her written offer were made simultaneously. There is no indication that she set any limit on the number of nurses in the mission, or that the 38 she took exceeded her notional optimal number. Here, as she was increasingly to do throughout her life, Miss Nightingale was moralising upon a fantasy of her own creation. After repeating the assertion that the doctors could not and would not employ the extra nurses, she added, inconsequentially,

> you have sacrificed the cause, so near my heart — you have sacrificed me, a matter of small importance now — you have sacrificed your own written word to a popular cry.
>
> I will not say anything of the cruel injustice to me.

She then raised the questions of where the newcomers were to be housed and the shortage of space in the hospitals. She would, she supposed, have 'to take a house in Scutari'. Five days earlier this choice had been 'impossible'. There they were to wait until 'you can employ them at Therapia [the Embassy compound, where there was nothing to do], or elsewhere – or till you recall them. Of course these unoccupied women will "go to the Devil".'

The climax of this letter was a consummate mingling of inferential blame and adumbrated threat:

> You must feel that I ought to resign, where [sic – when?] conditions are imposed upon me which render the object for which I am employed unattainable – and I only remain at my post till I have provided . . . for these poor wanderers . . . I must again refer to the deficiency of knives and forks here.[41]

When the Stanley-Bridgeman party arrived on 17 December Miss Nightingale, true to her threat, packed them off to Therapia. The nurses in the party rebelled that evening when they discovered they were to act as servants to the ecclesiastical ladies rather than minister to wounded soldiers. Rev. Mother Francis, bent upon establishing her independence from the outset, separated from the Therapia group and took her fifteen nuns across the Bosphorus to an already crowded French convent in Galata. The second Therapia house was apparently not considered. The nuns could indeed have been squeezed in at the first Therapia house. They stayed at the Maison de Providence until after Christmas, yet to meet Miss Nightingale. With characteristic inappropriateness Rev. Mother Francis confided in her diary: 'It was the best Christmas we ever spent . . . replete with spiritual joys and conformity to Him who came unto His own and His own received Him not.'[42] Until she and her party moved, the French nuns could not re-open their boarding school, on which their income depended.

Miss Nightingale tackled the interlopers by crushing Mary Stanley. After leaving her to stew for four days in the midst of the nurses' rebellion, she summoned her on 21 December. Miss Nightingale, clad in her black merino, spotless linen collar and cuffs, white apron, white cap with a black hankerchief tied over it, sat working at a small unpainted deal table in a small room, the door of which was screened by a heavy curtain. It was post day. Miss Nightingale kept Miss Stanley waiting through the morning while a stream of visitors entered before her. The crushing was easy. Miss Nightingale opened with a direct challenge, made in the presence of Mr Bracebridge and Dr Cumming.

She formally resigned and requested Miss Stanley to succeed her immediately. Miss Stanley, duly flustered, demurred and gabbled out 'every reason'. Miss Nightingale confirmed her victory by lending a suppliant Miss Stanley £90, to be followed later by another £90. That foolish, sybaritic Lady Bountiful and her party had spent all she had upon the best hotels and fare en route, and they had arrived penniless. The grants came from Miss Nightingale's private funds, that is, publicly subscribed monies which she controlled. Her sharp sense of legal niceties ensured that Miss Stanley and her people were given no 'official' money and Miss Nightingale saw to it that Dr Cumming made no official payments either. Stratford de Redcliffe, who was empowered to disburse official funds for good causes also refused Miss Stanley, but whether from reasons of fear of Miss Nightingale, inherent meanness, or prudence, or all three, I have not discovered.[43]

In the circumstances Miss Stanley's vague suggestions for the allocation of her people stood little chance with the lady superintendent. Miss Stanley hoped to place her ladies, under the chaplains' direction, as visitors to the sick and dying. They were not to 'nurse' the soldiery. The Catholic nuns were equally to be set under their chaplain, Father Ronan (who was yet to arrive after the Manning/Herbert/Bridgeman contretemps), 'supposing', Miss Stanley ventured, 'that Father Ronan . . . should approve and wish it'. The common nurses were not considered; presumably, until Miss Nightingale should change her mind, they were to continue to cook, sweep and wash for the ladies at Therapia. One among them, Jane Harding, who had served under Miss Nightingale at Harley Street, was expressly forbidden to communicate with her.[44] Irrespective of Father Ronan's likely views, Miss Nightingale rejected the plan. The British evangelical press — Miss Stanley noticed that Miss Nightingale's sofa was bestrewn with English newspapers — was already replete with lurid speculations about Puseyite and Papist sisters whose only object at the war must be to pervert British soldiers. Miss Nightingale could simply have ignored the abuse, as she had done hitherto, but it served her now to allege the practical and 'moral impossibility' of employing more females with dangerous religious labels.[45]

Four days later, on Christmas Eve, the lady superintendent summoned Miss Stanley again. Miss Nightingale was now equipped with a memorandum signed by Dr Cumming, cast in the now distinctive Nightingale format of close argument and secretarial mien. He formally requested the lady superintendent to select a total of 50 ladies and nurses, 'the number which you, in agreement with myself, have deemed sufficient for the proper working of the establishment, and beyond which you do not think yourself capable of managing as best to carry out the objects in view'.[46] This concession was Miss Nightingale's best option. It enabled her, with Miss Stanley's and Dr Cumming's acquiescence, to take women from both the Stanley and Bridgeman groups and thereby split them. Miss Nightingale chose thirteen of the ladies and nurses for Scutari. Another seven of the 31 in the Stanley party were sent in January 1855 to the General Hospital at Balaclava. The remaining eight apparently were left at Therapia.

Miss Nightingale offered to take five of the fifteen Bridgeman nuns. They were to replace the five Norwood sisters whom the lady superintendent planned to dismiss, thereby keeping the number of nuns constant. The Norwood sisters, apart from Miss Nightingale's complaints about their genteel ineffectiveness, had offended by flaunting their distinctive white habits. On joining the contingent in London they had arrived in discreet black, but once in France they blossomed in their normal white.[47] Miss Nightingale hated being tricked.

Rev. Mother Bridgeman proved a harder case than Miss Stanley. On 22 December Miss Nightingale had invited her, in writing, to place five of her nuns in the Scutari hospitals under the spiritual direction of Rev. Mother Clare, the Bermondsey superioress. Rather than negotiate on paper, Rev. Mother Bridgeman sailed over the Bosphorus to confront Miss Nightingale. This procedure had, after all, succeeded with Mr Herbert and Father Manning. Mother Mary Clare met the interloping superioress with icy formality. The lady superintendent duly kept her visitor waiting and then offered her lunch: 'a small remnant of musty cheese, a scrap of dirty butter in a bowl, some sour bread and some cold potatoes'. Rev. Mother Bridgeman, whose bulk implied a hearty appetite, was sufficiently piqued by this tactic to record it at length in her diary. None the less, Miss Nightingale failed to gain her point. Rev. Mother Brickbat, as Miss Nightingale henceforth called her — in reference to her complexion and manner — cited her agreement among her nuns confirming her headship and asserted the moral impossibility of setting part of her contingent under Rev. Mother Clare and thereby under Miss Nightingale.[48]

Rev. Mother Brickbat's behaviour and claims were impudent and legally unfounded. Father Cuffe, the senior Catholic chaplain, hinted that she should go home. Father Manning, writing a few days later, was fearful that the Irish contingent might indeed return in high dudgeon and warned them to stand fast. Rev. Mother Bridgeman, who neither needed nor heeded advice, decided to stay and fight. With Nightingalesque cunning she informed her nuns that anyone who wished to transfer to Rev. Mother Clare might write home for permission. Given the delays of the post, this move gave her three more weeks for parley. She must have been shocked when four nuns actually sought permission: but their temerity went unrequited; permission was refused for two of them and time ran out before permission arrived for the others. On Christmas Eve, two days after their initial encounter, Miss Nightingale renewed her offer to take five Bridgeman nuns and to house the remainder at Therapia. Rev. Mother Brickbat riposted by offering herself to go with four of her party to work under Rev. Mother Clare on condition that the lady superintendent separately housed the surplus ten nuns. The French nuns at Galata urgently wanted their rooms. Miss Nightingale's offer had explicitly excluded the Brickbat. Their confrontation continued until 5 January 1855 when the lady superintendent gave way and admitted Rev. Mother Bridgeman as an 'ordinary nun', like her four sisters, at the hospitals. Rev. Mother Clare put two of the Irish party into the kitchens, two to sort linen and left Rev. Mother Bridgeman unemployed and ignored. But by mid-January cholera had begun to ravage the overcrowded wards and all five Bridgeman nuns were finally enlisted as nurses.[49]

The Scutari female nursing venture rested on a fragile sectarian truce. Miss Nightingale, who had no firm denominational allegiance, was justifiably wary. But her predictions that the Irish sisters would proselytise in the hospitals were not borne out. The nuns were ostentatious in rounding up dying Irishmen, ostentatious enough to earn a rebuke from Rev. Mother Clare, and on one occasion they baptised a delirious terminal case whose affiliations were unknown, but they did not seek to convert known Protestants. Watchful Protestant chaplains and nurses would have remonstrated had they tried. The nuns for their part were quick to warn nominal Catholics to reject the ministrations of Protestant ladies, thereby provoking hitherto indifferent men into welcoming the ladies. The Anglican Sellonites were equally assiduous, if less officious, in mustering their nominal co-religionists. Presbyterian Scots and Irish were poorly supplied with both chaplains and nurses of their persuasion and some of them complained about the flaunting of Popery and pseudo-Popery in the wards, but the absence of overt sectarian conflict among the soldiers can be explained by their easy-going scepticism about the religious zeal of their betters. In December 1854 a dying man was given a medal by a Catholic chaplain. The man was idly fingering the medal, whereupon the chaplain accepted an offer of a piece of red tape from a hovering Sellonite and tied the medal around the patient's neck. Embarrassed, the man remarked to the Sellonite: 'I am what is called a Roman Catholic; I know no better. I would as soon be a Protestant if I knew how.' Near him lay Sam Gregg, aged 17, bereft since the Battle of Inkerman of his right arm and left hand, but described as 'cheerful'. He whispered smilingly to the Sellonite, Sister Terrot, 'I don't think much of that gammon! What good can a medal do to a dying man?'[50]

Had Miss Nightingale been able to coax rather than bully she would have defeated the Bridgeman challenge. Her remoteness from other human beings, her strident dealings with doctors, orderlies and ladies, their well-founded suspicions that she both saw through their inefficiencies and reported them home, all prevented her from cultivating useful friends and isolating the Irish nuns. Instead, the medical and purveying fraternity adopted Rev. Mother Bridgeman and her following as a weapon against their interfering, overbearing enemy. Miss Nightingale could neither risk the uproar if she sent the Irish party home nor cope with the Brickbat while they stayed. She could however, blame Sidney Herbert. She used Christmas Day to pen an eleven page reproach:

You have not stood by me, but I have stood by you. In this new situation, I have taken your written instructions as my guide ... Had I not done this, we should have been turned out of the Hospitals in a month, and the War Office would have borne the blame of swamping the experiment.

Aggrieved self-justification merged imperceptibly into outright threat:

Such a tempest has been brewed in this little pint-pot as you could have no idea of. But I, like the ass, have put on the lion's skin, and when once I have done that (poor me, who never affronted any one before), I can bray so loud that I shall be heard, I am afraid, as far as England.[51]

The Nightingale family had already begun to bray. They were practised in it, at least since October of that year, when Fanny and Parthe had told Mrs Gaskell several otherwise unsubstantiated anecdotes of Florence's childhood precocity as nurse and saint. Mrs Gaskell immediately broadcast them. Parthe's repertoire included a richly circumstantial story of Florence's devoted nursing, seven years before, of a dying child of a village woman. Mrs Gaskell recounted it, yet she observed, although the observation only half registered, that

> the father of this dead child — the husband of this poor woman — died last 5th of September, and I was witness to the extreme difficulty with which Parthe induced Florence to go and see the childless widow once . . . and though the woman entreated her to come again she never did.[52]

The intimacy between the famous Unitarian novelist and Florence Nightingale, which the family ardently desired, never developed after this episode. Within weeks of Miss Nightingale's arrival at Scutari the family propagandists were in spate. In November 1854 Parthe informed Monckton Milnes that 'in one week F has gained the confidence of all, the Doctors do her will, & the fund has poured . . . into her lap, tin pots, saucepans, jars, basons, sherry, combs, shirts, socks, sheets, coal, wooden spoons.' She also warned him, with the implied instruction to take counter measures among his political friends, that 'Dizzy is making trouble with (?) the RC and High Ch nurses.'[53] (No written evidence survives to substantiate this accusation. But it is consonant with Disraeli's character.) By the second week of December news reached the family from the Bracebridges of the flooding in of wounded and diseased soldiers from the Battle of Inkerman (which had occurred on 5 November, the day after Miss Nightingale's landing at Scutari) and of the loss of lives, provisions and hospital stores in the terrible Black Sea storm of 14 November, together with the first disclosures of strains between the lady superintendent, and unfeeling doctors, orderlies and nurses. 'The difficulties of her path thicken upon her', Parthe told Lizzie Herbert, '[but] . . . her heart does not quail.' 'May we', Parthe added, 'spread the Queen's letter a little?' Queen Victoria had informed Mr Herbert, in a letter written to Mrs Herbert, that she wished 'Miss Nightingale and the ladies would tell these poor, noble wounded and sick men that *no one* takes a warmer interest or feels *more* for their sufferings or admires their courage . . . *more* than their Queen'. This recognition was a triumph for the family; the Nightingales' dissenting, radical parvenu origins made it the more delectable. Florence saw to it that the Queen's message was read in the wards and placarded throughout the hospitals. She reported that the men said, '"She thinks of us", (said with tears)' and '"To think of her thinking of us"'. Burns, an Irish soldier, the only man from whom we have an identifiable verbatim report, expressed a more mundane view: 'It's very pleasant and proper, but I hope the good folks at home won't spend all their kindness in words, but will keep it up, and give us enough to keep the pot aboiling when we come back to them.' True to the family gift for evocative anecdote, Parthe ended her letter to Lizzie Herbert with 'a little story — Flo sat up all night with 5 Inkerman men — given up by doctors — she nursed them through — "saved by her" the Doctors say'.[54] This story is uncorroborated. Letters to William Nightingale from his friends at the Crimea praising Florence were copied by Parthe and distributed through their circle.[55] By mid-February 1855 the cheap serial *Illustrated History of the Expedition To The Crimea* contained the first portrait of the new heroine, although she was still too little known to compel the authors to mention her in their text. Their engraving is not a precise representation of its subject, but rather a generalised picture of an early Victorian, Frenchified young lady, plump-cheeked, with hair coiled around her ears like the young Queen, a cross on a chain encircling her neck, sitting reading a devotional work. By April 1855 such portraits were appearing in the soldiers' huts at the Crimea, cut from home papers. The sceptical young Protestant Irish medical man, Joseph Samuel Prendergast, who resented Miss Nightingale as a meddling Puseyite — perhaps even a secret Papist — yielded to the sentiments of his sisters at home and began, half-heartedly, to regard Miss Nightingale as a female martyr to duty. He duly pasted up in his mess hut the woodcut portrait they sent him and read the *Life Sketch of Miss Nightingale* they posted with it. But he was a conventionally-minded man and remained unconvinced: 'everyone . . . gives favourable accounts of her . . . I am certain I never said anything against her . . . [but] there is something in these Protestant maidens proceedings repugnant to some men's ideas of morality, decency & refinement'.[56]

The patriotic canonisation proceeded with the Rev. Sidney Godolphin Osborne's racy, opinionated glorification of Miss Nightingale in his reports to *The Times.*[57] He worked in the Scutari hospitals as a volunteer chaplain and medical helper. Osborne, was a knight errant who spent his life questing for objects to love and reform. Like Cobbett, whom he resembles, not least in his robust, compelling prose, he wrote on Tory-radical political reform, class mutuality, agricultural improvement, famine relief, sanitary reform and the Heroine of the Crimea. He was the first of a line of forceful men who found in her their Lady. Osborne, Russell the war correspondent,

A.W. Kinglake the historian, and other critics created The Lady with the Lamp as the living counter to the muddle and national shame of a war that failed public expectations of early glory. Russell's despatches brought direct to middle-class homes the horrors and mistakes of war and aristocracy's and officialdom's contempt for their common soldiery. Miss Nightingale projected herself and was projected by others as a mature, maternal symbol, the embodiment of common-sensical housewifely virtues, in contrast to infantile male parliamentary and military blundering. She became a neutral, safely non-political diversionary focus for the discontents that might otherwise have been concentrated by J.A. Roebuck, Augustus Stafford, Charles Dickens and other radical critics in their attacks on aristocratic dominance and mismanagement.

Resentment at Miss Nightingale's high-handedness festered throughout the winter of 1854/5. She was saved from an open rebellion by the drafting of the unemployed Therapian ladies and nurses, and the remaining Bridgeman nuns, to the Koulali hospitals (a few miles East from Scutari) which opened in January/February 1855, and the despatch at the request of the Commander in Chief, Lord Raglan, of ladies and nurses to two hospitals at the Crimea. Dissatisfied nurses also moved, when they could, beyond her reach. The lady superintendent opposed all these deployments, seeing in each a diffusion of her authority. Publicly she shed responsibility for them, privately she kept control of their funding.[58] Meanwhile she pressed Sidney Herbert and Lord Panmure, the new War Secretary, for a stronger statement of her powers, and suppressed mutinous nurses. In January the St Johnites complained about unequal work loads, the rules forbidding speaking with patients and reading to them without the chaplain's permission (the chaplains were especially wary of novels and High Church poetry), and 'the want of due consideration towards themselves' from the aloof lady superintendent, the haughty Mrs Bracebridge and the nagging Mrs Clarke.[59] The novelty of the enterprise and the frightful environment of its work demanded qualities of leadership and experience which no woman of the 1850s could have possessed. It is fair to remind ourselves that Miss Nightingale saved the mission from religious catastrophe and the ladies' fatuities. But she never won loyalty and instead met her subordinates' complaints with a mixture of unforgiving authoritarianism and tortuous self-justification. On learning of the complaints she issued instant 'letters of recall', which meant loss of wages, bonuses and 'characters'. She told the St Johnites' superiors that 'had they given me any opportunity of setting matters right, I might have convinced them of the impropriety of lightly taking offence', and then remarked that she was 'wholly unable to enquire into trifles', which in turn allowed her to conclude that the nurses' allegations were 'unfounded'. The council of St John's House acquiesed.[60]

On 27 April 1855 Miss Nightingale received from the War Office part of her much sought extended authority. She was named as almoner of the free gifts in all the British hospitals in the Crimea war zone. Within the week she sailed for Balaclava on the Crimean Peninsula, accompanied by an entourage which included Mr Bracebridge and Alexis Soyer, the great chef come to reform the soldiers' cooking.

Miss Nightingale's first act was to make an official visit to Lord Raglan. It happened that the Commander in Chief was absent from headquarters but her reception there none the less proclaimed her standing to the army. She spent the following days investigating the hospitals, especially those housing the Stanley ladies and St John's nurses. Thanks to the capable, hard-working nurses, and medical officers, helped by the lull in the fighting, the improvement in the weather and the enlarged supplies of food and clothing, affairs were less chaotic than accounts of the ladies' antics would have led her to expect. Miss Clough had left to follow a romantic whim to preside, uninvited, at the Highland Brigade Hospital on the heights above Balaclava. The Sellonite Mother Eldress at the General Hospital had suffered a mental collapse and spent her time praying while the nurses, orderlies and Turkish labourers made hay among the free gifts. Her successor, the tearful dithering Miss Wear, trailed around the hospital cradling a King Charles spaniel. Miss Nightingale's worst predictions about the Stanley party were being borne out.[61]

While at the Crimea Miss Nightingale established her credentials with Sir John McNeill, a distinguished civil administrator and medical man, the joint leader, with Colonel Alexander Tulloch, of the official inquiry into the commissariat of the army. She also strengthened her links with Dr John Sutherland and Mr Robert Rawlinson, the civil engineer, members of the second commission inquiring into the sanitary conditions of the army. Sutherland, one of the first sanitary inspectors appointed to the Board of Health in 1848, had already met Miss Nightingale when he inspected the Scutari hospitals. He was to become her devoted ally for the rest of his life. Sutherland was always more rigid in his thinking, more hardworking and more single-mindedly dedicated to sanitary improvement than Miss Nightingale. He was to subordinate himself to her and endure her slights and tantrums in the realisation that she had access to power to do good that he could never hope to tap. He brought a steadiness to their partnership that immeasurably strengthened its effectiveness.

Not surprisingly, McNeill, Sutherland and their colleagues found much to criticise among the unsuitable buildings used as hospitals, the collapse of primitive sanitary arrangements under the pressure of numbers and epidemic disease, and the dim, complacent timidity of overtasked doctors and purveyors sheltering behind regulations. Miss Nightingale cultivated the commissioners' esteem and fed them information. She was building for herself a defence against detractors and a means of publicly punishing those who stood in her way. Her alliance with the commissioners, themselves outsiders among the army men, was none the less an astonishing feat for a female with no official standing in the army.[62]

Miss Nightingale's powerlessness in the Crimea in relation to the ladies and nurses, imposed by the terms of her letter of appointment which specified only Turkey, was quickly exposed. Miss Wear and another zealot, Miss Fanny Taylor, especially, ignored Miss Nightingale's remonstrances. She ordered the ebullient Welsh cook, Elizabeth Davis, to cease cooking for the officers, but Davis, a survivor of trading voyages and shipwreck in the Pacific in the 1820s and 1830s, who relished the badinage of gentlemen of large fortune as they clustered around her cookhouse, boldly ignored the lady superintendent.[63] Miss Nightingale never wavered from the belief that her mission was to the common soldiery. With true wealthy upper-class Radical disdain, she declared that officers could look after themselves.

Within a fortnight of her arrival Miss Nightingale collapsed. The doctors were said to have diagnosed her sickness as 'Crimean fever', probably a form of typhus. This episode is mysterious. The date of the onset of the illness is not recorded and there are few records of its progress. Yet her illness was a public event. Soon after her collapse Miss Nightingale was conveyed in procession from her stateroom in a ship in Balaclava harbour up the hill to the Castle Hospital. Relays of soldiers carried her litter, Dr Anderson, Chief Medical Officer at the General Hospital, and her maid, Mrs Roberts, walked beside her, Soyer's secretary held a white parasol above her head and her uniformed message-boy, Robert Robinson, marched at the rear. The cortege launched rumours of her illness throughout the Crimea and evoked great sympathy among the troops. Officers like young Joseph Prendergast, who hitherto in his letters to his family had been facetiously dismissive of the lady superintendent and her female entourage, now became interested in her fate. Telegraphic bulletins about her illness reached the Queen and Lord Raglan, who paid Miss Nightingale a belated visit on 24 May, after she began to recover. Miss Nightingale is not recorded as showing the usual symptoms of fever whether of the typhus or typhoid varieties; that is, there is no record of diarrhoea, constipation, bleeding or pinkish spots. But she was delirious and unusually active for a person stricken with fever. Her hair was cut off, the normal treatment to reduce the heat of the brain in delirium. While at the Castle Hospital she wrote coherent-seeming notes about engines pounding in her head, persecutions from people crowding into her room demanding supplies, and the deceits of friends. The surviving letters do not mention nursing problems or the sufferings of the soldiers. On 21 May she wrote to Sir John McNeill to warn him that

> Last week a Persian adventurer appeared to me like a phantom, shewed me papers by which Mr Bracebridge seemed to have drawn upon me for £300000, I sent for him – He said very little, neither denied nor assented ... but said nothing (?) would even (?) that I had seen (?) the papers there for the first time ...
>
> Have you any advice to give? I come to you because you have shewn me much kindness.[64]

McNeill apparently returned the letter unanswered.

After about three weeks of illness Miss Nightingale's doctors decided she was sufficiently recovered to travel and they advised her to return to England to convalesce. She refused. About four months later, in October 1855, she alleged to the family, knowing they would spread the story,

> that Drs. Hall and Hadley sent for a list of vessels going home & chose one, the Jura which was not going to stop at Scutari ... and put me on board of her for England ... And that Mr Bracebridge and Ld. Ward took me out, at the risk to my life –. to save my going to England, though unconscious all the time.[65]

There is much confusion about this episode, not least in the presentations by recent biographers who muddle who said and did what. But a few salient elements are clear. Miss Nightingale was not 'unconscious all the time': she was sufficiently alert to reject the doctors' advice. Dr John Hall was devious — we know nothing about Hadley — but he was also cautious and punctilious. He was not the man to risk the uproar the lady superintendent would have aroused had he shanghaied her. There is no evidence that the officious, indiscreet Bracebridge made any allegations about the episode, as he would surely have done had he been involved as Miss Nightingale claimed. There is no record of Lord Ward remarking on it. I have been unable to discover whether the *Jura* did bypass Constantinople, but it seems inherently unlikely that a ship could not at least pause to allow important passengers to disembark. It is thinkable that Miss Nightingale, a poor sea-traveller, preferred to sail on Lord Ward's fast, well-appointed. steam yacht rather than on a tub like the *Jura*. Finally, the story first appears to have been told in October, four months after the event, by its central character who was 'unconscious' during its unfolding. October was the month when Miss Nightingale first clashed with Dr John Hall. The real oddity is the ready acceptance by historians, without conclusive evidence, of such an implausible accusation. Its real significance is its testimony to Miss Nightingale's novelistic imagination and her resolute effrontery in propagating stories to gain her ends.

After her return from the Crimea in Lord Ward's yacht Miss Nightingale took about six more weeks to recuperate and apparently did not return to the Scutari hospitals until about the middle of July. The feeding of the soldiers and the washing of the linen seems to have proceeded smoothly in her absence but the work of the nuns and nurses must have become even more peripheral to the daily regime of the hospitals because by the end of June only about five of the original 14 nurses, two of the six St Johnites and two of the five Stanleyites remained on the job. The others had proved to have 'unsuitable characters', a St Johnite confided to her chaplain.[66] Only the dedicated and disciplined contingent of Catholic religious remained undiminished. Although there had been a sudden rise in admissions in June due to another cholera outbreak, the overall number of patients in the Bosphorus and Crimean hospitals had fallen fairly steadily after January 1855 from 4,176 per 1,000 strength to 2,832 per 1,000 strength in July, while the death rate had diminished even faster.

Upon her return to business in mid-July Miss Nightingale used this decline as a new argument for asserting her overt control over the Stanleyites, escapee St Johnites and Bridgemanites at the Crimea hospitals. She opened negotiations with Dr John Hall, their nominal chief at the Crimea, to have them returned to the Scutari hospitals. The hot Crimean summer would damage their health, she suggested, and if Hall's reported intention to convert his Crimean hospitals into convalescent and staging depots was true, there was no need for female nurses. While seeking Hall's agreement and the exercise of his authority to return the nurses to Scutari, Miss Nightingale approached him as one commandant to another: 'I . . . hasten to apply for your advice on this subject – & trust that you will have the goodness as soon as possible to examine the question.'[67] The nuns and ladies were not to be consulted. But without their return to Scutari, the Nightingale mission would have virtually no presence. Hall's reply to Miss Nightingale was a cool, polite sidestep. Clearly he was under pressure from the Crimean ladies, Miss Wear especially, not to order them back to Miss Nightingale. He pleaded the necessity of the General Hospital, half-filled with seamen and other non-army patients with nowhere else to go, but he left it to the lady with the powerful friends to make the decisive move: 'If two nurses could be kept there it would be a convenience [Hall's idea of female nursing was as limited as Florence Nightingale's], but if you wish to withdraw them altogether we must endeavour to make some other arrangement.' The lady superintendent, outmatched by Hall's pliability, grudgingly agreed to leave Miss Dean and a nurse at the General Hospital.[68]

Miss Nightingale's return to business and the fall in the number of patients in the Kulali hospitals – there were now less than 50 – proved the last straw for Rev. Mother Francis. After obtaining permission from her bishop in Ireland she told Father Woollett, SJ, a chaplain at the front, on 2 September 1855 to advise Hall that she was ready to transfer her contingent, together with additional nuns whom she would bring from Ireland, to the Crimea to work 'under his direction'. In fact, Woollett had already sounded Hall, very likely at her instigation, and had found him cautiously compliant. Rev. Mother Francis now completed her entrapment of Hall with an ultimatum: 'I would not undertake again *to work with Miss Nightingale.*' Not that she had ever done so, but Hall plumped for the lesser of two inescapable rows.[69] Rev. Mother Francis alleged that she could no longer stand Miss Nightingale's low standards of hospital management, but after all, the Kulali nuns had been free for months to run their hospital in their own way. Given their advantage of a superior building and a much smaller press of patients, such reports as we have suggest that they had done little better than their colleagues at Scutari. The real precipitating cause of this secession appears to have been the proselytising forays of the recently converted Mrs Lawfield who was pressing her family during August 1855 to come over to Rome. Miss Nightingale found time to join the tug of war: 'I got her to talk to me as much as possible . . . as she otherwise falls into the hands of a silly little Priest here [Duffy?] & an unprincipled R. Catholic nurse whom I have dismissed'. [Nurse Wagstaff?] [70]

Hall accepted the Bridgeman offer, without informing the lady superintendent. She, after all, still had no official control over the allocation of female nurses outside Turkey. Rev. Mother Francis curtly informed Miss Nightingale of the new plan after receiving Hall's acceptance. 'I shall . . . be obliged to withdraw the Sisters from the General Hospital, Scutari . . . We hope to sail for the Crimea at the beginning of next week.' [71] This was more Bridgeman impudence. Miss Nightingale alone had the power to dispose of nuns and nurses at Scutari.

Miss Nightingale immediately sought to reinforce her authority. She approached Stratford de Redcliffe, who shied away and redirected her to General Storks, the newly appointed commandant at Constantinople, and to Rear-Admiral Grey. She also reiterated her demand to the War Office that her control over the female nurses should be extended throughout 'the East'. Storks, like the rest of his colleagues, tried to keep clear of the warring women. He ignored, as he was able to do in the absence of specific instructions, Miss Nightingale's call for extended powers. But he made a conciliatory gesture, within his and Grey's sphere of authority, by mildly rebuking Hall for requisitioning shipping berths for the nuns without obtaining permission. Yet Storks did not forbid the nuns' removal to the Crimea, although he added a warning that Miss Nightingale had decided to 'conduct' them to the Crimea in person. Hall returned a rather flippant, unrepentant note pointing out that Miss Nightingale had given the impression that she had washed her hands of the Irish nuns and the Crimea and 'if proselytism is what is dreaded, this is the very field for the poor nuns, as the greatest portion of their patients will be Turks, Jews, Greeks, & I fear, Infidels'. None the less, Hall was not a fool. He remarked that the contretemps was 'a very simple affair, tho' much I see, will be made of it'. After the row about Miss Wear and now this, he was coming to appreciate what he was up against. He would have been even more worried had he known that Storks would immediately supply Miss Nightingale with a full copy of his letter. [72]

The long sought strengthening of Miss Nightingale's mandate throughout the hospitals of the East arrived from Lord Panmure, the new Secretary for War, on 15 October, in the midst of these dissensions. It was less than she wanted: the permanent officials at the War Office were awake to the lady's pretensions. The order recognised Miss Nightingale 'as the General Superintendent of the female nursing Establishment of the Military Hospitals of the Army' and repeated that she was subject to the Principal Medical Officer, who was to give his directions through her. But the document left ambiguous her powers over the allocation of nurses outside Turkey. Such transfers were now subject to 'consultation' with Miss Nightingale but she had no absolute control. Disappointing though it was, Miss Nightingale brandished the document at her new enemy Hall on the day she received it, and she immediately set about establishing her version of the sequence of events, thereby warning Hall that the War Office was already informed of where the blame lay:

In September 1855 Mrs Bridgeman . . . who came out to serve under my orders in December 1854 . . . offered the services of herself & Sisters, without the knowledge or consent of [General Storks] . . . or my own, to you — which you accepted for the General Hospital Balaclava. that you had written to me (referring to a letter of mine dated some months previous proposing to withdraw the Nurses then there, a proposition at that time negatived by you) — desiring that this proposition should now be carried into effect, which I acceded to . . . that I immediately communicated with our Ambassador, who gave it as his opinion that I should be fully justified in calling upon Mrs Bridgeman not to undertake her intended voyage & upon Dr Hall not to receive her at Balaclava without my 'consent & permission' & that I 'should be entitled to the support of Brigadier-General Storks and Rear Admiral Grey in giving effect to my determination'. that, conceiving it to be injudicious to take such a measure and thus produce a breach between the Roman Catholic and Protestant elements, I consulted with . . . Storks . . . and came to the determination to bring Mrs Bridgeman and her sisters . . . to Balaclava myself. that, finding you of opinion that it was better for the arrangement to stand — viz. that the General Hospital . . . should be served by Roman Catholic Sisters alone, because the Patients in that Hospital at present consist chiefly of Roman Catholics, Jews, Turks, infidels and heathens — and referring to my instructions from the War Office placing me 'under the direction of the Chief Medical Officer' . . . I considered it to be my duty to acquiesce in your arrangement.[73]

Every sentence of this letter contains, as the reader will have perceived, a half-truth, lie or threat. Rev. Mother Francis did not come to serve under Miss Nightingale. The second sentence, refers to Miss Nightingale's proposal of mid-July to remove Miss Wear and her nurses, at which Hall temporised, and to her letters of 21 September repeating her proposal, to which Hall had explicitly replied: 'I do not want to get rid of Miss Wear and her nurses.'[74] Miss Nightingale's account of Stratford de Redcliffe's opinions is inherently improbable, given the ambassador's evasiveness and Storks's refusal to forbid the Bridgeman nuns' removal to the Crimea. It is equally improbable that consultation with Storks was needed to persuade Miss Nightingale to travel with the Bridgeman party. The quotation about the 'Jews and Infidels' from Hall's private letter to Storks was a nasty piece of bullying. And if Miss Nightingale was to hand over the Bridgeman nuns to Hall, as she protested that her War Office instructions impelled her to do, her journey to the Crimea was unnecessary.

Despite having surrendered the Bridgeman party to Hall, Miss Nightingale three days later besought Stratford de Redcliffe to cancel their permission to leave. 'What do I do – what do you direct? – I think you [must?] communicate to Hall and Bridgeman the instructions under which I act.' But the Ambassador was not to be inveigled. He duly undertook to advise the War Office to extend her authority, but he did nothing to forbid the Bridgeman venture.[75] Miss Nightingale's efforts to collar the Brickbat also failed. The latter coolly informed the lady superintendent that she 'never gave up the right to withdraw my Sisters from Scutari or elsewhere ... Were I about to place any of my Sisters in a hospital under your control, I should, of course, have referred the matter to you; but it is not so'.[76]

After a voyage of two days the *Ottawa* hove to off Balaclava in the midst of a storm. Bridgeman was determined to be first ashore. The rough seas did not permit a tug to approach the *Ottawa* but Rev. Mother Francis hoisted herself into a rocking small boat. Miss Nightingale was in her cabin. Immediately upon hearing that the Brickbat had got off, she rushed on deck and insisted upon plumping into a second small boat. The ladies landed at Balaclava together.

Miss Nightingale set about an inspection of the hospitals, looking for dirt and decay. Hall, with icy courtesy, regretted that he was unable to attend her. Miss Wear, who had signified her determination to stay at the Crimea, out of the superintendent's clutches, was now made to pay for her tenacity. Miss Nightingale removed Miss Wear's two allies – in reality they dominated her and did as they liked – nurses

Davis and Sheridan, and ordered Hall to replace them with 'two women', presumably soldiers' wives.

> As both your followers have alas! deserted you . . . I fear it cannot be very comfortable for you to remain at the General Hospital with the 'monks'.
> Would you not think it better to come up here . . . [the Castle Hospital — FN's temporary headquarters] And knowing as I do the Characters of your successors and of many of those with whom you have to do, I think it would be far pleasanter for you, better for your dignity, and might [avert?] much that may be and will be said both about our being spies . . . and of our pampering 'the monks'.

Miss Wear passed on to Hall Miss Nightingale's tormenting letter. He copied it. That canny man had begun to collect evidence for the defence. Miss Wear did not budge. Miss Nightingale was further incensed by discovering that she had taken up with the Brickbat and was sheltering behind her. The lady superintendent, after further futile badgering, at last requested Hall to order Miss Wear to the Castle Hospital. He politely offered to ask Miss Wear what she preferred. She preferred to stay.[77]

During this second visit Miss Nightingale established extra diet kitchens, saw that insulation felt was put in to the hospital huts to protect the inmates from the looming winter and besought the military authorities to set aside rooms as rest and reading rooms for the men. She had begun to look to the moral well being of the troops as well as to their care when physically disabled. She also closeted herself with each of the nurses, seeking private information about the behaviour of their colleagues.[78] Rev. Mother Francis and her nuns meanwhile set about stirrring up the orderlies to clean the General Hospital and run it efficiently.

In early November there arrived at Balaclava, while Miss Nightingale was in the midst of her battles at the Crimea, copies of *The Times* containing an extravagant attack on the army medical and purveying services, delivered in England as a public lecture by the newly returned Mr Bracebridge. Miss Nightingale was furious with him. She took to her bed alleging sciatica. Hall, too, was furious. He believed, wrongly, that Bracebridge's diatribe had been inspired by the lady superintendent. Miss Nightingale saw that Bracebridge's indiscretions also provided openings for the Irish Bridgeman faction. While in bed she wrote to scold Bracebridge and to warn him against launching into public denunciations of the Irish nuns. After all, she remarked, '"they can lie & I cannot". If you see well to tell this to Manning — I have no objection.'[79] She also primed Lizzie Herbert: 'Dr Hall does not think it beneath him to broil me slowly upon the fires of my own Extra Diet kitchen . . . Remember, please, that this is quite private, that I do not wish to complain of Dr. Hall, who is an able & efficient officer in some ways'. She went on to note incidentally that Hall had countermanded her order to supply eggs to non-officer patients.

> And, if Mr Herbert saw no impropriety in it . . . a private letter from some high authority to the Commander in Chief [Raglan had died — his successor, Codrington so far had ignored her] . . . to the effect that this work is not a silly display of feminine sensibility but an authorized set of tools.

Miss Nightingale also advised Mrs Herbert to press the War Office to send out more Bermondsey nuns 'to counterbalance . . . the Irish . . . who hate their soberer sisters with the moral hatred which, I believe, only Nuns and Household Servants can feel towards each other'.[80] The additional nuns were never sent.

Three weeks before this letter Miss Nightingale had had a final row with Rev. Mother Francis. Sister Mary Winifred, one of the Bridgemanites, although recruited from Liverpool, died of cholera at Balaclava. Miss Nightingale joined the group at her bedside and prayed with them. While praying she had also dispatched with her umbrella a large rat attempting to get at the dying nun. Miss Nightingale then joined the funeral procession to a prominent site on the Balaclava hills, and offered to build a cross upon the grave. Rev. Mother Francis delayed her reply until she had received and accepted a similar offer from the 89th Royal Irish Regiment. Miss Nightingale told Sidney Herbert: 'Mother Brickbat's conduct has been neither that of a Christian, a gentlewoman, or even a woman.' Miss Nightingale returned to Scutari, embattled on all fronts.[81]

Miss Nightingale had now reached the limits of the possible in her contributions to the internal working of the hospitals. Increasingly she looked beyond to the general management of army medical services. Her views on compelling the purveyors to work within a framework of standard issues of food, clothes and furniture and to make regular daily rounds to monitor the flow of their supplies, and on appointing house stewards and hospital commissaries on the French model, were all adopted by the War Office. Her scheme for the revision of the duties and pay of medical officers was adopted in the Royal Warrant of September 1855. She also conceived the idea of a school of army medicine early in 1855 and one was begun in a small way at Scutari.

On Good Friday 1856 (21 March) she returned for her third inspection of the Crimea. Her long awaited rescript proclaiming her full jurisdiction over 'the East' had finally arrived some days earlier.[82] Very likely Lord Panmure and the War Office had held it up until the end of the war was imminent. The peace conference had already begun. She was now equipped to stop Hall placing nurses without consulting her — she alleged that he had installed two nurses from Smyrna in the Crimea hospitals — and to stop Rev. Mother Francis extending her sway over the two Land Transport hospitals which hitherto had had no female nurses. Cholera had broken out there. Hall had invited Miss Nightingale to send nurses, but she was afraid that the Brickbat would preempt her. When Herbert sent news of the forthcoming rescript he counselled Miss Nightingale against wielding it too heavily upon Hall and the Brickbat; this would only provoke a 'damaging public row'. 'You need not be afraid that I shall molest the "Brickbat"', Miss Nightingale jauntily assured him through Colonel J.H. Lefroy. 'Above all, I am afraid of their resigning, & making Martyrs of themselves.'[83]

The row would have indeed been damaging. Hall, who had learned to deal carefully with Miss Nightingale's letters, supplied General Codrington and the War Office with copies of letters proving that she had offered the Smyrna nurses and that he had accepted them in good faith. As Miss Nightingale's future enemy at the War Office, the Deputy Secretary, Benjamin Hawes, remarked, 'Sir J. Hall has met the charge.'[84] She then adverted to an episode which her biographers have accepted as proving petty persecution from an aggrieved purveyor and Bridgeman ally at the Crimea:

As a practical woman, I think it a pity to give Mr Fitzgerald [Deputy-Purveyor at the Crimea] the pleasure either of refusing my Requisitions or of falsifying them to the W.O. I shall therefore take up everything with me which my Hospitals will want, leaving it to the Queen to supply such things only as bread & meat etc which I cannot make.

Had this man been one of our persuasion, he would have been brought to a Court Martial — But it is enough for a man to be a Roman Catholic for the Government to say 'Oh! do pray be quiet, don't tell of his lies'.[85]

David Fitzgerald had in December/January 1855/6 been deputed by the War Office to report secretly on the nursing arrangements at the Crimea. Although I have found no evidence to this effect, his commission might well have been part of a Hawes — Hall-Andrew Smith plan to counter Miss Nightingale. Fitzgerald commended the Bridgeman party for their efficiency and devoted service. He criticised Miss Nightingale for meddling, intriguing, and pretensions to dominate the whole hospital system.[86] In all, the report, which I could not find in the War Office papers — probably it was never officially filed — appears to have been a shrewd and fairly accurate survey, if unduly kind to the Bridgemanites, whose hospitals were as dirty and cholera-infested as the rest and whose impact on the orderlies was apparently about as marginal as the Nightingale party's. Fitzgerald gave a copy of of his report to Rev. Mother Francis — possibly she had helped with it because some of the detail in it could have come only from her (this also explains the strange survival of a copy in a Kinsale convent). Miss Nightingale knew by hearsay of the report but she had been unable to obtain it, even from Sidney Herbert, who very sensibly had refused her demand that he move for its tabling in the House of Commons. So, on Miss Nightingale's third visit to the Crimea, Fitzgerald was a marked man.

Within days of her arrival Miss Nightingale alleged to Sidney Herbert and other important people that Fitzgerald had refused food and shelter to the Bermondsey nuns whom she had brought with her. For over ten days she had to feed them and supply fuel from the special stores she had brought with her.

I tell you this not because I ask you to do anything. It is merely because I wish to leave on record some instance of that which nobody in England will believe or can ever imagine . . . You don't know what it is to have your 'children' short of food and warmth and to doubt whether you are not sacrificing them . . . for the good of the work.[87]

There is a novelist's perverted irony in these paragraphs. Miss Nightingale was beguiled by her own effrontery in playing the great power game. Astute Dr Hall had instructed his subordinates in writing to provide Miss Nightingale with everything she asked for; all was to be supplied according to rule by countersigned requisitions. But even this precaution was insufficient to thwart Miss Nightingale's outrageous stratagem which was, as she exulted, unimaginable at home – but only too believable to Hall. Dr Taylor had instantly agreed to place her contingent on full rations by requisition as things were required. She led him to believe that only part of the contingent had arrived and that he would be informed when the remainder from Scutari disembarked. He was never told that they were all at the Crimea. He never received a complaint about inadequate supplies. Moreover, he learned that potted meat supplied to the 'half' contingent had not, on Miss Nightingale's orders, been used. The ten obedient Bermondsey nuns, devoted to the lady superintendent in her struggle with the Brickbat, had fasted in silence. Miss Nightingale also drew upon her arrival a full allocation of tea, sugar and food from the purveyor's store but when the assistant purveyor asked her servant if they wanted more, the servant replied 'the Nurses had a sufficient quantity to last for a few days longer, and when necessary he would draw them altogether'. These further supplies were never requested. The assistant purveyor's statement was attested by three of his men. Miss Nightingale continued to broadcast the story throughout April: to Uncle Sam, to Parthe, to Sidney Herbert, to Sir John McNeill with the understanding that McNeill would bypass the War Office and Horse Guards and convey its gravamen to Prince Albert and the Queen. Parthe made copies and distributed them. In the Crimea, Hall finally countered by threatening to hold an open inquiry, but at home the lying went on.[88]

Miss Nightingale's arrival with her general order confirming her power throughout 'the East' brought the final collision with the Brickbat. Miss Nightingale wanted the Irish nuns to acknowledge her chieftainship and stay. She refused to accept Rev. Mother Francis's refusal and gave her twenty-four hours in which to submit. The Brickbat, backed by four Catholic chaplains, tendered her resignation to the newly knighted Sir John Hall. Miss Nightingale then tried to move Sidney Herbert to press Manning and the hierarchy to order them to stay, and pleaded hysterically with the Brickbat at a final interview, but the Brickbat and her nuns went home, leaving the key to their storeroom with Mr Purveyor Fitzgerald. Miss Nightingale posted herself outside the storeroom until an orderly gave in and fetched the key.[89]

After their departure Miss Nightingale brought four more Bermondsey nuns to staff a hospital rapidly emptying of patients and now containing only 98. Such aid as was needed was required at Scutari, caring for seriously ill men invalided from the Crimea. But Miss Nightingale had a point to make. She set about telling important people that the General Hospital held twice the number of patients which it had really held when she arrived, and that the numbers remained large long after they had in fact diminished. By May, Hall was able to close the hospitals, for want of patients. Her story was to become enshrined in official narratives. Something of the virulence of intra-Catholic hatreds shows in the treatment accorded the Bermondsey nuns by the Crimea chaplains. The chaplain to the Irish party, Father Michael Gleeson CM, declared that the Bermondseys' submission to Miss Nightingale was not 'for the good of religion'. He refused to visit them. Father Duffy SJ, refused them confession and holy communion. And lest Manning and the Irish bishops admonish the Bridgemanites for not standing to their post, Rev. Mother Francis saw to it that the four chaplains endorsed her decision to leave the Crimea.[90]

Miss Nightingale's private vilification of the Irish nuns began even before their departure. 'Your pig-sty is cleaner than ... the Hospital, as left by Mrs Bridgeman — The patients were grimed with dirt, infested with vermin, with bedsores like Lazarus (Mrs Bridgeman, I suppose, thought it holy)'. This letter, to Uncle Sam Smith, was copied by Parthe and sent to Sir John McNeill and Monckton Milnes, among others. Florence sent similar accounts to Lady Cranworth and Colonel Lefroy, one of the commissioners who investigated the hospitals at the Crimea. Lefroy, despite professing admiration for her work, refused to incorporate in his report her allegations against Fitzgerald and her charge that the Bridgeman hospital had squandered abnormally large amounts of rations. But he did imply that the Irish nuns fed their charges larger portions than the patients received at the Scutari hospitals. Hall privately denied to the War Office that the Bridgeman hospital was unusually dirty and, indeed, suggested the opposite. Miss Nightingale had spread the notion that he had been 'disgusted with the state of the Hospital'.[91]

The letter to the Puseyite, philanthropic Lady Cranworth contains a vivid example of that fine-toned double-bluff which had now become characteristic of Miss Nightingale, and of that distancing which issued in contempt for the pawns in her game:

I almost consider it a duty to add that, upon comparing the dirt, disorder, extravagance & carelessness which ... this Hospital, when just left by Mrs Bridgeman & her 11 nuns exhibited — with the working of our poor, despised & (I am sorry to admit it) too often exposing — themselves — to — be — dispised Nurses, I think that everybody who understands Nursing, must say 'rather one Nurse than 5 Irish nuns'.[92]

To other correspondents Miss Nightingale was, as we have seen with Mrs Lawfield and others, almost entirely dismissive of the common nurses.

Yet it was this passion to succeed, this assertion of the right to command, exemplified both in Miss Nightingale and Rev. Mother Francis, which did compel the doctors to exert themselves and the orderlies to improve their work. While the British hospitals consistently reduced their disease death rates after the crisis of the first terrible winter of 1854/5, the death rates in the French hospitals continued high and finally topped the worst British rates. The fifty French sisters of Charity were lowly, semi-literate drudges in the hospitals, unable to command anybody, and shared the insanitary habits of their patients and doctors. British doctors, none too fastidious themselves, were appalled at the filthiness of French hospitals, at the overflowing chamber pots which lay about uncovered and unemptied, at the soiled, reeking beds, at the typhus, scurvy and diarrhoea which ravaged the wards unchecked.[93] Miss Nightingale went to Scutari to emulate the French sisters, but she quickly surpassed them. It was a splendid achievement for her thin red line which only numbered 142 altogether and never more than 49 at any one time, constantly beset by illness and breakdowns.[94]

Miss Nightingale returned from the Crimea as the ministering angel, recognised by her sovereign. She had made valuable, influential friends in the Crimea, McNeill, Lefroy, and Tulloch. She had won the allegiance of able, biddable disciples, Drs Parkes, Sutherland, Alexander and Balfour, and Rawlinson the engineer. The Nightingale Fund, soon to rise beyond £40,000, was at her disposal. Sidney Herbert's political fortunes were now intertwined with her reputation. Lord Panmure could procrastinate, but ultimately was unable to withstand the political pressure she could mobilise. She was poised to make a new career in reforming the sanitary state of the British army to avenge the 11,000 men who, she believed, had died of disease and ill-attended wounds. Henceforth her enemies, Sir Benjamin Hawes, the prospective Permanent Secretary in the War Office who had seen through her tactics and had suffered from them, Sir John Hall, the generals at the Horse Guards, and the Commander in Chief, the Duke of Cambridge, would have to take extraordinary measures to stop this unleashed free-lance elemental force.

Notes

1. F.N. to Mrs Herbert, 14 Oct. 1854, quoted in Sir Edward Cook, *The Life of Florence Nightingale* (2 vols., London, 1913), vol. I, p.152.

2. Ibid., pp.148, 151.

3. F.N. to Mrs Herbert, 14 Oct. 1854, BL Add.Mss 43396, ff.11-12; Cook, *Nightingale*, vol. I, p.151.

4. S. Herbert to F.N., 14 Oct. [1854], Cook, *Nightingale*, vol. I, pp.150-1; Parthe Nightingale to R. Monckton Milnes, 'Monday' [16 Oct. 1854], Houghton Mss 18/158, Trinity College, Cambridge.

5. Cook, *Nightingale*, vol. I, p.151.

6. Margaret Goodman, *Experience of an English Sister of Mercy* (London, 1862), pp.57-60; Thomas Jay Williams, *Priscilla Lydia Sellon* (London, 1965), p.134.

7. Charlotte Willoughby Moore to C.P. Shepherd, 12, 15 Oct. [1854]; S. Herbert to Bishop Blomfield, 17 Oct. 1854; Blomfield to Shepherd, 14 Oct. 1854, GLRO HI/ST/NC3/SU/4, 2, 3, 5.

8. Evelyn Bolster, *The Sisters of Mercy in the Crimean War* (Cork, 1964), pp.17-21.

9. 'Memorandum of Agreement' GLRO HI/ST/NC3/SU/1; Grace Ramsay, *Thomas Grant first Bishop of Southwark* (London, 1874), pp.136-7; Sister Bolster quotes in *Sisters of Mercy* (pp.62-3) what seems to be a variant version of the 'Agreement' held in the Bridgeman Crimean War collection at the Convent of Mercy, Kinsale. I was not permitted access to this collection.

10. Bolster, *Sisters of Mercy*, p.27.

11. Ibid., pp.27-33.

12. Ibid., p.52.

13. Ibid., p.38.

14. Ibid., pp.49-51.

15. Ibid., pp.58-60.

16. Ibid., p.60.

17. Ibid., p.64.

18. Sidney Herbert to F.N., 19 Oct. 1854, BL Add.Mss 43393, f.1.

19. E.C. Rickards, *Felicia Skene Of Oxford* (London, 1902), p.111.

20. Cook, *Nightingale*, vol. I, p.158.

21. C.H. Bracebridge to T.B. Murray, 5 Nov. 1854; Selina Bracebridge to 'Dear Sir' [C.P. Shepherd?], 22 Jan [1855], GLRO HI/ST/NC3/SU/24, 7; C. Holte Bracebridge, *Shakespeare No Deerstealer* (London, 1862); C.H. Bracebridge, 'On the Mode of Inflicting the Punishment of Death', *Transactions of the National Association for the Promotion of Social Science*, 1866. (Hereafter *Transactions NAPSS*.)

22. F.N. to Sidney Herbert, 25 Dec. 1854, BL Add.Mss 43393, f.51; Mary Jones to F.N., 22 Dec. 1854, GLRO HI/ST/NC3/54/17.

23. Cook, *Nightingale*, vol. I, p.167.

24. Florence Nightingale, *A Contribution to the Sanitary History of the British Army during the Late War With Russia* (London, 1859), p.2; Return showing the Number of Officers and Men . . . in the Military Hospitals at Scutari . . . October and . . . November 1854, *H.C. Papers, 1854-55*, vol. XXXIII, pp.256-7.

25. F.N. to Sidney Herbert, Private, 10 Dec. 1854, BL Add.Mss 43393, ff.22-5; 1 May 1855, GLRO HI/ST/NC8/14d.

26. Elizabeth Davis, *The Autobiography of a Crimean Nurse*, ed. Jane Williams (2 vols., London, 1857), vol. II, pp.102, 128; F.N. to [Duke of Newcastle?] 10 May 1855, GLRO HI/ST/NC8/14d.

27. Emma Fagg to Madam [Mary Jones?] 4 Jan. 1855, GLRO HI/ST/SU/22; *Nurse Sarah Anne* [Terrot] *With Florence Nightingale at Scutari*, ed. Robert G. Richardson (London, 1977), p.88.

28. Elspeth Huxley, *Florence Nightingale* (London, 1975), pp.101-3; F.N. to Sidney Herbert, 25 Nov. 1854, BL Add.Mss 43393, ff.13-14.

29. Ibid., f.17; Dr A.J. Cumming to Sir John McNeill, 5 Nov. 1856 (copy); Sir John McNeill to F.N., 8 Nov. 1856, BL Add.Mss 45768, ff.21, 33-4; Stanley Lane-Poole, *The Life of . . . Stratford Canning* (2 vols., London, 1888), vol. II, p.383.

30. F.N. to Miss Gipps, 5 Dec. 1854, GLRO HI/ST/SU/14; Bolster, *Sisters of Mercy*, quoting Fanny Taylor, p.121.

31. Unknown correspondent to 'Dear Madam' [M. Jones?], 4 Dec. 1854, GLRO HI/ST/SU/15.

32. Marey Ann Coyle to Dear Madam [M. Jones?], 5 Dec. [1854], GLRO HI/ST/SU/16.

33. Ibid.

34. F.N. to Miss Gipps, 5 Dec. 1854; Mary Jones to F.N., 22 Dec. 1854, GLRO HI/ST/SU/14, 17.

35. Cook, *Nightingale*, vol. I, pp.182, 186; Sidney Godolphin Osborne, *Scutari and Its Hospitals* (London, 1855), p.25; William Usher to F.N., 24 Feb. 1895, GLRO HI/ST/NC2/V/1/95.

36. F.N. to Mrs Maria Hunt, 6 Sept. 1855; Elizabeth Kellett to F.N., n.d., GLRO HI/ST/NC1/55/4, NC/V10.55.

37. F.N. to Sidney Herbert, Private, 10 Dec. 1854, BL Add.Mss 43393, ff.22-5.

38. Ibid.

39. Alicia Blackwood, *Narrative of personal experiences . . . During a Residence on the Bosphorus throughout the Crimean War* (London, 1881), p.233.

40. Lord Stanmore, *Sidney Herbert* (2 vols., London, 1906), vol. I, p.365; F.N. to Sidney Herbert, 3 April 1856, BL Add.Mss 43393, ff.231-2; Sir Anthony Sterling, Assistant Adjutant-General of the Highland Division, complained that Miss Nightingale used far too many orderlies in the hospitals, Sir Anthony Coningham Sterling, *Letters from the Army In The Crimea* (privately printed 1857), pp.227, 314-5.

41. F.N. to Sidney Herbert, 15 Dec. 1854, BL Add.Mss 43393, ff.34-40.

42. Bolster, *Sisters of Mercy*, p.75; Helena Concannon, *The Irish Sisters of Mercy in The Crimean War* (Dublin, 1950), p.13.

43. Mary Stanley to Lizzie Herbert, 21 Dec. 1854, quoted in Stanmore, *Herbert*, vol. II, p.374; F.N. to Sidney Herbert, 21 Dec. 1854, 12 Feb. 1855, BL Add.Mss 43393, ff.40, 142-4.

44. Bolster, *Sisters of Mercy*, p.90; Jane Harding to F.N., 15 Aug. 1856, GLRO, HI/ST/NC2/V10/56.

45. F.N. to Sidney Herbert, 15 Dec. 1854, 25 Dec. 1854, BL Add.Mss 43393 ff.37, 46, Joseph John Gurney, *The "Record" and Miss Nightingale* (London, 1855).

46. A.J. Cumming to F.N., 22 Dec. 1854, BL Add.Mss 43401, f.23.

47. A Lady Volunteer (Fanny Taylor) *Eastern Hospitals and English Nurses* (2 vols., London, 1856), vol. I, p.66; Bolster, *Sisters of Mercy*, pp.99-100.

48. Bolster, *Sisters of Mercy*, pp.96-8.

49. F.N. to Sidney Herbert, 25 Dec. 1854, BL Add.Mss 43393 ff.47, 54; Bolster, *Sisters of Mercy*, pp.94-5, 99-101, 110.

50. [Terrot], *Nurse Sarah Anne*, pp.98, 115-6; [Sarah Terrot] *Reminiscences of Scutari Hospital in Winter 1854-55* (Edinburgh, 1898), pp.86, 89, 98.

51. F.N. to Sidney Herbert, 25 Dec. 1854, BL Add.Mss 43393, f.45.

52. Mrs Gaskell to Emily Shaen, 27 Oct. 1854, J.A.V. Chapple and Arthur Pollard (eds.) *The Letters of Mrs Gaskell*, (Manchester, 1966), p.319.

53. Parthe Nightingale to Monckton Milnes, n.d. [Dec. 1854?], Houghton Mss, Trinity College Cambridge, 18 149(2).

54. Cook, *Nightingale*, vol. I, p.215; [Terrot] *Nurse Sarah Anne*, pp.146-7; Parthe Nightingale to Lizzie Herbert, 9 Dec. 1854, (copy) BL Add.Mss 43396, f.14.

55. e.g. Dr Wallis to W.E. Nightingale, Jan. 10 1855, BL Add.Mss 45790, f.164.

56. Anon., *Illustrated History of the Expedition To The Crimea*, issue of mid-Feb. 1855, p.16; Joseph Samuel Prendergast to Frank Prendergast, 15-17 Feb., 4-6 March, 25-28 Apr. 1855, BL Add.Mss 59849, ff.35, 50, 82.

57. Osborne, *Scutari*, p.25.

58. F.N. to Sidney Herbert, Private 14 Jan., 22 Jan. 1855, BL Add.Mss 43393, ff.95, 105.

59. Elizabeth Woodward to [M. Jones?] 3 Jan. 1855, GLRO HI/ST/SU/20; F.N. to Sidney Herbert 15 Feb. 1855, BL Add.Mss 43393 ff.154-9. Bolster, *Sisters of Mercy*, p.156; [Terrot] *Nurse Sarah Anne*, p.133.

60. F.N. to Council of St. John's House, 11 Jan. 1854 [recte 5] GLRO HI/ST/SU/18.

61. Cook, *Nightingale*, vol.I, p.255; Davis, *Autobiography*, vol. II, p.136; Sidney Herbert to F.N., 10 Apr. 1859, BL Add.Mss 43395, f.155.

62. Cook, *Nightingale*, vol. I, pp.220-1.

63. F.N. to Aunt Mai Smith, 19 Oct. 1855, BL Add.Mss 45793, f.106; Bolster, *Sisters of Mercy*, pp.123, 147; Davis, *Autobiography*, vol. II, p.164.

64. Joseph Samuel Prendergast to John Prendergast, 31 Dec. 1855, BL Add.Mss 59849 f.1; F.N. to Aunt Mai Smith, 19 Oct. 1855, BL Add.Mss 45793, f.106; James S. Taylor, *Alexis Soyer A Chivalrous Chef* (Washington, 1921), p.15; Cook *Nightingale*, vol. I, pp.258-9; F.N. to Sir John McNeill, 21 May 1855, BL Add.Mss 45768, f.1.

65. F.N. to Aunt Mai Smith, 19 Oct. 1855, BL Add.Mss 45793, ff.108-9.

66. Mrs Mary Sansom to Rev. C.P. Shepherd, 28 June 1855, GLRO, HI/ST/SU/33.

67. Florence Nightingale, *A Contribution to the Sanitary History of the British Army during the Late War With Russia* (London, 1859), p.14; F.N. to Dr John Hall, 14 July 1855, BL Add.Mss 39867, ff.17-19.

68. Dr John Hall to F.N., 20 July 1855; F.N. to Hall, 24 July 1855, BL Add.Mss 39867, ff.20-22.

69. Rev. Mother M.F. Bridgeman to Father Woollett, SJ, 2 Sept. 1855; Woollett to Dr John Hall, 3 Sept. 1855; Hall to Rev. Mother Bridgeman (copy) 27 Sept. 1855, BL Add.Mss 39867, ff.27-9.

70. F.N. to Rev. C.P. Shepherd, 21 Aug. 1855, GLRO HI/ST/SU/36.

71. Bolster, *Sisters Of Mercy*, p.196.

72. General Storks to Hall, 8 Oct. 1855; Hall to Storks, 'Private & Confidential' [copy] 11 Oct. 1855, BL Add.Mss 39867, ff.42-3.

73. F.N. to Hall, 15 Oct. 1855; Copy to War Office instructions 155656/193, BL Add.Mss 39867, ff.44-6, 43401, f.11.

74. F.N. to Hall, 21 Sept. 1855; Hall to F.N., 27 Sept. 1855, BL Add.Mss 39867, ff.31-7.

75. F.N. to Lord Stratford de Redcliffe, n.d. [18 Oct? 1855]; Stratford de Redcliffe to F.N., n.d. [19 Oct.? 1855], BL Add.Mss 43401, ff.86-7.

76. Bolster, *Sisters of Mercy*, p.199. Sister Bolster gives no date for this letter.

77. A Lady Volunteer, *Eastern Hospitals*, vol. II, pp.163-7; Hall to F.N.,

19 Oct. 1855 (copy); F.N. to Mary Wear, 6 Nov. 1855 (copy); Hall to F.N., 28 Oct. 1855; F.N. to Hall, 7 Nov. 1855; Hall to F.N., 7 Nov. 1855 (copy), Mary Wear to Hall, 9 Nov. 1855; BL Add.Mss 39867, ff.52-63; F.N. to Hall, 27 Oct. 1856 [recte 5] PRO WO1/383/109.

78. Davis, *Autobiography*, vol. II, pp.185-6.
79. F.N. to C.H. Bracebridge, 4 Nov. 1855, BL Add.Mss 43397, ff.171-5.
80. F.N. to Lizzie Herbert, 17 Nov. 1855, BL Add.Mss 43396, ff.40-4.
81. Bolster, *Sisters of Mercy*, pp.212-14.
82. Cook, *Nightingale*, vol. I, pp.292-3.
83. Sidney Herbert to F.N., 4 Mar. 1856, F.N. to Sidney Herbert, 20 Feb. 1856, 21 Feb. 1856, BL Add.Mss 43393, ff.211-22; F.N. to Colonel J.H. Lefroy, 16 Mar. 1856, BL Add.Mss 43397, f.225.
84. Hall to General Codrington 12 Mar. 1856 (copy); minutes by Lefroy, J. Peel and Hawes, early Apr. 1856, PRO WO1/383, ff.105-16.
85. F.N. to Lefroy, 16 Mar. 1856, BL Add.Mss 43397, ff.225-6.
86. F.N. to Lefroy, 11 Jan. 1856, BL Add.Mss 43397, ff.205-6; David Fitzgerald to Hall, 23 May 1856, BL Add.Mss 39867, ff.156-8.
87. F.N. to Sidney Herbert, 3 Apr. 1856, BL Add.Mss 43393, ff.224-8.
88. Hall to F.N., 26 Mar. 1856 (copy); F.N. to Hall, 19 Apr. 1856; Dr G. Taylor to Hall, 21 Apr. 1856, Henry Powell (Acting Purveyor) to Fitzgerald, 23 Apr. 1856, Hall to F.N. 23 Apr. 1856, BL Add.Mss 39867, ff.100-28; S.M. Mitra, *The Life and Letters of Sir John Hall* (London, 1911), pp.441, 459-63; F.N. to Uncle Sam Smith, 17 Apr. 1856, BL Add.Mss 45792, ff.28-30; Parthe Nightingale to Sir John McNeill, n.d. [late Apr. 1856?] GLRO HI/ST/SU64; Parthe to ? with extracts from F.N.'s letter to Uncle Sam, 17 Apr. 1856, BL Add.Mss 45768, ff.14-5.
89. F.N. to Sidney Herbert, 3 Apr. 1856, BL Add.Mss 43393, f.229; F.N. to Uncle Sam Smith 17 Apr. 1856 and copy by Parthe, BL Add.Mss 45792, f.28, 45768, f.6.
90. F.N. to Lefroy, 5 Apr. 1856, BL Add.Mss 43397, ff.228-30; Bolster, *Sisters of Mercy*, pp.281-2.
91. F.N. to Uncle Sam Smith, 17 Apr. 1856, BL Add.Mss 45792, f.30; Parthe Nightingale to Monckton Milnes, [late Apr. 1856]. Houghton Mss., Trinity College, Cambridge, 18, 152 (A,B); Lefroy to F.N., 10-22 May 1856, BL Add.Mss 43396, f.231; Sir John Hall, 'Observations', (Oct. 1856) PRO WO33/3B.
92. F.N. to Lady Cranworth, 19 May 1856, BL Add.Mss 43397, f.109.
93. F.N. to Sidney Herbert, 28 Dec. 1854, BL Add.Mss 43393, f.58; F.N. to Douglas Galton, 5 May 1863, BL Add.Mss 45761, f.3; Charles Bryce, *England and France before Sepastopol, looked at From a Medical Point of View* (London, 1857); C. Shrimpton, *La Guerre d'Orient, L'Armée Anglaise et Miss Nightingale* (Paris, 1864), pp.4, 57; A.W., Kinglake, *The Invasion of the Crimea*, 8 vols., Edinburgh, 1883, vol. VII, pp.157-63, 440-3.
94. Lady Volunteer, *Eastern Hospitals*, vol. II, p.269.

3 THE CAMPAIGN FOR ARMY SANITARY REFORM

War is the opportunists' festival. Miss Nightingale's appointment had been a minor political expedient. She had seized the chance to enlarge her authority, but her relation to the army and War Office remained anomalous and insecure. With the ending of the war her career was in jeopardy. At 36 she was now a national heroine, the compeer of Grace Darling and Mrs Fry. The 'Lady-in-Chief' enjoyed the sentimental reverence of the nation and the palpable reward of the Nightingale Fund, together with a brooch from her sovereign, being the first woman to be so decorated for public services. The War Office, however, was resolved to end this meddlesome coadjuvancy. Moreover, the Nightingale family reported that her health was impaired. It seemed that her great public work must conclude and that she would retire, or return eventually, like any ordinary good woman, to the redcurrant jam of hospital management.

But Miss Nightingale had savoured the political game at the highest level. The commanding of others, the access to privileged information, the making of secret decisions, the entrapment of enemies and promotion of friends, canonisation by the public, had become the foci of her will, the pabulum of her imagination. She had to find a way of continuing in the power game. Her strength was her public standing and the admiration of some important persons; her resource was her capacity for indefatigable intrigue; her justification was the abolition of insanitary muddle in the army and the identification and punishment of those who had blundered. Within limits — the great personages who had per custom declared a war in which they themselves did not fight, who had mismanaged it, and who had botched the peace — they remained beyond Miss Nightingale's censure. She was no radical critic or leveller. She kept clear, for reasons both of faith and prudence, of patriot-agitators in the House of Commons like J.A. Roebuck and Augustus Stafford.[1] They wanted to stigmatise, rather than reconstruct. She, more than they, saw that it was a question of power. To join their campaigns, as a woman in their male parliamentary world, would entail oblivion. Her target comprised the men in the army and War Office who threatened her own reputation and the continuance of her secretaryship: doctors, purveyors, army officers, War Office officials, ministers of the crown. Many of their blunders had already been documented by

72

Sutherland's Sanitary Commission which had begun ordering improvements early in 1855 and by the McNeill-Tulloch reports on the commissariat in June 1855 and January 1856. All the commissioners found administrative confusion, laziness, timidity, callousness and stupidity. There had been shortages of food, clothing, animal fodder and shelter, but fundamentally the catastrophe of the first winter resulted from a breakdown in distribution ensuing from the High Command's unpreparedness to cope with a prolonged campaign in extreme climatic conditions. In terms of absolute numbers of dead the Crimean losses of 16,300 from disease and 13,000 invalided – compared with 1,760 dying from wounds and 2,660 killed in action – about 46 per cent of the 94,000 men who embarked for the East, amounted to a disaster comparable in modern times only with the calamitous campaign in the Netherlands in 1794-5. It was small consolation that the French losses, at about 70,000 dead and 65,000 invalided were absolutely and relatively greater, and that the uncounted Russian losses were probably larger still.[2] Miss Nightingale had much to be angry about. 'I stand at the altar of the murdered men, and, while I live, I fight their cause', she jotted in a private note of 1856.[3]

Her return to England in July 1856 coincided with the release of a report from the Enquiry of the Chelsea Board of General Officers which had been concocted by the Horse Guards to rebut the findings of the various commissions, especially the severe but balanced reports by McNeill and Tulloch. The Chelsea Board, composed of men who had never seen the Crimea, exonerated staff and regimental officers. 'Nobody was to blame.' The military Barnacles, abetted by ministers who wanted to extinguish a dangerous issue and a public become weary of yesterday's war, joined to bury the problem. Even McNeill and Tulloch, both at the end of their careers, were disposed to give up.[4]

Not so Miss Nightingale: within a fortnight of her homecoming she had wangled an invitation to visit the Queen and was busily prodding McNeill and Tulloch. She needed royal backing for her move to compel Panmure to institute an enquiry into the sanitary condition of the army, as a front for her work. The Queen was a ready tool, but Prince Albert proved difficult. He was, Miss Nightingale found, 'predisposed in favour of the Horse Guards'. She specially equipped herself with details, supplied by McNeill, about Mr Commissary Filder's false excuses about the want of transport to bring fresh meat to the Crimean soldiers, but Albert remained unconvinced. Panmure acquiesced, and then did nothing about it for six months, until March 1857, probably in the ill-founded expectation that Miss Nightingale would drop the matter. Miss Nightingale privately diagnosed him for her friends as possessing 'no courage or conscientiousness' and as 'the most bully-able of mortals'.[5] More accurately, he was a politician in a shaky coalition ministry, committed to reducing expenditure on the army now that peace had come, and adept at lying low on contentious questions. Moreover, Miss Nightingale's demands were extraordinary. She confronted Panmure as a private person with no official standing beyond that of public heroine, and a woman to boot, to demand official sanction for a commission of enquiry, the membership of which would be nominated by her, the procedures of which were to be determined by her, the objects of which were to be defined by her. The whole affair was to be independent of the War Office and Horse Guards, and yet it was to be paid for by government. Only a national heroine who could not imagine limits to her presumption, supported by a queen blind to the implications of that presumption, could have brought off such a coup.

Meanwhile Miss Nightingale was counter-attacking on other fronts. She learnt that Mary Stanley and other ladies were circulating rumours about her high-handedness. She arranged to see Lord Murray, 'amongst several other prominent persons', to tell him 'the truth'. 'You are the very person with whom I should like to make an exception to my rule of silence when attacked, yet I believe that you would be the very person who would advise me not to do so.' None the less, Miss Nightingale repeated that she was not going to enter into public controversy: by implication Lord Murray and other recipients of the truth were to do her fighting for her.[6] She had also heard that Dr Peter Pincoffs, a civilian who had served at the Barrack Hospital and whom she had lately snubbed, was contemplating writing a history of hospital services in the Crimea. Now, in October 1856, she sent him a long, warm invitation to visit her.

I will mention to you, in confidence, that I am under orders from the Queen, Lord Palmerston, and Lord Panmure to do the same thing in the form of a Précis to be presented to the Government . . . I expect that the consequences to me and the Service will be . . . great harm to my means of usefulness . . . But truth is truth & I shall tell it — my own object in thus writing to you, is to say that it is evidently of great importance that the Reformers should not appear to contradict each other — & therefore, if you would allow me a sight of your manuscript . . . with a hearing of your . . . explanations of it I should esteem it . . . a matter of great value to the Service.

Pincoffs's *Eastern Military Hospitals* is a well-informed account solidly based on the personal experience of a decent man. But several assertions in it, notably that Miss Nightingale won the confidence of most doctors, and that the high quality of the tiny medical school at Scutari owed everything to her, together with the vague hagiographical declarations which intrude into the narrative, suggest that Pincoffs belatedly revised his manuscript to please his new found patroness.[7] It also happens that these dubious assertions are just the ones used by Cook and repeated since by most biographers.

In November Panmure came to Miss Nightingale to settle the membership of her commission. He was now alert to her alliance with the Queen, her general support from Palmerston, the Prime Minister, and her hold over Sidney Herbert who was now out of office and ready to interfere. Panmure was well briefed by the War Office and the army medical authorities. They had equipped themselves with a long memorandum by Sir John Hall which refuted Miss Nightingale's wilder accusations about neglect, dirt and conspiracy.[8] There is no evidence that she knew of the existence of this document although she doubtless expected that Dr Andrew Smith and the War Office would look to their defences. Sidney Herbert was subsequently to use his position as head of the commission to supply Miss Nightingale with as many of Hall's letters as he could extract from the War Office. 'I send you Hall's correspondence. You know the matters treated with all the dates which I do not, and will see in them what I should not.' The proceeding was quite improper. Miss Nightingale relished it: 'I return your stolen goods. Pray keep them carefully. If ever we have to besiege the Army Medical Department, no Lancaster gun could be more formidable than this document.'[9] She took the initiative, confident that she could use the Queen, Palmerston and Herbert. Her list for the commission began with Herbert as president, and included General Storks, Dr Sutherland, Colonel Lefroy and Dr T.G. Balfour, assistant-surgeon to the Grenadier Guards, but a reformer, and former colleague of Tulloch's and already a distinguished medical statistician. Each was an ally, from the Crimea. She had been briefing some of them, at least, for almost a year, letting them think that the ideas were theirs.[10] It was a blatant exercise in packing but the quality was first-rate. Panmure, himself not averse to seeing the army medical service smartened up, proposed only Dr Andrew Smith, and vetoed only two of Miss Nightingale's more outrageous and costly suggestions. During their three hour meeting Miss Nightingale extended the scope of her proposed operations. As she noted afterwards in a triumphant personal memorandum on the interview:

Instructions: general and comprehensive, comprising the whole
Army Medical Department, and the health of the Army, at home
and abroad ... Smith, equal parts lachrymose and threatening,
will say, 'I did not understand that we were to inquire into this'. . .
　　You must drag it through. If not you, no one else.

Herbert now glimpsed glory in his prospective headship of the
commission and busied himself with preparing for it. Miss Nightingale
perceived her danger: 'My master jealous. Does not wish it to be
supposed he takes suggestions from me.' She countered by ignoring
him when issuing her orders to Panmure:

> (1) Col Lefroy to be instructed by Lord P. to draw up scheme
> and estimate for Army Medical School . . . I won.
> (2) Netley Hospital [the projected new military hospital near
> Southampton] plans to be privately reported on by Sutherland and
> me to Lord P. I won . . .
> (5) Sir J. Hall not to be made Director-General while Lord P. in
> office. I won.
> (6) Colonel Tulloch to be knighted. I lost.[11] [Tulloch was sub-
> sequently knighted and McNeill made a Privy Councillor after the
> government had blundered early in 1857 by trying to buy them off
> with £1000 each. They indignantly refused the offer and, egged on
> by Miss Nightingale, they made a public fuss, Herbert raised the
> matter in the House of Commons and the government gave in.]

In the event she also gained her two unacceptable nominees: Dr
Thomas Alexander, another Crimean reform ally, specifically recalled at
much expense from Canada; and Sir James Clark, the Queen's
physician, whom Miss Nightingale wanted because it was 'Agreeable to
the Queen to have him – just as well to have Her on our side'.[12]

Although she had no direct experience of high politics Miss
Nightingale moved effortlessly into the political game. Her forte was
annexation. In an age when ministers could be isolated from their
civil servants and, in a spirit of *noblesse oblige*, cajoled into entrusting
public business to high-born meddlers, her standing and determination
enabled her to gain ill-defined mandates over areas that ministers
deemed peripheral to national concerns. Once gained, the mandate
became the justification for further annexations embodied in particular
reform programmes launched without effective ministerial or financial
control. These she enlarged until she tired of them or until the costs

became so great that government became interested enough to override her. She was not an original thinker. She rarely was first to see what needed amendment and equally rarely did she foresee how the amendment was to be effected. But as a reformer she had four brilliant, unusual gifts. First, she repeatedly discovered and enlisted people with the skills to define problems and formulate solutions. Second, once briefed by her aides she could state the case with compelling clarity and marshall tremendous personal force and persistence in the ensuing battle with officialdom. Third, she possessed an unfailing alertness to the distribution of power and to the ambitions of others, although sometimes this sense was negated by her own ambition and her desire to boast. Finally she acted in the faith that whatever she believed and whatever she proposed to do was practically and morally right. Her memorandum of her interview with Panmure indicates her strengths and limitations. Only one of the main items on the list was her original contribution — the veto on Sir John Hall. Drs Pincoffs and Alexander and Colonel Lefroy, amongst others, had developed the idea of an army medical school and improved conditions of service for army doctors. Dr Sutherland did the critical work on the Netley Hospital designs. Even Tulloch's knighthood was a subject of dinner-table controversy before she took it up. Among her subsequent memoranda on the medical school, the projected courses on ambulance work, field surgery, sanitary reporting and climatology, amongst an impressively thorough list, were, with one notable exception, devised by Sutherland and Alexander. Their ingenuous exception formed the subject of Miss Nightingale's paper to the exclusion of everything else, even nursing: she projected a rigidly hierarchical government for the school that would make it independent of the War Office and effectively subject to her.

Her lust for authority always overset her concern for her policies. A secretary prepared to press reforms, yet vest their authority and prestige in existing government officials, might have found the task harder and might have achieved less in the short run. But Miss Nightingale set her reforms apart from official power and kept them dependent upon her personal force — a force that was really factitious and which often collapsed, taking her reforms with it — as her pretensions were exposed.

Miss Nightingale projected the Royal Commission into the sanitary condition of the army both as a further exposure of Hall, Smith, Fitzgerald & Co., and as an engine for further work on the army. Panmure procrastinated for six months and finally issued the warrant in May 1857.[13] There was, after all, every likelihood that her health would fail in the meantime. Unfortunately for Panmure, the frail Miss Nightingale did not yield and instead forced his hand. She had, she claimed, at their meeting with the Queen at Balmoral in mid-1856, been ordered by him 'in principle' to prepare a confidential report on the sanitary condition of the army. Panmure again had procrastinated until February 1857 before confirming this order. Miss Nightingale meanwhile had already compiled much of her draft. He surrendered to the inevitable and formally gave Miss Nightingale what she wanted – undefined scope. She was invited to discuss not only 'the medical care and treatment of the sick and wounded' but 'the sanatory requirements of the Army generally'. 'In principle', the report was to be confidential, but Miss Nightingale let it be known through Sidney Herbert that she retained the right to publish it if the War Office tried to bury it. In the event the report was absorbed by the Royal Commission, but not before Miss Nightingale had it privately printed and distributed among influential people, including A.W. Kinglake, the historian of the war, who was then beginning his work.[14]

The *Notes On Matters Affecting the Health, Efficiency, And Hospital Administration of the British Army . . . presented by request to the Secretary of State for War* amount to about 230,000 words over 830 pages. The presentation is the granite index of a strong ambitious mind: certainty of opinion at every point; inexorable argument against opponents; digests; recapitulations; numbered brief recommendations artfully planted among the sections; spontaneous audacity in proposing nothing less than a thorough reconstitution of the army medical and purveying departments based on exact detail and elaborate statistical charts to buttress the arguments, all presented in the mimic format of a parliamentary blue book. Three things stand out. The chain of authority planned for the newly independent army medical department would lead ultimately to Miss Nightingale, not to the Commander in Chief. The new Director-General and his subordinates were to report to a 'board of inspection' which was to comprise her nominees. Second, Miss Nightingale's novelistic gifts show both in her flashes of rhetoric:

> The observance of sanitary laws should be as much part of the future regime of India as the holding of Military position or as Civil government itself. It would be a noble beginning of the new order of things to use hygiene as the handmaid of civilization – [she was writing during the Mutiny]

and in her invention of an exploded piegraph to reinforce visually her assertions about the relative causes of mortality at Scutari through time. Such was her art that her certainties served, apparently incidentally, to highlight the faults of the enemy:

'typhoid fever' is well known to be pre-eminently due to foul air, arising from overcrowding and want of drainage; and, till the sanitary works at Scutari were executed [i.e. by Nightingale and the Sanitary Commission], it appears, by Dr. Cumming's own showing [i.e. his report on the varying incidence of diseases] to have prevailed there.[15]

Sanitary reform was her talisman. Only by pressing it as a better preservative of life than clinical treatment could she maintain her standing and keep the doctors and officers at bay. The fall in the death rate after March 1855, following the improvements in drainage and sewage disposal at Scutari, does support her case. But there were other important contributory factors which she played down or ignored. The improvement in the weather after March and the mild second winter must have helped, together with the relative quiescence of the war and the consequent opportunity to improve supplies and shelter for the troops. Miss Nightingale's impressive-looking statistical tables and exploded piegraphs hide these components. None the less her argument was rendered the more persuasive because the doctors were such easy targets. Menzies did ignore the blocked drains at the Barrack Hospital and the overflowing privies at the General Hospital. His notion of sanitation consisted in whitewashing walls. Hall and the purveyors did nothing to expedite the delivery of limejuice while scurvy was rampant. Hall's innate stinginess, reinforced by regulations which he revered both as shield and Holy Writ, led him to delay consignments of medical supplies, even during cholera outbreaks, until each amounted to a full load. Dr Smith let his subordinates assume that only preserved vegetables were to be used at Scutari; yet Scutari was adjacent to a city of 600,000 people who lived on vegetables. Similarly, the purveyors supplied green unroasted coffee beans to troops camped in Turkey where good coffee was the national drink. The Navy Board, Miss Nightingale pointed out, supplied antiscorbutic and fresh vegetables without trouble. Indeed, she had secretly been in touch with the Board while writing this part of her report.[16] But in the Navy anti-scorbutics had been for three-quarters of a century part of the normal food issue, whereas in the army they were 'medical' and therefore to be had only by doctor's requisition. Despite her vehemence on this point, Miss Nightingale's own notions on prevention of scurvy were as limited as the doctors'. She had 600-800 Scutari patients on her extra-diet rolls during the winter of 1854-5: scurvy and allied disorders were widespread yet, according to her own figures, her only contribution was eight quarts of lemonade. Like the doctors she made her stand-bys beef-tea, barley-water and rice puddings. During the summer she had, by doctors' requisition from the official stores, 8,200 oranges and 4,000 lemons, 57 apples and six pounds of quinces, to be distributed among several thousand patients. Her recommended recipe for lemonade for military hospitals was five lemons to 12 pints of water. (Mrs Beeton's 'Nourishing Lemonade' in 1861 requires the juice of 4 lemons and the rinds of 2 to every 1½ pints of water. Modern authorities on diet suggest a daily intake of vitamin C roughly equal to one lemon or orange a day.)[17]

Once she had established the doctors' and purveyors' guilt, Miss Nightingale dismissed them. The fault lay in 'the system'. There was no proper chain of authority, no precise allocation of responsibility, no codes for purchase and distribution of supplies. She brilliantly projected a new system in which every man, from Director-General to hospital orderly would have his set tasks and defined accountability. Medical officers were to be empowered not only to advise, according to an official code, on the siting and sanitation of camps but also they were to insist, upon threat of an official inquiry if things went wrong, that the commanding officer implement their recommendations. Should the commanding officer refuse he was to be required to do so in writing to the War Office.[18] At one stroke a new scale of authority was being planned for the army. (The Horse Guards saw the threat and blocked this provision.) Stewards and purveyors were to be made independent of medical officers' requisitions and were to become responsible for obtaining and distributing all supplies according to prescribed lists, subject only to the orders of the responsible general officers. All failures in supply and distribution were to be reported in writing. Miss Nightingale adopted this procedure from the East India Company hospital system; probably she learnt about it from McNeill, who had been a Company surgeon. Every element of army hygiene, diet, shelter, ventilation, latrines, clothing, rest periods, provision of orderlies, was to be codified. Miss Nightingale, drawing upon excellent advice from her Crimea cronies, provided the codes.

Together the *Notes* constitute an astonishing example of her gift for imagining palpable needs and assembling workable remedies. She was creating a self-acting, self-regulating system, embodying individual will-power in action, designed to secure the maximum output of useful work for the total money and manpower expended. 'Minuting', the War Office's method of gathering opinions and sharing responsibilities for decisions – and of muffling and delaying action – was to stop. Decisions were to be taken quickly, by identifiable officers. 'Minuting', moreover, kept information and decisions inside the War Office: decision-taking by single officials would open the Office to Nightingale influence. The 'minuting' process, in her view, both increased and hid the waste of time, men and materials that accompanied the merely ornamental tokens of status and misdirection and misappropriation of public resources endemic in the closed administrative system.[19] At one blow Miss Nightingale was proposing the transformation of a traditional hierarchical, haphazard and irresponsible yet hidebound establishment into a modern bureaucracy. Private business was to become public service. Miss Nightingale's inclusion of 'efficiency' in the title of her *Notes* is one of the first usages of the word in its modern sense (it did not enter the official military vocabulary until 1864); her use of the word, coinciding with the early moves to reform the civil service, universities, and local government, is a portent of things to come.

Even medical treatments were to be standardised. Miss Nightingale pointed out that at the Crimea, as in every preceding campaign, each surgeon observed the traditional decentralised practice of keeping to his own regimental wards and never officially exchanging reports with his neighbours. No army medical man had the opportunity to specialise. Only a new army medical school could provide the uniform, particularised training that would produce, as the navy medical school at Haslar already did, soundly equipped surgeons trained by experts who were enabled to pursue research. This research necessarily had to be founded upon the reports of a new army medical statistical department, also devised in detail by Miss Nightingale, drawing upon advice from the great statistician, Dr William Farr. Moreover, she pre-empted the findings of the professors and statisticians by providing for a future Barracks Improvement Commission to implement their recommendations about the removal of deleterious influences such as bad ventilation and ill-managed camp canteens.[20]

Each recipient of the report received his particular instructions with it. Earl Grey, for example, was warned that the report was 'confidential' and really intended only for Lord Panmure. Miss Nightingale tactfully directed his attention to the digests by assuring him that he need not 'go through the details ... but it would be the greatest advantage to our cause if you would give the weight of your influence in the House of Lords to such parts as you approve'. The third Earl, a cantankerous, clever man, upset Miss Nightingale's expectations and rebelled: 'I disagree with the emphasis of your report — it was the leadership — not the system — Raglan as compared with Wellington.' Wellington, he argued, dismissed officers who failed in their duty, whereas Raglan neither knew that Hall and Filder had failed nor dismissed them when he was finally informed about them. 'Your standing commissions ... will only *lessen responsibility* of Commanding Officers and Medical Officers', Grey remarked. The Navy had already reformed its medical services without commissions. Grey's precipient truculence endangered Miss Nightingale's whole position. Without the commissions she would have no standing. She immediately sent a vague, emollient reply which Grey graciously accepted as a surrender to his opinions. He was 'glad you think there is no great difference of opinion between us'. Yet she furiously annotated his letter with reiteration of her views: 'only a skilled trained Medical Officer can deal with ... diet, clothing etc.; 'Medical Officers did nothing at Scutari.; 'Army and Navy not to be compared — navy not in barracks and constantly see their men — in relatively stable conditions — army medical officers always confronted with something new'; and then, verging upon a direct negation of Grey's argument, 'must create separate sanitary Division of Army'.[21] Grey is not recorded as referring to her views in the House of Lords. Miss Nightingale was later to try to use him for other objects, but she and Grey never became allies.

She similarly failed to snare A.W. Kinglake. He was willing to make eloquent obeisance in his laborious history to the Lady with the Lamp, but he was much too shrewd to break his links with the War Office and the official clubland world and become a propagandist for the crusading female and her nondescript, elderly, unworldly supporters. Miss Nightingale was astute about people and she summed up Kinglake after their first meeting. She had sought to 'educate' him but he proved non-committal. 'I have been much worried', she told McNeill,

> by making the acquaintance of Kinglake, the historian (to be) of the late war — He had no judicial mind — not much feeling — not much conscience — & takes a superficial view of the whole thing. But his history will be as clever as everything he writes, and every body will read it and be deceived — He repeated to me all the *fadaises* of the Staff; & he gives the whole fund of unexamined commonplaces

(... about the non-supply of clothing etc and the QMGs Dept.) as historical material.[22]

She sent him, indirectly through Mrs Monckton Milnes, a book containing juxtaposed extracts from McNeill's report and the Chelsea Board. Her *Notes* arrived as reinforcement.[23] But Miss Nightingale's estimate that he would not use the critical evidence is borne out by the *History*. It is the first model bland war history: everyone is valiant and no one is to blame, and results are less important than the action. 'He is a good Counsel', she remarked, '[but] he strikes me as a very bad historian.'[24]

After these heady secret dealings with the Queen, Panmure, Lord Murray and other notables, the public Royal Commission on the sanitary state of the army at the Crimea was an anti-climax for Miss Nightingale. Once launched on her secret *Notes*, she had dismissed the projected Royal Commission as a mere public performance. She had not backed Herbert in urging Panmure to proceed with it; indeed, among her intimates she had denigrated Herbert's efforts. Yet when Panmure finally announced it, she insisted upon drawing up, in concert with Sutherland and Dr Alexander, the subjects to be canvassed and the men to be questioned.[25] During the sittings of the Commission she tended to leave the day-to-day management to Sidney Herbert. She proved lax about priming witnesses before they appeared before the Commission and Herbert had to undertake the major part of telling them 'what you want to get out'.[26] Herbert also took the initiative in isolating Dr Andrew Smith on the Commission by altering Smith's draft for the inquiry, without informing him. Miss Nightingale's letters to McNeill and her memorandum of the 1860s (written after Herbert's death) about the Royal Commission, claim that she 'shaped it's daily questions' and imply that she did the work while Herbert played the dilettante figure-head.[27] Their surviving correspondence from this period suggests the opposite: behind Herbert's back she was envious and disparaging.

During the sittings of the Commission Miss Nightingale's concern was to ensure that her spokesmen, Rawlinson, Sutherland, Balfour, Storks, McNeill and Tulloch, were enabled yet again to publish the shortcomings of Hall and his friends and to designate the work in sanitary improvement necessary to prevent such knaves and fools perpetrating another catastrophe. Hall's appearance as a witness posed a dilemma for Miss Nightingale. She wanted to punish him, but she could not risk a further alienation of the army's counter forces in

Parliament and the War Office. His examination had therefore to be as subtle as it was inexorable. She deputed Sutherland to do the job, coached by her after she had checked her brief and copies of Hall's reports with McNeill:

> Sir John Hall is to be examined next week. I have been asked to ask you to give some hints as to his examination . . .
>
> My own belief is that Hall is a much cleverer fellow than they take him for — almost as clever as Airey [Quartermaster-general at Crimea — he had by agreeing with the implications in every hostile question dextrously evaded the Commission's questions and exonerated himself a few days earlier] . . . I recall to you the long series of proofs of his incredible apathy . . . his not obtaining — lime juice Fresh bread Quinine etc and not denouncing salt meat . . . this man is (morally) the worst of liars. We do not want to badger the old man in his examination, that will only harm us — but we want to take the best out of him for our case.

As Miss Nightingale feared, Hall did well at his examination. He easily answered Herbert's rather vague questions. Sutherland remained mute, while Smith performed brilliantly in feeding Hall obviously prepared questions which enabled him to develop the argument that the death rate at Scutari fell during and after March 1855 because the numbers of sick men admitted to the hospitals fell from 6,000 to 3,000 and further declined thereafter. Miss Nightingale was vexed with Sutherland. 'He lets very inferior men put him down, owing to his want of pith.' Hall, Airey and Smith, by contrast, had lots of pith and were nimble too. In fact, the fair-minded Sutherland agreed with Hall's explanation and privately told Miss Nightingale so. Hall's escape, she lamented to McNeill, 'upsets the conclusion I want to impress on Mr Herbert'.[28]

This setback persuaded her that she must, in addition to having her *Notes* incorporated into the Commission's report, rehearse her main findings in the Commission's printed evidence. Her decision embarrassed Herbert. It was *outré* for a female to appear as an expert witness before a public inquiry. Mrs Caroline Chisholm had done so in 1847; but she was a married woman, and her appearances had been before a select committee of the House of Lords. Moreover, the Commission was Herbert's show. Miss Nightingale was likely to swamp it. But her popularity was such that he could not prevent her appearing should she decide to do so. He realised also that she was vulnerable.

Smith and Hall had demonstrated that the reduced death rates at Scutari could be attributed to causes other than her ministrations. Smith was a cool man. If she tried to hector him she might divide the Commission and ruin its standing. Herbert tried to restrict her to presenting evidence only on hospital construction.

> But this [she complained to McNeill] leaves untouched the great matters which will affect (& have affected) the mortality of our sick more than any mere Architecture could do ... People Government and Sovereign think everything has been remedied – but nothing has – It would be treachery to the memory of my dead if I were to seem to give in to the popular error ... Please advise.[29]

She did not want advice. She wanted McNeill's acquiescence in her decision to give evidence, and possibly a letter from him to Herbert approving her plan, because on that same day she sent an almost identical letter to Herbert announcing her intention to canvass the whole issue of disease, mortality and medical organisation in the army. She had also decided that she would not appear in person, but tender evidence in writing – thousands of words from the *Notes*, tables, graphs – a procedure as outlandish as a female expert giving evidence in person. Herbert then tried to persuade her to make her evidence 'confidential' and to leave it out of his report. She reluctantly agreed at first, but it appeared none the less.[30]

This episode is a signal illustration of the contrariety in her nature between the craving to dominate unseen and the impulse to enjoy public recognition of that dominance. She began by flattering herself with outright refusals, then played hard to get and finally made herself available for capture.

Her life is crowded with such contrarieties. At Scutari she repeatedly evaded requests from Jerry Barrett, the painter, to sit for her portrait. He had travelled specially from England to accomplish the feat. 'I have determined in no way to <u>forward</u> the making a show of myself or of any ... thing connected with that work though I cannot always <u>prevent</u> them from being made a show of.' She never refused Barrett outright. She visited his studio and although she would not sit for him she took a continued interest in his picture of 'Florence Nightingale at Scutari' and frequently came to study its progress.[31] The painting is now in the National Portrait Gallery and is reproduced on the £5 note. She never refuted Parthe's story that she refused to sit for or to look at the bust by John Steell, presented to her by the non-commissioned officers of the army in 1862. Yet she permitted the distribution of replicas.[32] In 1868 she refused a request for a photograph from Dr William Rendle, her ally in attempting to reform workhouse infirmaries. 'I never had one done, except once by command. [The portrait of 1856, taken for Queen Victoria.] I have a superstition, as far as myself am concerned, against "images made with hands" − & would rather leave no memorial . . . either of name or anything else − but only of God, whose unworthy servant I am.' Cook lists five portrait photographs taken before this letter was written. In 1887 she refused her 'ever dearest "Little Sister"', nurse Pringle, a photograph of a portrait statuette. Next year she gave one of the statuettes to a Scandinavian admirer.[33] These coy fluctuations in her projection of her self sometimes plunged into flamboyant self-extinction. Quite apart from her anonymous, celebrated return from the Crimea as Miss Smith and her unheralded but again celebrated return to Lea Hurst, she twice announced her impending death. In November 1857 she placed among her papers an envelope addressed to Sidney Herbert, marked 'to be sent when I am dead'. The letter comprises four pages of mingled recrimination, hints at reconciliation and arch withdrawal:

> I hope you will not regret the manner of my death. I know that you will be kind enough to regret the fact of it. You have sometimes said that you were sorry you had employed me. I assure you that it has kept me alive. I am sorry not to stay alive to do the 'Nurses' [Report on female nursing in army] . . . I must be willing to go now as I was to go to the East . . . Perhaps He wants a 'Sanitary Officer' now for my Crimeans in some other world where they are gone.

In February 1862 she prepared a similar letter, leaving directions about their future joint publications, for Dr Sutherland. The letters appear not to have been sent.[34] She survived on both occasions and there is no evidence to suggest that she had grounds for believing that she would die or commit suicide. Both letters appear to have half-stifled pleas for work and sympathy. Between 1864 and 1872 she separately told Mrs Bracebridge, Mary Jones, her High Church nursing disciple, and Dr Jowett of Balliol, that when she became infirm she wished to be taken to St Thomas's, left anonymously in a general ward 'and left there to die', thence to be buried anonymously. Each was 'not to breathe a word of this'. Apparently only Jowett was alarmed enough to try to dissuade her, or at least only his reply survives. He was down to earth. Her intention was 'eccentric'; besides 'it will kill you . . . and it will annoy your father'.[35] Jowett, like the rest of Miss Nightingale's friends, believed that she suffered from impaired health, the results of her privations at the Crimea. I shall return to this belief later.

Extinction of self also saved bother. Miss Nightingale regularly pleaded mingled modesty, pressure of business and ill health for refusing to allow her name to be used in connection with public committees and good causes. Moreover, as she explained to Richard Aspden, the secretary to the Manchester Clinical Hospital for Children which had elected her an honorary governor, she could not join organisations which she had not helped to create because there was always something wrong with them. In the Manchester case, she could not approve the rules by which they conducted their nursing.[36] Yet the self-hatred that issued from insecure narcissism ran very deep. Miss Nightingale, the stickler for accurate statistics, described herself in her return for the 1871 census as 'Imbecile & Blind'; and then boasted to Sutherland of having done so.[37] In 1872 she drafted a note to Aunt Mai remarking that she was glad she had never married and had children. Children ensured the continuance of self in the world, beyond the control of self and that was a prospect, in the light of Francis Galton's recent discoveries about heredity, 'immeasurably awful'.[38] 'Be of good cheer. I have overcome the world', she quoted St John of the Cross on a scrap of paper about 1873. 'Verily he has overcome all things in whom the pleasures of them excite no joy, & the bitterness of them no sadness.' That is 'indifference', she commented, 'not overcoming'.[39]

Sometimes Miss Nightingale thought herself to be the crucified Christ. At other times she thought herself to be an animate nothing, existing only in the will. But whether Christ recrucified or animate nothing, her will to work was continually thwarted by lazy, hostile men. Her struggle, she liked to tell others, was so much onerous because she was so womanly and diffident. She mused beguilingly to Jowett that she wished she 'had the combative faculty. It _is_ such a power to carry me [sic] through life.'[40]

The Herbert Commission's report fell flat. The press and the quarterlies were preoccupied with the Indian Mutiny, while Panmure, probably deliberately, tabled it in the House of Lords in February 1858 in the midst of the row over the Conspiracy to Murder Bill. The report was never debated in Parliament. The shaky ministries of the late 1850s did not dare upset the parliamentary colonels. The colonels' contributions to a short debate on a resolution moved by Viscount Ebrington, the sanitary reformer, deploring high mortality in the army, demonstrated the wrath that could descend from both sides of Parliament. The Commander in Chief, the Duke of Cambridge, received a special copy from Sidney Herbert. He very sensibly declined to give an opinion on it because it dealt with 'matters with which he is unacquainted'.[41]

Had the report been Miss Nightingale's rather than Sidney Herbert's, she would have busied herself promoting it. But she spent most of the autumn and winter of 1857 recruiting her health at Great Malvern. She left the task of arranging for favourable reviews in the quarterlies to Herbert and Edwin Chadwick, who had lately offered his services as sanitary ally to the great lady.[42] Late in December she casually told McNeill in a dictated letter — for she now declared herself too ill to write — that she 'had 10,000 copies printed — to circulate among medical and commanding officers'. In a draft in her own hand to McNeill, presumably made before the dictated note, the number was 2,000 and there was no suggestion that they had yet been printed. This idea she had presumably from Chadwick, who had used it to win acclaim for his Poor Law and Sanitary Reports. There is no evidence that she proceeded with the scheme. She was more concerned with having copies of her exploded piegraphs of army mortality framed, glazed and then sent to be hung at the Horse Guards, War Office and Army Medical Department. This gift was to be a 'flank march upon the enemy ... "God's revenge upon Murder"'.[43] When Chadwick confessed in March 1858 that he had made little headway with publicising the report and getting a cheap edition onto railway stalls, Miss Nightingale complacently told Sidney Herbert that it did not 'really matter ... Army matters are going on too well for that'.[44]

The commissions for army sanitary improvement, as provided for in Miss Nightingale's *Notes* and the report of the Royal Commission, were already at work. Panmure had finally conceded them official recognition in November 1857,

> with such ample instructions for 'preparing draft Instructions & Regulations defining the duties etc etc etc etc and revising the Queens General Medical Officers, Barracks, Purveyor's and Hospital Regulations' — as you may guess,

she crowed to McNeill, who had by now largely replaced her father as recipient of such confidences

> they were written by me — What a fool Panmure must be! Does he not see or does he not care where this will lead him? . . . All that is necessary now is to keep Mr Herbert up to the point . . . This new Sub-Committee [on Army Hospital organisation and management] entails upon me a labor I must gladly undertake.[45]

She had immediately repaired to Great Malvern, taking Aunt Mai with her.

Three days after Panmure's commission arrived, on 19 November 1857, Aunt Mai was compelled to finish a letter that her niece had begun but was unable to complete. The letter was to Lady McNeill. Aunt Mai had to

> say at her desire that her health is failing every week, and that she is compelled to give up any writing not absolutely necessary for business . . . She desires me to add . . . that it is of the utmost consequence to her, that no alarm concerning her health should be communicated to anyone. If it were to reach Mr Herbert he might from a desire to spare her, refrain from giving her the means of helping in the work, which would . . . fatal to [her] health, for which the only relief possible is advance in the work, to which she feels herself devoted.

The kindly, motherly Lady McNeill was expendable, unlike her husband. She was upset by the bad news and wrote to enquire more particularly about Miss Nightingale's illness. Aunt Mai replied that 'Dr [Walter] Johnson [the fashionable hydropathic practitioner] calls it "tension of the nerves" . . . Her head is as clear for work as ever . . . She is quite unable to do more than this, or you would hear from her . . . please ask Sir John to send copies of the Hospital Diets of Edinburgh Infirmary and tell him that she and Mr Herbert have fixed the Field Purveyorships.' (A second draft of this letter says that Herbert 'would not go far enough on the Purveyorships . . . and so the Report does not show this'.[46] This second version seems to be more correct. The recommendation was never pressed.)

It is universally accepted that Florence Nightingale endured a lifetime of debility and confinement to her bed after the Crimea. Sir George Pickering, in *Creative Malady*, argued that her illness, in common with that of other valetudinarian celebrities, gave her room to think and work. Sir George relied upon the evidence published by her biographers. Her unpublished papers suggest a more complicated story. Aunt Mai, the ill-used secretary, reported to Lady McNeill in January 1858 that Florence's health varied 'from week to week, with no real change or progress'. Yet she had 'very little treatment in the way of water cure, but the . . . comparative quiet makes it very suitable for her'. She remained in her room and saw no one 'except on business'. Aunt Mai thought that despite Florence's nervous tension, 'her head was never clearer or more able for business'. Miss Nightingale herself described her illness as 'nervous fever'.[47]

She was still hard at work on hospital matters in March 1859, when she wrote in her own hand to thank McNeill for data he had sent her. She invited him to visit her when next he was in London: there was 'much to talk about . . . Ministers are insecure.' (She was right. Lord Derby's second administration finally crashed in June 1859.) As an afterthought she invited Lady McNeill, too. But they had to come at a time of her choosing, when she was well enough to talk. She further stipulated that she was 'not able to see more than one person at a time, especially those who interest me so much' − to the end of her life she continued this practice of excluding witnesses − And she reinforced the prohibition by announcing that she was 'not able to sit up at all'. Nowhere in this letter does she say that she is ill.[48] Instinctively she had devised the perfect situation for compelling the attention of her chosen visitors and maximising the chances that the visitor would confide in her and undertake her behests. In mid-1861 she recruited as secretary her uncle Sam Smith, Aunt Mai's husband. (Aunt Mai had returned to her family in 1860, after two and a half years' absence, and thereafter Miss Nightingale refused to speak to her for almost 20 years.) He was directed to answer all letters from unimportant 'fools'. A few months later, in August 1861, she instructed him that she was too ill to see callers, 'especially Chadwick and the Herberts'. Uncle Sam was to give no one her address. In future he was to receive all her correspondence at his address, and bring it to her daily. She would leave the 'fools'' letters to him while, 'To anyone whom I want to see I can write myself.' Like others dismayed at her illness, impressed by her selflessness, and awed by her imperiousness, Uncle Sam acquiesced.[49]

Occasionally she diagnosed her indeterminate illness to suit her correspondent. In 1860 she drafted a note to Mrs Monckton Milnes telling her that a mutual friend had a 'weak heart and dropsy' and that he might 'die tomorrow – or live on for years to a painful death'. 'Alas', Miss Nightingale went on, 'it is [words deleted] in some respects the "prognosis" which has been made of me.' At other times she reported herself to be suffering from, according to Mrs Gaskell, 'over-pressure of the brain telling on the spine . . . necessitating rest' (1863); rheumatism of the spine and right elbow (1865); shortage of breath (1865) and 'spasms' of the lungs (1866), both on occasions when she had to visit her mother; chest 'attacks', which left her unable to speak, when Lizzie Herbert sought to call (1867); bereft of an 'ounce of strength' when she refused Chadwick's request to back him publicly in his parliamentary candidature (1868); 'feeling as if the top of my head was blown off' while excusing herself to Sutherland for being behindhand in correcting a draft (1869); 'too ill to move-probably' in 1870, when she put off a visitor, and instead travelled to the country on the day of the proposed visit; attacks of ague while discussing Indian ague with Sir Ranald Martin, 'completely knocked down with uncountable pulse and 90 hours of no sleep' again while she was visiting her mother, and forestalling another visitor (1879). In 1884, when apologising for being out when W.E. Gladstone called, she claimed to have a 'threatened return' of diabetes which she said she had first suffered in 1880. During the spring of 1888 she told Douglas Galton, her nephew and ally in sanitary reform, that she had had pleurisy for three months and been scarcely able to leave her bed, and was too ill to see him. Galton, as one of her team, had had his salary paid by the War Office. A dispute about this procedure had arisen in 1887 and Miss Nightingale had neglected to pull strings on Galton's behalf.[50] Miss Nightingale's 'Household Book' for 1888 shows that she ate heartily throughout that year. When she did suffer precise functional disorders, she did not broadcast the fact. In January 1877 she recorded with surprise that she had had 'diarrhoea all night'. (She seems to have come through the Crimea with no stomach disorders.) The diarrhoea attack did not prevent her from working all the next day. In 1873 she had the first intimations that her eyesight was impaired, but this disability did not seriously hinder her work until about 1884, when she was in her mid-60s; although her powers and interest in the world had begun to diminish about thirteen years earlier. In 1887, the jubilee, as she recalled, of Christ's first appearance to her and of her consecration to His work, she admitted to herself that 'old age had set in'.[51]

Before then her difficulty had been that she looked so well. During the mid-1860s she became plump and lost the wan spareness of her youth and Crimean years. Her journalist ally Harriet Martineau, herself an invalid who found that condition convenient, wrote silkily to Miss Nightingale in 1865 that an acquaintance had reported her to be looking very healthy: 'Julia has written that your face is deceptive, – that wld make uninformed people suppose you to be much less suffering than you are.' Miss Nightingale reassured her: 'I fail much. I never leave my bed, except to see my masters. My face is so swelled, especially when I make any such exertion, that I suppose this is what is meant by my "looking well".'[52]

Although she kept to her bed during interviews, she was always fully dressed and even into old age she sat upright unpropped by pillows.[53] Her indeterminate illnesses did not give her doctors much to work on. There is but one medical prescription among the Nightingale Papers: a general 'appetizing tonic' based on salicylic acid, phosphoric acid and sodium hypophosphate. She regularly purchased seltzer in 1877. Sir James Clark advised not to overstrain her brain in 1867 because that organ, if overworked, appropriated 'more than its own natural share of the nervous energy of the system', but nowhere in his diagnosis does he mention any general weakness or physical disability. Nonetheless, the family always reported her to be feeble, despite her looks, and her intimate, Dr Benjamin Jowett, when they took communion privately together, usually read her the lessons from the service for visitation of the sick.[54]

It remains indisputable that whenever Miss Nightingale announced herself to be ill she was busy. She told Rev. Mother Clare Moore in 1867 that she had been delayed in writing, because she had had a very bad 'attack on my Chest', which had prevented her from lying down 'for 17 nights'. Miss Nightingale added that she could 'scarcely . . . get on' with her work. This last was vexing because, 'We are having a very uphill fight about the workhouses.' Even when she complained of the rheumatism in the spine and elbow, and could not 'crook my finger and think to hold my pen', she did not stop writing 'for a single day'.[55] On official visits outside her house she travelled with great fuss in an ornate invalid carriage. When she went to Lea Hurst or Embley she took a special carriage on the train. Yet surreptitiously she walked in Hyde Park and there are two episodes which suggest that her weakness was feigned. Her niece, Rosalind Nash, recalled visiting her at South Street in the 1880s. Miss Nash encountered two of the junior servants racing each other down the stairs to the basement. One fell. 'I hurried upstairs to report, feeling very anxious . . . I opened the door, and there was Aunt Florence standing near me. I had always seen her half lying down . . . I was struck with wonder.' On another occasion, probably also in the 1880s, Miss Nash and her brother met their aunt in the garden,

> We should have kept out of the way . . . because of her health . . .
> I saw the reason, for she flushed at seeing us and for once looked
> slightly disturbed . . . She had been sailing along down the little
> glade . . . and I saw then how beautifully she walked.[56]

She had conscripted her very body in her cause. Despite her misuse of her flesh and bone she lived for ninety years. Like many great figures in history she possessed a frame that matched her will.

Disabled or not, her work in the later 1850s and through the 1860s was unremitting. In most of her campaigns Miss Nightingale was in the right. The War Office perpetrated its blunders blatantly and uncaringly, without regard to her advice. Panmure and his officials drew great applause for their decision to build a new military hospital worthy of the men of the Crimea. They proceeded to buy a site on marshy ground near a sewage outfall, at a grossly inflated price of £30,000. Then they built a hospital costing £300,000, about twenty times the amount then customarily spent upon such a project. Much of the money went on the facade and even more on the special foundations required for the unsuitable ground. The interior was skimped. Miss Nightingale criticised the nine bed wards as being too small for 'discipline', and she was the more offended because the authorities had ignored her suggestion that the hospital be designed on the pavilion system, to provide maximum ventilation and light to reduce infection. Each ward opened off a long central corridor and the beds were ranged along the dim, unventilated blank walls.[57]

  Sidney Herbert played a double game about the hospital. He had helped press for it and ensure that money was lavished on it. Once the scheme went wrong he sheered off and became a mild critic. Miss Nightingale meanwhile, having diagnosed the shortcomings, found herself blocked from effecting changes. Herbert, without telling her, finally secured from Palmerston in January 1857 an agreement to refer the plans to his Barracks and Hospital Improvement Committee.[58] She used the Committee to force through a redesign of the water closets, which had been provided without ventilation in the original plans, and a few other improvements. But it was Herbert who enlisted Douglas Galton, the future great engineer, to improve radically the

Netley ventilation system, and then Herbert boasted of it to Miss Nightingale.[59] But the damage was done. Netley Hospital never worked efficiently. Every winter the water froze in the washrooms along the corridor. Indian patients caught pneumonia. The floors, against her advice, were made of wood rather than encaustic tile, and were always damp.[60] Herbert's real interest in keeping Miss Nightingale at bay, apart from their rivalry for reputation as reformers, was to ensure that one of Mary Stanley's ladies at the Crimea, Mrs Shaw Stewart, a widow with impeccable social connections and High Church allegiance, should be appointed matron. She was a mettlesome woman, experienced in nursing and controlling staff, and she had clashed with Miss Nightingale at the Crimea. Mrs Shaw Stewart and Herbert together had stipulated, illegally, that the female nurses at Netley must all be Church of England by persuasion.[61]

After Herbert's death in 1861 Miss Nightingale found herself able to take a closer interest in Netley. Although she disliked Jane Shaw Stewart she consistently backed the matron in her endless rows with the army authorities. In a typical brush Miss Nightingale fought to get the matron the right to possess keys to the linen cupboards, hitherto held only by the purveyor.[62] When in the mid-1860s Mrs Shaw Stewart was finally driven out and the hospital reverted to male nursing management it fell into a dreadful state. There were no fixed times for dressing or feeding patients, bed sores became widespread and 'the medical cadets tried all sorts of "fancies" on [their patients] and no one interfered'.[63] A new matron, Mrs Deeble, and six nurses, all from St Thomas's Hospital, were appointed with Miss Nightingale's connivance, against the will of the Netley medical authorities. Mrs Deeble, trained in a hard school, soon put matters to rights. The timetable became effective and the bed sores and much else were reported in writing to the senior medical officer. She rebuked cadets in front of patients. Miss Nightingale rejoiced: 'They have caught a Tartar in her — Mrs S. Stewart was a dove![64]

The establishment of the hospital at Netley upset Miss Nightingale's plan for a large army medical school. She had wanted the new hospital to be built at Aldershot 'where the troops will be'. Ideally, it should have been added to the Woolwich hospital but this institution, so far as Miss Nightingale and Sidney Herbert were concerned, was a lost cause because it was controlled by Dr Andrew Smith. Netley's small wards and distance from London seemed likely to keep the numbers low. But delay could kill the project, so she settled for the inauguration of the medical school at Fort Pitt at Chatham and acquiesced in the decision that the school would move to Netley when the hospital there was sufficiently developed to receive it.[65]

Miss Nightingale and Herbert had succeeded in nominating old Crimean friends, Longmore, Martin, Parkes and Aitken, to the professorships. But the War Office contrived to appoint the safe Dr Gibson as Director-General. Throughout his regime he managed to hinder the researches of his colleagues and upset the female nursing staff. The school was never a success. The low status of surgeons in the army continued to deter good applicants. The teaching seems to have been mediocre. The senate of the school, dominated by Gibson and the War Office, regularly forestalled attempts to make hygiene a compulsory subject. Even Miss Nightingale's admirers among the staff were embarrassed by her attempts to institute a 'system of marks to be assessed on each day's work', a procedure she devised to rid the school of indolent 'Irishmen who can pass examinations'.[66] Its best teaching standards were probably attained during the early 1870s when, against Miss Nightingale's wishes, naval medical teachers and surgeons were introduced into the school. Its best practical results were probably achieved in India, where the army surgeons could apply the sanitary measures they had been taught. Miss Nightingale had insisted from the outset upon courses in hygiene but equally Parkes, Martin and their colleagues, devoted practical sanitarians all, would have emphasised such teaching without her dictation. After her influence waned in the later 1860s, contemporaneously with advances in antiseptic surgery and other clinical procedures, the Tory governments of 1867 and 1874-80 set about dismantling the Netley medical school and the succeeding Liberal government completed the destruction by enabling intending army surgeons to enrol at university medical schools. Edward Cardwell, as War Secretary, had already ended the old invidious regimental medical system in 1870 and had made all medical officers staff officers. The Netley school eventually moved to London and became an affiliate of the University of London medical schools. Miss Nightingale fought every move, striving to retain her grip on appointments and curricula, but from the later 1860s she lost every battle.[67] But she and Sidney Herbert had raised army medicine nearer to the level of navy medicine and without their lobbying it would have dragged on in its old routines a great deal longer.

Miss Nightingale's attempts to capture the whole army medical department through her projected supreme 'board of inspection' had equally mixed results. The War Office successfully fended off the board, which threatened their autonomy. They were unable to prevent

Sidney Herbert gaining a royal warrant to improve the pay and promotion opportunities of medical officers, but they managed to exclude guards' regiments' medical officers from it and thereby destroyed its effectiveness. The warrant failed Herbert's and Nightingale's hopes that it would raise medical officers' standing with their brother officers and thereby attract better men to the service. Medical officers of appropriate rank were still blocked from presiding at a board or in the mess. The warrant was finally withdrawn, under Horse Guards' pressure, in 1864.[68] Cardwell's reforms of 1870, which ended the regimental medical officer system, proved equally ineffective in raising the medical officers' standing.[69] Devious and authoritarian though her methods were, Miss Nightingale's priorities were right. But the inward-looking upper-class army headed by the stupid Duke of Cambridge would not learn. In every campaign during her lifetime, except the China War of 1857-8 when Crimean memories made the army careful in sanitary matters, disease continued to kill more men than battle.

Miss Nightingale's two main successes were associated with improvements that had been proceeding since the 1830s, in the collection of army health statistics, which T.G. Balfour had already organised, and in the improvement of barracks and camp accommodation. In both endeavours she drew on expert advice: from William Farr for epidemiological statistics and Douglas Galton for barracks construction. The War Office saw no threat in strengthening the statistical office of the army and Balfour, aided by Farr, went on to produce admirable sets of figures. Miss Nightingale's view of statistics was a simple one which she shared with her reforming contemporaries. Exact enumeration was the basis for the indication of exact social laws, from which the moral consequences of various forms of action could be predicted. Statistics were the unequivocal indicators of weaknesses and strengths in a system and the inescapable tests of the responsible human agents. Statisticians were the testers and moral guides.[70]

Barracks improvement really got under way in mid-1855 when Lord Shaftesbury took it up and induced Palmerston to provide some money for it. He, like Miss Nightingale, who came to the question in 1856, saw the problem chiefly as one of bad ventilation and filth which in turn produced physical and moral debility in the troops.[71] The Barracks Improvement Commission, comprising Herbert, Sutherland and Galton, worked extremely hard, visiting barracks all over England and recommending changes. At Wellington Barracks, for example, they urgently suggested ten additional baths, to cost £1,263; at St George's Barracks, additional latrines, baths and improved ventilation, at £5,786. G.C. Lewis, the Chancellor of the Exchequer, vetoed their recommendations. 'NCOs and Privates', he declared, did not 'understand the use of water closets.'[72] There were grounds for his opinion. At the Crimea the new WCs had been regularly blocked with old boots and food scraps. Miss Nightingale tried to evade this Treasury ruling, to Sidney Herbert's amazement, by launching a building programme and presenting the Treasury and War Office with a *fait accompli* when the bills came in. Apparently Herbert succeeded in warning her off.[73] But improvements did go forward. By 1862 the barracks at Chelsea, Gravesend, Colchester, York, Fleetwood, Pembroke, Malta and Gibraltar had variously received better ventilation, cookhouses and recreational dayrooms for the soldiers. Expenditure rose from £233,000 in 1854 to over £756,000 in 1859. By 1864 every barracks in England had 'ample water', one washbasin for every ten men and a bath for every 100. Unfortunately, there were still no regulations to compel the troops to wash themselves or their clothes.[74]

The Barracks Improvement Commission succeeded partly because it escaped Treasury and War Office control. It was chartered, like the Sanitary Commission and McNeill-Tulloch Commission at the Crimea, to institute improvements on the spot. This potentially enormously powerful breach in Treasury suzerainty had been conceived, not by Miss Nightingale or Sidney Herbert, but by Lord Shaftesbury, who had been appalled by the reports of mismanagement at the Crimea and had persuaded his step father-in-law, Palmerston the new Prime Minister, and the new War Secretary, Panmure, probably without any of them realising the constitutional implications, to send improvement commissioners with executive powers.[75] Shaftesbury also took a keen interest in the barracks question and travelled on tours of inspection, followed by Edwin Chadwick, in 1855. But possibly only Miss Nightingale glimpsed the opportunities that such commissions opened to outsider-reformers.

The improvements began to save life almost immediately. The death rate of the army at home fell from 17 per 1,000 in 1855 (double the rate of male civilians in comparable age-groups) to 9.95 per 1,000 in 1860 and to 8.86, or slightly above the comparable civilian average, in 1865.[76]

The Nightingale-Sutherland-Herbert barracks and hospital improvement programme rested upon the fixed idea that overcrowding and dirt were the prime and only generators of disease. Miss Nightingale had held this belief since at least her Harley Street days, when probably she had acquired it from Chadwick and other sanitarians writing in the 1840s. Subsequent speculations about the mechanics of the miasmic theory, whether the inhalation of putrescent substances oxidised and corrupted the bloodstream, or whether the exhalations of such substances or affected persons introduced poisons into neighbouring bodies, never interested her. Her objects were political, not scientific. Such speculations, especially theories about specific causative agents of specific diseases, and germ theory emerging in the 1860s, she detested because she perceived them as barriers to action, devices to enable medical practitioners to dabble uncontrolled whilst practical sanitarians were shackled.

Epidemiologists who questioned these assertions were attacked with lofty severity. In 1858 Dr E. Headlam Greenhow inferred from the history of measles epidemics in the Faroe Islands that there was an 'incubative' stage in disease 'carried by contagion'. He also argued that scarlet fever was a 'contagious' disease, that is, it developed from a specific illness-inducing agent transmitted from one infected person to another. Miss Nightingale, writing anonymously, rejected his theories.

> This is not sanitary doctrine and would be sustained ... by no careful observer ... It never appears to occur to the advocates of specific 'contagions' that there must have a <u>first</u> case in the world, which could not have received its 'infection' or 'contagion' from any other case; and hence, according to Dr Greenhow's doctrine, the Supreme Being must have directly infected it.

She went on to affirm that it was better to work on the proven rule that 'disease results from the infringement of known and unknown laws ... The cure for "infection", if there be "infection", is cleanliness and fresh air'. Miss Nightingale, self-proclaimed as a passionate statistician, did not attempt to meet Greenhow's figures. His so-called evidence was 'utterly futile ... All such alleged facts require to be tried by the ordinary rules of evidence, and when so tried, they fail.'[77] As we now know, Greenhow was right in his brilliant surmises. Miss Nightingale's scorn was the more virulent because Greenhow, recently appointed to the first lectureship in public health in the kingdom, at St Thomas's Hospital, was a dangerous rival. His paper was published as an official report to the Board of Health. He was also the ally of an even more threatening figure, Dr John Simon, then just beginning his great career as the proponent of scientific epidemiology and public health under the wing of central government.

The statistician, G.P. Neison, also challenged the 'sanitary-amateurs' by demonstrating, rather dubiously, that 'overcrowded' areas did not show significantly higher rates for consumption than uncrowded areas. His measures were crude, and his explanation, 'want of exercise', was even less commonsensical than the Nightingale-Sutherland argument that consumption resulted from 'shortage of good air' caused by overcrowding. The reply to Neison, published in the *Westminster Review* is signed, against the journal's custom, S(idney) H(erbert). But it reads as if it was drafted, at least, by Miss Nightingale. Typically, Neison's statistics pass unremarked. Instead the author simply reiterates that it is 'obvious . . . that the habitual admission of vitiated air will injure the lungs and produce pulmonary disease, just as the admission into the stomach of poisoned food will destroy that organ'.[78]

Apart from Herbert, Miss Nightingale marshalled other friends to write 'independent' condemnations of Greenhow's and Neison's papers. She tactfully indicated the lines of each reply and supplied its substance, her unpublished report on the army medical service in the Crimea. 'It is strictly private and confidential', she insinuated when sending a copy to Chadwick. 'I thought however I was in duty bound to send a copy to you who have always been our leader.' He duly seconded the Nightingale-Sutherland line at the Glasgow meeting of the National Association for the Promotion of Social Science in 1860. She often used Chadwick to bell cats, as he sought to use her reputation and money in his attempts to enter parliament. But she regarded him as a lightweight who was 'not scientific'; he was among those forbidden to visit her.[79] He in turn frequently defaulted on his promises as publicity agent: she equally refused to support his campaigns publicly. They were wary rivals, allied by necessity in promoting their separate careers as sanitary reformers.

Miss Nightingale continued throughout her life to support defenders of the miasmic theory. Diehards such as Douglas Galton in the 1870s, (he quietly changed his mind in the mid-1880s) Sir J. Clarke Jervoise in the 1880s and Dr Elizabeth Blackwell in the 1890s were inspired by her example when disputing specific germ disease theory.[80] Each advance in germ theory diminished the sanitary reformers' opportunities to advocate work that won public esteem. Miss Nightingale liked to say that 'facts are everything – doctrines are nothing'[81] but the fight during the 1860s about the classification of disease data shows how doctrines can create facts. Dr Farr and Miss

Nightingale fought to retain generalised 'zymotic' categorisations – engendered from outside from dirt and other avoidable conditions – which implied a rebuke to government and a need for preventive action. Dr Simon and the medical profession, including Dr Balfour who proved traitor to the Nightingale group on this issue, pressed for a less politically charged, more precise 'gridiron' classification listing the disease, the parts affected in every case, and as many special pathological features as could be conveniently included. Simon won.[82]

Quarantine also posed threats to Miss Nightingale's usefulness and she fought it equally vehemently and unavailingly. Despite increasing evidence to the contrary, especially in relation to smallpox in Britain and cholera in India, she never departed from the assertion that 'Quarantine is a complete failure.' Quite apart from its restrictions on individual freedom and international trade, quarantine implied official endorsement for contagionist theory and, as the Ottoman Empire demonstrated, an excuse for authority to evade its sanitary duties.[83] Depending upon her correspondent, she could even make contagion theory and quarantine anti-Christian. She informed Jowett that whenever the facts were established 'in Science ... those facts will show a "moral" – the best "moral" ... [showing] best the perfect God, leading men to perfection. "Contagion" would then shew God a Devil.' When smallpox broke out in Oxford in 1871 she instructed Jowett to ensure that the college rooms were 'thoroughly aired'; this would obviate the need to send the undergraduates away.[84]

The Herbert-Nightingale work for army sanitary reform had become firmly established by the time of Herbert's failure in health in late 1860 and ensuing death in August 1861. Their partnership, thanks to Miss Nightingale's and her biographers' celebration of it, is one of the most famous in British history. The surviving evidence suggests a more precarious alliance. Until the Crimean episode, Miss Nightingale had been closer to Mrs Herbert than to her husband. In 1849, two years after their first meeting in Rome, Florence called her 'the Spirit of Love'.[85] Miss Nightingale found Lizzie Herbert a useful mouthpiece during the Harley Street escapade, but their intimacy turned cold when Lizzie succumbed to Mary Stanley and abetted the Anglo-Catholic party at the Crimea. Thereafter Florence's career demanded that she cultivate Sidney Herbert rather than his wife. He was a genuine reformer imbued with a mixture of *noblesse oblige* due to family piety and Peelite impatience with muddle. Doubtless he would have moved independently to improve the army medical service and camp accommodation after the Crimean débâcle but he proved dilatory even under Miss Nightingale's goading and rivalry and his efforts would have been limited and weakly pursued. Above all, Miss Nightingale established for him what had to be done. He needed her to lend momentum to his cause but in acceding to the alliance he found himself gundog to an inexorable and untiring huntress.

Herbert had been unwell since at least January 1858 when he complained to Miss Nightingale that he suffered 'neuralgic headache and tic in the temple and jaw'. He was inhaling and, as he remarked, making himself sick with, 'Christchurch Remedy' – a mixture of chloroform and camphor, topped off with numerous glasses of brandy. She apparently countered by claiming to suffer the same affliction. Herbert's ailments left Miss Nightingale unmoved.[86] Behind his back she waged a quiet battle for the total allegiance of their shared factotums. 'Sidney Herbert is very forgetful', she warned young Captain Galton in 1860. He had failed to move on the 'Cape Hospital Huts (which you are to design) . . . No one appreciates as I do Mr Herbert's great qualities. But no one feels more the defect in him of all administrative capacity in details.'[87]

The worse his illness became, the more exigent she became. She needed him to reform the War Office before he became incapable. Her view of 'reform' meant removing the Permanent Under-Secretary, Sir Benjamin Hawes, and other obstructionists and replacing them with men 'of business from outside'. She did not complain about their competence: simply they were in the way of her ambition to plant her nominees in the Office, to abolish 'minuting' and to make all officials directly responsible to the Secretary for War, who would report to her. In place of 'minuting', all important documents bearing upon soldiers' health were upon completion of drafting or receipt to be sent to her for perusal. Dr Sutherland was, of course, already in the Office, but effectively he was seconded to her service and he spent most of his time working at her home. Similarly, Captain Galton called with papers and to receive instructions almost every morning. Sir Edward Lugard, Military Under-Secretary, was also a Nightingale devotee. Some of the old guard were now in their sixties and probably they were tired, although Miss Nightingale never remarked on it. The Peninsula War veteran, Sir John Burgoyne, Inspector-General of Fortifications, was to be edged out in favour of Galton, who was to take 'Buildings' (including barracks etc.), while Major Jervois, another rising young engineer, was to have 'fortifications' which was unimportant in her scheme. The reactionary Commander in Chief, the Duke of Cambridge, was beyond her reach but she intended to neutralise him by replacing his private secretary, W.F. Forster, with a more amenable go-between.[88]

Apart from dilatory Herbert, the man who stood between her and this audacious coup was Sir Benjamin Hawes. Miss Nightingale's biographers have uniformly accepted her characterisation of him as devious, procrastinating and self-serving. The little evidence we have suggests that Hawes deserves better. At the time of the Crimean hospital crisis he was imaginative and innovative. He instigated I.K. Brunel, his brother-in-law and dearest friend, to design and superintend the construction of the hospital at Renkioi, much the best hospital in the East. The hospital was designed in the pavilion style linked by covered walkways. The 22 wards were prefabricated, with special provision for ventilation, ducted heating and plumbing. It is little celebrated in the literature but, more than the cumbersome and inefficient Lariboisière in Paris, it is the first modern hospital and yet another proof of Brunel's manifold genius. Renkioi's lack of fame partly results from Miss Nightingale's silence about it, yet pavilion hospitals with protected ways and sound plumbing became her trademark as the authority on hospital design.[89]

Hawes was equally creative in working to reform the Army Medical Board and army medical education. Himself a political radical, he was fully aware of the inefficiency of the Horse Guards. He wanted to free the Board and Medical School both from the grip of Miss Nightingale and the old Crimean gang, and to ensure that it functioned at the highest standards of civilian practice. To this end he proposed that H.W. Acland, who already possessed a great reputation and was newly appointed Regius Professor of Medicine at Oxford, join with an unnamed leading London specialist to review the proposals for the army medical school, and that a civilian medical man of the first rank should be invited to join the Board. The threat of such unmanageable expertise was too much for Miss Nightingale and Sidney Herbert, who fended it off by asserting that Hawes's proposals were meant only to delay the project. Possibly, but they would also have improved it by bringing army medicine nearer to the best practice.[90]

Hawes's third and greatest offence was his resistance to Miss Nightingale's takeover of part of his department and the wrecking of his authority. Her scheme that every senior official in the division handling matters that affected health, clothing, contracts and buildings should by-pass their permanent head and report directly to the minister, could and did lead to chaos, when such a system effectively came in after Hawes' death in 1862 and prevailed until Cardwell reorganised the office in 1870.[91] Only a full-scale study of the War Office will reveal the truth about Hawes but such little evidence as we currently have suggests that he is a maligned man. Perhaps Herbert recognised Hawes' virtues, despite Miss Nightingale's nagging. He temporised with her but never removed Hawes.

When in December 1860 a leading British authority on diabetes, Dr Henry Bence Jones, advised Herbert to retire from public life, Miss Nightingale worked hard to reverse the verdict. She argued with Herbert but initially failed to persuade him. He had decided to put his young family first. Florence then approached Lizzie Herbert, but failed with her too. However, within a fortnight Miss Nightingale had induced Herbert to retain the War Office, while moving to the House of Lords. 'The doctors don't give him a year unless he retires from the House of Commons', she confided to Harriet Martineau, who wrote for the *Daily News*. Although Herbert was 'no statesman' and had 'no organizing capacity', he did possess 'great persuasiveness', and 'he alone could carry the Estimates we wanted ... [and] the reorganization of the War Office'. 'I feel it so important just now that "D. News" should help him through [Martineau had lately attacked Herbert in the *Daily News* for a minor scandal concerning army promotions] ... We must get Hawes out & Herbert is not the man to turn him out but no other Secretary of State would turn him out either.' Miss Martineau duly wrote to order.[92]

But it was too late. Herbert had received a fresh medical ultimatum and decided to retire. In desperation Miss Nightingale besought Bence Jones to change his prognosis. The letter is a remarkable example of ruthless wheedling:

> I have seen both Mr Herbert and Mrs Herbert ... since I saw you
>
> I know him so very well that I can see that the strong impression, (somewhat falsely derived from your words) is upon his mind *viz.* that he is the subject of hopeless disease, that, ... he cannot expect to live a year — that he ought to have devoted this year to retirement and his children — altho' he has yielded to our prayers that he would retain office ...
>
> I am sure that we must all of us bless you for having the means of prolonging his life by <u>pulling</u> him out of the Ho: of Commons & that we do not wish one word unsaid which you did say.
>
> But, if you would just say to him now what you did to me viz.

that you have known worse cases recover, that, because a man is told to prop up his house he need not think it <u>must</u> tumble down. I am sure that you would not make him more careless, but that you would give him more vitality.

Indeed his wife asked me to ask you to do so. [This might be true, in a literal sense. But there are indications that Lizzie would have preferred him to have retired altogether.]

For the sake of sparing your time, I have written. But, if you liked to call here, I would give you the circumstances.

Common sense tells me never to interfere between a Physician & his Patient.

So that I hope and trust you will not think this is interfering

And above all, that, whatever you may think it right to say to Mr Herbert, you will not let him know that I have written to you . . . He is so very peculiar in temperament that I think scarcely any man knows him.[93]

During the following month Herbert became unable to walk upstairs without distress and his condition continued to deteriorate through the spring, although he kept on working and attending the House of Lords. Apparently he was living on brandy. On 7 June, after discussing ventilation and sanitary commission matters, he told Miss Nightingale that he intended to resign the War Office and leave for Spa to recoup his health. She was furious: 'You have left no impress of yourself on the War Office. You have not even coloured it . . . No man in my day has thrown away so noble a game as Sidney Herbert with all the winning cards in his hands.'[94]

Upon his death eight weeks later she produced at least five heavily corrected drafts of an anonymous obituary, each emphasising his sainthood and her discipleship and the necessity to continue his work. For the first time she projected Herbert as 'her dear master'. Each draft covers about 16 pages: in each about 11 pages deal solely with Miss Nightingale's labours for the army. He, she said, was an 'ideal' man, but she alone knew 'how to <u>do</u> things'. Miss Nightingale also secretly supplied the funeral sermons to be preached at the official service.[95]

With Herbert gone, she set out to recruit W.E. Gladstone. His efforts to reduce Herbert's service estimates and his opposition to barracks and hospital improvement made Gladstone an unpromising quarry, but he was a Peelite, a High Churchman and former personal friend of the Herberts, and he was obviously the coming man. She sent Gladstone her draft obituary and begged him to take up the great work.

But prudent Gladstone replied that he accepted Lizzie Herbert's view that Sidney's work was done. Miss Nightingale was irate, but canny enough not to attack Gladstone direct:

> She has made a natural blunder between administrative reforms and organization — a blunder which he never made — He did improve the War Office administratively at every step. He did not re-organize it. And alas! he knew it . . .
> Deep disappointment with himself, especially as regards his not having reorganized the War Office according to his plan . . . hastened, I am certain, my dear Master's end . . .
>   You will not let a word of this go beyond yourself to any human being . . . My dead master would at this moment approve of what I am doing in appealing to you . . . His was the purest ambition I have ever known.

Gladstone returned a sober, detailed description of the 'beautiful' funeral. Miss Nightingale had declared herself too ill to attend and had 'never even thought' of going to view the body. The pith of his letter is a consummate piece of Gladstonian filigreed evasion:

> I read last night with profound interest your important paper [Miss Nightingale's draft panegyric]. I see at once that the matter is too high for me to handle. Like you I know that too much would distress him, too little would not. I am in truth ignorant of military administration . . . It is your knowledge and authority more than that of any living creature that can do him justice, at the proper time, whenever that may be.

As for the War Office, Gladstone professed himself 'reluctant to touch that subject . . . for fear I should spoil it'. But meanwhile, as insurance, he 'ventured' to keep a copy of her paper. Miss Nightingale confided to McNeill that she had written another letter to Gladstone (which I could not trace) 'asking him whether I should ask him to help in it for S. Herbert's sake. The reply was truly Gladstonian — cautious, cold, complimentary, yet eloquent — but evidently intending to do nothing.' Undeterred, she sent Gladstone her memorandum on Sidney Herbert and War Office reform 'to be dealt with at your own discretion . . . I understand that it is at your request I am sending you this. My only stipulation is that, if you think it necessary to mention my name in connection with the paper, you will say that it was drawn up at your request, not volunteered by me.' Gladstone appears never to have used her paper. In 1863 and 1864 she again attempted unsuccessfully to enlist him, but finally in 1869 after he backed a nurse training scheme in Ireland without consulting her she dismissed him as 'the most unsanitary brute that ever was'.[96]

After her first rebuff from Gladstone Miss Nightingale began to broadcast Sidney Herbert's famous last words: 'Poor Florence — our unfinished work'. The provenance of these, like many famous last words, is doubtful. Herbert's physician, Dr Williams, reported the death-bed in detail to Miss Nightingale. He mentioned Herbert's taking leave of his family but he did not transmit, as he surely would have done had he heard it, any final message for her. Lady Catherine Dunmore, Herbert's sister, also recounted the death-bed tableau to Miss Nightingale. She said that Williams arrived 'too late to hear His Expressions of perfect Happiness, his Gratitude to God ... his Blessings to his Wife & Children & to all of us', She, too, does not report a last message for Miss Nightingale. The first record of these words, in a variant of the usual version which came from Miss Nightingale, occurs in a conciliatory reply from Lizzie Herbert dated 12 August 1861, ten days after the death: 'I send you some of his last words — those to you were "Poor Florence! Poor Florence! Our joint work unfinished!"' The phraseology of both versions is implausible, although the first reflects Florence's curt style and the second Lizzie's gushing wordiness. Implausible or not, Miss Nightingale immediately inflated the purport of the phrase and circulated it. 'His last words, several times repeated were: "Poor Florence — & our work unfinished"' was the version she confided to McNeill.

Simultaneously, and instinctively, she appropriated Herbert's reputation and denigrated his work by interpreting the death-bed scene.

His wife & his sisters interpret his death-bed in their own way. And great pains have been taken to represent it as a 'glorified death'. I understood him as no one else did. I loved him & served him as no one else — I have letters from him, as long as he could hold a pen at all, up to the last fortnight. [The last letter I have found is dated 7 June — his announcement of his retirement — for which Florence castigated him by return, nine weeks before his death. There is no reason why he should have written after that — and she would have kept the letter had he

done so.] And his death, had it been as they represent, would have
been purely selfish, going to heaven himself & leaving 'us in the
storm'. But it was not. He died with manly cheerfulness, because
he felt he had no more work in him — but with a deep regret for
failure.

She sent Douglas Galton yet another version of the last words (this
time 'said . . . twice') coupled with an admonition to hold tight at the
War Office, keep an eye on Herbert's successor and bring her as many
of Herbert's recent War Office papers as he could lay hands on. 'This
is the last opportunity I shall ever have of carrying out my poor
Master's wishes.'[97]

When preparing her memoir Lady Herbert had asked Miss
Nightingale's permission to read his letters to her. The request
put Miss Nightingale in a rage. In the midst of a rambling,
incoherent 24 page letter to McNeill she sought to justify her refusal
to herself:

> I have hundreds of Sidney Herbert's letters — I cannot give them to
> Lady Herbert or refuse them to her —
>   Up to this time I could not burn them because they have stood
> in good stead about some things at the War Office.
>   His letters will prove . . . his failure . . . they will prove (to use his
> own words) that 'all that' he 'had done' he 'had coined out of
> "my brain"'. [I have found no letter which says this] . . . I will
> never be the one to tell to his wife or his fellow-Ministers what he
> did not tell himself.

Miss Nightingale intended to refuse Lizzie's request 'by hiding . . .
away'. Lizzie asked again in 1890 when the family was gathering
materials for the projected biography. Florence's reply is
quintessential Nightingale: insidiously unctuous, effortlessly evasive,
thoroughly egotistical and iron-hard, glossing a lifetime of deceit and
cherished enmities:

> Dearest, Indeed that loss, unspeakable, irreparable, is always before
> me . . . Would that I could help you in giving you materials for the
> proposed 'Life' as you ask — But alas! I cannot. I am altogether
> unable, I am sorry to say, to do what you wish & what I should wish
> so much.
>   I have no letters from him that I could lend you. His letters while

I was in the Crimean War, were not on very important business, & not such as one cared to preserve. [Many, probably all, of these letters are among the Nightingale Papers in the British Library.]

Afterwards, there were the five years, all but a week from August 7 1856 ... to August 2 1861 ... the day that took him home to minister to still greater works for his, for our Heavenly Father — you know — who better? — how it was — letters do not pass between those who see each other day after day ... during the whole period there were no letters or none kept and not a line of record or of copy have I ...

How sorry I am to have to say this to you you will know ...

After this, perhaps you will hardly wish to see me, as you kindly offer. My illness is so much increased that I am not equal to the work constantly increasing upon me. And I hardly see anyone not closely connected with that present work.

I hope you are pretty well ...

ever your old friend
F.N.[98]

Miss Nightingale paid a small penalty for withholding the letters. Stanmore's biography of Herbert is a rare instance of a contemporary work which treated Miss Nightingale as a little lower than the angels, and indeed found her 'jealous', intolerant and 'censorious'.

Nonetheless, by the time of Herbert's death her aggression and his careful work had ensured that in the short run at least, War Office business was conducted less haphazardly and that greater attention would be paid to the well-being of the common soldiers. Between Herbert's resignation and Edward Cardwell's advent at the War Office in 1868, the Duke of Cambridge and the Horse Guards were to undo many of the administrative reforms, but the improvement in army sanitary arrangements was a more permanent gain. Thousands of men in the British army at home and abroad lived healthier, longer lives in better conditions because she had acted the bully for them.

Notes

1. F.N. to [Sidney Herbert?] draft, n.d. [June 1856?], BL Add.Mss 43401, ff.201-4; F.N. to McNeill, 1 Mar. 1857, GLRO HI/ST/SU/75.

2. 'Return Relating to the late Army in the East', *Parliamentary Papers*, 1857, vol.IX, pp.1-4; R. Thompson Jopling, 'On the Mortality among Officers of the British Army in the East', *Report of British Association for the Advancement of Science, 1856*, p.144; Thomas Longmore, *The Sanitary Contrasts of the British*

and French Armies during the Crimean War (London, 1883), pp.5-14; J.S. Curtiss, *The Russian Army under Nicholas I, 1825-1855* Durham, NY, 1965), pp.249, 359, has a critical discussion of the various estimates for the Russian losses. The Russians did not collect figures on disease in their army until 1859.

3. Sir Edward Cook, *The Life of Florence Nightingale* (2 vols., London 1913), vol. I, p.318.

4. Report of the Board of General Offices appointed to inquire into . . . the reports of Sir John McNeill and Colonel Tulloch . . .' *PP*, 1856, vol. XXI; War Office minute on McNeill and Tulloch Report, n.d. [Oct. 1856], PRO WO33/3A; Florence MacAlister, *Memoir of the right hon. Sir John McNeill* (London, 1910), p.404.

5. F. N. to McNeill, 4 Sept 1856; F.N. to Lady McNeill, 7 Oct. 1856, GLRO HI/ST/SU65-70.

6. F.N. to Lord Murray, 24 Sept. 1856 (draft), BL Add.Mss 43401, f.252.

7. F.N. to Peter Pincoffs, 'Private & Confidential', 21 Oct. 1856, BL Add. Mss 45796, ff.92-3; Peter Pincoffs, *Experiences of a Civilian in Eastern Military Hospitals* (London, 1857).

8. Hall 'Observations . . . on the Medical Department of the Army' Oct. 1856, PRO WO33/38 *The Panmure Papers*, ed. George Douglas, and George Dalhousie Ramsay (2 vols., London, 1908), vol. II, pp.305-6, 321.

9. Cook, *Nightingale*, vol. I, pp.356-7.

10. Sidney Herbert to F.N., 16 Jan. 1856, BL Add.Mss 43394, f.3; Lefroy to F.N., 28 Aug. 1856, in Cook, *Nightingale*, vol. I, pp.322-3.

11. Cook, *Nightingale*, vol. I, p.329-31.

12. Cook, *Nightingale*, vol. I, p.330.

13. F.N. to Sidney Herbert, 6 Jan. 1857, BL Add.Mss 43394, ff.1-2.

14. Cook, *Nightingale*, vol. I, pp.335, 442-5; F.N. to McNeill, 16 Nov. 1857, GLRO HI/ST/SU94; F.N. to Monckton Milnes, 3 May 1857, Houghton Mss, Trinity College, Cambridge 3793(2).

15. Florence Nightingale, *Notes on Matters affecting the Health, Efficiency, And Hospital Administration of the British Army, founded chiefly on the experience of the late war* 'Presented by request to the Secretary of State for War' (London, 1858), pp.566, XXVI.

16. F.N. to Sidney Herbert, 20 May 1857, BL Add.Mss 43394, ff.45-6. Miss Nightingale shared with contemporaries and with later historians a belief that the navy was much healthier than the army. It might have been so, but convincing evidence is lacking. The navy's procedure of paying off seamen after each tour of duty and then recommissioning only the able-bodied greatly enhances the sickness and mortality figures. Cf. Sutherland to Edwin Chadwick, 15 Oct. 1883, Chadwick Papers, University College, London, CP1920.

17. F.N., *Notes*, pp.XXII, XXXV, 156, 205, 323, LIV.

18. F.N., *Notes* pp.350-65, Appendix 7, pp.XXXV-IX.

19. F.N. to Sidney Herbert, 24 Mar. 1859, BL Add.Mss 45768, ff.88-9.

20. F.N., *Notes*, pp.188-90, 287-301.

21. F.N. to Lord Grey, June-July 1857, BL Add.Mss 45796, ff.205-30.

22. F.N. to McNeill, 3 May 1857, GLRO HI/ST/SU79.

23. F.N. to Mrs Milnes, 3 May 1857, BL Add.Mss 45796, f.190.

24. F.N. to McNeill, 3 May 1857, GLRO HI/ST/SU79.

25. F.N. to McNeill, 1 Mar. 1857; 3 May 1857, GLRO HI/ST/SU/75, 79.

26. Sidney Herbert to F.N., n.d. [23 May 1857?], BL Add.Mss 43394, ff.47-8.

27. Sidney Herbert to F.N., 26 Apr. 1857; F.N. Memorandum on Royal Commission, n.d. [1861?]; BL Add.Mss 43394 f.29; 45823, f.1.

28. F.N. to McNeill, 12 June 1857; 27 June 1857, GLRO HI/ST/SU/85, 86; 'Report of the Commissioners appointed to inquire into the . . . Sanitary

condition of the army . . .'. *PP* 1857-58, vol. XVIII Qs.5343-73; F.N. to McNeill, 25 June 1857; Sutherland to F.N., 7 Sept. 1857, BL Add.Mss 45768, ff.55-6; 45751, f.45.

29. F.N. to McNeill, 7 July 1857, GLRO HI/ST/SU/87.

30. F.N. to Sidney Herbert, 7 July 1857, 21 July 1857; Sidney Herbert to F.N., 20 July 1857, BL Add.Mss 43394 ff.95-8, 112, 116.

31. F.N. to Jerry Barrett, 18 July 1856, GLRO HI/ST/SU/193; Henry Newman, 'Letters from Scutari, 1856', in *Friends' Quarterly Examiner*, Oct. 1910, pp.550-2. (Newman accompanied Barrett to the Crimea.)

32. Parthe Verney to McNeill, 3 Apr. [1862?] GLRO HI/ST/SU/112; F.N. to Benjamin Jowett n.d. [mid-Sept. 1865?] Jowett Papers, vol. I, Balliol College, Oxford.

33. F.N. to [William Rendle?], 1 Dec. 1868; F.N. to 'ever dearest "Little Sister"' (Miss Pringle), 21 Oct. 1887, GLRO HI/ST/NCI/68/4, 87/47; Ulricke M. [Lienicke?] to F.N., 27 Oct. 1888, BL Add.Mss 45809, ff.10-11.

34. F.N. to Sidney Herbert, 26 Nov. 1857, F.N. to Sutherland, 2 Feb. 1862, BL Add.Mss 43394, ff.190-4, 45751, f.205.

35. F.N. to Mrs Bracebridge, Jan. 1864, BL Add.Mss 43397, f.195; F.N. to 'very dearest friend' (Mary Jones), 12 Sept. 1869, GLRO HI/ST/NCI/69/2; F.N. to Jowett, 22 Jan. [1872?] Jowett Papers, vol. IV, Balliol College, Oxford.

36. F.N. to Richard Aspden, 8 July 1867, GLRO HI/ST/U26/67.

37. F.N. to Sutherland, 31 Mar. 1871, BL Add.Mss 45755, f.198.

38. F.N. to Aunt Mai Smith, 30 Aug. 1872, BL Add.Mss 45793, f.222.

39. F.N. Note, n.d. [1873?], BL Add.Mss 45841, f.84.

40. F.N. to Jowett, n.d. [late July 1865?] BL Add.Mss 45783, f.41.

41. *Parl. Debs.* 3/vol.CL cols. 474-95; F.N. to Monckton Milnes, 25 Feb. 1857, Houghton Mss, supp. 3543, Trinity College, Cambridge; Sidney Herbert to F.N., 26 July 1859, BL Add.Mss 43395, f.192.

42. Chadwick to F.N., 31 July 1857, F.N. to Chadwick, 11 Feb. 1858; Chackwick to F.N., 16 Feb. 1858, BL Add.Mss 45770 ff.5-15.

43. F.N. to McNeill, 27 Dec. [1857?], GLRO HI/ST/SU/100; F.N. to McNeill 27 Dec. [1857?] (draft), BL Add.Mss 45768 f.72. The phrase comes probably from John Reynolds, *The Triumph of God's revenge against the crying and execrable Sinne of Murther* (1621).

44. F.N. to Sidney Herbert, 12 Mar. 1858, BL Add.Mss 43395, f.5.

45. F.N. to McNeill, 16 Nov. 1857, GLRO HI/ST/SU/94.

46. Mary Smith (Aunt Mai) to Lady McNeill, 19 Nov. 1857, 2 Dec. [1857?] BL Add.Mss 45768, f.252, 254. Another draft is at GLRO HI/ST/SU/96-8.

47. Aunt Mai to Lady McNeill, 29 Jan. 1858 F.N. to McNeill, 10 Oct. 1857, GLRO HI/ST/SU/101, 93.

48. F.N. to McNeill, 19 Mar. 1859, GLRO HI/ST/SU/110.

49. F.N. to Uncle Sam, 28 June 1861; and [Aug. 1861?], BL Add.Mss 45792, ff.197, 229.

50. F.N. to Mrs Milnes, 18 Aug. [1860?], Houghton Mss, Trinity College Cambridge, Supp. 354(2), Mrs Gaskell to C.E. Norton, 13 Jan. 1863, in J.A.V. Chapple and Arthur Pollard (eds.), *The Letters of Mrs Gaskell* (Manchester, 1966), p.707; F.N. to Rev. Mother Clare, 28 Feb. 1865, BL Add.Mss 45789, ff.43-4; F.N. to Lizzie Herbert, 19 July 1865 BL Add.Mss 43396, f.193; F.N. to Mary Jones, 23 Sept. 1866, GLRO HI/ST/NCI/66/16; F.N. to Lizzie Herbert, 21 Feb. 1867, BL Add.Mss 43396, f.206; F.N. to Chadwick 7 Nov. 1868, Chadwick Papers, University College London, CP1490; F.N. to Sutherland, n.d. [early Jan. 1869?] BL Add.Mss 45753, f.165; F.N. to Sutherland, n.d. [July 1870?], BL Add.Mss 45753, f.239; F.N. to Martin, 23 July 1874, BL Add.Mss 45803, f.233; F.N. to Miss Mackenzie, 11 Sept. 1879, GLRO HI/ST/79/4; F.N. to Gladstone, 4 Dec. 1884, BL Add.Mss 44488, f.202; F.N. to Galton, 5 May,

19 June 1888, BL Add.Mss 45766, ff.60-1, 93.

51. F.N. 'Household Book' 1888, BL Add.Mss 45849; F.N., Diary, 9 Jan. 1877, BL Add.Mss 45847, ff.48-9; F.N. to [Sutherland?] 22 July 1873, BL Add. Mss 45803, f.86; F.N. to Gladstone, 3 Dec. 1884, BL Add.Mss 44488, f.196; F.N 'Note , 6 Aug. 1887, BL Add.Mss 52427, f.4.

52. Harriet Martineau to F.N., 23 Jan. 1865, GLRO HI/ST/VI/65; F.N. to Martineau, 12 Feb. 1865, BL Add.Mss 45788, f.283.

53. Mary Scharlieb, *Reminiscences* (London, 1924), p.46.

54. Dr C.B. Williams, prescription, 24 July 1870, BL Add.Mss 45802, f.164; F.N , Diary 1877, BL Add.Mss 45847, f.55; Clark to F.N., 31 Mar. 1867, BL Add.Mss 45772, f.199; F.N., Diary, 3 Feb. 1877, BL Add.Mss 45847, f.51.

55. F.N. to Rev. Mother Clare, 1 Mar. [1867?]; and 28 Feb. 1865 BL Add. Mss 45789, ff.51, 43.

56. Rosalind Nash, 'I Knew A Man', typescript, GLRO HI/ST/NC12/14, pp.5-6.

57. F.N. — signed by Herbert, Sutherland et. al., 'Objections to Netley, 12 Mar. 1858, PRO WO 33/6A.

58. Herbert to F.N., 2 Jan. 1857, BL Add.Mss 43394, f.224.

59. F.N. to Sutherland, n.d. [June-July 1857?], BL Add.Mss 45751, ff.30-3; Herbert to F.N., 12 Feb. 1859, BL Add.Mss 43395, f.144; [FN?] anonymous leader on Netley Hospital in the *Builder*, 24 July 1858, p.493.

60. F.N. Memorandum of interview with Mrs Deeble, matron at Netley, [24 Feb. 1870?], BL Add.Mss 45754, f.89.

61. F.N. to Sutherland, n.d. [16 July 1861?] BL Add.Mss 45751, f.195.

62. F.N. to Sutherland, n.d. [July 1861?] BL Add.Mss 45751, f.198; F.N. to Galton, 17 Jan. 1865, BL Add.Mss 45763, f.12.

63. Sir Edward Lugard, Draft report to War Office on Netley Hospital, 26 May 1868, BL Add.Mss 45774, f.101.

64. F.N. to Sutherland, n.d. [10 Dec. 1869?], BL Add.Mss 45754, ff.35, 89.

65 F.N. *Notes*, p.11; F.N. to Martineau, 23 Jan. [1859?], BL Add.Mss 45788, f.21.

66. E.A. Parkes to F.N., 17 Jan. 1861, BL Add.Mss 45773, f.25; F.N. to Galton, 7 Apr., 3 Nov. 1864, BL Add.Mss 45762, ff.92, 237.

67. F.N. to Acland, 31 Mar., 8 Apr., 17 Apr., 12 July 1876, 29 Jan. 1881, Acland Papers, Bodleian Library, Oxford, d.70, ff.70-87.

68. Herbert, 'Regulations for Medical Organization of War Office', 9 July 1858. PRO WO33/6A; F.N. to McNeill, 24 Mar. 1859, GLRO HI/ST/SU/III; F.N. to Clark, 7 Oct. 1863, 7 Apr., 8 Apr., 11 Apr., 5 June 1864. BL Add.Mss 45772 ff.174-90; F.N. to Galton, 29 Nov. 1864, BL Add.Mss 45762 ff.64-6; 22 June 1866, BL Add.Mss 45763, f.192-4.

69. G.J.H. Evatt, *Army Medical Organization* (London, 1878), p.28; J.M. Grant, Memorandum ... on Hospitals, Dec. 1878, PRO WO33/33; Anon., Report on Shortage of Recruits to Army Medical Department, 1879, PRO WO33/32.

70. F.N. Notes for 'Suggestions', n.d. [late 1850?] BL Add.Mss 45842, f.51; John M. Eyler, *Victorian Social Medicine* (Baltimore, 1979), esp. Chapters 2 and 7.

71. Shaftesbury, Diary, 2 June 1855, Broadlands Mss, National Register of Archives, SHA/PD/7.

72. Report of Barracks ... Commission, 15 Oct. 1858, pp.1, 22, PRO 33/6A.

73. Herbert to F.N., 20 Aug. 1857, BL Add.Mss 43394, f.143.

74. Alan Ramsay Skelley, *The Victorian Army At Home* (London, 1977), p.36; War Office memo. 'Condition of the Soldier', n.d. [1862?] Broadlands Mss, National Register of Archives, ND/B/21/5; Sutherland to Chadwick, 15 Aug. [1864?] Chadwick Papers, University College, London, CP1920; *PP*, 1857-58,

vol. XXXVII, p.1. The expenditures given here are conservative. Higher totals are printed in *PP*, 1857, vol. IX, p.167 and *PP*, 1860, vol. XLI, p.95. Presumably, they vary according to the time of year at which they are calculated, amongst other factors.

75. Shaftesbury, Diary, 15 Feb. 1855. Broadlands Mss. PRO, SHA/PD/6.

76. *PP* 1857-58, vol. XVIII, p.527; *PP* 1862, vol. XXXIII, pp.5-6, 33; *PP* 1867, vol. XLIII, pp.5, 24-5.

77. E. Headlam Greenhow, *Builder*, 5, 30 Oct., 20, Nov. 1858; (F.N.) *Builder*, 6 Nov. 1858; F.N. to Chadwick, 11 Aug. 1858, Chadwick to F.N., 21 Aug. 1858, BL Add.Mss 45770, ff.32, 43.

78. F.G.P. Neison, 'On Phthisis in the Army', *Report of British Association for the Advancement of Science 1858*, pp.189-92; (SH) 'The Sanitary Condition Of The Army', *Westminster Review*, vol. 51, 1859, pp.668.

79. F.N. to Chadwick, 7 Oct. 1858, BL Add.Mss 45770, f.35; Chadwick to F.N., 27 Sept. 1862 BL Add.Mss 45771, ff.62-4; F.N. to Balfour, 28 Sept. 1858, BL Add.Mss 50134, ff.47-50.

80. J. Clarke Jervoise, *"Infection"*, 2nd edn (London, 1882); Elizabeth Blackwell, *Why Hygienic Congresses Fail* (London, 1892).

81. F.N. to Walker, 10 Apr. 1866, GLRO HI/ST/NC1/66/4.

82. Farr to F.N., 23, 25 Apr. 1860, BL Add.Mss 43399, ff.109-12.

83. F.N. to R.J. Ellis, draft, n.d. [Aug. 1867?] BL Add.Mss 45782, f.100.

84. F.N. to Jowett, [draft] n.d. [1866-67?], BL Add.Mss 45783, f.142; and 3 Oct. 1871, BL Add.Mss 45784, f.1.

85. F.N. to 'Dearest' (Lizzie Herbert) 4 Sept. 1849, BL Add.Mss 43396, f.5.

86. Herbert to F.N., 2 Jan. 1858, BL Add.Mss 43394, ff.227-8.

87. F.N. to Galton, 24 Apr. 1860, BL Add.Mss 45759, ff.36-8.

88. F.N. to Galton, 1 Sept. 1860, 8 June 1861 *'Burn This'*, BL Add.Mss 45759, ff.51-3, 223.

89. L.T.C. Rolt *Isambard Kingdom Brunel* (London, 1970), pp.292-8. Brunel is masked as Bonnel in George Douglas and George D. Ramsay (eds.), *Panmure Papers*, (2 vols., London, 1908), vol. II, pp.401, 405.

90. Lord Stanmore, *Sidney Herbert*, (2 vols., London, 1906), vol. II, 153-61.

91. F.N. to McNeill, 24 Mar. 1859, BL Add.Mss 45768, f.88-90; F.N. to de Grey, 16 May 1862, BL Add.Mss 43546, f.19. Edward M. Spiers, *The Army and Society 1815-1914* (London, 1980), pp.157-200.

92. Herbert was probably suffering from renal disease as well as diabetes. Tests of his urine disclosed very high and increasing proportions of albumen, which baffled his doctors. P.E. de Strzelecki to McNeill, 5 Nov. 1861, BL Add. Mss 45768, f.161; F.N. to Lizzie Herbert, 5 Dec. 1860, BL Add.Mss 43396, ff.89-95; F.N. to Martineau, 4 Jan. 1861, BL Add.Mss 45788, ff.103-10.

93. F.N. to [Dr. C.B. Williams?] [draft?] 7 Jan. 1861, GLRO HI/ST/NC1/61/1.

94. Herbert to F.N. 7 June 1861; F.N. to Herbert, n.d. [9 June 1861?] BL Add.Mss 43395, ff.303-9.

95. F.N. drafts of obituary, BL Add.Mss 45818, [Aug. 1861?] ff.8-210; Rev. R.S.C. Chermside to F.N., BL Add.Mss 45797, f.254.

96. F.N. to Gladstone, 8, 9 Aug., 25 Nov. 1861; Gladstone to F.N., 10 Aug. 1861, BL Add.Mss 44397, ff.28-50, 188-9; F.N. to McNeill, 21 Aug. 1861, BL Add.Mss 45907, f.24; F.N. to Sutherland, n.d. [March 1869?], BL Add.Mss 43573, f.202.

97. C.B. Williams to F.N., 2 Aug. [1861?], BL Add.Mss 45797, ff.246-7; Dunmore to F.N., n.d. [4 Aug. 1861?] BL Add.Mss 43396, f.147; Lizzie Herbert to F.N., 12 Aug. 1861, BL Add.Mss 43396, f.153; F.N. to McNeill, 21 Aug. 1861,

BL Add.Mss 45907, ff.22-3. F.N. to Galton, 16 Aug. 1861, BL Add.Mss 45759, ff.255-7.
   98. F.N. to McNeill, 21 Aug. 1861, ff.28-29; F.N. to Lizzie Herbert, 24 Feb. 1890, BL Add.Mss 43396, ff.226-9.

4 INDIA

Miss Nightingale took up India when her leverage on army medical services and barracks slackened during the early 1860s. With Sidney Herbert's death she lost her *point d'appui* on the War Office and government. The War Office regained the initiative and army sanitary improvement settled into a slow bureaucratic routine. She yielded readily enough, behind a barrage of complaining letters. The battle for power always engaged her more than the business that ensued in its aftermath.

She had discovered India during the Mutiny in 1857. In the midst of her post-Crimean enterprises, she had half-heartedly asked McNeill to 'advise' her whether to go to India to nurse the British soldiers. Apparently he rejected the idea and she acquiesced.[1] She had noted also the need for sanitary reform in India but it was Sutherland who formulated the justification for an Indian sanitary crusade. In September 1857, on the occasion of her nephew leaving with other unseasoned troops for India, he remarked that there would be much sickness among them. 'The whole sanitary work in India will require reconsideration in the altered state of matters.' Native soldiers could no longer be trusted; henceforth British troops would have to hold the country, and that could be effected only if their sickness and mortality rates were reduced:

It would be a beautiful thing to do it, and I am certain it could be done, and India kept in hand . . . by the Anglo Saxon race.

It would be a greater thing to do than it was to conquer Hindoostan.[2]

Miss Nightingale adopted the project in the autumn of 1858 after her *Notes on the Army* . . . were finished. In August she began pressing the argument on Edwin Chadwick, hinting that he propagate it in the quarterlies. This was cool, because Chadwick, who probably had picked up the notion from Sutherland and Farr, had already sketched it for her only a month before. Chadwick had given the Indian scheme his distinctive emphasis: he urged sanitary reform as the cheapest way of maintaining a white Indian army. He probably supplied Dr Andrew Wynter with the impressive-looking figures used to back the idea in his anonymous article in the *Quarterly Review* for January 1859.[3] Wynter asserted that about 100,000 British soldiers had died of disease in India between 1815 and 1855. At an estimate of £100 per man for training and experience, their untimely and unnecessary deaths, measured by rates of about 76 per 1,000 in 1836 declining to 41 per 1,000 in 1855 among an average strength of 25,000 men, represented a loss of ten million pounds to the British empire. If the 1855 rate persisted among the 95,000 men stationed in India since the Mutiny the ultimate monetary cost would be prohibitive. There is reason to believe that the figures were overstated, but the argument remains powerful.[4]

Miss Nightingale's Indian campaign followed the lines of infiltration of the War Office. During the spring of 1859 she secured a Royal Sanitary Commission for India. Lord Stanley, the Tory Secretary for India, temporised for eight months, but gave way when it appeared that his government was doomed: a Nightingale commission would be an irritating legacy to his Liberal successor. His permanent officials at the India Office were opposed to her meddling and their fears were justified by the membership of the Commission: Herbert as chairman, Sutherland, Sir R. Martin, Farr, Alexander, and two inescapable gestures to the Indian Council, Sir Proby Cautley and Sir R. Vivian. Fortunately her uncle Sam was friendly with the latter: 'Vivian must be soaped', she told him, 'so as not to let him think we undervalue his opinion.' Chadwick had sought nomination but Miss Nightingale and Stanley ignored him.[5] The composition of the Commission reflected her isolation from men possessing recent Indian experience; Martin, Cautley and Vivian were big names and great men, but they were nearing the ends of their careers — her reputation as Crimean heroine cut no ice with younger Indian bureaucrats and soldiers.

The work of the Commission fell to Sutherland and Farr and it soon turned out to be frustrating. The officials at the India Office prevaricated for six months over a request for mortality and sickness figures. Even after Farr secured an order from the Secretary for India, Sir Charles Wood, the Office stalled. Stalling was easy because there were no reliable health statistics for civilians and natives in India. There had been no effective censuses, there was no regular registration of deaths, estimates on the incidence of disease among natives were made randomly from records of admissions to native hospitals. The situation was ready-made for Miss Nightingale to create her own data. In consultation with Sutherland, Farr and McNeill, she devised an extensive questionnaire and sent it to 200 British stations in India.[6]

The questionnaire is a remarkable example of Miss Nightingale's pertinacity, practicality and sense of the actual, honed by Sutherland's grasp of medical possibilities and Farr's mastery of vital statistics. The ruling assumption is that ill-health is caused by bad environmental factors which can be identified and remedied. There are fourteen sections, covering 'topography', 'climate', 'sanitary condition of station', 'health of the troops', 'intemperance', 'diet', 'dress, accoutrements, and duties', 'instruction and recreation', 'military prisons', 'field service', 'statistics of sickness and mortality', 'hospitals', 'burial of the dead', and instructions for a general report from each Presidency. The questions are precise and searching: for example, number four among the fourteen relating to topography asks,

> At what distance from the station is the nearest water, whether sea, river, lake, marsh, nullah, or canal? Is the vicinity liable to overflow of water? if so, at what season, and how long does the overflow last? Is there any broken ground, or are there any ravines or water pits near the station, and what is their effect on health?

Amongst the 23 questions about the sanitary conditions of the station the respondent was required to supply sketches of the ground-plan of the camp, the barracks, kitchens, urinals, drainage system, and to state the distance from the barracks at which animals were slaughtered, the regulations governing the practice and how the offal was disposed of, and if 'nuisance is experienced . . . how you propose to prevent it'.[7] Nothing attests so vividly to Miss Nightingale's gift of accendency as her presumption that every dutiful Indian medical officer and military engineer would labour to answer the questionnaire in full. She seems not to have understood that an honest respondent might endanger his career. The miracle is that there are so many detailed, critical replies. No modern army would permit it.

The evidence must have fulfilled her expectations. Nearly 1,000 pages of small type, it amounts to a massive, intricately informed phantasmagoria of poor water supplies, damp badly-sited camps, ill-built, hot and grubby barracks adjoining filthy native bazaars, endemic fever and (amongst British troops) venereal disease, a total want of field sanitary regulations, culminating in omnipresent, stolidly accepted death. Only drunkenness, which the doctors reported as rare, did not meet the stereotype of the pre-Nightingale army. She had provided an outlet for dozens of technicians and junior officers, many of them Scots, whose aspirations and expertise had been slighted by their superiors. 'The medical officer has no power in these matters' (camp-sites etc.), reported army surgeon Cox from Muttra on the Jumna river south of Delhi, 'and he would lay himself open to rebuke if he interfered'. Assistant-Surgeon Howell of the Madras Engineers, reporting from Cuddapah, complained that his superiors consistently camped their men in paddy-fields, ignoring the rising ground on either side, which left the camp in up to six inches of water after rain. Dr Joseph Ewart, of the Mewar Bheel Corps at Kherwarrah, recounted similar stupidities and asked that sanitary officers be given 'executive and responsible functions' to be exercised independently of their immediate commanding officers. Dr Duncan Macpherson, Inspector-General of hospitals for the Madras Army, rehearsed, perhaps unconsciously, to Miss Nightingale's commissioners the lesson she had sought to teach:

in England, the last place where sanitary considerations obtained a hearing was in those influential quarters where rests the highest military authority. The terrible ordeal of the Crimea came and laid bare to the world the defects of our system ... it is for us to profit by this great example, and to hasten to amend what is faulty in our system here.[8]

The embattled subordinate improvers had found a champion in Miss Nightingale and she found in them a network — though many soon defected — of irregulars who would abet her in her skirmishes with the India Office and Presidency governments.

Early in 1862 Miss Nightingale took to bed for four months — she was 'much worse' she told McNeill in the course of a business letter and unable to come to felicitate his daughter on the birth of her child — while she arranged the evidence, prepared coloured graphs displaying the gross extent of preventable mortality, digests and recapitulations of the evidence and statistics, together with a reprinted volume of 'Observations' on the *Report*, reiterating its main findings. The Treasury and State Paper Office baulked for six months at the cost of the Blue Book but Miss Nightingale finally overrode them, and the *Report* appeared in mid-1863. She herself paid for the figures and wordcut illustrations. She sent special copies of the 'Observations' to the Queen and other notables and ensured that prominent members of both houses of parliament asked for the *Report* and 'Observations' in their respective libraries. She also arranged for favourable reviews in the daily press and quarterlies.[9] Beyond this she produced a brilliant précis of the 'Observations' entitled *How People May Live and not Die in India*, for presentation to the Edinburgh congress of the National Association for the Promotion of Social Science. The Prince Consort attended the session and the gathering concluded with cheers for Miss Nightingale. On every front the result was a triumph for her pertinacity. Two powerful Indian proconsuls, Sir John Lawrence and Sir Bartle Frere, were confirmed as disciples.[10] Temporarily at least she had outflanked the India Office.

Miss Nightingale and Sutherland proposed in the *Report* to establish for India a system of sanitary reconstruction, modelled on their Army Sanitary Commission, designed to maintain their authority distinct of the India Office. There were to be three new bodies, ranked vertically. At the base there was to be a 'public works executive' in each of the three presidencies, composed of sanitarians and engineers. They were to oversee small local improvements and to execute the larger schemes approved by their respective presidency sanitary commissions. These last were to comprise leading sanitarians, senior medical officers and government officials. Their role was vaguely described as 'consultative and advisory'. Above them there was to be a 'home commission' composed, although Miss Nightingale did not say so, of her cabinet drawn from the War Office. 'The function', she equivocated, 'could of course be consultative only.'[11] Her practice soon proved that she expected all Indian sanitary projects to be referred home. Moreover the 'public works executive' was to implement instantly, without awaiting local permission, such improvements as the home commission might direct.

This audacious mechanism impelled Miss Nightingale into endless intrigue. Almost two years before the Royal Commission even reported, she had tried to send 'Instructions' about Indian barracks improvements and soldiers' day-rooms through Earl de Grey during his brief stay as Indian Under-Secretary in 1861. He quietly held up despatch of the 'Instructions' while in office and then evaded her demand that he commend them to his successor. His Indian Office officials meanwhile adapted the 'Instructions' to fit the little money available and sent them to India as their own invention. Miss Nightingale was furious. Moreover, the India Office had acted without informing the War Office, thereby declaring their refusal to be directed by Miss Nightingale through her War Office agents. The India officials also moved to ensure that papers were retained in their office and not circulated to the War Office, thereby blocking her sources of information. The India men had effectively negated her bid for control.[12] The three-tiered sanitary commission was not finally instituted until September 1863 and even then it remained inactive.

Lord Stanley, her chosen replacement for Herbert as her agent, was little help. He was both in Opposition and lacking in Herbert's graces. Jowett, when advising her about possible recruits, had characterised him as 'a cold ill mannered Radical Aristocrat rather [?] cut off from the religious world & equally from the jolly world, but still a man with higher aims than any other politician.'[13] He proved a languid go-between. He 'does nothing for us', Miss Nightingale complained to Harriet Martineau in July 1863. 'I have to do it all . . . a poor invalid woman'.[14] Stanley had once at her behest persuaded the Secretary for India, Sir Charles Wood, to forbid alterations to the Bombay Hospital until the plans had been referred home. This small intervention taught Stanley a lesson. Miss Nightingale moved to have the alterations redesigned by the fashionable, expensive Matthew Digby Wyatt. Stanley struggled to hold her to their initial understanding that the plans were to be studied by the War Office architects. The project apparently was stalemated. The hospital was not rebuilt until much later and there is no evidence that Wyatt was ever called in.[15] After this episode Stanley evaded her demands with vague but coy conspiratorial notes. He made no commitments although at important dinner-tables he readily boasted of his acquaintance with her.

Her drive to get things done, her secrecy and her craving for recognition and proprietorship made her a shifty ally. Even the faithful Sutherland was quietly denigrated. In October 1863, for instance, she privately hinted to Galton that he should correct the implications of an India Office minute she had seen on a document he had spirited out for her. The minute noted that Miss Nightingale's summary of some report from Ceylon was 'merely a résumé' of fuller notes compiled by Dr Sutherland. This 'curious minute', she protested, 'put [her] into a very false position'.

All the original Ceylon documents are in my hands – in my house at this moment – were all abstracted by me It was only in my house that Dr Sutherland could, or did, consult them – He made his 'Notes' from the original documents . . . I mine. I saw his 'Notes' – he mine – as we always do – But I did not look at his 'Notes' even – while writing mine. I had not got them.

This is not very clear. Her explanation becomes more confused as it proceeds:

> I had rather my handwriting (or name) had not appeared at all in this matter ... I have given Dr Sutherland the whole credit, if that be an object, of the India Commission, and have got him £1500 [through Stanley] for it ...

She faced a future of resentful toil at the periphery, of being less and less in the know, of wielding less and less power: 'But I have had a great deal more to do with the original documents than he has ... also why do we only see this minute of 10/7 on Oct 28?'[16] Galton, too, had his future to look to, and he had no right to show her documents.

Suddenly, before the year was done, Miss Nightingale came in from the cold. The surprise nomination of Sir John Lawrence as Governor-General was announced at the end of November and she pounced immediately. His appointment gave her 'a most unexpected hold on India', she exulted to McNeill '... few have had such extraordinary chances as I have had – twice – a Secretary of State and a Governor-General delivered, as it were, into my hand'. The great-hearted saviour of Delhi during the Mutiny would 'play ... [the] noble ... game ... as Sidney Herbert ... had not played it'.[17] After Lawrence's death in 1879 she was to tell Gladstone that:

> Sir John Lawrence came to me in those last hurried days [he sailed for India within ten days of his appointment] we sketched out the whole plan of Sanitary proceedings not only for the Army but for the native populations for all India, which he carried out ... thank God for it.

They met at her house on 4 December. The meeting had been arranged by Stanley. Their talk was about sanitary reform for India:

> I have had the great joy of being in constant communication with Sir John Lawrence – she told Farr on 10 December – and of receiving his commands to do what I had almost lost all hope of being allowed to do – viz. of sending out full statements and schemes of what we want the Presidency Commissions to do. I should be glad to submit to you copies of papers of mine which he desired me to write ... They are, of course, confidential ... with Sir John Lawrence's commands we feel ourselves empowered to begin the Home Commission ...[18]

Biographers have accepted Miss Nightingale's fiction and presented her and Lawrence as united in their pursuit of the grail of salubrious India. There is no evidence that Lawrence acceded to any of her overtures. His responses which survive suggest that he was non-committal and that his subsequent actions in India were consistent with his knowledge of what was possible rather than with Miss Nightingale's dream of making India a clean, sober Arcady. He remarked of her terrible descriptions of native towns in the *Report* that though their state was generally bad much had been done to improve them. Moreover, 'the cost of improvements . . . is great, and the great bulk of the people are very poor'. Miss Nightingale asserted that 'opinion' was unanimous that spirits should be banned from Army canteens and grog-shops in the bazaars. Lawrence was 'inclined to think it would not answer absolutely to prohibit the sale in canteens'. After all, canteens helped finance the army. Six months later he bravely reduced the rum issue to one dram per day. This hardly fulfilled Miss Nightingale's boast that 'he . . . carried out everything we suggested'.[19]

Lawrence used Miss Nightingale's reputation and the expertise of her team when it suited him. He adopted her — or Galton's — plans for stone or brick two-storied, white-washed barracks. He envisaged rehousing the 25,000 white troops who had arrived since the Mutiny and were still crowded into existing dilapidated barracks and temporary cantonments. But Lawrence was a careful spender and in no hurry, especially as he encountered opposition on every front. In India his permanent officials were bent upon reducing taxation and expenditure and had moved decisively to that end just before his arrival. At home the Horse Guards, the India Office and War Office, locked in inter-departmental warfare, were united in wanting to retain a cheap army and doubly united in keeping out Miss Nightingale.[20] In India Lawrence named men to Miss Nightingale's projected Presidency Sanitary Commissions, but then delayed the announcement of rules upon which they could proceed. This allowed local medical men, suspicious of the new commissioners, to develop the habit of refusing to supply information, in which they were backed by suspicious army officers who regarded the new Commissions as threats to their independence. The senior civil officials did not like the Commission either. As John Strachey loftily informed Miss Nightingale, after telling her that the 'draft' rules followed her suggestions, 'no measures involving an immediate large expenditure could have any chance of being adopted'.[21]

In the event the few army building programmes begun during

Lawrence's regime were restricted to some urgent works in Calcutta and to his beloved hill-stations, especially Simla. He disagreed fundamentally with the Nightingale team on the strategy for holding India, a disagreement that had been manifest since at least 1861. Lawrence believed that the Indian plains could never become healthy and habitable for white troops and that the alternative was to establish permanent settler-garrison forces on the climatically more equable, and therefore salubrious, hills. Miss Nightingale, Farr and Co. argued that the key to India lay in the plains which carried the communications, rivers, railways and roads, and which contained the great towns, the breeding grounds of sedition. The white army must be stationed near these strategic points and therefore the plains must be rendered wholesome. Lawrence never wavered in his preference: he directed such little money as he had to the hill-stations. Miss Nightingale never admitted to herself that she was dealing with a strategic, sanitary heretic.[22]

Her moral improvement plans for the soldiers were part of her design to make the plains habitable. They hinged on the barracks building programme, and failed. Her 'dayrooms', on the Crimea model, to encourage troops to pass their free time reading, letter writing and playing innocent games, were to be housed in the ground floor space of the new barracks. Very few seem to have been built. There were also to be 'workshops' for hobbies, and garden plots allocated to the men. These foundered on the niggardliness of the Indian Government and War Office. The army would not supply tools or instructors, the gardens required water which was scarce and expensive. Moreover, with reveille at four each morning, the men preferred an afternoon siesta to toiling in stifling sheds or sun-baked gardens: such work was native work, anyway. Miss Nightingale, who never understood that India was very hot, ascribed the failure to want of leadership from officers; and, indeed, no general order was ever issued to compel men to work in the sheds or gardens. Everywhere beset by procrastinators, she longed for the power to work miracles of obliteration: as Christ would have done 'if Christ had had to work through Pilate!'[23]

Her tie to Lawrence was strained further by the counter attack by senior Indian medical officers upon the statistics in the *Report*, published in August 1864. The doctors' ignorance and former neglect now served them. Miss Nightingale and Farr had indeed made statistics without straw. It emerged that the Nightingale figure silently omitted two Presidencies, Madras and Bengal, because estimates were

unavailable, yet the *Report* by implication covered all India. There were
no figures for 1857 and the year following because statistical work
ceased during the Mutiny. This too was glossed in the *Report*. It
emerged that the Nightingale team had estimated the recent sickness
and death rates by calculating from the numbers of troops sent out to
India, without allowing that these numbers were inflated by the move
to build a post-Mutiny white army. The doctors asserted that the 71
per 1000 death rate of 1836 was exaggerated and unprovable and that
the assumption that the 41 per 1000 rate had continued undiminished
since 1855 was false; as was the average over the period of 69 per
1000. They declared that the death rate had been dramatically reduced
from about 1859, and quoted their figure for 1863, 20 per 1000,
without adding that it had been an extraordinarily fever-free year.
None the less, the doctors' figures for the post-Mutiny period were
probably closer to the real order of magnitude than those publicised
by the Nightingale team. Her angry claim that the army had cut the
Indian mortality and sickness rates by a new, secretive policy of
invaliding home much larger members of troops at earlier stages of their
illness was an admission, although she made it look like a rebuttal.[24]

'We have been replying with all our might', Miss Nightingale told
Harriet Martineau, when seeking her journalistic support, 'The
opponents are always stronger than the supporters of good.'[25] Miss
Nightingale fought, as she had done when her tuberculosis statistics
were impugned, passionately on every front. She sent Lord Stanley
to Sir Charles Wood to persuade him to withhold two of the Indian
critiques, by Messrs Norman and Baker, from the House of Commons.
Wood, who neither cared much about Indian death rates nor liked
parliamentary rows, readily complied. Miss Nightingale rejoiced to Farr
that craven Wood had 'wisely held his tongue'.[26] She also quickly
revised and reprinted her pamphlet on *How People May Live ... in
India*, incorporating into it a letter from Sir Hugh Rose, the
Commander-in-Chief in India, praising the *Report*. Rose had written his
letter to the Horse Guards, in reply to one from the War Office drawing
his attention to the *Report*. It is very probable that Galton sent this
uncharacteristic War Office memorandum to Rose, at Miss Nightingale's
instigation. Galton then spirited Rose's reply to Miss Nightingale. She
incorporated his letter, before asking Galton's permission. She went
further, somehow:

The letter has been quoted in the 'Times'. By the way I did not send
it to the Times. I sent the 'Abstract' and 'Suggestions' to Mr Delane

[the Editor] through Count Strzelecki, & told them of the existence of Sir Hugh Rose's letter and got those articles written. But I did not give them Sir H. Rose. Probably they came to you for it.

Why did she tell Galton he had given it, if he had given it? Galton's short, cool reply ignored the point.[27]

The *Report*'s most dangerous critic was Dr A.C. Leith, chairman of the Bombay Sanitary Commission. He was a capable man who resented the carping tone of the *Report*, and who had independently kept figures on army health (which he must have withheld from the Royal Commission). Like his colleagues he argued that the *Report* overstated recent mortality and illness rates. His estimate for the recent army mortality rate for Bombay was 12/1000. Miss Nightingale apparently heard about Leith's threatened reply from a newly returned Indian official. She secretly obtained a copy from J.J. Frederick, an official at the War Office and secretary to the Army Sanitary Commission, who had illicitly borrowed it from Sir Proby Cautley – Miss Nightingale cultivated Frederick with gifts of game and subscriptions to his favourite charities. In India news of Leith's criticisms had appeared in the Bombay press. She moved first to capture Leith by sending him a sweet letter, accompanied by 'valuable books' and 'suggestions'. Among the latter was an invitation to send his findings to her Indian Barracks Committee rather than to the India Office. Leith professed himself flattered by her interest, but he stolidly evaded capture and even fought back, remarking that, 'It is easy to point out what is required but there are many delays . . . as everything . . . has to be submitted for approval to those without local knowledge.' Stanley was alarmed: Leith was a person of consequence who could not be brushed aside. Stanley proposed that he be openly 'answered', courteously and cautiously and not be made 'an enemy'. Miss Nightingale ignored this unsubtle suggestion and – without telling Stanley that she had already tried to silence Leith – advised Stanley to prompt Sir Charles Wood 'privately' to invite Miss Nightingale to inform him about the errors in Leith's report. She supplied a draft. Stanley dodged: it would be wrong to 'put my name to a letter I have not written'. He suggested that she write. She refused. Finally, they agreed that Sutherland should write to Wood. Stanley and Miss Nightingale might then write to support him. In the event Miss Nightingale prevailed upon Stanley to write; Wood agreed to refer Leith's report to the Indian Barracks and Hospital Improvement Commission.[28] Miss Nightingale then mobilised Farr to devise answers to Leith's 'statistical objections' and urged Galton, a member of the Barracks Commission, to have the report referred to Sutherland, in accordance with 'Lord Stanley's desire'. Their replies were to be officially printed. She would send copies to influential people, beginning with Lawrence. Miss Nightingale also set out to split the Bombay Commission and isolate Leith by warning their secretary, Surgeon J.P. Walker, 'strictly in confidence', that Wood was on her side. She undertook that the draft replies would be circulated among the full membership of the Barracks Commission; but after they were completed on 5 December 1864, she insisted that they go into type on that very day. Stanley, as chairman, did not even see the draft until three weeks later.[29]

Cautious Sir Charles Wood learned from this episode. He directed that all correspondence between India and the Barracks and Hospital Improvements Commission should go through him. Stanley and Miss Nightingale then promptly agreed that she would have to work through the Governor-General, who was not a 'sanitary commission'. After delicately hinting that Wood was likely to approve, she asked Lawrence,

Would you not think it well that papers which involve sanitary principles of permanent importance ... all the papers from the Bengal Sanitary Commission ... should be sent home officially through Sir Charles Wood to the Barracks and Hospital Improvement Commission?

Wood meant well, she allowed, but he was 'very ignorant of sanitary matters' and it 'does not do to depend upon the life of one person'. After delaying his reply for six months Lawrence declared himself honoured by her faith in his capacity and promised to help where he thought her plans were 'plausible'. But as for addressing sanitary reports to her through the India Office, 'you will think me timid – but ... only the Secretary of State for India can do that'. Miss Nightingale savagely marked this part of his letter.[30] 'Our difficulties', he informed her in another evasive letter, 'are ... very much beyond your conception.' The British, he explained, were 'birds of passage' and did not look to a long-term future. The natives were apathetic, and even opposed to sanitary changes. The European townspeople were united to blocking increased taxation to pay for new water and drainage schemes.[31] Moreover they could always drum up support back home. From this time onward, India was beset by cyclones, drought, famine and commercial collapse and Lawrence dismantled his sanitary commissions and virtually ceased to communicate with Miss Nightingale.

The unhappy Leith row continued throughout 1865. Farr was persuaded by Leith's calculations; so too was Stanley. Miss Nightingale urged Farr to alter his report: 'otherwise people will miss the point. e.g. they think we told the lie'.[32] But it seems that Farr quietly stuck to his figures. Poor Galton was in trouble after it emerged that Miss Nightingale had seen Leith's report before Wood had released it, (thanks to Frederick, of course), Galton found her unsympathetic and resistant to accepting some blame: 'All I regret is my excessive discretion (which indeed is my besetting sin).' She accused him of siding with the forces of unsanitary, complacant truth: 'it would be far better if the temporary 12 per 1000 had remained at 69 per 1000, if people are to be deluded by it into the belief that any material improvements ... have been made'. She then proposed that the team attack another damaging report, by Colonel Norman, but this time they all seem to have backed off.[33] The Leith and Norman episodes suggest that the men on the spot were achieving a much greater saving of life, with only limited resources, than Miss Nightingale and the writers who have followed her, have allowed.

In December 1865 Miss Nightingale heard that Lord de Grey, an upright Christian reforming aristocrat, was likely to succeed the ailing Wood as Secretary of State for India. She immediately cast her nets. She had, she told de Grey,

> been busy with Sir John Lawrence ... He was most strongly of the opinion that your 'home' Commission should begin operations at once − in sending our plans of Barracks & Hosps, with complete 'instructions' − this was his own word ... I urged repeatedly that it would be much less offensive (to India authorities) if this were done by the home Commission under a direct instruction from the Secretary of State for India. And he answered repeatedly − Just the reverse − you have lost time − you should volunteer all this ...

There is no evidence for this version, and much evidence to indicate that it could not have happened. As usual Miss Nightingale began with a reverie of desire and ended with a dramatic imperative. The letter continues for twenty pages. Miss Nightingale, once more faced with dislodgement from business, was desperate to hang on. Manipulation was her very being. She apologised by implication for the rambling, repetitive missive and explained that a short plea 'cannot go down on its knees − And that is ... my position (morally) at this moment to you'. De Grey rebuffed her.[34] Six months later she finally lost Stanley.

He came into office in July 1866. He had been ready to tinker while in Opposition but now he tartly informed her that he had no time to help in sanitary matters and, besides, he could 'not interfere in a colleague's department'.[35] They never collaborated again.

The colleague at the India Office was stern Lord Cranborne, later Lord Salisbury. He was an intelligent reactionary, outside Miss Nightingale's ambience of Whiggish, reforming aristocrats. She did not know how to collar him and drafted several approaches, varying from fully 'flattering' to fully businesslike. Finally she must have sent a business letter, because he curtly replied that he had no time to attend to her proposals. Miss Nightingale tried again in the following year: 'weak as I am I should be glad to have the opportunity of discussing the subject [cholera in India] with you when you could conveniently do so'. Cranborne never came. Meanwhile he quietly countermanded a despatch from his predecessor, de Grey, permitting a start on minor sanitary works — 'finance must come first'. Miss Nightingale blamed Galton and Sutherland. Their laziness in 'Indian sanitary matters [had] lost my <u>locus standi</u> with Cranborne — bequeathed by Stanley'.[36] Here, as she often did when defeated, Miss Nightingale constructed a world in which she was both heroine and victim, betrayed by her acolytes. It seems to be that in these situations her lies, as told to acolytes and prospective supporters, lose their ordinary connotation as being intended to deceive and instead become the materials for a fantasy which was real enough to her as she wrote. And so it might have seemed to Galton and Sutherland, who accepted her reproaches and continued loyal to her.

Even at this desolate stage in her career Miss Nightingale exemplified for many Britons the spirit of reform: of preservation and improvement of human life as a means to national strength and therefore true economy under God's laws of incorporation of the British and Indian masses into British middle-class norms of cleanliness and sobriety as a way to national perfectibility under Providence. As had happened before with Sidney Herbert, Sutherland and Jowett, like-minded spirits consecrated themselves to her unexpectedly at critical points in her pilgrimage. Sir Bartle Frere, the former Governor of Bombay, returned to England in the early summer of 1867 and joined the Council of India. He was a kindred visionary to Miss Nightingale. He too was a spender. In Bombay he had defied the financial control of the central government and built lavishly, employing expensive home architects and setting his crest on his public buildings. He had also upset local British dignitaries and their wives by entertaining native gentlemen and their ladies at Government House. Miss Nightingale obtained from Galton Frere's London address and advice on how to approach him. After Frere's visit to South Street she indulged herself in a small but characteristic piece of superfluous deceit. The great man came, she boasted to Galton, of all people, 'by his own appointment'. The meeting was a success. 'I think perhaps we start at a fresh advantage now.' Frere's faith, she discovered, was 'save . . . lives, cost what it will, then we can work'.[37]

Bartle Frere became her spy in the India Office. He provided her with copies of Cranborne's minutes to despatches. His 'rummaging through . . . papers' supplied Miss Nightingale with proof that the Indian government was building hospitals with ventilation systems which ignored her Barracks and Hospital Commission's prescriptions. She and her commission, working by English precedent, were keen on fully opened windows allowing air to sweep along the corridors. The Indian hospital builders, mindful of the heat, designed verandah-shaded windows which could be closed during the sweltering afternoons and through dust storms. Frere, who had in effect been sacked by Lawrence, turned Miss Nightingale against him. Lawrence, he alleged, did nothing but commission reports. The Governor-General was niggardly with money, even in cases of obvious need. He was afraid of offending the home government.[38] A romantic egotist, Frere was determined to fulfil the destiny that had been thwarted in India. 'He offered', Miss Nightingale confided to Sutherland, 'almost with tears in his eyes, to be "our aide de camp".' Together, they decided to press the new Secretary of State, Sir Stafford Northcote, a pressible man, they believed, to create a public health department in the India Office, headed by Frere and comprising Sutherland, Galton and Farr.[39]

This project revived Miss Nightingale's hopes of by-passing the Indian Government and India Office by having Indian sanitary matters directly referred home, to her. She intended the department to rule on the 'doors and windows' question, thereby correcting error and avenging the slight she had suffered from Indian army engineers and doctors. Above all, the department would enable her to see papers and know what was going forward. Frere's hopes paralleled hers. He envisaged the department as a mechanism for enabling Presidency governments to ignore the Indian central government. The department would approve, in the name of the India Office, local budgets for 'public' improvements.[40]

Northcote was to be edged into granting 'confidential' permission to Frere to send on papers to Sutherland and Galton in the War Office, and thence to Miss Nightingale. But Sutherland, Miss Nightingale scoffed, turned 'etiquette-ish' about the scheme. He was worried about losing his job. Enmity between the War and India Offices made his position awkward and he was already suspect from his association with the bothersome lady. He sought a 'formal' agreement between Northcote and his War Office chiefs. This did not suit Miss Nightingale.[41] An open agreement would alert the senior officials of both camps: each group would work to evade the agreement while both would collaborate to ensure that she saw only trivia, and those belatedly. Besides, she enjoyed espionage. She instigated moves, through Galton at the War Office, to get at documents even before Northcote was approached. Galton offered to the India Office on behalf of a 'sub-committee' of the War Office (presumably himself and Sutherland) to exchange information as a prelude to renewing co-operation. Miss Nightingale then wrote to Northcote commending this enlightened magnanimity and suggesting that the India Office reciprocate. Her proposal offended the tradition of departmental insularity. She never understood that rationality was not enough and was surprised when Northcote, whom she deemed weak, hedged on agreeing and fled on holiday.[42] It is a measure of his weakness that he did not refuse outright. Meanwhile Frere and Galton, aided by the prevailing inefficiencies of their respective offices, had already begun to abstract and exchange papers, which duly came to South Street.[43]

Northcote gave way within the month. On 20 August 1867 he accepted the Nightingale-Frere department within the India Office and undertook to instruct local Indian sanitary bodies to defer to it. Having won the victory Miss Nightingale despised the vanquished: 'He is very well intentioned – but he has not the elements of Sanitary', she recorded for herself, forgetting the noun; and indeed, 'Sanitary' for her was a means to power rather than a science. She thought he would carry out his undertakings because he was too soft to break them. He obeyed her summons to visit her. 'He kept his eyes shut all the time – and I kept my eyes wide open', she recorded after the interview. Ruthlessly, she seized her chance to pursue a larger dream:

Then I began about Nurses [for army, European civilian and native hospitals]. He said he was pestered by private persons with their philanthropic schemes about India (like Miss Carpenter, he said). [I wonder if he did. I shall return to Miss Carpenter later.] I said – I'm not a philanthropic person. It's <u>they</u> who are pestering me.[44]

After years of evasion and rebuffs from Sir Charles Wood, Lord de Grey and Lord Cranborne, she now had half under her thumb at least, a Secretary for India, a potentate who could deliver up to her not only the army, but India. The great plan she had shared with Sutherland since the Mutiny, and which had since lain quiescent, of regenerating native India and thereby justifying British suzerainty to God and man, now sprang to life. Having gained her public health department and received no outright rejection of her nurses, she informed Galton that our 'work will really be introducing the elements of civilization into India'.[45] Miss Nightingale had emerged as an imperialist.

Miss Nightingale rejected the philanthropist tag because she presented herself as being inside government, as an engine propelling 'national' efficiency, in contrast to outsiders who self-indulgently and ineffectually busied themselves with uplifting individuals or special groups among the poor. Her family standing, wealth, tenacity and good luck had enabled her to worm further into government than other improvers, especially female ones, but she was more like other philanthropists of her time than she cared to admit. They vied for the same fiefdoms and pursued indistinguishable strategies. While Stafford Northcote was merely 'pestered' by them, her rivals threatened her very purpose in living — by threatening her unique eminence as a reformer. Among these rivals Mary Carpenter and the National Association for the Promotion of Social Science are worth discussing because they impinged upon Miss Nightingale's career, they illuminate certain of her ambitions and they are interesting in their own right. Miss Carpenter, moreover, has been the beneficiary of almost as much ill-founded hagiography as Miss Nightingale.

In mid-1867 Miss Carpenter had emerged as Miss Nightingale's main competitor for India. Like Miss Nightingale, she had first had her hopes raised by Lawrence's appointment, then had been rebuffed by Wood, tried de Grey and Cranborne and failed, and then had tackled Northcote, whom she found, she informed Miss Nightingale possessively, 'very amenable indeed'.[46] Like Miss Nightingale again, her ambition was to use government to implement, that is, build and pay for, her chosen innovations — the emancipation of Indian women, the introduction of children's reformatories and a strict regime in Indian gaols, and sanitary reform. They began to circle one another in April 1867. Miss Carpenter opened by seeking Miss Nightingale's acquiescence in her projected visit to India. Miss Nightingale turned to Jowett, who knew everybody, for his usual shrewd malicious appraisal of the interloper.

He pronounced her 'worthy — but a terrible bore'.[47] Prospectively, she was a formidable competitor. She was thirteen years older than Florence Nightingale and had already become famous as an anti-slavery advocate and Ragged Schools manager almost a decade before Miss Nightingale went to the Harley Street Institution. Miss Nightingale found herself 'terribly busy' and postponed Miss Carpenter's intended visit until it became impossible for the lady to come: 'It is very good of you', Miss Nightingale purred, 'to think of me during your short & busy stay in London.' When she finally permitted a meeting, she refused to be impressed. She noted after the visit; 'Well — Miss Carpenter came here . . . on very serious business. She began by telling me what every one knows but which seemed to have struck her as something new — the awful state of the Indian women . . . She wants to put me into communications with divers people at Madras and Bombay.'[48]

Like Miss Nightingale herself, Josephine Butler, the campaigner against the Contagious Diseases Acts, Lord Shaftesbury and other Victorian reformers, Mary Carpenter was given to dedicating herself in God's name to her successive causes, and to recounting that determination on paper. Lawrence's preferment, as it did with Miss Nightingale, alerted her to new opportunities. She recorded on 12 January 1864:

> my solemn resolve that henceforth I devote my heart and soul and strength to the elevation of the women of India . . . I shall obey the remarkable call which has been given me so unexpectedly . . . Without any . . . apparent change of plan, I shall watch openings . . . and later — A grand and new life appears opening upon me, Heavenly Father, by tokens drawn from the marvellous workings of Thy providence.[49]

She had lit upon India after venturing successively on Home Visiting, Ragged Schools, children's reformatories and convict reform projects. In each she had made the rules, done the managing and taken the credit, but rarely actually worked in the enterprise. She was domineering, sentimental and cruel, suspicious of fellow reformers and intolerant and inept in handling her subordinates and her charges. Each venture increased her power and reputation, but there is no evidence to show that the subjects of her endeavours were made happy or better.[50]

Again like Miss Nightingale she had a father who had educated her, whom she publicly esteemed but privately despised. He had been a

Unitarian clergyman. He was 'lost at sea' in 1840 (when Mary was 33), while on a Mediterranean tour recovering from a nervous breakdown. She disliked her mother and sister and was 'not lonely' when they died. They envied, she said, her 'secret consciousness of having performed . . . any service . . . better than others would have done'.[51] As a child she had insisted on running her own Sunday School. Before she was twenty she knew that God had chosen her for 'distinguished' work. Her earthly reward was public 'affection and gratitude'. She never married. In serving her heavenly father she made reparation, she believed, to the earthly father whom she could not love, indeed to her unloved self, for, as she often recalled her mother telling her, she was very like her father in mind and body. The parallel with Miss Nightingale extends even further. Miss Carpenter adopted a little girl, whom she apparently left, as did Miss Nightingale, to be raised by others: 'a little girl of *my own*! . . . Ready to my hand and nicely trained, without the trouble of marrying etc., etc.,'.[52] Rarely can two egotisms have been so mirrored. Florence Nightingale's and Mary Carpenter's restless possessiveness, their attitude to their respective fathers, their craving for fame through self-sacrifice, illuminate the motivations of other Victorian females who adopted bizarre, unpopular causes — Ellice Hopkins, the social purity campaigner, for instance, or her crony, Sarah Robinson, 'the soldier's friend', or another Unitarian campaigner, Octavia Hill. Social isolates from childhood, their work is characterised by voyeuristic condescension, complacent parsimony and an unwavering resolve to use the state to underwrite their pursuits and coerce the subjects of their careers. The stock explanation for the involvement of spinsters in Victorian social reform, the 'superfluous women' argument, is inadequate to explain the sheer drive and flair of these crusaders who remained unmarried apparently by choice.

When Miss Nightingale refused to treat, Miss Carpenter countered by appealing to the National Association for the Promotion of Social Science, where Miss Nightingale had earlier made her triumphant plea for India. The NAPSS had been created in 1856 by a vigorous, newly graduated briefless barrister, George Woodyatt Hastings, the son of a founder of the British Medical Association. Hastings used the prestige of old Lord Brougham, the first president of NAPSS, to bring about a coalition of old Benthamites, social statisticians like Farr and William Newmarch, sanitary reformers like John Simon and Lord Shaftesbury, law and education reformers such as Brougham, James Kay-Shuttleworth and M.D. Hill, earnest paternalist aristocrats like Lord Ebrington and Stanley, representatives of the Unitarian and Quaker reforming cousinhoods, Howitts, Taylors and Sturges, and social work careerists like Mary Carpenter and her juvenile reformatory and convict discipline rivals. Hastings succeeded in recruiting almost every great name in the reform calendar, including Miss Nightingale.

The NAPSS provided a platform for amateurs working from outside Parliament, or at least the Cabinet and the bureaucracy, to forward their particular objects. The celebrated annual meetings, held at a succession of provincial cities, provided opportunities for public oratory and displays of concentrated reforming strength. The sub-committees and deputations enabled individuals to press their particular aims and arrange cabals. Rivalries between crotcheteers were particularly sharp on the timing, size and presentation of deputations to important people. The published reports of special committees and the *Transactions* were intended to sway governments and municipal corporations through reproduction in the daily press. The NAPSS was open to ladies, even to their speaking publicly at the congresses. Women could not serve on the Council, but at the 1858 meeting they comprised one-third of the 1500 participants. The journal was printed, at higher than ruling rates, by Emily Faithful at the Victoria Press.[53] The NAPSS's model was the British Association for the Advancement of Science. 'Social Science' for the members of NAPSS neither carried its contemporary Comtist meaning of progressive sociology nor its modern connotation of controlled social inquiry into social and class structures. NAPSS members already knew the answers: their problem was to rouse 'public opinion' and make government act. Hastings paid lip-service to prevailing orthodoxy in the first issue of the journal:

> Advancing knowledge has proved an inseparable connexion between the various branches of physical science, and disclosed to us, as Newton foreshadowed ... a unity throughout creation, a vast expansion of purpose, based on a few simple laws ... as promulgated by ... the ... Divine Legislator.

But he immediately qualified this profession by remarking that the NAPSS's strength was 'the practical knowledge and actual experience of social reformers'. Indeed, Hastings off-handedly foisted 'social science' on the Association – in the midst of arguing against the intention of some of the founding fathers to have 'law' in the name of the proposed journal: 'People so hate the name of *law* ... whereas under general social science a good deal of law & legislation might be worked in & made popular.' Ambitious Hasting's chief concern was that the infant Association should be 'National'.[54] And so it became: within ten years NAPSS had 1600 members, almost double the enrolment of the British Association.[55]

The reformers' practical knowledge found expression through the five original departments: Law Amendment, Education, Punishment and Reformation, Public Health, Social and Political Economy. The members' object was not to change the world but to manage it. They intended, now that Old Corruption and Chartism were defeated, to produce rationales for middle-class control over the urban masses who were now beyond village tutelage, whose ignorance, turbulence, criminality and poverty were faults or misfortunes within themselves, not their society. The NAPSS had considerable influence on protective legislation for the middle classes during the 1860s and 1870s: reforms in the law of bankruptcy and other areas of commercial law including patents; married women's property; the Endowed Schools Act; reform of the law of evidence and innovations in prison discipline; the Public Health Act of 1875 and compulsory notification of infectious diseases; and the great report on strikes in 1860 which crystallised a view of trade union activity which has endured to the present. The NAPSS also led in creating international associations in statistics, weights and measures and, especially, international law. This remarkable organisation is now largely forgotten, partly because it petered out in the mid-1880s as its founding generation dropped away and their particular line of indirect state interventionism became unpopular among the harshly polarised advocates of anti-statism and socialism, and partly because Hastings, the very embodiment of the NAPSS, was disgraced in 1892 when he was sentenced to five years imprisonment for fraud.[56]

From the outset Miss Nightingale deemed the NAPSS a rival for public interest. She lent her name to the Association, Hastings's assemblage of big names did not permit her to do otherwise, but privately she disparaged it: 'If the whole of the 1st vol. of the Transactions had been burnt, the world would have been none the worse', she confided to Chadwick, another old hand threatened by the new organisation.[57] None the less, she offered to present a paper at the next congress in Liverpool. She had the paper on 'The Sanitary Conditions of Hospitals' read, but she did not appear despite allowing rumours to circulate that she would; her paper duly appeared in the second volume of the *Transactions*. Her contributing lent *éclat* to the journal but she spoiled the effect and upset Hastings by issuing the article as a separate pamphlet before the *Transactions* appeared, and then again as a book, padded with material from the Army Sanitary Commission.[58] Her paper, which developed into *Notes on Hospitals* in its third edition of 1863, remains a brilliant polemic. She vividly rehearsed the evils of overcrowding, bad ventilation and lighting as correlatives to yet another denunciation of the belief that 'hospital diseases' were spread by contagion. Her argument now looks bizarrely simplistic, but set in its context of seedy, grubby hospital buildings, doctors and patients, it becomes apt and beneficial. Miss Nightingale used the NAPSS as a rostrum on three more occasions. The committee was glad to have her name, but after her brush with Hastings over her premature pamphlet both sides kept their distance.

Her feud with Mary Carpenter over India continued through the 1860s. In 1867 Miss Nightingale used her kinsman and acolyte, Henry Bonham Carter, to dissuade Miss Carpenter from delivering an Indian paper, probably on female education and its promise for sanitary reform, at the forthcoming NAPSS congress in Belfast. The letter, signed by Bonham Carter, warned 'that no good is to be done in the way proposed' because it would 'induce misdirected efforts which might embarrass your present negotiations or relations (whatever they may be called) with government'. Bonham Carter offered to draft, 'for Miss Carpenter' to read at Belfast, an alternative document stating general principles but rejecting immediate action. She delicately riposted by addressing herself directly to Miss Nightingale: 'your letter ... is really right', and noting her particular obligation to Miss Nightingale for enclosing a copy of Miss Carpenter's original letter declaring her intention to speak at Belfast — signals sent and received. Miss Carpenter then feinted beautifully. She claimed to have lost her voice and therefore could not 'undertake to read any papers aloud at the meeting'. Indeed, she hinted that her illness would prevent her from attending. A week later in Belfast, doubtless to Miss Nightingale's vexed surprise, Miss Carpenter delivered two papers on India, the first concerned with prison discipline, the second, given 'extemporaneously' to ringing applause and the encomium of her chairman, the influential Lord Dufferin (of the War Office, formerly of the India Office, and future Governor-General of India), on Miss Nightingale's forbidden subject, 'Female Education'.[59] Miss Nightingale had met her match.

Their next and last confrontation occurred two years later, in September 1869, when Miss Carpenter sought to enlist Miss Nightingale's support for her Indian Association for the Promotion of Social Science, a body she had created among British civil officials, Bombay Parsees and a few Hindu gentlemen. Miss Carpenter had plunged into India with almost as little knowledge and understanding as Miss Nightingale. Her experience on her first and second journey had disabused her of the notion that simple proselytism among deferential natives would lead to the introduction of cleaner, classified prisons and female education among Hindus. The government would not provide money for the first and Hindu fathers, husbands and mothers, resisted the second. Such female schools as existed dated from long before her visit and indeed were upset by her interference. Apparently only one of the schools she launched survived: she had nominated herself Lady Superintendent of the Bombay Normal School but typically had immediately left the running and teaching of the school to subordinates – who in this case turned out to be effective. Miss Carpenter found native gentlemen to be complaisant but unreliable. She moved in 1869 to circumvent them by proposing a separate women's section of the Indian NAPSS. It would also circumvent British officials like Sir Alexander Grant, the Director of Public Instruction in Bombay, who blocked her requests for money after discovering that her schools were to inculcate Christianity. A ladies' section, Miss Carpenter confided, would engender '*sympathy* . . . without any *possibility* of suspicion *Private* on the part of the *natives* . . . or of the *government* of absurd fanaticism'. Miss Nightingale was invited to endorse, but not annex, the proposal: 'of course I do not suppose that you can take any part, but it will be a . . . benefit if you will write me a few lines of sympathy which I may read to the ladies'. Miss Nightingale pleaded ill-health and inability to hold a pen. Miss Carpenter begged. Miss Nightingale provided 'something'. Miss Carpenter returned 'many thanks for your loving note'.[60] There is no evidence that she used it. She would have had small opportunity to do so: agreeable Indian gentlemen such as Keshub Chunder Sen, now revered as fathers of the Indian freedom movement, proved wholly unenlightened when it came to allowing their own womenfolk to join Miss Carpenter.

Miss Nightingale found Miss Carpenter's interventions singularly disturbing because they emulated at every point her own discovery that India provided a multifarious, unspoiled field for a woman of business. (At first sight, it is strange that they did not try Ireland which was closer and obviously in need of improvement, but both ladies, like most of their colleagues, avoided Ireland. There, government was already in the field, the proud Anglo-Irish gentry appeared hostile and the common Irish were uncouth, resistant to advice and ultimately hardly worth preserving. As Miss Nightingale once remarked, Hindus were gentlemen, compared with the Irish.) Lawrence, partly because of the army sanitary improvements already achieved and largely because he was parsimonious, had disappointed Miss Nightingale's ambitions but she had early realised that she could by-pass him and his officials by tackling sanitary, civil and economic problems among the native population. Prison reform, nursing, village institutions, irrigation and canal building, and control of cholera had all been added to her agenda before Miss Carpenter took to India.

In each case Miss Nightingale herself was belatedly adopting initiatives already taken by dedicated medical men and engineers in India. The earliest evidence of Miss Nightingale's interest in prisons comes from mid-1864, when she began to demand of Lawrence's private secretary Dr Charles Hathaway – significantly, she did not raise the issue with Lawrence – that the Indian government produce accurate prison death rates. Hathaway had earlier been the Inspector of Prisons. Her demand was an implied rebuke.[61] The Inspector-General of Prisons in Bengal had already calculated death rates of about nine per cent of inmates per year, compared with a one per cent rate in British gaols.[62] Indian prisons were dilapidated, overcrowded, ill-ventilated, undrained, filthy and supplied with poor food. The inmates, unsegregated by age or crime, had, according to Sutherland, 'low resisting power . . . they do not stand penal work as our men do'.[63] Local reformers and English activists such as Miss Carpenter were bent upon building panopticons and children's reformatories (there were only 400 child prisoners in all India in 1868) and introducing new graduated dietaries and punishments. Lawrence vetoed their plans. Privately he agreed that there were 'no good jails here', but warned that the reformers' ambitions would 'cost millions'. He added resignedly that prisoners were 'at least as well off as the rest of the people'.[64]

Miss Nightingale was interested in building new gaols to preserve life, not in new regimes of discipline for prisoners whose average expectation of life wearing 60 pound punishment chains was 15 days.[65] She went further than other reformers, too, in campaigning for redesigned lunatic asylums, which she was told were worse than the gaols. She wanted Lawrence to ask her Sanitary Commission to draw up schedules for cell sizes, latrines, bedding, airing and exercise. She was indifferent to the actual shape of prisons, but settled for the Pentonville model because it promised that surveillance and discipline would entail regular cleansing, meals and exercise. After Lawrence failed to seek her Sanitary Commission's advice she sent detailed plans and schedules anyway. She also intended to 'bring in the India Office somehow ... they hold the purse strings'. They had lain low during the eighteen months that the prison issue had been canvassed in England. Miss Nightingale professed to be surprised when shortly after this letter *The Times* began to print the horrible details of Indian prison life and to advocate reforms. She told Galton that she had not furnished *The Times* with the information, 'however it makes our path much easier'.[66] She prodded Stanley into speaking to Sir Charles Wood, the Secretary of State, and supplied him with information for Wood's instruction. But Stanley was lukewarm — 'our suggested reforms are very costly' — and Wood did nothing. Stafford Northcote again proved more pliable. A NAPSS deputation waited on him and he told Lawrence to start on new gaols, on the basis of NAPSS assertions that they could be erected for £4. 10s 0d a cell. No building ensued. As General Strachey, Inspector-General of Irrigation and a senior member of the Governor-General's Council, remarked:

> When I think of all that has to be done in India for the honest part of the community, how roads and railways and canals have to be made ... and 10,000 works of improvement to be carried out, it seems to be monstrous that we should have to discuss these schemes, which I can only characterise as ... petty sentimentality.[67]

But clearly a clean-up did occur. Possibly fortuitously, cholera virtually disappeared from the prison compounds. At Bhagulpore prison in Bengal the annual death rate fell from an average of 16 per 100 inmates over the period 1844-65 to 1.9 per 100 in 1866 to 0.4 per 100 in 1869. The Madras gaol reported an improvement from 12.6 per 100 in 1865 to 5.3 per 100 in 1867 and 1.7 per 100 in 1871. Apart from the cheaply installed but apparently efficient new water storages in the gaols, and hence isolation from cholera (with luck), the British foreshortened the problem by unobtrusively halving the admissions.[68] Miss Nightingale's influence was indirect, but by lending her reputation to local reformers such as Doctors Mouat and Walker, who were trying to enforce cleansing schedules, she helped them to persist and gain a little from complacent, penny-pinching officials. This battle won, Miss Nightingale showed no interest in Indian prisons after the 1860s. Her interference had been well justified: she had helped break the terrible sequence which had made imprisonment in India a near certain death sentence.

Miss Nightingale's brief involvement with female nursing in India also arose from reaction to local initiatives. Early in 1864, in the first flush of his governor-generalship, Lawrence had permitted Dr Walker to proceed with his ambition to create a trained female nursing service in Bengal. Walker had decided upon his plan before he 'officially' informed Miss Nightingale of the project in November 1864. Apparently he intended to recruit Eurasian Christian women — Hindu and Moslem women were unavailable — and instal them in regimental hospitals to be trained effectively by the medical officers. Soldiers' widows, European and Eurasian, were already employed, untrained. This chain of authority broke Miss Nightingale's cardinal rule about the independence of the matron.[69] She also saw it as a challenge to her eminence as the authority on nursing. She made a take-over bid for the project by printing and circulating her own more elaborate scheme. She let it be known that Lawrence had asked her to despatch 66 head nurses and 112 assistants for regimental hospitals. There is no such request from Lawrence among the Nightingale Papers. There is not even a letter 'sanctioning', as Miss Nightingale oddly put it, such a plan. She also envisaged creating training schools in civilian general hospitals. 'There is a private and most pressing invitation to me to go out. If the Doctors would give me six months there, I would go', she confided to McNeill in the reasonable expectation that the story would spread, as it did. In all the Nightingale Papers, which preserve so much trivia, no such important invitation exists. Miss Nightingale admitted the fantasy of her plan in a concluding sentence in the letter to McNeill: her scheme was impossible because no trained nurses were available in England, but it served its purpose in smothering Walker's more feasible project.[70]

Eighteen months later her interest revived when Mary Carpenter threatened to move in on the nursing question:

Be assured that I never think you neglectful for not answering letters, [Miss Carpenter proffered] I am well aware that you have long turned your attention to India, & doubtless your efforts have produced valuable fruit. But I have seen no effort to train nurses, & there is a universal want of . . . decent nurses in the hospitals etc. [Then Miss Carpenter, fresh back from India, turned the screw] I believe that little is done in India by correspondence.

She added that she had secured Frere's support.[71] Miss Nightingale now moved to stop the intrusion. She obtained somehow the minutes of the governor-general's council on the nursing proposal and littered them with savage marginalia. She mobilised McNeill against the plan, warning him that she had 'always been against' placing nurses in regimental hospitals – a reversion to her old Crimean battles but a false affirmation in its present context. She even wrote to Lawrence. After three drafts, each declining in vehemence, she finally begged him to delay his decision and seek her help. Her plea must have crossed with the news that Lawrence had indeed vetoed the grandiose – though less grandiose than Miss Nightingale's own proposed contingent of 178 – scheme devised locally by Major G.B. Malleson and espoused by Miss Carpenter.[72] Miss Nightingale now countered with a reduced plan for a core contingent of four lady-superintendents to travel from England under contract from the India Office to recruit and train local women, an idea she had earlier totally opposed. She had lately despatched a similar core group to Sydney to begin training locals there. Again she remarked that she 'fain would' go to India to establish the system herself, 'then we should not have to worry', but this time she did not claim to have been invited. Again the Indian government vetoed this plan.[73] They were preoccupied with famine and flood and falling revenues. Miss Nightingale gave up. In her hard-headed way she recognised that so long as the government and the army could use slave labour and the chain of command remained unbroken, nothing could be done: 'Englishmen command Hindoo males and Eurasian subordinates – who give orders to the poor coolies – who do the actual nursing.'[74] Thereafter attempts by well-meaning governor's ladies, Christian missions and presidency governments foundered under lack of money and avoidance by Englishwomen 'who lose all desire to exert themselves', Eurasians who were too proud and 'native women' who were 'too ignorant'. When Miss Nightingale was last consulted about the problem, in 1889, matters had not changed.[75] Only with the coming of women doctors and a sufficient number of lady-superintendents for independent mission hospitals in the 1890s did effective nursing training and management really begin.

Miss Nightingale always preferred the larger arena of public preventive sanitation. The indications for action were straightforward because the laws of health and cleanliness were simple and proven. The monetary outlay was relatively small and it was more than repaid by the strengthened national efficiency which resulted. Even in crude terms of lives preserved for money spent, her priorities, as against expenditure upon large hospitals and a highly skilled medical service, both in her own age and during the century since, were the right ones.

Ineluctably and not unwillingly, her concerns with barrack building, public sanitation and protection from cholera led her into Indian social and economic questions about which she knew little. Her ignorance never hindered her from making pronouncements, yet her common sense generally saved her from the callous inanities promulgated by better informed but more owlish authorities.

Miss Nightingale's opinions about cholera varied through time, but she passionately held to whatever notion happened to occupy her mind and always tried to forbid the propagation of rival theories, even if they were theories she had lately espoused. In 1854, she had drawn upon her transitory — or mythical — experience at the Middlesex Hospital to inform Mrs Gaskell that cholera was not contagious, that is, in her view, transmitted from victim to victim by contact. Miss Nightingale 'never had a touch even of diarrhoea'. By 1861 she had come to believe that sufferers caught cholera by drinking dirty water; she tried to stop the professors at the Army Medical School acknowledging any other hypothesis.[76] Cholera was endemic in India, she told the NAPSS Congress in 1863, because the army stations and bazaars lacked clean water and 'when men drink water, they drink cholera in it'.[77] But she soon perceived that this doctrine narrowed her field of operations by diverting attention from overcrowding, lime-washing of barracks, street cleansing and removal of sewage. In mid-1864 she warned Dr Hathaway that 'Dr. Budd's paper (the classic demonstration that cholera is a water-borne infection) is of no practical value ... It is purely theoretical.'[78] Many eminent medical men shared her reaction to Budd's work, but her peculiarly exposed position as a non-medical, unbeneficed sanitary advocate made her edgily strident in her dogmatic confusion — especially when authority ignored her. During an epidemic at Mean Meer (now Lahore) in 1863 the government had withdrawn all troops to barracks and thereby created great overcrowding: but they ignored the Indian Sanitary Commission's rules about isolating cases within the compounds; privies stayed foul and water supplies remained unimproved. Miss Nightingale was further put out because the report had been secretly supplied to her and she could not attack the government without exposing Walker, her go-between.[79]

India is the home of cholera and epidemics flared regularly at pilgrimages, fairs and festivals and accompanied the famines that recurred every three or four years during the last third of the century. Cholera death rates are only available after 1881 and they represent gross under-registration but still they record that between 1881-1900 6-8 per cent of all registered deaths were cholera cases representing nearly one million victims.[80] Government, faced with the impossible task of providing safe water supplies, resorted to quarantine: when cholera appeared soldiers were confined to barracks, afflicted villages and towns were isolated, pilgrimages forbidden, festivals terminated. Miss Nightingale dismissed these improvisations – although they indisputably saved thousands of lives – because they treated natives 'like infants', instead of employing them as adults 'to clean up and exercise responsibility', and because, she alleged, quarantine was unscientific.[81] By October 1865, after another bad outbreak in India, she reverted to the old miasma theory. Herding people together under quarantine only fortified the 'cholera influence'. Thus strengthened, it 'may extend hundreds of miles atmospherically from the Centre . . . The moral is: that, unless you improve the sanitary condition of the Civil populations, you cannot insure immunity for the Soldiers.'[82]

To this end she composed a new set of rules to be issued by the Indian Sanitary Commission in 1866. Ventilation, strict allowances of cubic feet of air per man in barracks, drainage, water supply, were all prescribed but the new emphasis was on strict and immediate removal of ordure. She pressed Galton to ensure that the War Office and India Office endorsed the new regulations, so that Indian officials would be less free to ignore them. After all, she prompted Galton, 'you have the first authority in Europe as to preventive action (about Cholera) in Dr Sutherland. After him and Grainger (who is dead) [Dr R.D. Grainger wrote a valuable report on cholera in 1850] I don't think you have any better authority than I.' She was, she boasted to Galton, 'not modest'. She relished knowing she was right and delighted in the espionage required to help her prevail. Two days later she returned 'with the greatest reluctance', some Indian papers Galton had purloined from the War Office for her, and signed herself 'Betsy Prig'.[83]

Her new rules were largely ignored. At home, after the epidemic of 1866 even Dr Farr defected to the water-borne camp, admitting to her belatedly – he had sought to hide his disloyalty – that 'the case against the water was very strong'. In India even stalwart allies like Dr T.G. Hewlett, the Health Officer for Bombay, settled for quarantine.[84] Miss Nightingale then set about outflanking them. At home she sounded influential people including Frere, de Grey and Napier of Magdala, the Indian military hero, on a proposal to establish a separate Indian Sanitary Service, independent of the medical officers and subject to her India Office Sanitary Committee. The fact that the medical profession had plumped for a specific water-borne causative agent for cholera proved that they had lapsed into 'contagionism' and thereby demonstrated that they were 'declining in ... accurate observation and deficient in theory ... The present decline in India dates from ... when a mere theory of a Bristol contagionist [Budd] was printed in an Indian government report & was accepted as a truth.'[85] In India she stirred a leading — and now lonely — believer in the miasma theory, Dr Cunningham, to write a report condemning the specific agent, water-borne theories and reliance on quarantine, and restating the case for thorough-going reconstruction and cleansing. The India Office, despite her efforts, buried the report.[86] Thereafter she, Galton and Sutherland, echoed unhelpfully by Chadwick, continued to preach the miasmatic doctrine. They reinforced the conservatism of like-minded medical men in India and the United States and at home.[87] But official opinion ignored them. Quarantine met the limits of what was possible; yet Miss Nightingale was never content with the possible when others defined it.

It is hard to be infallible, even when one is on the sidelines. Miss Nightingale's pronouncements upon Indian canals, irrigation and drainage always sounded authoritative but they slewed with each blunder and according to the allegiance of the particular high underling she was trying to catch. Her problem was to find work for her London sanitary committee and to give directions on matters highly disputed among medical men and engineers. In 1865 she commissioned the great analyst, Dr Robert Angus Smith, to produce a simple set of procedures for 'finding out how much dirt there was in water'. Smith proved characteristically cautious, changeable and slow in writing his recommendations. He rewrote the paper, she said, six times in five months and then destroyed it in order to begin anew. But Miss Nightingale trapped him by obtaining a draft and secretly setting it in type at her expense. Her object was to compel the Indian sanitarians to get on with their work *her* way, not necessarily the best way. Her timing was unfortunate. Smith was apparently groping his way towards a qualitative analysis rather than a straightforward quantity count, with the object of establishing differentials between kinds of 'dirt' according to their varying contents of disease-inducing agents. Advanced doctors in India were doing the same and they rejected Smith's report as old-fashioned. The War Office and India Office, too, had reservations about the report, which promised only expensive trouble. Miss Nightingale moved quietly to order the printing of up to 2,000 copies, at government expense. Without waiting for India Office approval she despatched copies of the proofs to Dr Walker in Calcutta. India Office approval was irrelevant because, she informed Walker, the report had been 'written at your instigation'. She reassured him that the Office liked the report, but would take 'two years' to get around to sending it to India. Meanwhile she had already sent 100 copies 'privately'. Her machinations appear to have been in vain. The India Office never ordered that Smith's procedures be followed and local officers seem not to have adopted them.[88] By backing the local officers' assertions of independence of higher Indian authority she had necessarily but inadvertently increased their independence of her commands. Despite her protestation that Smith's report represented 'the last and most perfect knowledge on this subject', the report was not even Dr Smith's 'last word'. I could not discover what Smith thought about Miss Nightingale's perfidy, but his dealings with her ceased soon afterwards.

Miss Nightingale was equally expeditious with drainage problems. Rawlinson, her engineering coadjutor from Crimean days, warned her that India was geographically various and everywhere poor. He plumped for a series of pilot schemes, employing diverse sizes of pipes and systems. This did not suit Miss Nightingale. Too much was left to local decision and no role remained for the home sanitary committee. Rawlinson, she said, was unhelpfully pessimistic, too.[89] The India Office ignored her overtures for instructions to her committee to provide drainage rules. She sent them none the less. Her rules betray a complete want of understanding. Pessimists alleged the 'impossibility of water drainage in a country with dry seasons', but this was 'no problem'. Water to flush the pipes had simply to be pumped from the rivers. Malta and Gibraltar were 'drier' than India (as indeed they are in terms of annual rainfall, compared with say, Calcutta) but their towns and British stations had no difficulties. As for the system, 'earthenware or iron pipes are now so universally introduced ... that it is only necessary to name them'. With sublime aristocratic disdain she ignored costs and difficulties in survey, land tenures and taxation, water flow, plumbing skills, in a sub-continent short of trained men and notorious for jobbery and extravagance. The sewage could readily be used in 'sewage irrigation, as in England' – where it had largely failed – or be emptied into the rivers and sea by gravity flow. Miss Nightingale's severely logical, sanitary mind lapsed into ambiguity: 'A few thousand gallons ... per day are nothing in India. If the latrines were discharged after sunset, there would hardly be the vestige of the water next morning'. She issued these dicta ten years after the outcry about sewage pollution of the Thames and midst growing criticism of the fouling of British bays and estuaries. 'Native habits', she admitted, were dirty, but piecemeal expedients devised by local incompetents would only pander to them. After all, she continued, she knew orientals and their practices, having been in the Crimea. Only an 'entire scheme' designed by her and her advisers could serve India.[90]

No one took any notice. Miss Nightingale retreated to offering advice about water filters and building brick tops to wells to prevent permeation. Meanwhile the men on the spot extended their dry earth closet systems, the only kind possible within the available money and water supplies, and pressed on with concrete open canal drains.[91] Miss Nightingale's last powerful comrade in India, Lord Napier, Governor of Madras, yet another duty-ridden, simplistic proconsul attracted to the national heroine, defied the central government and his advisors by ordering the building of a sewage farm and an underground sewage, drainage system. (Like others among her proconsul friends he faithfully obeyed her injunctions to burn her letters, and wrote regularly about their conspiracy to better India in a coyly flirtatious style whenever his wife was away in the hills.) The sewage farm proved inefficient and the six-inch pipes in the underground system, recommended by Miss Nightingale upon 'the best advice', could not cope in the wet season and blocked during the dry.[92] Cawnpore's sewers, built (it was believed) according to the specifications of Miss Nightingale's committee (there is evidence that Chadwick had a hand in it), proved disastrous. However, Bombay's cleansing system of deep open drains, devised against Nightingale-Rawlinson principles, also worked badly. The ratepayers and government were never prepared to pay for any sufficient system.[93] But Miss Nightingale never recognised this obstacle. In 1871, when she began to lose interest in the subject, she was still accusing local planners of inability to 'see the consequences of a fact and realize them in practice'.[94] Like the local doctors, the local engineers never took Miss Nightingale and her sanitary committee seriously, and she hated them for it.

By extension from her interest in drainage, Miss Nightingale took the side of the canal-irrigation interest in the controversy with the railway promoters. Fundamentally the conflict divided two kinds of imperialist: the canal builders saw themselves justifying British dominance in India by controlling the great rivers, expanding irrigation and thereby enabling the natives to work the land for the more effectual production of food and cash crops. River and canal transport was cheap and within the range of the natives. Men like Richard Temple, the great civil servant, and Arthur Cotton, the canal builder, were possessed by a vision of managing great waters and feeding the millions. Returns on government capital investment would be low but they would be certain. But above that stretched the prospect of using the state to achieve a design that would gloriously loft the British Empire above its pagan Roman predecessor by, as one engineer privately exulted, realising 'the gift of Providence in a well supplied river, turned to its proper account'.[95]

Railway men also protested the grandeur of their aims but their plans were more prosaic. They boasted 'Private Enterprise' but they required government support for construction loans raised among British capitalists and government guarantees on passenger traffic and freight rates. They argued that in times of famine they could bring food quicker. More attractively, at least to the War Office and sections of the India Office, they asserted that their trains could convey troops faster and in larger numbers than the river boats. They were, as Miss Nightingale put it, the 'merchants' of imperialism; her canal people were, like the Romans, the 'civilizers'. Behind the scenes and unbeknownst to her, the canal promoters were as hungry for government guarantees as their railway rivals.[96]

Railway advocates alleged that canals bred fever. Doubtless they were right. But Miss Nightingale's home sanitary commission and the presidency commissions were never empowered to investigate the charge. She was undeterred. The natives, she instructed Lawrence, must be directed to plough in the irrigation water and not let it stagnate. Rice farmers would have to change their ways. Napier warned her that there was small scope in India for innovation in agriculture: 'The more you see of the country the more you are struck with the practical simplicity and appropriateness of the native methods.'[97] But non-interference as a principle of administration was alien to Miss Nightingale.

She finally lost her irrigation friends when she circulated the proofs of a pamphlet on the subject in 1874. They could offer only embarrassed criticisms. Contrary to Miss Nightingale's' assertion, no navigation or irrigation system made a profit. Her declaration that navigation and irrigation were simultaneously practicable throughout the year on every system was untrue of all except the lower Ganges. She had had the current Viceroy, Lord Northbrook, in view when preparing her text. Its errors gave Northbrook the opportunity to fob her off completely. Miss Nightingale's last resort was to charge Lord Salisbury, now returned to the India Office, with producing shoddy figures on canal and irrigation finances. The returns were poorly kept and possibly the losses were smaller than the railway lobby, especially, alleged but they remained losses to the general revenue rather than profits. Salisbury was a railways man. When he told Miss Nightingale that he did not know the precise figures and had no intention of collecting them she was baffled: 'And they call me a "dangerous man"!!!'[98]

From this point Miss Nightingale and other 'civilizing' imperialists began to devise ways of supporting irrigation in India that by-passed the authorities. They placed their hopes in the ryots, the agricultural peasants. The famines and disturbances of the mid-1870s had revealed the ryots as unwilling to take government water because they could not pay for it and because irrigation transactions further subjected them to the extortions of petty officials and zemindars. Miss Nightingale proposed that the government, through a co-operative land bank, lend money to the ryots, at seven per cent interest, to enable them to pay off their creditors, buy their land, and purchase government water. Thereby they would find self-respect, feed themselves and become forever faithful to their British emancipators. Their villages would become stable, efficient units. To this end she became a keen advocate of strengthened village councils and through this allegiance she moved, as did many other 'civilizers', into supporting the nascent Indian National Congress and towards a form – in the far future – of Indian Home Rule within the Empire. In pursuit of this ideal in 1882 she secretly advised the Queen not to accept a petition from the 'European ladies of Calcutta' against the Ilbert Bill, a measure (which failed), designed to enable Indian magistrates and sessions judges in country districts to try European settlers. Again the British and Indian governments moved slowly and reluctantly, and the proposed land bank remained a dream. As G.H.R. Hart, an official in the India Office, remarked, it would demean government to sponsor a *'mont de piété'*, and the ryots would never repay their loans from a land bank.[99]

The village development scheme needed honest intermediaries. Miss Nightingale and Arthur Cotton developed an idea that she had discussed with Frere in the 1860s: there were to be two new ranks of officials. First, a corps of capable, respectable, properly paid natives had to be trained in India to oversee local agricultural practices and village accounting; there were too few Europeans to do the job. To this end, agricultural and 'public works' colleges had to be established in India and several were opened in the later 1870s. Second, a corps of British district officers had to be created to direct the native officials and keep them honest. Jowett – whose two brothers had died young in India –

backed the scheme and carried the statutes that enabled Oxford University to lead in establishing in the early 1880s agricultural education courses for candidates for the Indian Civil and later the Colonial Service. Half of the early, disappointingly few, probationers were Balliol men.[100] It was the small, unheralded beginning of a great force for good during the next seventy years.

These new cadres could have become Miss Nightingale's missionaries, but by the 1880s she was too old and out of touch to use them. By 1881 she was getting tired, Sutherland's hearing had failed and Galton had been promoted out of her reach. Her old Crimea allies were now feeble and in isolated retirement. The Liberal government led by Gladstone, the man she could not catch, first ignored her Army and Indian Sanitary Commissions and then in 1881 began to dismantle them. She drummed up sufficient support to save them but neither the War Office nor the India Office referred matters to them and they ceased to work. The Tory government finally abolished them in 1889.[101]

In India tens of thousands continued to die each year from malnutrition, typhoid fever and cholera, but thousands more lived because Miss Nightingale coached successive Secretaries of State, Viceroys and local medical men in what had to be done and how it could be done. She was never alone in seeing the problems nor in devising solutions but she used her reputation in Britain and India to make expenditure on such projects seem necessary and right. The public debt almost doubled from £90 millions in 1860 to £160 millions in 1880, while the land revenue rose by only a sixth, from £18.7 million to £22 million.[102]

Yet she never grasped the complexities of Indian geography, caste, poverty and social inertia. She dimly recognised them as prodigious obstacles but in her determination 'to do' she readily pretended that they did not exist. Only in 1898, midst a lucid interval during her encroaching senility, did she have a revelation of the problem that was India. Prince Aga Khan visited her. He talked much, she noted afterwards, of 'spirituality'. He asked doubtfully 'do you think that Sanitation can make much difference in life?' 'To him', Miss Nightingale added, 'sanitation is unreal and superstitious ... I never understood before how really impossible it is for an Eastern to care for material causes.'[103] And then, quite out of character, she did not condemn him.

Notes

1. F.N. to McNeill, 15 July 1857, BL Add.Mss 45768, f.60.

2. Sutherland to F.N. 'Friday' [11 Sept. 1857?] BL Add.Mss 45751, f.49.

3. F.N. to Chadwick, 11 Aug. 1858; Chadwick to F.N., 12 July 1858, BL Add. Mss 45770, f.23, 18.

4. (Andrew Wynter), 'Lodging, food, and dress of Soldiers', *Quarterly Review*, Jan. 1859; Chadwick to F.N., 8 Oct. 1858 BL Add.Mss 45770, f.58.

5. F.N. to McNeill, (copy) 9 May 1859, BL Add.Mss 45768, f.98; Chadwick to Stanley, (copy) 23 May [1859?] Chadwick Papers, University College, London, CP1871; W.C.B. Eatwell to Farr, 9 Sept. 1859, Farr Collection, British Library of Political and Economic Science, London, vol. I, ff.36-42; Farr to F.N., 4 Dec. 1860, BL Add.Mss 43398, f.255.

6. Farr to Sutherland, [June 1859?], 30 Oct. 1859, BL Add.Mss 45751, ff.136-7, 140-1; F.N., Five Drafts of Questionnaire n.d. [late 1859?] BL Add. Mss 45824, ff.1-30.

7. 'East India (Sanitary State of the Army). Report . . .' *PP*, 1863, vol. XIX, pt. II, p.4; pt. III, p.20.

8. 'Report', *PP*, 1863, vol. XIX, pt. II, pp.311, 214-5, 519, 295, 654.

9. F.N. to McNeill, (copy) 15 Apr. 1862, BL Add.Mss 45768, f.170; Farr to F.N., n.d. [16 Sept. 1861?], F.N. to Farr, 17 Sept. 1861, BL Add.Mss 43399, ff.44-7; F.N. to Galton, 15 Aug. 1863, BL Add.Mss 45761, f.69;

10. Sir Edward Cook, *The Life of Florence Nightingale*, (2 vols., London, 1913), vol. II, pp.26, 158.

11. 'Report', *PP*, 1863, vol. XIX, pp.159-60.

12. F.N. to Galton 'Burn', 2 Nov. 1863, BL Add.Mss 45761 f.190.

13. Jowett to F.N., n.d. [late 1861?] Jowett Papers, Balliol College, Oxford, vol. I.

14. F.N. to Martineau, 19 May, 8 July, 22 July 1863, BL Add.Mss 45788, ff.186-91.

15. Stanley to F.N., 30 Apr. 1863, BL Add.Mss 45781, f.79.

16. F.N. to Galton, 28 Oct. 1863, BL Add.Mss 45761, ff.187-8.

17. F.N. to McNeill, 17 May 1864, GLRO HI/ST/SU/152.

18. Cook, *Nightingale*, vol. II, pp.45, 50; F.N. to Gladstone, 6 July 1879, BL Add.Mss 44460, f.234.

19. Lawrence — notes on galleys of F.N.'s Report on barracks [Dec. 1863?] BL Add.Mss 45829, ff.103-6; Lawrence 'General Order', 21 June 1864, BL Add. Mss 45798, f.239; F.N. to McNeill, 17 May 1864, GLRO HI/ST/SU/152.

20. F.N. to Galton, 21, 26 Dec. 1863, BL Add.Mss 45761, f.245, 264; Lawrence to Wood (copy), 1 July 1865, Mss EUR F90/30, India Office Library; F.N. to Stanley, [22 Apr. 1863?] BL Add.Mss 45781, f.5; F.N. to Lord Mayo, 23 Mar. 1870, BL Add.Mss 45754, ff.124-6; Sutherland to Chadwick, 5 Feb. 1870, Chadwick Papers, University College, London, CP 1920.

21. Strachey to F.N., 21 Sept. 1864, BL Add.Mss 45798, f.264.

22. Farr to F.N., 22 Apr. 1861, BL Add.Mss 43399, f.20; F.N. 'How People May Live and not Die in India' *Transactions of the National Association for the Promotion of Social Science*, 1863, pp.501-2; Hyde Clark, 'On The English Settlement Of The Hill Regions Of India', *Journal of the Society of Arts*, 21 May 1858.

23. F.N. to Charles Hathaway (copy) 'Private', 27 June 1864, BL Add.Mss 45782, f.156.

24. F.N. to Hathaway, 18 Apr. 1864, n.d. [mid-June 1864?] BL Add.Mss 45782, ff.152, 156; John M. Eyler, *Victorian Social Medicine* (Baltimore, 1979), p.175; Dr McClelland to Sir Charles Trevelyan, 13 Jan. 1864, BL Add.Mss 45798, ff.214-5.

25. F.N. to Martineau, 20 Feb. 1865, BL Add.Mss 45788, f.288.

26. Stanley to F.N., 25 Oct. 1864, 2 Nov. 1864; India Office to Stanley, 4 Nov. 1864, BL Add.Mss 45781, ff.144-7; F.N. to Farr, 5 Aug. 1864, BL Add. Mss 43399, f.204.

27. Cook, *Nightingale*, vol. II, pp.52-3; F.N. to Galton, 'Private', 19 Sept. 1864; Galton to F.N., 21 Sept. 1864, BL Add.Mss 45762, ff.208-14; *The Times*, 23 Aug. 1864.

28. J.J. Frederick to F.N., [Marked 3 Oct. 1865-recte 4?] BL Add.Mss 43397, ff.23-4; F.N. to Galton, 10 Nov. 1864, BL Add.Mss 45762, ff.243-4; A.H. Leith to F.N., 27 Sept. 1864, BL Add.Mss 45798, f.267. Stanley to F.N., 25 Oct. 1864, 26 Dec. 1864, BL Add.Mss 45781, ff.144, 149.

29. F.N. to Galton, 10 Nov. 1864, 5 Dec. 1864, BL Add.Mss 45762, f.243-4, 279; F.N. to Walker, '(strictly in confidence)', 19 Dec. 1864, BL Add.Mss 45781, f.258; Stanley to F.N., 26 Dec. 1864, BL Add.Mss 45781, f.150.

30. Stanley to F.N., 12 Jan. 1865; 20 Feb. 1865, BL Add.Mss 45781, ff.153, 157; F.N. to Galton, 26 Jan. 1865, BL Add.Mss 45763, ff.15-17; F.N. to Lawrence, 'Private', 26 Dec. 1864; Lawrence to F.N., 6 July 1865, BL Add.Mss 45777, ff.58-63.

31. Lawrence to F.N., 7 Apr. 1865, BL Add.Mss 45777, ff.64-5.

32. Farr to F.N., 28 Mar. 1865, 8 May 1865; F.N. to Farr, 10 May 1865, BL Add.Mss 43400, ff.24, 42-4; Stanley to F.N., 21 Oct. 1865, 25 Oct. 1865, BL Add.Mss 45781, f.177-8.

33. F.N. to Galton, 26 Jan. 1865, BL Add.Mss 45763, f.17.

34. F.N. to de Grey, 11 Dec. 1865, BL Add.Mss 43546, ff.88-94; F.N. to Galton, 'Private', 6 Jan. 1866, BL Add.Mss 45763, ff.123-4.

35. Stanley to F.N., 4 July 1866, BL Add.Mss 45781, f.195.

36. F.N. to Cranborne, drafts [July 1866?], Cranborne to F.N., 17 July 1866, F.N. to Cranborne, draft, [Feb. 1867?], BL Add.Mss 45779, ff.1-7, 198; F.N. to Galton, 28 May 1867, BL Add.Mss 45764, ff.70-1; 24 July 1867, BL Add.Mss 45752, f.198.

37. F.N. to Galton, 10 June, 16 June [1867?], BL Add.Mss 45764, ff.75-6.

38. F.N. to Sir Bartle Frere [10 May 1867?], BL Add.Mss 45780, f.2; F.N. to Sutherland, reporting conversation with Frere, [14 June 1867?] BL Add.Mss 45752, ff.179-80.

39. F.N. to Sutherland, 22 July 1867, BL Add.Mss 45752, f.188; Reginald Bosworth Smith, *Life of Lord Lawrence*, 6th edn. revised, (2 vols., London, 1885), vol. II, pp.316-20.

40. F.N. to Stanley, (draft) [10-11 July 1867?] BL Add.Mss 45781, ff.198-9; F.N. to Galton, 24 June 1867, BL Add.Mss 45764, ff.82-6.

41. F.N. to Galton, 24 June 1867, BL Add.Mss 45764, f.84.

42. F.N. to Galton, (draft) [16 July 1867?] BL Add.Mss 45764, f.88; F.N. to Sir Stafford Northcote (draft 3) 25 July 1867, Northcote to F.N. 30 July 1867, BL Add.Mss 45779, ff.93-101.

43. Frere to F.N., 27 July 1867, BL Add.Mss 45780, ff.13-17; John Martineau, *Life and Correspondence of Sir Bartle Frere* (2 vols., London 1895), vol. II, p.39.

44. F.N. Memorandum of interview with Northcote, 20 Aug. 1867, BL Add. Mss 45752, ff.216-19.

45. F.N. to Galton, 20 Aug. 1867, BL Add.Mss 45764, f.107.

46. Mary Carpenter to F.N., 7 June 1867, BL Add.Mss 45752, f.177.

47. Jowett to F.N., 22 Apr. [1867?], Jowett Papers, Balliol College, Oxford, vol. II.

48. F.N. to Carpenter, 21 Aug. 1867, Carpenter Collection, Bristol Archives Office, 12693/24; F.N. Memorandum of conversation, 7 June 1867, BL Add.Mss 45752, f.175.

49. J. Estlin Carpenter, *The Life And Work of Mary Carpenter* (London,

1879), pp.298-310.

50. Her biographers have glossed the sadism, deceit and self-righteousness revealed in her journal of her management of the Red Lodge, her female reformatory. On 15 April 1857 she noted that Crawford, Petty and Burke had all been in 'solitude for a week ... The ... house has been going on very promisingly'. In mid-June of that year she had put 'a strong case of hysteria ... feigning' in the cells. The case was later found unconscious and then to be dying. Miss Carpenter ordered it to be placed in an unused bedroom, out the way of 'common use', otherwise there 'might be a painful association'. The child died on 17 June. 'There was no sigh, no struggle! ... Never before did I desire to remember death rather than life.' Miss Carpenter preached a death sermon to the girls: 'said I had forbidden her the garden to save her health'. The body was laid out by five senior – i.e. about 14-year-old – girls and all the inmates were conducted in to see it. 'I preached that evening on the parable of the virgins ... It seemed to me that I had never loved my children so tenderly or they me'; but so as not to spend 'an unnecessary penny' Miss Carpenter denied their request for black ribbons and instead 'brought out my old crepe'. The coffin was left for three days in the main Oak Room of Red Lodge. Miss Carpenter preached again as the coffin was removed on Saturday 20 June. The girls erupted into a 'violent burst of sorrow' but, privately, Miss Carpenter recorded 'Solemn but not unhappy thoughts, She had not left Red Lodge to sin.' The next day Miss Carpenter went to London to attend to 'a call ... which I felt it right to attend to'. The trustees of Red Lodge were apparently never summoned to discuss the death.

Before Miss Carpenter's departure on the Sunday 21 April, another girl had been found to be dying. Miss Carpenter wrote her 'a long farewell'. The funeral was rushed and private. The girls were forbidden to see the body and were refused permission to attend the funeral. Again, there was no inquiry into the death. Miss Carpenter's absence was, she reflected, 'probably [erased] best for all ... when the last pains [?] of mortality and the last rites were passing. After her return, we (MC and her sister [?], who had buried the child) wept together at what had passed.' Carpenter Collection, Bristol Archives Office, 12693/1, Apr., June 1857.

51. Ruby J. Saywell, *Mary Carpenter Of Bristol* (Bristol, 1964), p.4; Carpenter, *Life And Work*, p.385.

52. Carpenter, *Life And Work*, p.252.

53. G.W. Hastings to Lord Brougham, 18 Sept. 1864, Brougham Papers, University College, London, BP 13032.

54. *Transactions of the National Association for the Promotion of Social Science*, vol. I, 1857, pp.XXVI, XXI; Hastings to Brougham, 5 Nov. 1857, Brougham Papers, University College, London, BP 13109.

55. Leone Levi, 'On the Progress of Learned Societies ...' *Report of British Association ... 1868*, pp.171-2.

56. G. Shaw-Lefevre. 'Presidential Address', *Transactions of National Association for ... Social Science, 1884*; B. Rodgers, 'The Social Science Association, 1857-1886', *Manchester School*, vol. XX, 1952, pp.283-310; Philip Abrams, *The Origins Of British Sociology: 1834-1914* (Chicago, 1968), pp.44-52.

57. F.N. to Chadwick, 11 Oct. 1858, BL Add.Mss 45770, f.60.

58. Farr to F.N., 16 Oct. 1858, BL Add.Mss 43398, f.83; Hastings to F.N., 29 Oct. 1858, BL Add.Mss 45797, ff.27-9.

59. Henry Bonham Carter to Carpenter, draft n.d. [15 Sept. 1867?], Carpenter to F.N., 17 Sept. 1867, BL Add.Mss 45789 ff.122-4; *Transactions, the National Association for ... Social Science, 1867*, pp.239-45, 405-18.

60. Carpenter to F.N. 15 Sept. 1869, 24 Sept. 1869, 27 Sept. 1869, BL Add. Mss 45789, ff.152-5.

61. F.N. 'Note on Irish Disestablishment' [late 1869?] BL Add.Mss 45754,

f.59; F.N. to Charles Hathaway, 18 June 1864, BL Add.Mss 45782, f.154; Richard Temple, *Men And Events of My Time In India* (London, 1882), pp.75-6.

62. Dharmapāla Mahājana, *The Administration of Sir John Lawrence in India, 1864-1869* (Simla, 1952), pp.103-4.

63. Sutherland to Chadwick, 21 Apr. 1883, Chadwick Papers, University College, London, CP 1920.

64. C.E. Gover, 'Memorandum on Juvenile Reformatories in Madras Presidency', 29 Jan. 1868, Chadwick Papers, University College, London, CP 87; Lawrence to Wood, 16 May 1865; Lawrence to Northcote, 21 Mar. 1868, Mss EUR. India Office Library, F90/30, f.63; F90/31/f.113; Mahājana, *Lawrence*, p.104.

65. Judge Gopal Rao Pauvery [?] to Carpenter, 14 Feb. 1876, Carpenter Collection, Bristol Archives Office. 12693/25.

66. F.N. to Hathaway, (copy) 18 June 1864, BL Add.Mss 45782, f.154; F.N. to Galton, 3 Oct 1864, 20 Oct. 1864 BL Add.Mss 45762, ff.224-5, 235; F.N. to Walker, 18 Dec. 1865, GLRO HI/ST/NCI/65/27.

67. Stanley to F.N., 22 Apr. 1865, 15 May 1865, BL Add.Mss 45781, ff.163-4, Northcote to Lawrence, 9 June 1867, Mss EUR, India Office Library, F90/31 f.98; Mahājana, *Lawrence*, p.104.

68. Dr F.J. Mouat to Chadwick, 10 Feb. 1873; Sutherland to Chadwick, 13 Feb. 1873, Chadwick Papers, University College, London CP. 1451, 1920.

69. Dr J. Pattison Walker to F.N., 21 Nov. 1864, BL Add.Mss 45781, f.251.

70. F.N. McNeill, 7 Feb. 1865, GLRO HI/ST/SU/156.

71. Carpenter to F.N. 2 June 1867, 7 June 1867, BL Add.Mss 45789, ff.104, 108.

72. Minutes of Governor-General's Council of India, 10 June 1867, BL Add. Mss 45782, f.246; F.N. to McNeill (copy) 21 Sept. 1867, BL Add.Mss 45768, f.216; F.N. to Lawrence (draft) n.d. [26 Sept. 1867?] BL Add.Mss 45777 ff.148-56.

73. F.N. to R.S. Ellis (draft) Aug. 1867, BL Add.Mss 45785, ff.93-6; F.N. to McNeill, 10 Sept. 1867, GLRO HI/ST/SU/157; Ellis to F.N. 26 Jan. 1868, BL Add.Mss 45782, ff.105-8; D.G. Bowd, *Lucy Osburn* (Windsor, NSW), 1968.

74. F.N. to Galton, 22 May 1882, BL Add.Mss 45765, ff.115-17.

75. Mary Carpenter, *Six Months In India* (2 vols., London, 1868), vol. I, p.150; Miss C.G. Loch to F.N., 28 Jan. 1889, BL Add.Mss 45809, ff.99-100.

76. Dr E.A. Parkes to F.N., 1 Dec 1861, BL Add.Mss 45773, f.42.

77. *Transactions of National Association for . . . Social Science, 1863*, p.505.

78. F.N. to Hathaway, 18 June 1864, BL Add.Mss 45782, f.155.

79. John Strachey and J. McClelland, *Memorandum on Cholera*, 23 Mar. 1863, [Bombay]; Walker to F.N., 9 Aug. 1864, BL Add.Mss 45781, f.227.

80. India Office, *Imperial Gazetteer of India* (Oxford, 1907), vol. I, p.521.

81. F.N. to Frere, (draft) 27-8 Aug. 1867, BL Add.Mss 45752, f.222.

82. F.N. to Walker, 18 Oct. 1865, GLRO HI/ST/NCI/65/19.

83. F.N. to Galton, 13 Jan. 1866, 15 Jan. 1866, BL Add.Mss 45763, ff.141-3.

84. Farr to F.N., 2 Aug. 1868, BL Add.Mss 59786, f.27; Hewlett to F.N., 28 Sept. 1867, BL Add.Mss 45782, f.8.

85. F.N. to Frere (draft) 30 Mar. 1869, BL Add.Mss 45780, ff.150-6; F.N. to de Grey, 11 Feb. 1869, BL Add.Mss 43546, ff.130-1; F.N. Memorandum of interview with Napier, 4 Dec. 1869, BL Add.Mss 45754, ff.41-2.

86. Sutherland to F.N., 8 Nov. 1870, BL Add.Mss 45755, f.90; F.N. Notes of interview with Cunningham, 18 Feb. 1870, BL Add.Mss 45754, ff.79-83; 'Report of Army Sanitary Commission on Dr Brydon's report on Cholera in India, 20 May 1870, BL Add.Mss 43397, f.60.

87. F.N. 'Letter on Cholera', *New York Herald* [1883?] undated cutting in Chadwick Papers, University College, London CP 66; Galton, 'On Sanitary

Progress in India', *Journal of Society of Arts*, 28 Apr. 1876, p.528; Sutherland to F.N., 15 Mar. 1873, BL Add.Mss 45757, ff.75-6; Edwin Chadwick, *The Precautions To Be Taken Against Cholera, (Principles of Central Action)* (London, 1871, reprinted in part, 1883); Golaub Sing, *Hindu View Of Cholera* (London, 1871).

88. F.N. to Galton, 30 Oct. 1865, 7 Dec. 1865, BL Add.Mss 45763, ff.87-9, 106; F.N. to Walker, 18 Dec. 1865, GLRO HI/ST/NCI/65/27; Sutherland to F.N., 6 Dec. 1870, BL Add.Mss 45755, f.134.

89. Rawlinson to F.N., 30 Dec. 1862, BL Add.Mss 45769, ff.90-1.

90. F.N. to [Stanley?] (draft), [late Nov. 1863?] BL Add.Mss 45781, ff.106-9.

91. F.N. to Walker, 'Private' (copy) 18 June 1864, BL Add.Mss 45781, f.225; Hector Tulloch, *Report on . . . the Drainage Of . . . Madras* (Madras, 1865).

92. Napier to F.N., 22 Sept. 1867, 'Burn it!' 8 July 1868, BL Add.Mss 45779, ff.199-202, 219-20.

93. Sutherland to Chadwick, 27 Jan. 1875; Tulloch to Chadwick, 6 Feb. 1869; [5 Nov.? 1869] Chadwick Papers, University College, London, CP, 1920, 1998; Rawlinson to Acland, 24 Feb. 1868, Acland Papers, Bodleian Library, Oxford, d.66.

94. F.N. to W. Clark [an engineer in Calcutta?], 3 Nov. 1871, GLRO HI/ST/SU/71/12.

95. Colonel Playfair to Frere, 30 Nov. 1866, Mss EUR. F 90/45. India Office Library.

96. F.N. to Chadwick [draft – early 1865?] BL Add.Mss 45771, f.65. Francis William Fox, 'On Indian Railways and Indian Finance', *Report of British Association . . . 1875*, p.210; Lieut-General McMurdo, 'Settlement and Military Colonisation in India', *Journal of Society of Arts*, 22 Mar. 1878, pp.344-7.

97. Major Malleson, Memorandum on F.N.'s letter to Lawrence, 2 June 1866, BL Add.Mss 45782, ff.212-6; F.N. to Lawrence [draft Oct. 1868?], BL Add.Mss 45777, f.173; Napier to F.N., 13 Dec. 1868, BL Add.Mss 45779, ff.228-9.

98. Napier to F.N. [28 April. 1874?], BL Add.Mss 45779, ff.244-7; Frere to F.N., 14 Jan. 1875; F.N. to Frere [draft Jan. 1875?], BL Add.Mss 45780, ff.279-87, 292; Salisbury to F.N., 19 Sept. 1877; F.N. to Sutherland, 23 Sept. 1877, BL Add.Mss 45758, ff.64-71.

99. F.N. to Louis Mallet [draft Feb. 1878?], BL Add.Mss 45779, ff.148-55; F.N. to W.R. Robertson (Superintendent-General of Farms in Madras Presidency), 7 Mar. 1879, Mss EUR B.263, f.122, India Office Library; F.N. to Gladstone, 7 July 1879, BL Add.Mss 44460, ff.242-8. G.H.R. Hart, Memorandum on Monts de Piété and a National Bank for India, [Aug.-Sept. 1879?] Mss EUR F86/27, India Office Library.

100. Frere to F.N., 7 Sept. 1867, BL Add.Mss 45780, f.66; F.N., Memorandum of conversation with Galton and Dr Poore. [Nov.-Dec. 1888?], BL Add.Mss 45766, f.207; F.N. to Galton, 16 Dec. 1893, 23 Jan. 1894, BL Add.Mss 45767, ff.106-22; F.N. to Arnold Toynbee, (copy) 20 Oct. 1882, BL Add.Mss 45807, f.14; Jowett to F.N., 26 Feb. 1886, Jowett Papers, vol. VII, Balliol College, Oxford.

101. Sutherland to Chadwick, 10 Dec. 1887, Chadwick Papers, University College, London, CP 1920; F.N. 'Memorandum on Indian Sanitary Executive Boards', 18 July 1889, BL Add.Mss 45836, f.73; Memoranda of conversations with Sir Thomas Crawford, 6 Dec. 1889, 7 Mar. 1890, BL Add.Mss 45772, ff.104-15; F.N. to Galton, 2 Aug. 1888, 28 Aug. 1888, 31 Aug. 1888, 9 Sept. 1888, 16 Jan. 1889, BL Add.Mss 45766, ff.118-214; J.A. Godley, India Office, to Stanhope, 13 Feb. 1889, PRO WO 32/6069.

102. John and Richard Strachey, *The Finances and Public Works of India*

From 1869 to 1881 (London, 1882), pp.6-9; Richard Temple, *The Statistics of the Indian Empire* (London, 1881), pp.4, 15.

103. F.N., Memorandum of conversation with Prince Aga Khan, 5 July 1898, BL Add.Mss 45827, ff.192-3.

5 NURSING

Miss Nightingale's gift to nursing was to identify it in the public mind with sanctified duty. Contrary to nursing folklore, she neither invented modern nursing behaviour nor even the idea of nursing as a calling. But by bestowing her *imprimatur* upon secular vocational nursing she gave it standing in Victorian Britain and throughout the world. And, of course, she secured the benison of female nursing in army hospitals.

The regimen of sexual purity, punctuality, cleanliness and obedience to matron's orders coupled with skills in directing scrubbers and porters, surveillance and control of patients, applying dressings, leeching and administering enemas to both females and males, had been developed by the Anglican nursing orders in the London voluntary hospitals during the later 1850s, although expectations about hospital nurses' conduct had been rising in many hospitals, especially St Thomas's, since at least the 1830s.[1] Miss Nightingale assimilated and published as her own the knowledge supplied her by several very able, unsung women. Mrs Jane Shaw Stewart possessed considerable continental experience. She was a searching judge of hospital design and practice and did the detailed investigations of the Lariboisière which later, unacknowledged, served Miss Nightingale when advocating the pavilion system. Mrs Shaw Stewart was also, Miss Nightingale told Uncle Sam privately, the source of 'most of the ideas' on female military nursing.[2] Mrs Roberts, Miss Nightingale's stalwart in the Crimea, had been working to improve nursing at St Thomas's since 1830. Rev. Mother Clare, Rev. Mother Bridgeman and above all Mrs S.E. Wardroper also educated her in nursing matters. Mrs Wardroper, matron at St Thomas's between 1854 and 1887, was the main progenitor of the matron's role as manager of nurses, with a distinct sphere of authority within the hospital in contrast with the older role of housekeeper subject to the governors and steward; thereby she developed the type of quiet, stiffly humane, ladylike efficiency with due obedience to matron and the doctors that constituted 'Nightingale' nursing.[3] Miss Nightingale's famous *Notes on Nursing*, first published in 1859, is full of pithy good sense and vivid anecdotes about quiet, food, light and reassurance for patients and percipience in nurses. But it is wholly directed to home, not hospital, nursing. Miss Nightingale never produced a comparable guide for hospital work. She later supported district nursing, as an extension of domestic nursing, but she showed no interest in advancing other kinds of specialised nursing, of children, for example, or the insane.

Indeed, the practice of nursing was never among Miss Nightingale's prime concerns. As the history of the Nightingale Fund demonstrates, she preferred patronage, and surveillance of nurses' lives, to guiding their professional work. The Fund was opened as a thanks offering in November 1855. When it closed two years later about £44,000 had been collected, £9,000 of it by compulsory levy on the troops at the Crimea, although as General Codrington assured the Secretary of War, the authorities had made it 'appear <u>voluntary</u>'.[4] The money was transferred to Miss Nightingale without strings, upon the understanding that the Heroine Nurse was to use it to fulfil her professed intention of opening a nursing school. The Romish renegade, Mary Stanley, had proposed such a school in her *Hospitals and Sisterhoods* (1854) and her advocacy of nurses under Christian vows and gushing eulogy of the Catholic and Anglican sisterhoods in the Crimea was, to those who knew, a rebuke to Miss Nightingale. But Mary Stanley had no money and her chances were spiked by the announcement of Miss Nightingale's plan in November 1857.[5] This achieved, Miss Nightingale returned to her main interest of defending her role in the Crimea and hounding Drs Hall, Smith and other enemies.

She had sought confirmation of her envisaged nursing plan from Mrs Shaw Stewart and Dr Sutherland, both of whom took the hint although the former, outspoken as ever, remarked that Miss Nightingale possessed neither the experience nor the staying power to conduct such an institution — a damaging comment on Miss Nightingale's pretensions, given Mrs Shaw Stewart's authority in nursing matters.[6] Miss Nightingale appears to have never afterwards sought Mrs Shaw Stewart's opinions on anything. Instead she launched many ill-substantiated (though not wholly unfounded) anecdotes about Mrs Shaw Stewart's cantankerousness and evaded a specific request to return her letter.[7] Nightingale biographers have repeated these rumours while ignoring the lady's estimate of their heroine. The Fund then lay idle for eighteen months during which time Miss Nightingale pondered various ways of spending it including building a model barracks, bequeathing it to St Thomas's Hospital as a private fund for training nurses, and salting it away for the posthumous publication of her 'Suggestions For Thought'.[8] After this flurry, the Fund lay unused and unconsidered for another eighteen months. Early in 1859, over two years after the Fund had opened, Sidney Herbert, one of the trustees, had become embarrassed by the delay and moved to use the Fund to underwrite a nurse training agreement between the St John's nursing institution and King's College Hospital. But when Miss Nightingale flared at his impertinence, he apologised and dropped the matter.[9] The decision which she finally took in late 1859 was hastened by yet another challenge, this time from the redoubtable Mrs M.A. Baines of the Leeds Nonconformist Liberal clan who was prominent in the Ladies Sanitary Association. They also wanted to create a nurse training scheme but had been hampered by lack of money. Mrs Baines privately sought cash from the Fund and threatened to ask again publicly if she was refused. Miss Nightingale instructed Aunt Mai to answer this 'impudent woman' and drafted a savage reply for either her or Uncle Sam to sign. Mrs Baines hoped she might 'be pardoned'. Miss Nightingale told Aunt Mai: 'Certainly Not', and added that she was to tell the lady that she would publish her ignorant, intruding letter if she persisted. Mrs Baines gave up.[10]

Herbert was right to be concerned because the press was beginning to question the trustees' inactivity. Miss Nightingale had initially demanded the establishment of a board to manage the Fund because she was too 'ill' to do it. Yet she chose the members of the board. It was a distinguished group. They included, in addition to Herbert, Sir James Clark, the Queen's physician, General Sir Joshua Jebb, the prison builder and the ubiquitous Mr Bracebridge. Unbeknownst to the public, clause 13 of the trust deed, drafted by Miss Nightingale, permitted her to define her powers in relation to the trustees, while the remainder of the deed bound the trustees 'to handle money as I direct'.[11] Criticisms of the board finally prompted them in May 1859 to issue an ultimatum to her, through her father-figure, Sir John McNeill, to start something. She riposted by creating an inner executive of three members and appointing Arthur Hugh Clough, her cousin by marriage, now broken in health and unemployed, secretary at £100 a year.[12] A further delay of six months ensued while Miss Nightingale havered about the Fund. The trustees' attempts to hurry her were met with the reply that she was too ill to act. Suddenly, in December 1859 she plumped for a nurse training scheme at St Thomas's Hospital. Sidney Herbert and Elizabeth Blackwell, who had had their plan for King's College Hospital ready for almost a year, were ignored, and thereby rebuked for their officiousness. St Thomas's had been under consideration since at least April 1859, but no full arrangement had been worked out and the trustees of the Fund apparently preferred the King's College Hospital plan. The Board of Governors of St Thomas's Hospital accepted willy-nilly into the hospital the cuckoo of the Nightingale Fund for Nurses. Indeed, it was only McNeill's last minute advice which stopped Miss Nightingale from commandeering the whole hospital.[13] The scheme was to be implemented in the hospital, conducted by their matron and the house surgeon, Mr Whitfield. But the Governors were to be excluded from the selection of Nightingale probationers, (Miss Nightingale's careful choice of noun — she did not want 'novice' with its overtone of religious orders.) The Governors were to have no disciplinary powers over them, the wards in which the Nightingales trained were to be wholly given over to them and the money which sustained them was to remain separate from the Hospital accounts. A less sacrosanct, less combative cuckoo would have been turned away.

Officially, Miss Nightingale had no standing in the arrangements. Privately, she made the rules. She apparently dictated them from her sickbed to McNeill who conveyed them to the Fund committee for their unconditional assent. Like the regime at the Harley Street Institution, Miss Nightingale's ordinances were about power, her power, and they are silent about what the probationers might learn or do. All pupils were to be registered, with a detailed physical description of each, 'as may afford the means of identifying them at a future time'. All were to live in at the Hospital and

> be subject to such . . . regulations as to dress — hours of attendance on the sick — hours of attendance at lectures — hours of relaxation — hours of repose — etc as may be established by Miss Nightingale — The Matron to be responsible for the strict observance of all the rules which shall have been established for her pupils . . . The Matron to keep a . . . Discipline book in which shall be entered daily every instance of misconduct or act in omission calling for punishment or serious reprimand . . . with the consequent proceedings of the Matron thereupon.

Each nurse was to record in a daily 'ward book' her duties and her observations of patients. These were to be sent monthly to Miss Nightingale. The 'ward books' together with the entries in the discipline register were to be reviewed before any certificate was issued by the Fund committee, that is, Miss Nightingale. She managed to inspect each set of reports and each probationer until at least 1881, when she was 61 and failing in health. The monthly discipline returns unnervingly display Miss Nightingale's steely, precise grasp of indirect control. Each printed sheet is divided into two main sections, the first covers, amongst other qualities, 'Trustworthiness', 'Personal Neatness', 'Quietness' and 'Ward Management' with spaces for marks specified between 'Excellent, good, moderate, imperfect and O'; the second section includes 'Sobriety', 'Honesty' and 'Truthfulness'. Here Miss Nightingale ruled 'no degree admissible ... first dereliction ensures dismissal'. As an addendum to this initial formulation Miss Nightingale also required Matron Wardroper 'to furnish confidentially' to her 'a list of nurses to be dismissed to make way for the Nightingale Fund Nurses'.[14] She was not going to allow her probationers to suffer possible moral contamination from matron's old cronies. Equally secretly, patients had to be ousted to make room for the Nightingales. The Fund committee was uneasy and doubtless the St Thomas's governors were perplexed but Miss Nightingale went to bed, seemingly 'badly failing' and demanded immediate acceptance of her terms as requisite for her survival. The parties agreed immediately.[15]

The lady probationers were to be selected by Mrs Wardroper, subject to vetting by Miss Nightingale should she so decide. They were to be aged between 25 and 35 and to have character testimonials from their family physicians. Deserted wives, who had often turned to nursing, and had formed a valuable part of the Crimean contingent, were excluded. Their training was to last one year and be completed within that year. Each successful candidate was to receive a certificate. Probationers were to receive £10 during training; £2 at the end of the first quarter, £2 10s 0d at the ends of the two next quarters and £3 at the conclusion. The Fund was to supply them with lodging, including tea and sugar, washing and their outer uniform. The uniform was brown [like the Crimean uniform] with white cap and apron. Each Nightingale was to have her own sleeping cubicle, although all had to pray together, twice every day, eat together and collectively attend the service of the Established Church at 11 a.m. on Sundays. (Presumably the patients were left unwatched.) But there were to be no religious tests for admission. They were not to scrub floors, set fires or clean grates. This was work for the underclass of women scrubbers. Miss Nightingale was determined that nursing should be honourable. The income from the Fund permitted a recruitment of 15 pupils each year. They could expect hospital appointments at the end of their training at £20 to £25 per year plus board and lodging.[16]

Miss Nightingale's other ambition for the Fund was to train midwifery nurses. She had trouble in settling upon an acceptable training institution but in 1862 she finally arranged with the council of St John's House to train Nightingale midwives under St John's auspices in King's College Hospital. This course was for women who 'intend to pursue the calling as a business' as distinct from 'ladies'. They were to receive full board, and £10 per six months' course, in advance. Each applicant had to produce a 'certificate of health' and 'strict references as to character'. Trainees were subject to instant dismissal for 'misconduct', an all-encompassing term; the dismissal notice was to be forwarded to the offender's referees and the £10 was to be repaid. The twelve vacancies each year were rarely filled. Midwives in practice did not want the qualification and intending midwives neither could nor would delay gaining an income for six months. The scheme languished until 1867 when it finally closed, after an unusually severe outbreak of puerperal fever in the Nightingale training annex. Miss Nightingale, after years of procrastination, had plunged into the arrangement with the hospital. She ignored the hospital sanitation rules she had made famous in 'Notes on ... Hospitals' (1858) by permitting the authorities to designate as the lying-in ward a third floor section immediately above surgical wards which housed endemic erysipelas. A hospital rule forbade students engaged in the surgical wards or in dissection from entering the lying-in ward but the rule was disregarded and puerperal fever soon infested the third floor.[17] The doctors were helpless and thought that the miasma of the disease travelled up the ventilator shafts. By the time the Nightingale project ceased in the autumn of 1867 it had killed about 28 mothers, or about 1 in 28 of the inmates. Evidence is scarce about the number of midwives trained between 1862 and 1867, but in 1864 £60 was spent. Extrapolating from that, the Fund produced about 30.[18]

Miss Nightingale privately acknowledged that she had known about the heavy maternal death rate since early 1866, and very likely she knew of it long before that. Yet she did not stop the project until late November 1867. She announced then that she had intervened 'immediately' upon discovering the mortality rate.[19] Sir Edward Cook accepted this explanation, although he characteristically planted a clue to the real sequence of causes in a stray, allusive footnote (vol. I, p.159). Later writers repeat Cook's explanation, yet they compress the time-gaps in a half-conscious attempt to make it fit their heroine's concern with nursing and death rates.[20] But the King's College Hospital scheme really collapsed because of the spiritual tribulations of Miss Mary Jones.

Miss Jones had been lady superior of St John's House in 1854 when Miss Nightingale had been collecting nurses for the Crimea. They formed an effusive, intimate friendship, with Mary Jones as the adulatory dependent partner. Miss Nightingale sent her 'Dearest Friend' nosegays. Miss Jones assured her 'beloved Friend and Mistress' that she treasured them so much that she could not 'part with one flower even'. Her visits to Miss Nightingale were her 'one indulgence and greatest pleasure'. Miss Jones was one of the very few persons admitted to the presence during Miss Nightingale's days of illness and work in the 1860s.[21] In 1856 Miss Jones led the group of St John's nurses who took over King's College Hospital, and it was her incumbency that persuaded Miss Nightingale to locate her midwives' training scheme there. A High Church devotee, Miss Jones had decided by the summer of 1867 that her six nurses should take open vows, that she should become their acknowledged spiritual head, and that the High Church hospital chaplain, Mr Giraud, should set up an altar in her hospital room and expose the sacrament on it. Protests by Evangelicals prompted Tait, the Bishop of London, to forbid these proceedings. The embarrassed hospital authorities sided with the Bishop and asked Miss Jones to desist. She countered by offering to sever her connection with St John's House, to which the Bishop was both Visitor and Chairman of the Committee, and thereby remove herself and her sisters from his jurisdiction. She argued that fuller participation in the sacraments would make her sisters better nurses.[22]

Miss Nightingale let her heart rule her head and backed Mary Jones. Against her experience at Harley Street and Scutari, and against her known opposition to professed sisterhoods she denounced – to herself – 'ecclesiastics [who] always oppose women who do anything well', which was not the point of the dispute. Against even her private advice to her 'Dearest Friend' not to succumb to the Roman Catholic iniquity of subjecting women to their confessors, she publicly upheld Mary Jones's claims to govern her sisters' relations with their chaplain in her own way. Secretly through her intermediary, Sir Harry Verney, she warned the Bishop that 'if Miss Jones goes – I'll take our midwifery school away & bestow it wherever she goes'.[23] The Bishop and hospital authorities held firm and Miss Jones and her sisters withdrew in November 1867. Miss Jones subsequently opened a private nursing home. Miss Nightingale was surprised and upset that her friend should have persisted, against her advice, with her Romanising follies. She cut Miss Jones for most of the following year and only permitted a resumption of their intimacy after that lady humbly pleaded for it.[24]

The hospital authorities first considered approaching the High Church Clewer sisterhood to replace the St Johnites, but Miss Nightingale vetoed that. The Clewer women were associated with the

formidable Louisa Twining and Miss Nightingale sensed trouble from
her. Bishop Tait proposed what Miss Nightingale dismissed as 'those
idiotic Deaconesses' led by their obstreperous founder, Rev. Thomas
Pelham Dale. Miss Nightingale wanted them even less than the Twining
lot. The prospect of Pelham Dale, who had fomented the Jones trouble,
backed by Tait and the Hospital surgeons, was particularly daunting:
'How I wish there were no men', she lamented. After her two vetoes
the hospital council, without telling Miss Nightingale, turned to the All
Saints' sisters who were ensconced in University College Hospital, and
their lady superior accepted. They came, despite Miss Nightingale's
threat to remove her Fund.[25] Outmatched, Miss Nightingale withdrew,
and began to talk about the puerperal fever death rate. When Mary
Jones died in June 1887, Miss Nightingale memorialised her to herself:

> She is my oldest friend in the Nursing Cause. When dying &
> apparently speechless, she said in all at once in a distinct voice to
> her two oldest Sisters, kneeling by her: 'Little Children, keep
> yourselves from idols.'[26]

Miss Nightingale's failure with midwives' training impelled her to
thwart the plans of others. In 1869 she opposed a move by the Ladies'
Medical College to train 'skilled Lady Midwives'. The college's proposed
tuition was elaborate and thorough. Miss Nightingale, who hitherto
had urged such thoroughness, now denounced the scheme because it
would produce over-trained women who would evolve into lady doctors
and forsake ordinary midwifery. Her Fund could have saved the
project; her authoritative opposition certainly helped to destroy it.[27]
She also rejected as impractical and restrictive a contrasting take-over
bid by the Obstetrical Society to register midwives, limit their
ministrations to 'natural labours' and compel their attendance at 25
deliveries before registration, that is, more than four times the number
required of medical students.[28] This scheme foundered too. Meanwhile
coroners continued to report the sad outcomes of the ministrations
of incompetent, grimy midwives. In 1873 the General Medical Council
was asked to back a revised plan by the Obstetrical Society to register
practising midwives after they had received some minimal instruction
in cleanliness, anatomy, obstetrics and nursing at London and
provincial hospitals. The teachers were to be volunteer medical men
and hospital matrons; the tuition was to be free and given at times
to suit the midwives. Proponents of the scheme on the Medical Council,
such as the well-meaning Professor W.D. Acland, knew from the

difficulties that the Nightingale Fund and Ladies Medical College had experienced that the main problem was to attract midwives to the courses. Miss Nightingale, having condemned the Ladies' Medical College plan for being too elaborate, now condemned this course for being too rudimentary. She specially sought evidence from Berlin and Vienna to prove that five months was the minimum period of instruction required in advanced nations. Throughout 1872-3 Acland, her spy on the General Medical Council, sent her the confidential minutes and drafts of the Council under the illusion that he and she were allies in the cause of improving midwives. Most of the Council were opposed to becoming involved with the midwives' question. They were able to demolish the proposal after Miss Nightingale, having refused to return to Acland some illicitly supplied documents, leaked information that she was privy to the Council's deliberations and disapproved them. She even scolded Acland for carelessness after the Council inadvertently included in a printed report some abusive marginalia which she and Bonham Carter had added to one of the purloined papers.[29] At this point Acland gave up. Had Miss Nightingale lent her authority to a midwives' training scheme, however elementary in its inception, a worthwhile system of instruction and registration would have emerged long before it finally did in 1902. There was widespread support for such a scheme among middle-class women, medical men, parliamentarians, and some midwives. Partly thanks to Miss Nightingale's obduracy, thousands more parturient women were to endure needlessly prolonged pain, mismanagement and death before the midwife situation began to be remedied.

However, Miss Nightingale did attempt to mend the hospital puerperal fever death rate, if for the wrong reason. In 1871 she and Sutherland belatedly published a trenchant survey of maternal mortality rates in lying-in and general hospitals. With their usual verve they covered a wide range of institutions, reproduced plans of wards to demonstrate overcrowding and bad ventilation, and concluded with sets of model plans and rules for hospital procedures. Their statistics were defective, but they got the general proportions right: women were safest when delivered at home and most at risk when confined in lying-in hospitals. Similarly, the Nightingale-Sutherland rules about cleansing wards and changing bed linen are sensible and practicable, despite their dependence upon the maxim, under challenge by 1871, that 'The smallest transference of putrescing miasm from a locality where such miasm exists to the bedside of a lying-in patient is most dangerous.' Yet again Miss Nightingale had founded right practice on wrong principles. Behind the scenes she was still working to stop the introduction of carbolic acid antiseptic procedures into hospitals, on the grounds that they made doctors careless and scrubbers lazy. The disturbing feature of *Notes on Lying-In Institutions* is the casual way in which five years of bad results at King's College Hospital are reported. It is indicative of Miss Nightingale's small concern with nursing and the operation of the Fund that she appears to have remained complacent about the hospital reports or even to have ignored them completely. In 1866 she had asserted that confinement at home was twice as safe as delivery in hospital yet she did nothing to apply the lessons of this to the Fund's ward at King's College Hospital.[30] But it is also fair to say that *Notes on Lying-In Institutions* provoked interest in its subject and accelerated the improvements in cleansing, rebuilding and antiseptic procedures that were beginning in maternity hospitals and wards about 1870. Yet the lethargy Miss Nightingale and Sutherland showed when writing the book, the nonchalance she displayed at its slow publication, and their unwontedly cool tone when handling horrifying statistics indicate that she at least regarded the *Notes* as a cover-up for her blundering connection with King's College Hospital and as a screen for her real reason in breaking with the hospital. None the less, her devious pursuit of self-satisfaction happened to issue, as it commonly did with Miss Nightingale, in public good.

The Fund's production of trained lady nurses was also modest, measured against the acclaim which the scheme received. Dropouts and expellees seem to have constituted a third of each year's intake and in some years, 1864 for example, as few as four survived. The annual reports of the Fund are uninformative and there were at least two major attacks upon its management. During the 1860s, at least, the unfilled places meant that income from the Fund was simply reinvested. Cynical contemporaries like the journalists on the *Pall Mall Gazette* asked publicly where the money went, and received no answer.[31]

But the money which was spent was well spent. The Fund sustained about 100 working nurses over the first decade and certified about 1900 all told between 1860 and 1903. Possibly because their numbers were small and Mrs Wardroper and Miss Nightingale constituted such a formidable duo of teacher and inquisitor, their quality was superb. The Nightingales carried with them throughout the world Mrs Wardroper's concern with cleanliness, exactitude, neatness and personal solicitude for every patient, reinforced by secure self-esteem based on confidence in their skills and status, and backed by the cachet of association with the national nursing heroine and the dedication she evoked. Miss Nightingale ensured, too, that the dedication was maintained: her nurses were directed to posts by the Fund and were subject to secret reports to the Fund from their employers. They were forbidden 'for a certain number of years' (which had become three by the 1880s) to take situations for themselves.

On the other hand, the widows, the religious seekers, the searchers for satisfying employment, the spinsters by choice and the unloved found a home in St Thomas's, a family in living and praying and working together, and parents in Mrs Wardroper and Miss Nightingale. Sister Sybil Airy, who went to nurse British troops in Alexandria during the Sudan campaign of 1884, is an example. With great courage she nursed a smallpox case and enteric fever cases in a makeshift hospital. On Easter Day 1884 she wrote to 'Dearest Miss Nightingale' describing the day's work and religious services:

> We had our little Easter Service this evening at 5.30 with Holy Communion. I am *organist* (but only a very poor one) so I had the privilege of playing the dear *old* Easter Hymn 'Jesus Christ is risen to-day' ... We decorated the Church a little with Palm branches, and exquisitely *sweet Roses* — eight pink, and eight yellow. While thus occupied my thoughts flew to dear old St Thomas's, and I wondered if Mrs Wardroper had decorated the Chapel there as beautifully as she used to in days gone by ...

In 1887 Nurse Airy lost her baggage and personal possessions when the *Tasmania*, which was carrying her and the other nurses home, foundered on the south coast of Corsica. She took charge of the shipwrecked party, men and women, organised them to find shelter on the shore, built a fire, and obtained provisions by using sovereigns she had sewn into her stays. Miss Nightingale replaced the watch she lost in the wreck; once back at St Thomas's Miss Airy led the probationers in special prayers of thanks to Miss Nightingale.[32]

A large proportion of the Nightingales, perhaps even the majority, were not 'ladies'. Too few of these offered themselves, and Miss Nightingale and Miss Wardroper were obliged to take 'women' from the respectable lower-middle and working classes. Observers considered them to be physically stronger than the 'ladies', more obedient and readier to do unpleasant tasks and less flighty and 'tall-talk' especially in religious matters. They were also said to get on better with the working-class under nurses, who did most of the washing and feeding of patients, and with the scrubbers.[33] But anyone who stayed the course must have possessed determination, resilience and self-control. Before the 1860s were out the Nightingales had carried the evangel to Netley, Edinburgh, Liverpool, Salisbury, Lincoln, Leeds, to St Mary's and the Westminster among the London hospitals, and to Sydney.[34] Before she died, Miss Nightingale had the satisfaction of seeing 'her' standards introduced into Scandinavia, Italy, Russia, the United States and throughout the Empire. Rarely can such a beneficial revolution in the lives of so many people — patients and women — have been wrought on the basis of sheer reputation. Mrs Wardroper's young women, and the young women they trained in turn, made possible the modern curing, caring hospital and the modern district nursing service. Doubtless Miss Wardroper, even without Miss Nightingale's patronage, would have produced disciples to spread the ideal of effective nursing but the Nightingale money meant that there were more of them, and the Nightingale name ensured that they rose rapidly to matronships and to acknowledged domains of authority and expertise within the hospitals.

Snobbish, genteel rivals such as Elizabeth Garrett — later Dr Garrett Anderson — saw Miss Nightingale's elevation of 'women' as a capitulation to lower standards and as yet another disappointing closure of a promising field for employment of middle-class ladies. Miss Garrett, insecure *nouveau riche* like many of her sisters, argued that all probationers should pay premiums and that the salaries of superintending nurses should be low enough to discourage interlopers from below the 'governess' level. Her plea was taken up by Dr A.P. Stewart, a spokesman for the doctors, and hospital administrators hopefully echoed it. Miss Nightingale, *nouveau riche* too, but patrician in her values, rejected their arguments as 'disgraceful to . . . common sense'. She wanted good nurses regardless of their origins, and with a patrician grasp of financial realities she declared that *all* nurses should be 'highly paid' because they performed duties which required special skills. Besides, premiums and lower salaries would only diminish the already inadequate supply of recruits.[35] The genteel critics' vision of broods of well-born would-be nurses being elbowed aside by upstarts was destructive fantasy. Still, Miss Nightingale feared that a public debate would harm the nursing cause and while she fumed privately she left it to Farr and others to spread her message at dinner tables. We commonly blame Florence Nightingale for the traditional low pay for nurses, but some of the guilt should fall elsewhere. But it must be added that Miss Nightingale took no positive action to raise nurses' salaries and, indeed, was so ill-informed about them that she regularly overstated them publicly by about 10 per cent. Of course this might also have had the effect of raising the going rate in hospitals controlled by governors unversed in the matter.[36]

The publicity won by the Fund confirmed Miss Nightingale's standing as the national authority on nursing and women's work. Between 1860 and 1890 she was involved, welcome or not, in every major controversy over nursing in Britain and she had to be invoked, even consulted, on almost every major question about women's rights.

Other London and provincial hospitals soon developed training schemes in emulation of St Thomas's. Their nurses were beyond Miss Nightingale's control. From the late 1860s, as their numbers grew, these nurses combined with some restive spirits among the Nightingales to press for the creation of an autonomous nursing college to grant certificates, to bind the emergent 'profession', control entry and salary scales and, most important, inaugurate a superannuation scheme. Acland and the reformers on the General Medical Council realised that general standards had to be set and he undertook to persuade the Council to back a nursing college. All these proposals directly challenged Miss Nightingale's suzerainty and she fought them like a tigress.

She seized on the suggestion that general certification entailed formal examinations. These, she asserted, could never prove fitness to nurse. Doctors would set questions which inculcated 'contagion theory', and thereby blind nurses to the 'real causes' of disease. Moreover, lectures could never develop 'character', which came only from 'practical training'. Examinations could never replace the 'continuous assessment, weekly record, notices of character progress, practical work in ward' and matron's monthly reports which made for Nightingale conditioning. After all, musicians and painters were accepted for their 'work', not their examinable, theoretical knowledge. But behind these persuasive arguments lurked Miss Nightingale's real antipathy to examination schemes: they would 'fatally interfere with discipline'.[37]

During the next twenty years she used these arguments to beat back a succession of registration proposals. Public acceptance of the lady nurses and the associated emergence of the new curative hospital enabled royal ladies to busy themselves as patronesses. Naturally they consulted Miss Nightingale, who used them to repel the would-be certifiers. In 1877 Elizabeth, Princess of Roumania, sought advice about forming a nursing service for her country's soldiers. Miss Nightingale told her to select only persons of character and not mere examination nurses. She warned the Grand Duchess of Baden in 1883 that nursing attracted 'many apples, few good ones', but then she consoled the Duchess with the observation that Germany contained many women who retained the 'moral discipline' and 'Devotion to home duties' which was the 'best preparation for high devotion to Hospital life'. These worthy middle-class souls compensated for Germany's want of ladies, by comparison with Britain where primogeniture and inequality of fortunes within the family induced many ladies to turn to nursing to support themselves, but not, Miss Nightingale added, 'from the highest motives or from any great fitness'.[38]

Despite her rearguard activity her control gradually slipped away. In 1881 the Ratcliffe Infirmary, as Miss Nightingale chose to call it, had the temerity to reject for their superintendent's post the lady dispatched to them by Miss Nightingale and Mrs Wardroper (Miss Airy, later of Alexandria — the shipwreck heroine) and instead to 'select . . . a woman who knew absolutely nothing'.[39] Also in that year Miss Nightingale was not consulted when a District Nursing Association, backed by the Duke of Westminster, was established to train nurses to work with local provident dispensaries.[40] Six years later, her former ally William Rathbone, the nursing reformer from Liverpool and Sir Henry Ponsonby, the Queen's private secretary, combined to stop her getting hold of the Queen's Jubilee Fund in order to under-write her plan for training district nurses. They intended instead to use the money as the basis for a superannuation fund. Her response was that 'nursing is a duty – not a reward'. Rather than be excluded, she then espoused the idea and began to suggest extremely shrewd ways of making it work — under her aegis. Rathbone was inclined to admit her to the organising junta, but Ponsonby would have none of her. After this final rebuff she dismissed it — the first substantial advance in providing effective superannuation — as 'another mischief-making & pauperizing charity'.[41]

The Queen's Jubilee Fund inspired the creation of other nursing bodies to bid for the spoils. A committee of matrons, about which Miss Nightingale had not been consulted, began to meet to discuss nursing matters and to seek money. Miss Nightingale was against it: the gatherings would 'only breed spite'.[42] But they continued. A more ominous challenge came from the proposed British Nursing Association.

This body was created by a committee comprising doctors' wives — a remarkable instance of their new respectability — hospital matrons and insurance promoters, under the patronage of Princess Christian. Their object was to make nursing 'a legally constituted profession', that is, to obtain a charter to enable the BNA to create a register of certificated nurses, set standards and control entry.[43] Miss Nightingale did not fight the BNA openly. But she let it be known that she disapproved and drafted pamphlets against the proposal, to be signed by her acolyte, Henry Bonham Carter. 'I'm staying out of the fray', she told Acland confidentially, 'but I send a pamphlet against the BNA scheme.' With a remarkable assumption that Acland might dismiss from his mind his knowledge of its origins at South Street, she added, 'We agree with this pamphlet.'[44] But Acland was disposed, timidly, to support the BNA. So did many Nightingales. Its professional advantages were too obvious to be denied. Marie C. Redpath wrote in 1889 to her 'old chief' from Kimberley in South Africa, to confess that she had joined the BNA 'with a view (to setting up a private nursing Home and School here) . . . and I think it will be useful (if the Charter is obtained) . . . but I am afraid you don't approve of the movement as I see no St Thomas's names on the Committee nor your own among the Patrons, and gathered so from Mr Bonham Carter's pamphlet', which Miss Nightingale had sent to her in common with all the Nightingales.[45]

Divisions among the sponsors of the BNA and the creation of a rival body, together with Miss Nightingale's known opposition, allowed the government to stall on granting the charter until 1893, two years after Miss Nightingale had lost interest in the affair. Thereafter she steadfastly refused invitations, even from Princess Christian and Louisa, Grand Duchess of Baden, to become a patroness of the Royal British Nurses Association.[46] Ironically, the bitterly won charter turned out to be full of loopholes and sadly disappointed its patient begetters. Even more ironically, most nurses believe, despite the real story being told first by Cook and since in Professor Abel-Smith's authoritative *History of the Nursing Profession* (1960), that they owe their present chartered status to Miss Nightingale.

One particular nursing episode provides a vivid display of Miss Nightingale's annexational, secretarial prowess. In 1864 she learnt of two moves to introduce trained nurses into workhouse infirmaries. In London Dr E.H. Sieveking, who had been concerned with the problem for almost a decade, made yet another attempt to develop a training system for poor and pauper women to equip them to nurse in the infirmaries and among outdoor paupers. In Liverpool, William Rathbone, the philanthropist, anonymously offered £700 to create a training scheme in the town's workhouses. Miss Nightingale, using Sutherland to write the letters, approached both men with advice and offers to supply the lady superintendents. Sieveking abandoned his project rather than have her take it over. Rathbone accepted her offer of a lady superintendent, but only that.[47] Even so, it was a slack period for the Nightingale Fund scheme and Miss Nightingale had no nurses available. By the autumn of 1864 negotiations were suspended. But in December a pauper in the Holborn Union, Timothy Daly, died in sufficiently public and horrifying circumstances to cause a scandal that could not be hushed up.[48] Miss Nightingale struck. She told C.P. Villiers, the president of the Poor Law Board, that 'poor Daly's' death made imperative a full inquiry into workhouse nursing. She promised to help the inquiry with all her strength. They could begin by emulating Liverpool where 'one noble man [was] putting up £1,200 [sic]'. Villiers, a wily old politician, smoothly rebuffed her. He informed her that the only inquiry envisaged was a departmental one into the immediate circumstances of Daly's death. The nursing issue was ignored. However, in deference to the great lady he added an ill-considered postscript: 'I'll see you about a possible enquiry if you want.' She hooked him by return mail:

From the PS to your letter it appears that you desire to have personal communication with me on the subject. I am hardly able to see anyone, but I consider the case of such importance that I would make an effort to see you if you should happen to desire it.

She concluded her letter with the heads of discussion for his visit: nursing as 'an acquired art' and not 'a natural gift' and the 'Liverpool experiment'. Villiers came to South Street in January 1865 and was complaisant.[49] By February when it became clear that Villiers had not acted to his promises and was evading her, Miss Nightingale turned yet again to Harriet Martineau to revive the flagging workhouse reform campaign in the *Daily News* and the quarterlies.

I have also had to see Mr Villiers and, at Mr Villier's desire, Mr Farnall [a poor law board inspector] to confer about introducing Trained Nursing into London Workhouse Infirmaries. They are much more frightened at the death from the Holborn Union than they 'let on'. I was so much obliged to that poor man for dying.

Villiers needed reminding, Miss Nightingale added, that he must attend to powerful representatives of opinion outside Parliament, lest they join his enemies inside the House of Commons.[50] Through H.B. Farnall, sickened by the misery he observed but could not alleviate, she received a secret flow of documents from within the Poor Law Office detailing frightful overcrowding, privation, cruelty and filth in London workhouses. She also obtained secret intelligence from Douglas Galton, whom the Poor Law Board consulted about the design and fabric of workhouses. This information she passed on to Harriet Martineau, to the *Saturday Review* and, through Jowett, to G.C. Brodrick, a Balliol man then on *The Times* staff.[51] They used these reports to add substance to their editorials and news items as a succession of horrifying cases similar to Timothy Daly's came to light.

In the short run this campaign failed. The *Daily News, The Times* and *The Saturday Review* had not mobilised public opinion and Villiers was secure in the knowledge that the great majority of MPs remained uninterested in radical reform of the Poor Law. Miss Nightingale had provided him with the heads of a bill that would have transformed the Poor Law and the management of the sick poor and which, indeed, prefigured developments for the next 60 years. She proposed the establishment of a new central authority, separate from the Poor Law, to levy and spend a general metropolitan rate for the sick poor. All workhouse infirmaries and suburban hospitals were to be transferred to the new authority. These steps were to inaugurate a dismantling of the workhouse system, the abolition of labour tests, and the ending of outdoor relief for the able-bodied poor.[52] Her plan was not original. Its elements and general shape were similar to various schemes for 'state medicine' promulgated by radical medical men since the 1840s. Her distinctive contribution was to put the elements, medical attendance, non-parochial taxation and central control together in a particularly simple-looking, coherent way. None the less it was too much for Villiers. He knew that any proposal to destroy local control of taxation and spending on the poor would create violent opposition. Miss Nightingale was in touch with at least one MP interested in radical reform of the system, Arthur Mills, a paternalist Tory; but Villiers adroitly delayed the committee stages of his bill until after midnight and thus easily outflanked the tiny clutch of disunited critics in a near-empty House of Commons. Miss Nightingale's admirably drafted motion prepared for her brother-in-law, Sir Harry Verney, never came on.

Her motion is a lucid summary of her concerns as an improver and vividly expresses her disregard both of sentiment and political realities:

> That inasmuch as the question of the due care of the sick poor in the metropolis is neither one of local rating nor of local management but of administration it is expedient that for the sake of economy, uniformity and efficiency that there should be one central and responsible administration to undertake the entire medical relief of the sick poor.[53]

Although she ignored immediate political realities, her motion went to the heart of the matter: about three-quarters of the 168,000 inmates of London workhouses were there because they were sick and their condition would remain scandalous until more money was spent upon classifying them, nursing them and building infirmaries for them — which was exactly the point that Villiers and his fellow MPs would not face. Even Farnall was frightened by the implications of Miss Nightingale's proposals. Without telling her, he and his fellow officials delegated to investigate workhouse conditions settled for improved ventilation, and dodged the rating and nursing questions. She was furious when she learned of his treachery from Villiers, who now was in Opposition and ready to make trouble for his Tory successor.[54] (Villiers used Miss Nightingale to see the papers Farnall was removing from the Office.) She was the more angry because Farnall, Villiers and the new president of the Poor Law Board, Gathorne Hardy, misunderstood her intentions. She wanted a reallocation and eventual reduction of expenditure, not an increase. The extra money that was to be spent on the sick poor was to be provided by a reduced expenditure on malingerers and the non-incapacitated sick, who would be discovered and declared ineligible for relief by a centralised, efficient medical authority bent on economy.

'FoolHardy' (Villier's name for his supplanter when writing to Miss Nightingale) was 'pompous ... & foggy' as his subordinate, Farnall, said.[55] His Metropolitan Poor Bill of 1867 tinkered with the rating provisions and created opportunities for local unions to co-operate in building ventures. But 'foolHardy' remained deaf to suggestions from Sir Harry Verney, J.S. Mill, Villiers, Farnall, and the British Medical Association that he extend his bill to create a central building fund and provide for nursing. He transferred Farnall to Yorkshire and midst the MPs' preoccupation with parliamentary reform ignored Verney and Mill.[56] When it became clear that the bill would pass unaltered Miss

Nightingale, desperate but still carefully negotiating through an intermediary, begged Gathorne Hardy to permit the Nightingale Fund to train lady nurses in workhouses. He rejected her offer and deepened the humiliation by entertaining a rival bid from Miss Louisa Twining and her Workhouse Visiting Society to train pauper nurses. But this too came to nothing.[57]

Just when Miss Nightingale seemed relegated to impotent officiousness on the workhouse question a chance event enabled her to reassert her pre-eminence as nursing heroine and thereby compel attention from important people. On 19 February 1868 Miss Agnes Jones died of typhus fever in the Liverpool workhouse. She had been the lady superintendent in charge of nurse training, installed and paid for by William Rathbone. Her death caused Miss Nightingale to change her attitude to Miss Jones from private contempt to opportunist public adoption, tinged throughout with puzzlement at such unrelenting self-abnegation.

Agnes Jones was born in 1832 into an evangelical Anglican military family. Her childhood was spent in Mauritius, where she decided to be a missionary when she grew up. She was given to hiding, and evincing 'silent hysterics'. By her fourteenth birthday her family were back in England. She recorded in her diary: 'When I look back at the past year, I see nothing but sin, depravity and unhappiness.' At sixteen she 'blossomed' when she became 'greatly attached' to one of her teachers, Miss Mason, who with her particular friend, Miss Bellingham, had been Protestant missionaries in Ireland. Under Miss Mason's influence Agnes became a teacher at a Dublin ragged school. Two years later in 1853, she visited Kaiserswerth, that magnet for British Protestant *devotes*, and then returned to Ireland to take up visiting the sick. This lasted until 1859, when she was caught up in the Evangelical revival and became a full-time 'home visitor', tract distributor and Bible reader. After the revival ebbed in 1860 she retreated to Kaiserswerth.[58]

In 1861 Miss Jones sought admission as a Nightingale pupil at St Thomas's. Miss Nightingale opposed her entry, but was outflanked by Miss Jones, who surreptitiously gathered support from other members of the Fund committee. Miss Nightingale told her confidante Mary Jones that Agnes Jones's

peculiar character . . . is want of character. She is always under some one's meridian . . . I told . . . Mr Rathbone . . . that I thought Miss A. Jones, with many excellent & even endearing qualities, would never have the moral authority necessary for his purpose — & would get herself into ludicrous scrapes.[59]

At the end of her training Agnes Jones nursed in at least three London hospitals within three years: her 'low state of general health' and 'partial nervous deafness' apparently prevented her from securing a continuing appointment.[60] In mid-1864 she seems to have been the only applicant for Rathbone's Liverpool workhouse post. The Liverpool board of guardians had hedged Rathbone's initiative with crippling conditions. They made the lady superintendent subject to the workhouse master in all disciplinary matters relating to nursing and gave her no standing in the workhouse on matters deemed separate from nursing. But it was Dr Sutherland who worried about Miss Jones's mental and physical unfitness for the appointment and her acceptance of rules which breached Miss Nightingale's code giving hospital matrons clear authority in the nursing sphere. Miss Nightingale expected only failure from the experiment and held aloof from it.[61]

The Liverpool workhouse infirmary at the time of Miss Jones's arrival in early 1865 was a typical large urban pauper infirmary of its period. It contained between 1,200 and 1,500 inmates crowded into wards built to house many less, sleeping three to a bed. Violence was common, cross infections were endemic and deaths were frequent. The staff comprised 50 pauper nurses, mostly wholly untrained, and 150 scrubbers.[62] The workhouse master resisted Miss Jones from the outset and the guardians gave her no support. Every day she finally got to bed at 1 a.m. and rose again at 5.15 a.m. Her tearful entreaties and prayer sessions made little impact on hard-boiled, resentful nurses and she soon found herself doing much of the routine toil herself. Even after contracting typhus in early February 1868 she continued to work herself to exhaustion and succumbed within a fortnight.[63]

Within hours of learning of the death Miss Nightingale was busy: 'Of course a good many arrangements fall upon me', she answered Mary Jones's letter of condolence. 'It is something like saving from a wreck . . . Please return thanks for her — as you have prayed for her. You can't think how much good your letter of divine sympathy for her did me.'[64] Miss Nightingale wrote a eulogy of Miss Jones and employed a firm of advertising agents to foist it on every major newspaper and weekly in Great Britain. At first only the *Daily News* accepted it — although that paper did not normally carry obituaries — but the agents 'got an influential man on the job' and the obituary subsequently appeared ubiquitously.[65]

Before any request arrived from Liverpool Miss Nightingale had begun to interview likely replacements for Miss Jones. She and Mrs Wardroper finally agreed upon Mrs Kidd. As before, their choice was limited. One of Miss Jones's workhouse visiting friends in Liverpool found Mrs Kidd to be 'energetic . . . but not superior', and predicted that she could not succeed where even the saintly Miss Jones had been 'overwhelmed'.[66] And indeed Mrs Kidd failed. She was dismissed in March 1869 for drunkenness and it soon emerged that she had been a drunkard long before her appointment. Miss Nightingale privately blamed Mrs Wardroper for the disaster. The Liverpool authorities pointedly ignored Miss Nightingale when choosing Mrs Kidd's successor and let it be known that their future nurse training would not be on the St Thomas's pattern. Miss Nightingale indignantly predicted that this would bring catastrophe. With marvellous inconsistency she declared: 'We believe that vice cannot exist without discovery among our trainees.'[67]

Miss Nightingale's obituary of the 'workhouse saint' quickly brought her the reverence she craved. Dr Bowman told her that he knew 'she [Agnes Jones] was one of the very few who enjoyed your full confidence, & whom you looked to for carrying on your system for the future . . . you have heavy blows'. Henrietta Walker, a nurse at the Liverpool workhouse, filled several pages with incoherent grief and religiosity and ended by 'consider[ing] you . . . the highest lady in the land, next to the Queen'.[68] Miss Nightingale published an expanded version of the obituary, entitled 'Una and the Lion', in *Good Words*, the Edinburgh Presbyterian monthly, in June 1868. She sent offprints to numerous friends, including her old Indian ally, Dr J.P. Walker. Her covering letter to him began with a long recital of her illnesses and administrative trials, and continued:

> this very year has seen the death of the best & dearest of my pupils, my 'Una' [Miss Nightingale reduced Agnes Jones into an anonymous, mythical *Faerie Queen* 'being' in the *Good Words* article] . . . Now my 'Una' is gone, I cannot think how I could ever be unhappy when she was doing God's work so gallantly at Liverpool Workhouse . . . I don't know that I ever wrote so much about my own things before — But your kindness encourages me.[69]

The article in *Good Words* is a remarkable piece of autobiographical wish-fulfilment, half-conscious projection of herself, outright mendacity and calculated pleading. The autobiographical wish-fulfilment dwells on sainthood:

> One woman has died ... attractive and rich, and young and witty
> [Agnes had none of these attributes]; yet a veiled and silent woman,
> distinguished by no other genius but the divine genius — working
> hard to train herself in order to train others to walk in the footsteps
> of Him ... She overworked because others underwork ... She lived
> for life, and died the death, of the saints and martyrs.

The projection focuses upon concealment of self:

> I do not give her name! were she alive, she would beg me not ...
> Of all human beings I have ever known, she was the most free from
> desire of the praise of men ... she preferred being unknown to all
> but God; she did not let her right hand know what her left hand
> did ...

And lies:

> In under three years she brought 'discipline' to one of the most
> disorderly hospital populations in the world ... At St. Thomas's
> she was our best pupil ...

Completed with calculated pleading: 'there is no "amateur nursing"
[a blow at Louisa Twining and her pauper nursing schemes]. We need
more women to train as nurses ... we challenge England ...'[70]
'Una' caused a sensation. Ladies of 'a far higher class' flocked to
St Thomas's and within the year Miss Nightingale had sufficient
Nightingales to 'occupy' the St Pancras workhouse and Netley Hospital
and, subsequently, Highgate workhouse.[71] Harriet Beecher Stowe,
a correspondent of Miss Nightingale's since Crimean days, also received
an offprint. According to Miss Nightingale, she publicised 'Una' in the
United States and undertook to launch a poorhouse nursing scheme.
If she did, I could not trace it. Miss Nightingale also claimed that Henry
Ward Beecher, Mrs Stowe's brother, reissued 'Una' as a pamphlet with
a preface by himself, extolling Miss Nightingale. This appears to have
been wishful thinking by Miss Nightingale: there is no record of such a
pamphlet. Meanwhile she revelled in interviewing, choosing and drafting
her newly augmented following. 'I cannot think of her even now
[1870] without tears, which I have no time to shed.'[72]
This euphoria was broken in 1871 when a memoir of Agnes Jones by

her sister was announced, prefaced by Miss Nightingale's 'Una' and incorporating her name on the title-page. She secretly threatened the publisher, Alexander Strachan, with heavy punishment if he used her name or reproduced 'Una', or even issued the book. It does seem true that 'Una' and Miss Nightingale's name were used without her knowledge or permission; although, as Strachan was also the publisher of *Good Words* and presumably held copyright in 'Una', the position is not clear-cut. But she really wanted the withdrawal of the whole book and legally she had no case. Her vanity prevented her from doing what was possible, that is, ensuring that her name and 'Una' were deleted. Her real fear was that, having appropriated Agnes Jones and depersonalised her − 'I do not give her name; were she alive she would beg me not' − and absorbed her into her own reputation, she would lose her to this interloping sister. Strachan ignored her protests. She made Sutherland issue further threats − 'It is so hard to make me write another letter And I have no one to act for me' − but the book emerged unaltered.[73] The *Memorials* did indeed restore Agnes Jones as a saint in her own right. Thereafter Miss Nightingale kept silent about her and Miss Jones slipped from public memory.

The celebrity Miss Nightingale achieved with 'Una' also served to re-establish her links with government. The new president of the Poor Law Board, G.J. Goschen, an innate economiser and more active than Gathorne Hardy, was looking for ways to reduce Poor Law expenditure and he readily responded to an invitation in December 1869 from Miss Nightingale to visit her to be coached on the problem. She summed him up, present and future, in one unsparing, accurate paragraph:

> I don't think he will ever do much. He is a man of considerable mind, great power of getting up statistical information and Pol. Econ. but with no practical insight. It is an awkward mind − like a pudding in lumps. He is like a man who has been Senior Wrangler and never anything afterwards.[74]

She produced a scheme partly new, partly old, calculated to appeal to such a clever-simple politician. The new element envisaged the removal of able-bodied paupers to the provinces and the Colonies under a state subsidised emigration plan. Those who refused to go should be 'offered help to support themselves. Everybody ... women and children ... can produce to some extent'. The children were to be trained in state supported industrial schools. The old part was her familiar project of reclassifying the sick to reduce their numbers. Those with families were to be redefined out of pauperdom and made the responsibility of their families. The residuum were to be centrally redistributed through a metropolitan system of specialist institutions maintained by a metropolitan rate.[75]

Goschen recoiled from the emigration proposal: it was 'semi-communistic'. He argued that whatever the state did for the poor they would not do for themselves and thereby the state sapped 'the power of self-help'. He also betrayed Miss Nightingale's hopes by procrastinating on the metropolitan rate and the new system of pauper infirmaries. Miss Nightingale hated Goschen's 'stupid brutal cry for economy'. He and the Liberal government, she told Jowett, 'know no more of what the people of England are, or of what they ought to be, than the Man in the Moon'.[76] But the general reclassification and reduction of paupers could be quickly effected and win ratepayers' applause. During 1870 and then to 1874 under Goschen's successor, James Stansfeld, the number of paupers in England and Wales was cut by 18.5 per cent, or 194,000. They turned up again as 'unemployed' and in the queues at hospital out-patient halls, but in the short run Goschen and Stansfeld appeared to have conducted a triumphant piece of Liberal reform.[77] Miss Nightingale was not solely responsible for such a grotesque scheme but by encouraging Goschen, in particular, she shares responsibility for its implementation and its cruel results.

In nursing, as in all her enterprises, Miss Nightingale's achievement was mixed. She gave nursing a public standing and independence within the medical hierarchy that it would otherwise have taken much longer to consolidate. Her emphasis upon common sense care, pithily expressed in *Notes on Nursing*, was invaluable and she greatly strengthened the vocational aura of nursing by her posturing, but she added nothing to the details of technical proficiency required in a nurse's daily tasks. In workhouse nursing she had far-sighted ideas but she proved ready to abandon them for the immediate satisfaction of petty intrigues with Poor Law Board officials, and the practical results of her advice were malign. But then, she was less interested in the workhouse question, indeed in general nursing, as her delays with the Nightingale Fund prove, than her contemporaries and later biographers have believed. Miss Nightingale served the cause of nursing less than it served her.

Notes

1. Edward James Edwards, *Nursing Association For The Diocese Of Lichfield* (London, 1867), p.39; (Mary Stanley) *Hospitals and Sisterhoods* (London, 1854), pp.1-2.

2. Jane Shaw Stewart to F.N., 27 July 1858, 10 Nov. 1858, GLRO HI/ST/V2/58; F.N. to Uncle Sam Smith, 11 Nov. 1857, BL Add.Mss 45792, f.74.

3. Brian Abel-Smith, *A History Of The Nursing Profession* (London, 1960), pp.20-1.

4. *Lancet*, 4 July 1857, p.15; Codrington to Panmure, 1 Feb. 1856, PRO WO1/381, f.959.

5. Sir Edward Cook, *The Life of Florence Nightingale* (2 vols., London, 1913), vol. I, p.443.

6. Shaw Stewart to F.N., 13 July 1857, GLRO HI/ST/NC2/V35/57; Sutherland to F.N., 25 Aug. 1856, BL Add.Mss 45751, f.1.

7. F.N. to 'Dearest Friend' (Mary Jones) n.d. [early 1865?], 23 Sept. 1866, GLRO HI/ST/NC1/64/24; 66/15; F.N. to Sutherland [16 July 1861?] BL Add.Mss 45751, f.195.

8. F.N. to Uncle Sam Smith [6 Nov. 1857?], 11 Nov. 1857, BL Add.Mss 45792, ff.68-9, 72.

9. Herbert to F.N., 22 Mar. 1858, BL Add.Mss 43394, f.21; *Lancet* 3 Apr. 1858, p.346.

10. F.N. to Aunt Mai [19 Dec. 1859?], M.A. Baines to F.N., 19 Dec. 1859, BL Add.Mss 45793, ff.194-9.

11. 'Proper Trust Deed' of Nightingale Fund, Houghton Mss 18/120, Trinity College, Cambridge.

12. McNeill to F.N., 25 May 1859, BL Add.Mss 45768, f.100; McNeill to Herbert, 25 May 1859, GLRO HI/ST/SU/117; Herbert to McNeill, 15 Dec. 1859, 19 Dec. 1859, GLRO HI/ST/SU/121, 122.

13. McNeill to F.N., 11 Apr. 1859, BL Add.Mss 45768, f.94.

14. McNeill, 'Notes for service of Nightingale Fund nurses at St Thomas's', [19 Dec. 1859?] GLRO HI/ST/NCI/SU/123; Nurses Monthly Record Sheets – Nightingale Papers, 'Miscellaneous Photographs and Pamphlets' – BL; A.L. Pringle 'Some Recollections of Miss Nightingale ...', GLRO HI/ST/NC12/4, p.76; (Mrs Ellis) 'Something Of What Florence Nightingale ... Is Doing', *St. James's Magazine*, vol. I, 1861, pp.38-9.

15. Herbert to McNeill, (copy) 15 Dec. 1859, BL Add.Mss 45768, f.106.

16. F.N. to Mary Jones, 15 May 1860, GLRO HI/ST/NCI/60/3; Sir Joshua Jebb, 'Statement of the Appropriation of the Nightingale Fund', *Transactions of National Association for ... Social Science, 1862*, pp.642-7; *Lancet*, 23 June 1860, p.626.

17. Jebb, 'Nightingale Fund', pp.644-5; F.N., 'Notes on the Sanitary Conditions of Hospitals ...' *Transactions of the National Association for ... Social Science*, 1858; *Lancet*, 13 Dec. 1862, p.662.

18. *Lancet*, 31 Mar. 1866, p.353, 4 Apr. 1868, pp.437-8, 1 Aug. 1868, p.154; *Pall Mall Gazette*, 23 Mar. 1866, pp.5-6, 11.

19. Nathaniel Powell to F.N. 29 Jan. 1868; F.N. to Powell, [draft 1 Feb. 1868?] BL Add.Mss 45800, ff.213-6; F.N. to Sutherland, [12 Mar. 1867?] BL Add.Mss 45752, f.252; F.N. to [Acland?] [draft, early Feb. 1868?] BL Add.Mss 45800, f.219.

20. cf. Cecil Woodham-Smith, *Florence Nightingale* (London, 1950), pp.473-4.

21. F.N. to [Mary Jones], 23 Sept. 1866, GLRO HI/ST/NCI/66/15; Cook, *Nightingale*, vol. i, pp.448, 502.

22. F.N., Memorandum on King's College Hospital dispute [Sept. 1867?], BL Add.Mss 45752, f.237.

23. F.N. to Mary Jones, 7 Nov. 1866, GLRO HI/ST/NCI/66/17; F.N., Memorandum [13 Oct. 1867], BL Add.Mss 45752, f.240; F.N. to Harry Verney, 15 Feb. 1867, BL Add.Mss 45791, ff.70-1.

24. F.N. to Sutherland, BL Add.Mss 45753, f.1; F.N. to Mary Jones, 19 Oct. 1868, GLRO HI/ST/NCI/68/12.

25. F.N., Memorandum, 12 Oct. 1862; F.N. to Sutherland [12 Nov. 1867?], BL Add.Mss 45752, ff.239, 253-5.

26. F.N. Memorandum, 3 June 1887, BL Add.Mss 52427, f.43.

27. F.N. to Acland, 20 July 1869, Acland Papers, d.70 ff.15-20, Bodleian Library, Oxford; Jean Donnison, *Midwives And Medical Men* (London, 1977), pp.76-7.

28. F.N. to Braxton Hicks, 23 Jan. 1872, GLRO HI/ST/SU 72/1; Donnison, *Midwives*, p.78.

29. F.N. to Dr Gottwald (copy), 26 Apr. 1872; Frau Littra to F.N., 24 May 1872, GLRO HI/ST/NCI/SU72/4, 8; Acland to F.N., 28 Mar. 1873, BL Add.Mss 45786, ff.30-2; F.N. to Acland, 31 Mar. 1873, Acland Papers, d.70, ff.41-57, Bodleian Library, Oxford.

30. F.N. *Introductory Notes on Lying-In Institutions* (London, 1871); F.N. to Sutherland [20 July 1870?] BL Add.Mss 45754, f.244; F.N. to Acland [25 Nov. 1865?] GLRO HI/ST/N4/66/20.

31. *Pall Mall Gazette*, 23 Mar. 1866, pp.5-6; *Lancet*, 25 Aug. 1883, p.343, 14 July 1884, p.81.

32. Sybil Airy to F.N., 13 Apr. 1884; 15 June 1887, BL Add.Mss 45775, ff.149-50, 173; *The Times*, 19 Apr. 1887.

33. A.P. Stewart, 'Hospital Nursing', *Transactions of the National Association for . . . Social Science, 1866*, p.591; F.N., 'Notes for Dr Stewart' [Oct. 1866?] BL Add.Mss 45818, f.31; F.N. to Sutherland, 12 Sept. 1870, BL Add.Mss 45755, f.47.

34. J.S. Bristowe, *How Far Should Our Hospitals Be Training Schools?* (London, [1884?]), p.12.

34. Elizabeth Garrett, 'Hospital Nursing' *Transactions of the National Association for . . . Social Science, 1866*, pp.473-4; F.N. to Farr, 13 Oct. 1866, BL Add.Mss 43400, f.111.

36. 'A Lover of Truth & An Old Nurse' to F.N. [June 1868?]; William Heathcote [Governor? of Hampshire Hospital] to F.N., 11 Apr. 1868, BL Add.Mss 45801, ff.8, 86-7.

37. F.N. to Acland, 'Private & Confidential', 20 July 1869, Acland Papers, d.70, ff.9-14, Bodleian Library, Oxford.

38. E.B. Mawer to F.N., 5 June 1877, BL Add.Mss 45750, ff.192-4; F.N. to Grand Duchess of Baden, (draft), 26 May-9 June 1883, GLRO HI/ST/SU83/2.

39. F.N. to Galton, 6 June 1881, BL Add.Mss 45765, f.13.

40. G.R. Trevelyan to F.N., 25 Feb. 1881, BL Add.Mss 59786, ff.52-3.

41. F.N. to Rathbone, 14 Aug. 1887, 1 Sept. 1887, 13 Oct. 1887, 14 Oct. 1887, 10 Dec. 1887, Henry F. Ponsonby to Rathbone (copy), 6 Oct. 1887, BL Add.Mss 49625, ff.5-21.

42. F.N. to Pringle, 21 Oct. 1887, GLRO HI/ST/NCI/SU/87/47.

43. Ethel Fenwick to F.N., 11 Feb. 1888, BL Add.Mss 45808, f.33.

44. F.N. to Acland, 7 July 1889, Acland Papers, d.70, f.127, Bodleian Library, Oxford; Henry Bonham-Carter 'Secretary of the Nightingale Fund', *Is a General Register for Nurses Desirable?* (London, 1888).

45. Marie C. Redpath to F.N., 12 Mar. 1889, GLRO HI/ST/NCI/V6/89.

46. F.N. to Rathbone, 3 June 1891, 5 June 1891, 27 Jan. 1891, 4 July 1891,

GLRO HI/ST/NCI/SU/91/3-13; F.N. to Acland, '6 a.m. confidential' 22 July 1893, 25 Mar. 1894, GLRO HI/ST/NCI/SU93/6; 94/2. F.N. to HRH Helena, Princess Christian . . ., 17 May 1894; F.N. to Louisa, Grand Duchess of Baden, 14 Apr. 1896, BL Add.Mss 45750, ff.98-100, 187-8.

47. E.H. Sieveking to F.N., 31 Dec. 1864, BL Add.Mss 45799, ff.68-70; Rathbone to F.N., 25 Feb. 1864, GLRO HI/ST/NCI/SU/151; F.N. to Rathbone (draft in Sutherland's hand) 30 July 1865, BL Add.Mss 45752, f.41; Louisa Twining, *Recollections of Workhouse Visiting and Management* (London, 1880), pp.17-19.

48. *The Times*, 4, 16 Feb. 1865.

49. F.N. to C.P. Villiers [draft 30 Dec. 1864?] [draft, early 1865?] Memorandum for discussion with Villiers [Jan. 1865?]; Villiers to F.N. 31 Dec. 1865, BL Add.Mss 45787, ff.54-66; Cook, *Nightingale*, vol. II, pp.130-1.

50. F.N. to Martineau, 12 Feb. 1865, BL Add.Mss 45788, f.280.

51. Sutherland, 'Notes for Conversation with Farnall', April 1865; F.N., 'Notes of Conversation with Farnall' [late April-early May 1865?], BL Add.Mss 45752, ff.11-34; F.N. to Farnall [drafts May 1865? early 1866?] BL Add.Mss 45786, ff.180, 197; F.N. to Galton 'Private & Confidential Burn' 17 Aug. 1866, BL Add.Mss 45763, ff.221-33; Jowett to F.N., 5 Dec. 1865, Jowett Papers, Balliol College, Oxford, vol. I; *Pall Mall Gazette*, 14 Feb. 1867.

52. F.N. to [?] draft [May 1865?], BL Add.Mss 45752, ff.1-2.

53. A. Mills to F.N., 15 June 1865; F.N., draft of motion on Poor Law [early June 1865?], BL Add.Mss 45799, ff.119-21.

54. F.N. to Galton, 20 Oct., 31 Oct., 9 Nov., 14 Nov. 1866, BL Add.Mss 45763, ff.234-56.

55. C.P. Villiers to F.N., 30 Jan. [1867?], BL Add.Mss 45787, f.72; Farnall to F.N., 27 Jan. 1867, BL Add.Mss 45786, ff.212.

56. Verney to F.N., 11 Mar. 1867; Verney to Gathorne Hardy, 12 Mar. 1867; Gathorne Hardy to Verney, 12 Mar. [1867?] BL Add.Mss 45791, ff.77-81; Mill to Chadwick, 5 Mar. 1867, Chadwick Papers, University College London, CP1401; Farnall to F.N., 6 Mar., 11 June 1867, BL Add.Mss 45786, ff.239-43.

57. F.N. to Gathorne Hardy, [draft Mar. 1867?] has read his bill 'with much satisfaction'; F.N. to Villiers [draft, Mar. 1867?] the Bill 'is a disaster', BL Add.Mss 45787, ff.132-41.

58. J. Jones, *Memorials of Agnes Elizabeth Jones, By her Sister* (London, 1871), pp.2-100.

59. F.N. to [Mary Jones?], 24 May 1861, GLRO HI/ST/NCI/61/3.

60. Sutherland to F.N. [early July 1864?] BL Add.Mss 45751, f.241.

61. Sutherland to F.N. [June 1864?] BL Add.Mss 45751, f.242.

62. Margaret E. Tabor, *Pioneer Women* (London, 1927), pp.112-4.

63. Sutherland 'Notes on Liverpool Workhouse', 13-17 Sept. 1865, BL Add.Mss 45752, ff.50-2; E. Gilpin to F.N., 8 Feb. [19 Feb.?] [1868?] BL Add.Mss 45800, ff.220, 243.

64. F.N. to 'Dearest Friend' (Mary Jones), 20 Feb. [1868?], GLRO HI/ST/NCI/68/3.

65. Rathbone Bros. and Co. to Verney; Rathbone Bros. to F.N., 25 Feb. 1868, BL Add.Mss 45791, ff.102; 45800, f.254.

66. Thomas Henry Satchell to F.N., 24 Feb. 1868; F.N. to Satchell [draft 25 Feb. 1868?]; Gilpin to F.N. 2 Mar. [1868?] BL Add.Mss 45800, ff.252-7, 270-3.

67. F.N. to Sutherland [late Mar. or early Apr. 1869?], BL Add.Mss 45753, f.230.

68. Bowman to F.N., 3 Mar. 1868; Henrietta Walker to F.N. 19 Mar. [1868], BL Add.Mss 45800, ff.261-3.

69. F.N. to Walker, 10 Aug. 1868, GLRO HI/ST/NU/68/8.

70. F.N. 'Una And The Lion', *Good Words*, June 1868, pp.360-3, reprinted in Jones, *Memorials of Agnes . . . Jones.*

71. F.N. to 'Dearest Friend' (Mary Jones), 5 Feb. 1870, GLRO HI/ST/NCI/70/3; F.N. to Sutherland [21 Dec. 1869?] BL Add.Mss 45754, f.43.

72. F.N. to Verney, 3 May 1872, BL Add.Mss 45791, f.142; F.N. to Mary Jones, 5 Feb. 1870, GLRO HI/ST/NCI/70/3.

73. F.N. to Sutherland, 24 Mar. 1871, BL Add.Mss 45755, f.183.

74. Thomas J. Spinner, Jr., *George Joachim Goschen* (Cambridge, 1973), pp.31-2.

75. F.N. to G.J. Goschen (draft) Dec. 1869, F.N. Memorandum on Poor Law [early 1871?], BL Add.Mss 45802, ff.94, 271; F.N., Memorandum of interview with Goschen [29 Dec. 1869?] BL Add.Mss 45754, f.52.

76. Spinner, *Goschen*, p.32; F.N. to Jowett [Dec. 1869?], BL Add.Mss 45783, f.147; Jowett to F.N., 26 Dec. 1869, Jowett Papers, Balliol College, Oxford, vol. III.

77. F.B. Smith, *The People's Health* (London, 1979), pp.383-4.

REPUTATION AND POWER

In August 1866 when her Indian and Poor Law pursuits were faltering Miss Nightingale was visited again by God. 'What has thou to do with rest & ease', He asked in good Authorised Version style. Her account does not record an answer. Instead, Miss Nightingale's next sentence reports her apparently addressing herself: 'It may be that they [official hindrances] only came as messengers — that it is really God who has need of you.' Her report of His appearance on 7 May 1867 also ends in tangled syntax. The day was, she recalled mistakenly, the fifteenth anniversary of His summoning her 'to the perfection of my service (to be a Saviour)'. When He came a third time at 6.30 p.m. on 28 July 1867 He reminded her, quite incorrectly, that she had, like Him, spent three unrequited years each at Harley Street and Scutari. Her vision of His head, crowned with thorns and bathed in light, merged with hers: 'I think that I am another Himself . . . another *en état de victime*.' A picture of Christ crowned with thorns hung in her bedroom.[1]

These reported experiences are the more strange because Miss Nightingale did not pray, did not attend divine worship, and only took the sacrament when Jowett brought it. She read the Christian mystics, only to disagree with their passivity, although she esteemed St Teresa of Avila. She did not believe, in any orthodox sense, in the Incarnation, the Atonement, Revelation, or Salvation through faith or works. She twice declared that she believed in an existence after death but that she had no concern with it because her business was with this world. Her future state existed, she affirmed, independently of her wishes and of any covenant with God. She reserved to herself a half-flippant, Whiggish scepticism. She jotted on a scrap of paper probably about 1866-7; 'I should like above all Eternities, to work in Hell . . . "to save the puir burning bodies". But to be shut up with Dean Scott etc etc. & Bishop etc etc . . . for 1000 years . . . the spirit shrinks appalled.'[2]

Her beliefs, in so far as she recorded them, have an Arian, Unitarian core. She wavered between regarding God as person and as idea. Generally she inclined to the latter, having decided in about 1850 that she preferred the 'Egyptian' system of belief which revered the attributes of God to the 'Greek' system deifying the faculties of man.[3] Her *Suggestion for Thought* are a jumbled, repetitive attempt over three volumes of print to develop two linked arguments: that 'God' exists as 'idea' in advanced civilisations like that of nineteenth century Britain, and that the proof of His existence and perfection lies in His creation of those natural laws by which man, using his intelligence to discover and free will to adopt, could work out his own happiness and advance towards perfection. Miss Nightingale, like many other Victorian improvers, was deeply worried by the impasse to good action presented by inexorable laws of human behaviour and the incidence of disease as revealed by statistical data. 'Free will', defined as the capacity to learn from the data and contrive adjustments, was her way, in common with other Victorians, of surmounting that impasse.

> Crime, disease and death, by God's law, always go together. Therefore, insensible but immense progress has been made through Dr. Farr's branding of a certain class of diseases with the word '*zymotic*' (and its association of 'preventible') towards the abolition of [these?] evils ... Man has power to realize all that is right and good, not by prayers to another Being to do *his* work, not by a mysterious 'self determining' power through which he shall 'will' to do it, but by taking God's appointed means.[4]

She knew the appointed means: 'It is a religious act to clean out a gutter and to prevent cholera, and ... it is not a religious act to pray (in the sense of asking).'[5] Moreover, she was divinely appointed to know. Ultimately, her faith was a sacralised egotism. She reminded Jowett that the 'most extraordinary' fact that she – a woman – should be uniquely possessed of 'all the practical knowledge of Army organization', united with the will to devote 'every instant' of life to it, proved that she was uniquely 'part of God's plan'. God had created her like Himself, 'a Trainer', in a world which was 'a training school'.[6] Her task was to declare God's laws of sanitation and virtue, and to aid and measure each person's adherence to those laws and thereby guide the world's slow march towards perfection. Her religious experiences and writings on religion – the *Suggestions* – are justifacatory exercises and corroborative arguments for her election as Trainer: they do not express her primary impulse to work in her chosen way. That impulse we can vaguely trace in her behaviour but its precise nature remains hidden in her psychopathology.

The 'Stuff' (her label for the *Suggestions*) occupied Miss Nightingale for thirty years. It is both a religious testament and a vindication of her rejection of her family. Her attacks on her family, as the quotations in Chapter 1 illustrate, are vivid and unfair. The disquisitions on metaphysics are clumsily argued, ill-informed and almost unreadable.

Jowett, whom along with several other great men she coerced into reading the 'Stuff', evaded direct criticism, but he privately told A.H. Clough that Miss Nightingale's arguments were thoroughly muddled, especially her various depictions of God as 'legislator', which were at once 'too vague' and too limiting because they rendered the 'universal God ... a finite entity'. Jowett subsequently dodged her repeated requests to edit the work. The material on the family is thrust into volume two, completely disrupting the discussion of religion in volumes one and three. As Jowett warned Clough, 'the book [is] ... too full of antagonisms'.[7] At its heart lay acute problems of personality that were alleviated only in work, deceit and paranoia.

Miss Nightingale also sent copies of the manuscript to her father, Sir John McNeill, John Stuart Mill, Monckton Milnes and Uncle Sam Smith, seeking their endorsement of her metaphysics and praise for her philosophical prowess. She hinted to each that he was the sole recipient of her confidence. She also supplied each with a pretext for the work. She told McNeill in May 1860, for instance, that in 1852 she had had

> a large and very curious acquaintance among the Operatives of the North of England, & amongst those ... called Holyoake's party [G.J.H. was a working class secularist] in London. The most thinking and conscientious of our enormous artisan population appeared ... to have no religion at all.
>
> I then wrote the first part of what I have ... [sent] you, without the least idea of every publishing it. And it was read in manuscript by some of them ... No one knows of it. And, till after my death, I would never have it published, certainly not in my name.[8]

She told Milnes that she 'had read' the manuscript 'to one or two', and Jowett that the 'artisans ... have implored me to publish something for them', with the implication that they had neither read nor heard it beforehand.[9] There is no evidence for any of these claims: some circumstantial evidence, indeed, suggests that they are false. Had she known Holyoake he would, as an assiduous tuft-hunter, have boasted of their acquaintance in his memoirs. But his own reference to her implies that he never met her. There are no letters from her among his papers and he would surely have preserved them had she written to him. Nor are there any Holyoake letters among her papers and had there been any it is uncharacteristic of her to have destroyed them. Furthermore, there is no evidence for any contact with artisans in the North of England even had she had time and opportunity.

Indeed, in August 1861 she told McNeill, having forgotten what she had told him fifteen months earlier, that she was considering a new venture teaching the *Suggestions* to the artisans of the East End of London. Altogether, it was an odd explanation to produce because there is nothing in the *Suggestions* about the working classes. It probably originated from Miss Nightingale's acquaintance with the wife of Edward Truelove, the Owenite free thought bookseller. Mrs Truelove made a hat for Miss Nightingale in 1867. Miss Nightingale had presented her with *Notes on Nursing* in 1860 and Stanley's *Life of Arnold* in 1861.[10]

Her correspondents were less gullible than her later biographers. Their responses offer insights into their characters and into the problem that, at one stage or another, afflicted many eminent Victorians – how to deal with a great national heroine who was also importunate and unbalanced. Her father was characteristically kind and flattering and, faced with the diatribe in volume two, embarrassed and defensive: 'Was ever sentence truer than yours? – "God's plan is that we make mistakes."' He then turned to tell her about the family cats. McNeill tactfully if unconsciously ambiguously – after a silence of four months – called the *Suggestions* 'a mine' and warned her off the working classes. They would find her arguments 'too abstruse'. Milnes, that radical friend of the working-men, suavely jibbed: 'Alas I have such a morbid horror of teaching on these subjects with what people call the lower classes'. Jowett, having condemned the *Suggestions* privately, humoured her. She must have informed him that she was already teaching in the East End because he replied that he was 'glad you see the Artizans'; her response that 'Elisha must have a new mantle', (II Kings 2) must have given him pause.[11]

Only good, grave John Stuart Mill – who had never met her – directly annotated Miss Nightingale's text. She asked him in September 1860 to read a 'religious work', adding the bait that it had been written years before for the 'irreligious artisans' but had not then been published because her 'health broke'. Her letter is in a laboured schoolgirl hand quite different from her usual flowing copperplate, on cheap ruled paper instead of her usual luxuriant headed wove. She added a dash of schoolgirlish flattery, too: 'Your "Logic" – especially as regards "Law" "Free Will" and "Necessity" – has been the forming influence of it and of "me".' A few weeks earlier she had used Chadwick to try and inveigle Mill to meet her at breakfast but he had refused and by way of apology had half-heartedly suggested that Miss Nightingale write to him direct. Now he was caught.[12]

Mill scrutinised her manuscript like an indulgent, careful but remote and very clever supervisor of a doctoral candidate. He noted small, and some great, errors of fact, logic and grammar, quibbled about matters of taste, but evaded quarrelling with her central propositions about the existence of God. He generally ignored her discussion of her family; although he appropriated for *The Subjection of Women* (1869), at the price of a delicately allusive compliment, several of her examples and ideas about women's trivialising duties within middle-class families, and women's relation to the arts and intellect. He is known to have begun his essay in 1860 and it seems likely that Miss Nightingale's sprawling, logically undisciplined effort spurred him to it.

Her text of the 'Stuff' and his marginalia comprise a fascinating serio-comic antiphon.

Nightingale: Some of those called the most highly cultivated of the human race, Descartes, Laplace, Hume, have not been able to conceive of a God at all.

Mill: There must, I think, be some mistake . . . about Descartes. He not only believed but thought he had proved the existence of God *a priori*.

Nightingale: Never let us give our belief unless our reason, feeling, conscience, are all satisfied; even though we cannot satisfy reason, feeling, conscience, by any other belief.

Mill: How do we know that the constitution of the world must be such as to satisfy our feelings and conscience?

Nightingale: between God and men there is no . . . agreement. Man did not ask to be born. God never asked man whether he would take charge of himself or not . . . But He is too good a Father to put it into His children's power to refuse it. If He were to do this, timid spirits would resign at once. According to the theory of responsibility, suicide would be justified. For a man may put an end to his service, if dissatisfied with it.

Mill: not if he has taken his wages.

Nightingale: That a man is blind implies some ignorance of physical law, either on his own part or on that of those who preceded him.

Mill: What if he is struck by lightning?[13]

After this encounter Mill never repeated his mistake. In 1867 he refused her plea to join the Indian Sanitary Commission.[14]

Mill's labours on the 'Stuff' and the adverse advice from her other correspondents went for nothing. Without waiting for their comments Miss Nightingale had an unrevised, anonymous version entitled *Suggestions For Thought to The Searchers After Truth among the Artizans Of England* privately printed in three volumes in blue book format by Eyre and Spottiswoode, the HMSO printers, early in 1860. Thomas Carlyle was one of the few to notice the work. He dismissed it as the bleating of a sheep lost in the wilderness.[15] Nearly seventy years later some of her mordant reflections on her relations with her family were reprinted as an appendix to *The Cause A Short History of the Women's Movement in Great Britain*, (1928) by Ray Strachey, a member by marriage of the clan with whom Florence Nightingale's reputation was to be linked over two generations. Miss Nightingale's piece, entitled *Cassandra*, has become the *locus classicus* of radical feminist opposition to the traditional family – a strange fate for an article by a woman who was but a lukewarm supporter of the emancipation of women in her lifetime and who believed in subordinating everybody else.

Miss Nightingale's was one of the first big names that campaigners for women's rights sought to add to their petitions and letterheads. Equally, the maintenance of her reputation as a great woman rested in part upon her association with such causes. But the relationship was always delicate and shifting: the campaigners wanted her name but not her interference. Their apprehensions were unfounded. When Miss Nightingale decided to move into an area of philanthropy already occupied, as in workhouse nursing in the mid 1860s, she preferred to mount a new distinct, rival operation, rather than try to capture the organisations already in the field. She rarely bestowed her name anyway. She had to be convinced that her association with an alien cause would enhance her reputation.

The crucial issue was women's suffrage. Miss Nightingale, like the Twining sisters and Mary Carpenter, could not afford to withhold her support but privately she was sceptical of the cause and disposed to belittle its campaigners. During the latter stages of the passing of the Second Reform Act in 1867 she boasted to Sutherland and to Mill that irrespective of the size of the male electorate she 'had more political power than if I had been a borough, returning two MPs'.[16] Indeed, she had one MP in her pocket: Sir Harry Verney, and therefore she was still much better off than the vast majority of her contemporaries, male and female. About this time John Stuart Mill asked her to support the movement to enfranchise women. Miss Nightingale was ingratiating, but evasive. She thanked him for his special invitation and continued:

> That women should have the suffrage I think no one can be more
> deeply convinced than I. It is so important for a woman to be a
> 'person' as you say . . .
> But it will be years before you obtain the suffrage for women. And
> in the meantime there are evils which press much more hardly on
> women than the want of the suffrage . . . Could not the existing
> disabilities as to property & influence of women be swept away by
> the legislature as it stands at present? [so far as property is concerned
> she proved right − the law was made more equal before women
> achieved the vote] . . . Is it possible that, if women suffrage is
> agitated as a means of removing these evils, the effect may be to
> prolong their existence? . . .
> As to my being on the Society you mention, you know there is
> scarcely anything which, if you were to tell me that it is right
> politically, I would not do. But I have no time. It is 14 years this
> very day that I entered upon work which has never left me 10
> minutes' leisure not even to be ill . . . If you will not think me
> egotistical, I will say why I have kept off the stage of these things.
> In the years that I have passed in Government offices, I have never
> felt the want of a vote . . . And I have thought that I could work
> better for others off the stage than on it. Added to which, I am an
> incurable invalid, entirely a prisoner to my room.[17]

In 1868 Miss Nightingale signed a petition for the suffrage, after 15,000
other women headed by Mary Somerville, the writer on science, had
already signed it.[18] But privately she refused to try to register as a
voter. In 1870 she subscribed to the National Society for Women's
Suffrage and allowed her name to be added to the General Committee
in 1871, but she remained inactive. In 1878 she permitted the
movement to print a brief statement by her supporting women's
suffrage on the Millite grounds that they were householders, ratepayers
and 'persons'. But she added that she did 'not expect much from it'
because women voters were unlikely to be any more enlightened or
progressive than men.[19] She had begun to swing against women's
suffrage, as others of her kind, Octavia Hill and Beatrice Potter among
them, were to do. In June 1889 she refused to sign a women's suffrage
petition. However, she also held aloof from the revolt of the female
Unitarian-Quaker-Positivist-Intellectual cousinhood that erupted into
print during that month. She did not join that high-minded galaxy −

Mrs Matthew Arnold, Mrs W. Bagehot, Mrs Russell Barrington, Mrs E.S. Beesley, Mrs J.H. Bridges, Lucy Cavendish, Mrs W.E. Forster, Mrs T.H. Green, Mrs Frederic Harrison, Mrs Courtenay Ilbert, Mrs Lynn Linton, Miss Christina Rossetti, Mrs Leslie Stephen, Mrs Alma-Tadema, Mrs Humphry Ward — who with 90 others declared their opposition to women's suffrage in the *Nineteenth Century*. Miss Nightingale wrote, probably after reading their protest, that women were 'too ignorant of politics . . . look at Women Unionists and Home Rulers — furious and ignorant'. They knew nothing of 'what is feasible, what has been done, what has failed, what is historically true or historically false' — a just observation on Mrs Lynn Linton, Mrs Humphry Ward and Mrs Russell Barrington, at least.[20] Miss Nightingale found the ultimate proof of women's political incapacity in the campaign to register nurses without her consent, thereby demonstrating that women voters would be moral wreckers. But beyond this disquiet, Miss Nightingale had presciently glimpsed that women would not vote to further their special interest, but would follow their husbands into party divisions that only hindered the advancement of women.

Like most extra-parliamentary reformers, Miss Nightingale was impatient with party politics. She understood and was well informed about the daily parliamentary round but she remained disengaged. She took a poor view of most politicians, especially when they crossed her. In 1871 when Edward Cardwell, an efficient, reforming War Secretary, blocked her access to his Office she attributed his action to simple political malice and belittled him as a time-saver, with 'no type of greatness in his mind'. She wanted what neither Cardwell nor anyone else could accomplish against the colonels and the Horse Guards, a wholesale reorganisation of the army, the cutting down of the Guards regiments, elevation of the engineers and promotion by merit throughout. She dismissed his Army Regulation Bill and the abolition of purchase as 'toys'. Both his Liberal Party and the Tories existed only 'to register popular feeling, to satisfy popular ignorance, to make a scene in effect before the pit', and in this they were abetted by the press. They were forsaking 'solid practical administrative things for glittering politics'.[21] Only the few, she wrote in another private memorandum, probably in the late 1870s, could make the great reforms. Yet the few were increasingly thwarted by the newly augmented majority, who were inevitably 'fools'. The work of the innovative few had become 'as difficult to reconcile with party government, as . . . the "survival of the fittest" with Christianity'. The few were being driven even further into 'expediency'; although expediency was morally justified 'when it is incarnating the eternal idea into the earthly form . . . of practical good'. She saw the minority as invariably right and the majority as invariably wrong, not because the minority was open-minded, creative and pluralistic and the majority was the reverse, but because the minority was ordained by God to lead.[22]

Her notion of the 'eternal idea' expressed in practical good meant that Miss Nightingale had no fear of the growth of the central state. Here she differed from philanthropists of inferior rank who had had to build their empires with less state aid. Mary Carpenter and Louisa Twining, for example, looked to the state to provide 'pecuniary support and coercive power' to their private philanthropic ventures. In this way, they argued, they actually contained the secular state by taking its money and using its police, while retaining for private middle-class Christian persons responsibility for the efficient, humane, immediate management of the lower orders, thereby enabling each individual to fulfil her ultimate Providential role. The central state was augmented in service but not enlarged in power.[23] Miss Nightingale, by contrast, sought to make the state coterminous with her private concerns. Her procedures aped the standard reform tactics of male parliamentarians. They sought select committees and Royal Commissions to investigate particular abuses and to produce evidence to back the legislation they envisaged. She contrived her own select Committees and Royal Commissions and, like her parliamentary counterparts, stage-managed the flow of evidence to fit the report she had commonly drafted beforehand. Like them, too, she looked to a central authority delegated by government to enforce the uniform rules she had devised, with the difference that she herself privately sought to control that statutory central authority, which she also endeavoured to keep independent of ministers, and superior to local units whether in hospitals or in Indian army barracks. Her peak period for such operations, the decade between the later 1850s and later 1860s, coincided with the peak period for more orthodox Royal Commissions. Reformers of prisons, schools, universities and trades unions proceeded in a similar way but none did it with so much finesse, confronted such formidable male bastions, or achieved such a widespread preservation of life.

Miss Nightingale's extraordinary ability to avoid public controversy yet win moral approval shows vividly in her dealings with the anti-Vaccination and anti-Contagious Diseases Acts agitations. Her guile in the latter, especially, is positively Gladstonian.

The campaign to end compulsory vaccination against smallpox

never engaged her. When the campaigners sought her public backing she delayed her replies but finally wrote privately agreeing with their allegations that vaccination occasionally harmed people, although only permitting herself to be quoted as saying that the problem needed further study. In the mid-1870s, however, when the Ladies Sanitary Association began to press for a Royal Commission Miss Nightingale could not resist supplying them with the right questions:

does Vaccination retain its power against Smallpox?
does compulsion under two years work?
does Vaccination introduce disease?
can the present system of employing and paying public Vaccinators be bettered?
would pure cow lymph be better?

Miss Nightingale was not original in thinking these were the crucial issues but as usual she made them curt and clear and they were the questions ultimately addressed by the Royal Commission of 1889. Yet, having defined the questions, she refused to sign any petition for the Commission. Of course, she said, she agreed with the objects of the petition, but the overriding importance of her general sanitary aims was such that she could not risk offending 'those whose co-operation I desire [who] might hold different views'.[24] Fundamentally, she disliked vaccination because it was beyond her control and threatened her sanitary province.[25] She never supported it in India. In the mid-1890s, at the time of one of the recurring rows about compulsory vaccination in England, she told Sir William Wedderburn, the old India hand, that

Vaccination (in India) I don't much care about — the greatest authorities in England believe that the diminution of smallpox has resulted more from Sanitation than from Vaccination (But I don't dare say anything about it).[26]

This is both an incorrect and wrong-headed comment on one of the signal successes of medical intervention in nineteenth century Britain. It is cruelly unfortunate for her reputation and for some of those who died that she did not lend her reputation to spreading vaccination, in India especially.

In common with many other Victorians Miss Nightingale was both fascinated and appalled by the moral questions raised by the Contagious

Diseases Acts. Female prostitution negated the ideal of chaste womanhood to which she and other Victorians subscribed. Her interest in the problems of prostitution and venereal diseases long predated the passing of the first Contagious Diseases Act in 1864. In about 1852, amidst one of the flurries about Anglican Sisterhoods and prostitute rescue work, she told Henry Edward Manning that poverty, not innate depravity, was the cause of prostitution and that rescue work had to include training in gainful skills, caring for silk worms, printing, weaving, farm work which would sustain a girl when she left the retreat and equip her for emigration. 'Anything' was 'better than needlework' which was underpaid and would 'take them back . . . to their old habits'. She was against continuously preaching at them, as the Clewer sisters and chaplains did. Instead she advised a 'variety of work, less food, especially meat, to "lower their tempers", and to compel them to "wash all over with soap" . . . [because] personal purity is so necessary to mental purity'.[27]

Late in 1857 some medical men and army officials began to work for legislation to protect soldiers against venereal diseases by inspecting prostitutes in garrison towns and controlling those found to be infected. A sensationalist, inaccurate book by Dr William Acton on prostitution was the pretext for, and indeed was possibly occasioned by, the campaign. It also seems a reasonable supposition that the move was intended as a diversionary counter-attack upon Miss Nightingale's revelations about the Crimea and army death dates from disease. By the end of 1860 the War Office and Sidney Herbert were ready to join the agitation.

Miss Nightingale was opposed to this Continental system of licensing immorality. It proved yet again that the authorities regarded common soldiers as 'unmanageable animals'.[28] She wanted positive inducements to the soldiers to forego vice: encouragement of marriage within the service, full support of army wives and children, and greater provision of rest-rooms and leisure activities for unmarried soldiers. Her arguments were rational and were proved right by events. She declared firstly that inspection had not diminished venereal disease in France and that there were no grounds for believing that it would diminish disease in the United Kingdom. In Gibraltar, the Ionian Islands and Malta where the system already obtained, there had been no measurable decrease in the incidence of disease among the soldiery. Secondly, she argued that the proposed legislation was unfair because it penalised the prostitute while exonerating her customer, and unnecessary because it would be simpler and more effective to enforce and strengthen local laws against brothel-keeping and living upon immoral earnings. Miss Nightingale was not lenient towards prostitutes but she did believe that the law should be equal in its incidence and that every individual should be protected against arbitrary arrest and degrading treatment by authority. Repressive though she wanted the law to be, she also admitted that prostitution could not be stopped – anymore, she said, than she could stop her cat lapping milk. Rather than spending public money upon punitive lock hospitals she preferred the establishment of more effective curative wards in general hospitals.[29] These persuasive arguments, however, were only embellishments to her fundamental conviction that inspection and control were the outcome of a wrong-headed belief in contagion. Throughout the later 1850s and early 1860s, as I remarked in Chapter 3, she was embattled on the smallpox and tuberculosis fronts and her resistence to every attempt to include venereal diseases among the contagions was part of that battle. 'There is no satisfactory evidence', she asserted, 'that syphilis is propagated only by contact with infected persons . . . It rests exactly on the same evidence as does the presumed origin of small-pox solely from contagion.' In fact it rested on much less. Nobody knew what syphilis was or how it was caused or cured. But the doctors were more right than she was when she scornfully dismissed their description of it as a 'specific poison', especially when she went on to assert that 'all evidence tends to show that venereal disease is generated by vice not . . . propagated by infection'. She justified this assertion by the example of 'demoralized' France where disease increased under the regulation system because 'demoralization' damaged bodily functions in the same way as physical miasma, and thereby induced disease 'between persons who have no disease'. Even her allies were apparently unimpressed with her claim that she knew 'more about it than most men'.[30]

Her boasts notwithstanding, Miss Nightingale's arguments were better than those of the regulationists. They had no evidence to support their claim that compulsory inspection had reduced the incidence of venereal disease in France and there was much circumstantial and anecdotal evidence to suggest that regulation was ineffectual as a sanitary measure. They had no sound evidence for their assertion that venereal disease had increased dramatically in the British army and navy about 1860, although there are plausible grounds for thinking that they might have been right. It is likely that the better care of the troops that followed the post-Crimean rows, thanks in part to Miss Nightingale, meant that fewer men died from other severe infections, while the increase in the number of European soldiers stationed in India might well have led to a sudden rise in venereal disease, or at least a better reported incidence because of the closer medical inspection that better care involved. The regulationists believed that the statistics – which with hindsight look worthless – made intervention imperative; and ironically their most powerful argument was derived from the lesson which they had learned from Miss Nightingale and her coadjutors, Chadwick and Farr. This was the assertion that venereal diseases intolerably lessened efficiency, and raised costs in the army and navy.[31]

In 1861 Herbert bowed to the Horse Guards and War Office in adding, without telling her, a lock ward to the Devonport Military Hospital in readiness for voluntary inspection and the incarceration of prostitutes. She unwisely turned to Lord de Grey, the new War Secretary, and W.E. Gladstone, 'at their own request', for support and even threatened them in 1862 with instigating Sir Harry Verney to raise the matter in the House of Commons. She was desperate because she apparently knew that a secret inter-departmental committee was studying the problem and she found herself unable to influence it. 'You are known to have seriously considered the growing evil in Civil life', she prompted Gladstone. De Grey, although he avoided giving Miss Nightingale a direct answer, favoured compulsion, while Gladstone, who for the next twenty years was to evade declaring himself on the Acts, dismayed Miss Nightingale by shilly-shallying and then admitting that he leaned, in her words, towards 'direct coercion'.[32] Miss Nightingale in common with almost every other Victorian reformer, female ones especially, persisted in the hopeless quest of enlisting Gladstone, and like her rivals she was always disappointed. His circuitous utterances always promised that he was for them, but never said he was with them.

The inter-departmental committee met during 1863 and reported early in 1864. It upset everyone's expectations with a majority report along Nightingale lines, recommending voluntary lock hospitals, improved barracks and recreation facilities for the soldiers and sailors and more strict enforcement of local laws against brothel-keeping and living from immoral earnings, and ended with a declaration that the Continental system was ineffective in France and inappropriate for the United Kingdom. Miss Nightingale, although she never claimed the honour, might well have assisted the majority to arrive at these conclusions by rehearsing her arguments in her anonymous *Notes on the Supposed Protection afforded against venereal disease, by recognizing Prostitution and putting it under Police Regulation*, privately printed in blue-book format early in 1863. She sent copies to important people including Sir George Lewis at the War Office. She put Sutherland's name on this copy and when he was reprimanded for attempting to browbeat his chief she left him to carry the blame. She also once more enlisted Harriet Martineau to reproduce her arguments and statistics in the *Daily News.*[33]

The committee's findings were suppressed and instead a dissenting report advocating regulation by Sir John Liddell, Director-General of the naval medical department, was leaked to the press as the full committee's report. The War Office reinforced this manoeuvre by planting letters supporting regulations in *The Times* and other newspapers.[34] Miss Nightingale was beaten at her own game. The Contagious Diseases Bill which ensued from Liddell's report was poorly considered and badly drafted. When it was referred to a Select Committee Sir Harry Verney succeeded in having its police powers better defined and limited, but the measure passed in Parliament without debate or public scrutiny in July 1864.

Almost immediately the authorities found it necessary to create a commission to implement the Act, although the Act did not provide for one. Miss Nightingale boasted to Miss Martineau that she had been 'asked to name the War Office member upon it . . . and to write the Instructions'. In fact, unasked, through Galton she nominated two men, Graham Balfour and Longmore, and attached a list of 'instructions' proving that regulation did not and could not succeed.[35] Balfour was included in the commission but it seems likely that he was chosen for his statistical expertise, despite Miss Nightingale's support. Longmore was ignored. However, Balfour justified her hopes by entering a dissenting report in October 1864 recommending the Nightingale-secret committee line of more certain implementation of existing laws curbing prostitution and closer inspection of soldiers. The majority report of the commission admitted that the Act was unworkable because it was almost impossible to detect and conclusively diagnose venereal disease in women. It too recommended enforcement of existing laws and more 'cheerful . . . camps and hulks' for the men, equipped with savings banks and libraries.[36] The legislation was amended in 1866 and 1869, but it never proved fully effective. There is no evidence that Miss Nightingale took much interest in these developments. She had abandoned the issue in 1864 when she realised that the first Bill could not be stopped.

The campaign to repeal the Acts also developed independently of her. She followed a policy towards it similar to the one she had taken towards women's suffrage. She permitted herself to be loftily associated with the cause and joined Harriet Martineau, Mary Carpenter and Josephine Butler and over 100 other women in signing a protest against the Acts on New Year's Day 1870. She also readily, if anonymously, fought in print her old enemies, the hard lady doctors such as Elizabeth

Garrett and Elizabeth Blackwell who supported the Acts.[37] But she held aloof from becoming identified with the daily round of theatrical agitation headed by the beautiful, charismatic Josephine Butler.

The organisation of which Mrs Butler was the luminary, the Ladies' National Association, first asked Miss Nightingale to become a Vice-President in August 1870. The LNA was a thoroughly expressive organisation. When the Government had offered a Royal Commission on the Acts as a compromise in May 1870, the LNA had pledged non-co-operation. Miss Nightingale was disposed to rebuff them but, as usual, she used Sutherland as a sounding board:

> What do you advise me to do about 'giving' 'my' name as Vice-President
> My feeling is this: My horror of this legislation is, if possible, yet stronger than ever, − there being ... scarcely a tittle of evidence in favour of its doing what it promises. But ... if anything could have supported the objectionable legislation, it is: the blunder of this Association − especially their public protest against an enquiry ... there is scarcely a person of the least weight among them ...
> I should not like to join them as Vice President. Yet I should not like to refuse to join them without telling them that I am unchanged in opposition to the C.D. Acts ... But above all, I don't want a correspondence with them. I have suffered too much from Mrs Butler.[38]

Sutherland duly gave her the advice she half wanted: to decline the Vice-Presidency − and say 'not from want of interest − but feeble health'. A fortnight later, she still had not done so and wrote again to Sutherland who was now himself seriously ill − 'I am sorry you are ill. But, I suppose, as I have not heard again, that you intend me to believe that you are either well or dead' − to confirm her view that she should refuse. The Butlerites were getting much publicity, she added wistfully. But she declined their invitation.[39]

Behind the scenes she continued to badger Home Secretaries and correspond with Mrs Butler. Occasionally she nearly got caught, as in November 1872, when the Council for the National (Repeal) Association sought her permission to publish a phrase she had unwisely used in a letter to Mrs Butler, 'that ... compulsory examination' was 'monstrous': 'As your influence is so great, we are very anxious to ... use ... this extract ... as showing that you are still as heartily opposed to the Acts as ever.' Miss Nightingale turned to Sutherland: 'Please say

— It was you who approved this sentiment.' Sutherland jibbed for once. He told her to tell the National Association that her opinion remained unchanged 'but that from your peculiar position you find that you must keep clear of controversy.'[40] She did not remark publicly upon the suspension of the Acts in 1883 or their repeal in 1886. But, as with women's suffrage, she gradually changed her opinion. In 1896, after sensational allegations of a rise in venereal disease in India with the ending of compulsory inspection the year before, doctors and army officers agitated for the reimposition of the Acts there. Miss Nightingale signed a ladies' memorial calling for regulation, although she added a reservation seeking an independent inquiry. Mrs Butler was back in the fray with a passionate pamphlet: *Truth before Everything.* Miss Nightingale privately dismissed her old rival: Mrs Butler was one of the 'shouting ladies'. 'She does not want to hear facts; she wants to be enthusiastic.'[41] Miss Nightingale always had the facts on her side.

From about 1871 Miss Nightingale ceased her pursuit of power. Occasionally, as with the battle about registration of nurses, or supplying female nurses for the campaign in the Sudan in 1882-5, or a succession of fights about architects' plans for hospitals and women's colleges, she revived as the tricky, dogmatic, wheedling manipulator of the 1850s and 1860s. But her efforts lacked their former drive and each was short-lived. Her compulsion to work was gone.

The death of her father and the decrepitude of her mother and Parthe seemed to ease her private difficulties. She had once described herself, when she was about 27, and yet to find her way, as 'the Moon' to her family, 'the Earth'. 'The Moon revolves round her, moves with her, never leaves her. Yet the Earth never sees but one side of her; the other side remains for ever unknown.'[42] Now the moon was preparing to reveal her unknown side to herself, at least. Her need to identify with other people, to enter and possess their minds, ebbed away. On 14 September 1877 she told herself in her diary that 'Everything henceforth shall be between God and me — no need to think other people's thoughts at all — No help from people'.[43]

None the less she remained dependent upon the effusive affection and admiration of women. During the 1880s she frequently invited to stay with her and sent presents to matron A.L. Pringle, her 'ever dearest "Little Sister"'. In 1888 Miss Nightingale was desolated when Miss Pringle went over to Rome. The 'Nightingale Fund' removed her from St Thomas's.[44] She also took up nurse Pirrie and felt bitterly deceived when her 'un-friend' revealed that she intended to marry.[45] In 1872 she had spent a whole fortnight trying to persuade matron Torrance not to marry 'that wretched little Dowse'. She was furious when Torrance finally told her to mind her own business.[46] Later, she always made time, even when she was 'very ill' or had to 'put off the other lady', to see 'my Goddess', matron Rachel Williams of St Mary's Hospital. When Miss Williams volunteered as an ordinary nurse for the Suakim Expedition in 1884 Miss Nightingale, unasked, wangled her promotion to superintendent. Miss William's announcement of her engagement during the following year shocked Miss Nightingale: 'O dearest Miss Williams this is bitter & grievous indeed.' Miss Nightingale sought a meeting to talk her out of it, but Miss Williams apparently refused to see her. Miss Nightingale was reduced to pleading: 'I crave to see you once more ... he will see you all his life', adding the bait that Sir Harry Verney had 'gone straight to W.H. Smith' (the War Secretary) with Miss Williams's complaints about the 'chaplain's laxity in Egypt'; but there are no more mentions of Miss Williams.[47]

These rebuffs drove Miss Nightingale further back upon herself. The unsparing appraisals she had formerly made of others she now made of herself: 'You have never been "mother in chief" to St. Thomas's. You take the Cross ... and you use it as a club to give blows with.' 'I have never been Thy servant. I always seek my own glory — not Thine.'[48] By late 1893 all her old male 'wives' as she called them, with the exception of ailing Sir Harry Verney who was to die in February 1894, had predeceased her. Her mother and Parthe were dead. She had lost her 'dearest friends', Mary Jones, dead in 1887, and nurses Pringle, Pirrie, Williams and Torrance. Belatedly, in 1893, she besought the Holy Spirit to 'make me learn sympathy with them by my own troubles and illness — instead of making me think that they should allow for me. I have never prayed for any of them I only talked of them.'[49] Pondering the departed again in 1899, and her own approaching translation, she asked herself, 'What is the language ... spoken at the "Last Judgement"? What is the language or languages spoken in Heaven?.'[50]

Heaven had to wait another eleven years. Meanwhile she made and re-made her will, began numerous small, anonymous acts of philanthropy and, perhaps, continued her rediscovery of her self. Miss Nightingale was wealthy, although she continued to tell people that she was poor. Apart from her minor share of the family estate she made a lot of money from her books, especially *Notes on Nursing*. She was to leave £36,127, £35,000 of it in personalty. She ate well and lived comfortably, although she secretly skimped on the sanitary arrangements of her own house. Her establishment at Number 10 South Street comprised a cook, four housemaids and a commissionaire.[51]

During lucid intervals she continued her practice of eliminating as beneficiaries under her will persons who offended her, and making them aware that she had done so. In 1872 she had struck out her main medical ally at St Thomas's, Mr Whitfield, for 'carrying on' with nurse Butler.[52] In 1897 she docked £2,000 from Francis Galton's portion which had been earmarked for a Nightingale Professorship of Applied Statistics — 'Social Physics' — at Oxford. She had discovered both that the amount was insufficient for a full professorship and that Galton had become untrustworthy because he admitted to a belief in germ theory. Poor matron Pringle's Romish perfidy was similarly penalised. The twenty pounds she was allotted to enable her to buy a 'small gold . . . cruxifix' was withdrawn in 1901.[53]

In her will of 1896 Miss Nightingale ordered that her private papers be 'destroyed without examination'. And in 1901 she revoked the order. Meanwhile, as she had done with Lizzie Herbert, she resolutely fobbed off seekers after letters in her possession and besought holders of her letters to destroy them. Her view seems to have remained unaltered from 1860 when she asked Monsignor Manning, 'Dear Sir or dear friend', to burn her letters to him. 'I have alas! met with such treachery in my poor life that any carelessness on the part of those whom I <u>know</u> to be friendly to me might easily be turned to bad account.'[54]

A generation later she rebuffed Mrs [T.H.?] Green who approached her on behalf of Evelyn Abbott, Jowett's biographer, seeking copies of Jowett's letters to her. Miss Nightingale was in top evasive form. The projected biography was 'so dear to my heart', but she had to select out the private unimportant letters which would only encumber Mr Abbott's researches. She would have liked to have accepted Mr Abbott's kind offer to call but unfortunately she was too ill to receive him. Moreover, the 'real difficulty' was that she had 'not the strength' to select out the private letters.[55] The biography appeared without them. Miss Nightingale's reply was not all evasion. Her manuscripts and papers were littered throughout the first floor of the house, inside piano stools, behind coal scuttles, under sofas, on bedroom wash-tables. Such order as had prevailed had been Sutherland's, and once he departed — nearly 80 and worn out — about 1887-8, her bundles of drafts of letters to various correspondents, packets of envelopes bearing pencilled or orange crayoned memoranda, sheafs of letters from correspondents around the world, boxes of annotated parliamentary papers, slipped into chaos. Time was when she knew where things were but by the 1880s she had lost control. Her careful drafts of letters and copies of memoranda were no longer available for reference and had become superfluous. The vertical filing cabinet would have been her salvation but it was developed in the 1890s, too late for her. Moreover that vivid sense of the sequence and particular thrill of past events which sustain hoarders of memorabilia had faded and the events had blurred and lost significance. Often she reverted to the Crimean days, oblivious of listeners, babbling and shouting incoherently about half-recalled conflicts.[56]

The puzzle remains why she did not effect the destruction of evidence that was so damaging to her reputation, and which she knew to be damaging, as we know from her correspondence with Mrs Green, Lizzie Herbert and Manning. Possibly her manuscripts survived intact because she never found criteria for distinguishing the 'public' – the successes, army sanitary reform, Indian sanitary reform, the development of hospital nursing – from the 'private' – the failures, her monstrously unfair depreciation of her family and her ingratitude for the support they lavished on their 'swan', her bigotry about cholera, her double-dealing with Dr Hall, Rev. Mother Brickbat and Agnes Jones, her duplicity about King's College Hospital and midwives' training. Beyond that we can only speculate that Florence Nightingale, like Mr Richard Nixon and his tapes or Donald Crowhurst and his false sailing records, was so possessed by the habit of deceit, the savouring of special private information against the world, and the conviction that the full, or near-full record would compel posterity to vindicate all her actions, however aspersed during her life, that she could not bring herself to destroy material which had become part of her identity. Having brazened out lies in life she would brazen them out in death.

After all she had successfully beaten back attacks on her reputation by Parthe in pre-Harley Street days, by Fanny Taylor, Mary Stanley and Elizabeth Davis in the 1850s and 1860s, by medical men such as Greenhow and Leith who had criticised her statistics and her dogmatism about contagion and Indian sanitary policy. She had been fortunate that those who possessed evidence which contradicted her claims, Rev. Mother Bridgeman, Sir John Hall, Lizzie Herbert, Cardinal Manning, Sir John Lawrence, the fifteenth Earl of Derby (Lord Stanley), held their peace, respectful of her national standing, fearful of her vindictiveness and mindful that each was implicated in the machinations by which her reputation had been built. Not until

Stanmore's *Memoir of Sidney Herbert* finally appeared in 1906 did anyone dare to describe her publicly as a little lower than the angels. Through E.T. Cook (1913) the family made an astutely ambiguous, effective response. In this study I have tried to construe that species of fallacy that Cook half exposed, but which later writers, excepting Lytton Strachey, have embraced and obscured again — that doers of good deeds must necessarily be good in themselves.

Perhaps Miss Nightingale hoped too that she might in old age by re-reading old letters and re-living old controversies find the key to the mystery of that divided self which had impelled her to fight, to cheat, to bully, to boast and to save lives. The text which hung in her bedroom must always have been at once a comfort, a warning and a conundrum to her, as it is to any reader of her papers: 'It is I; be not afraid.'[57]

Notes

1. F.N., Memoranda, 2 Apr. 1867, 28 July [1867?], BL Add.Mss 45844, ff.4-8.

2. F.N., Note, Nov. 1845, BL Add.Mss 43402, f.34; F.N. to Jowett, Oct. 1868, BL Add.Mss 45783, f.145; F.N., Note [late 1860s?] BL Add.Mss 45844, f.215.

3. F.N. to her parents, 29 Apr. 1850, BL Add.Mss 45790, f.23.

4. F.N. *Suggestions For Thought to The Searchers After Truth among The Artizans Of England* (3 vols., privately printed, 1860) (drafts − 1852-3, 1859-60) vol. I, p.172; Reba N. Soffer, *Ethics And Society In England* (Berkeley, 1978), p.96.

5. F.N. to Jowett [copy, 1 July 1862?], BL Add.Mss 45783, f.7.

6. F.N. to Jowett [draft, 1880s?] BL Add.Mss 45783, f.65.

7. Jowett to Clough, 22 July [1860?], 9 Aug. 1860, BL Add.Mss 45795, ff.19-24.

8. F.N. to McNeill, 17 May 1860, GLRO HI/ST/NCI/SU/130. The copy of this letter in the BL varies in some important details, BL Add.Mss 45768, f.112.

9. F.N. to Milnes [1860?] Houghton Mss 18/131, Trinity College, Cambridge; F.N. to Jowett [draft, early 1860?] BL Add.Mss 45785, ff.104-5.

10. F.N. to Mrs Truelove (copy), 5 Nov. 1860, BL Add.Mss 45979, f.147; F.N. to Mrs Truelove [1861?] BL Add.Mss 45798, f.44; F.N. to Mrs Truelove, 5 Sept. 1867 in Sue Goldie, *A Calendar of the Letters of Florence Nightingale* (London, 1980), number E.859.

11. Sir Edward Cook, *The Life of Florence Nightingale*, (2 vols., London, 1913), vol. I, p.504; McNeill to F.N., 31 Aug. 1860, BL Add.Mss 45768, ff.120-3. Milnes to F.N., Jan. 1860, Houghton Mss 18/121(2), Trinity College, Cambridge; Jowett to F.N. 17 Nov. [1859?] Jowett Papers, vol. I, Balliol College, Oxford; F.N. to Jowett [draft early 1860?] BL Add.Mss 45785, f.104.

12. F.N. to J.S. Mill, 'Private', 5 Sept. 1860, BL Add.Mss 45787, f.1-2; Mill to Chadwick, 7 Feb. 1860, F.N. to Chadwick, 31 July 1860, BL Add.Mss 45770, ff.128, 148-53.

13. 'Suggestions', BL Add.Mss 45840, ff.13, 35, 53, 34.

14. F.N. to Chadwick (copy), 30 May 1866, BL Add.Mss 45771, f.97; Stanley to F.N., 27 July 1865, BL Add.Mss 45781, ff.173-4.

15. W.J. Bishop and Sue Goldie, *A Bio-Bibliography of Florence Nightingale* (London, 1962), p.121.

16. Louisa Twining, *Thoughts On Some Social Questions* (London, 1903); J. Estlin Carpenter, *The Life and Work of Mary Carpenter* (reprinted Montclair, New Jersey, 1974), p.429; F.N. to Sutherland, [after 17 May 1867?] BL Add.Mss 45752, f.63; F.N. to Mill, drafts, 11 Aug. 1867, BL Add.Mss 39927, f.62.

17. F.N. to Mill, 11 Aug. [1867?], Cook, *Nightingale*, vol. II, pp.215-17.

18. Helen Taylor to F.N., 22 Apr. 1868, BL Add.Mss 45801, ff.37-8.

19. F.N. to Sutherland, 2 July 1868, BL Add.Mss 45753, f.46; Mentia Taylor to F.N., 26 Apr. [1870?], BL Add.Mss 45802, f.130; Cook, *Nightingale,* vol. II, pp.217, 451.

20. F.N. to [?] (draft), 30 June 1889, BL Add.Mss 45809, f.160; *Nineteenth Century*, June, July, Aug. 1889, pp.781-7, 104-5, 356-84.

21. C. Edmund Maurice (ed.), *Life Of Octavia Hill* (London, 1913), pp.262-5; F.N., Memorandum [May 1871?] BL Add.Mss 45843, ff.35-9; F.N. to Milnes, 18 May 1880, Houghton Mss 18/142/2, Trinity College, Cambridge.

22. F.N., Memorandum, 5 Nov [early 1870s?], BL Add.Mss 45844, f.234; F.N. to Jowett, (drafts mid-1880s), BL Add.Mss 45783, ff.203-6.

23. Carpenter to Chadwick, 26 Nov. 1860, Chadwick Papers, University College, London, C.P.445; Carpenter, 'The Education of Neglected Children', *Congrès International de Bienfaisance*, 1862, Tome II, pp.89-90. William Carpenter, (ed.), *Voices Of The Spirit and Spirit Pictures*, Bristol, 1877, p.ix; Louisa Twining, *Recollections of Workhouse Visiting and Management ...* (London, 1880), pp.29-39; Louisa Twining, *State Organisation And Voluntary Aid* (London, 1882), p.1.

24. H. de Noailles to F.N. [1876?], F.N., draft reply, n.d. GLRO HI/ST/NCI/V2/76.

25. F.N. to Sutherland, 6 Mar. 1872, BL Add.Mss 45756, f.162.

26. F.N. to Sir William Wedderburn, draft [Dec. 1896?] BL Add.Mss 45814, f.40.

27. F.N. to Manning [1852?] BL Add.Mss 45796, ff.2-7.

28. F.N. to Balfour, 10 Dec. 1860, BL Add.Mss 50134, ff.90-2.

29. (F.N.) 'Private and Confidential' '*Note on the Supposed Protection afforded against venereal disease, by recognizing Prostitution and putting it under Police Regulation*, [1863?]

30. *Note*, p.2; F.N. to Galton, 12 Apr. 1862, BL Add.Mss 45760, f.64; 25 June 1861, BL Add.Mss 45759, f.232.

31. Paul McHugh, *Prostitution and Victorian Social Reform* (London, 1980), pp.35-52; F.B. Smith, 'Ethics and Disease in the Later Nineteenth Century: The Contagious Diseases Acts', *Historical Studies*, vol. 15 (1971), pp.123, 132. Indeed, there is one set of superficially plausible figures which shows that reported venereal diseases were diminishing by about 7 per cent per year during the early 1860s, before the first Contagious Diseases Act in 1864, Benjamin Scott, *A State Iniquity* (London, 1890), p.13.

32. F.N. to Galton, 25 June 1861, BL Add.Mss 45759, f.235; F.N. to Martineau, 25 Aug. 1863, BL Add.Mss 45788, f.208; F.N. to Gladstone, 26 Apr., 4 May 1862, BL Add.Mss 44389, ff.213-14, 239-40; McHugh, *Prostitution*, pp.36, 48.

33. Report of a committee comprising Samuel Whitbread, J. Liddell, T.G. Logan, Tom Taylor, E.H.F. Pocklington, 15 Dec. 1862. PRO WO33/12/188; F.N. to Martineau, 25 Aug. 1863, BL Add.Mss 45788, ff.208-11.

34. *Lancet*, 19 Mar. 1864, pp.327-9; 'Report', p.4.

35. F.N. to Martineau, 31 Aug. 1864, BL Add.Mss 45788, f.275; F.N. to

Galton, 22 Aug. 1864, BL Add.Mss 45762, ff.184-5.

36. 'Report of a committee on the Contagious Diseases Act', October 1864, PRO WO33/17A.

37. McHugh, *Prostitution*, p.56; *Pall Mall Gazette*, 25 Jan., 3, 18 Mar. 1870.

38. F.N. to Sutherland, 22 Aug. 1870, BL Add.Mss 45755, ff.40-1.

39. F.N. to Sutherland, 12 Sept. 1870, BL Add.Mss 45755, f.46.

40. Mrs F. Pennington to F.N., 22 Nov. [1872?]; F.N. to Sutherland, 24 Nov. 1872; Sutherland to F.N., 25 Nov. 1872, BL Add.Mss 45757, ff.41-2.

41. *The Times*, 25 May 1897; George W. and Lucy A. Johnson (eds.), Josephine Butler, *An Autobiographical Memoir* (Bristol, 1913), pp.232-3; Cook, *Nightingale*, vol. II, p.408.

42. Cook, *Nightingale*, vol. I, p.59.

43. F.N., Diary, 14 Sept. 1877, BL Add.Mss 45847, f.84.

44. F.N. to Pringle, 21 Oct. 1887, GLRO HI/ST/NCI/87/47; Jowett to F.N., 31 Dec. 1888, BL Add.Mss 45785, ff.100-1; Lizzie Herbert to F.N., 9, 18 Mar. 1890, BL Add.Mss 43396, ff.230-8.

45. F.N. to Miss Pirrie, 21 Dec. 1885, GLRO HI/ST/NCI/85/13; F.N., 'Note', 31 Oct. 1897, BL Add.Mss 45844, f.190.

46. F.N. to Sutherland, 'Most private', 21 Oct. 1872, F.N. to Bonham Carter, 9 Nov. 1872, GLRO HI/ST/NCI/72/25, 44.

47. F.N. to Rachel Williams, 20 Mar. [1873?]; 11 Jan. 1885; 23 Sept. 1885, GLRO HI/ST/N3/SU180, 129, 149.

48. F.N., Notes, 1-2 Feb. 1890, 9 Jan. 1891, BL Add.Mss 45844, ff.44, 50.

49. F.N. Notes [Oct. 1893?] BL Add.Mss 45844, f.116.

50. F.N., Note, June 1899, BL Add.Mss 45844, f.196.

51. *The Times*, 31 Nov. 1910; *Westminster Gazette*, 2 Nov. 1910; F.N. to Galton, 26 July 1870, BL Add.Mss 45764, f.286; F.N. to Mrs A.E. Hawthorn, 23 Apr. 1890, BL Add.Mss 45776, f.273.

52. F.N. to Bonham Carter, 15 Oct. 1872, GLRO HI/ST/NCI/72/22.

53. F.N., Will, Somerset House; F.N. to [?] draft [Aug. 1897?], BL Add.Mss 45815, f.124.

54. F.N. to Manning, 25 Feb. 1860, BL Add.Mss 45797, f.103.

55. F.N. to Mrs [T.H.?] Green, 17 Oct. 1894, BL Add.Mss 45812, ff.200-1.

56. Helena Gleichen to Miss Lloyd Still (copy), 31 July 1930, GLRO HI/ST/NC5/4.

57. *The Times*, 13 Aug. 1937.

SELECT BIBLIOGRAPHY

Florence Nightingale was an indefatigable correspondent, recorder and hoarder. Two enormous collections of her letters and papers are held at the British Library and the Greater London Record Office. There is also a valuable collection, which includes copies of documents held elsewhere, at the Wellcome Institute for the History of Medicine, London. Her peculiar method of working upstairs, with her secretariat of Sutherland, Galton and other downstairs and at the War Office, resulted in the setting down of a vast amount of day-to-day business, then normally conducted by conversation and now handled by telephone. Moreover, her early universal fame and the ensuing correspondence with notables led to wholesale preservation of her letters; there can hardly be a large manuscript repository in the world which does not boast at least a handful of her beautiful copperplate autographs.

Her letters crop up among the papers of many other eminent Victorians, but most pertinently and/or plentifully in the following collections:

Acland Papers,	Bodleian Library, Oxford.
Carpenter Collection,	Bristol Archives Office.
Chadwick Papers,	University College, London.
Farr Papers,	British Library of Political and Economic Science, London.
Frere Papers,	India Office Library.
Gladstone Papers,	British Library.
Herbert Papers,	British Library.
Houghton Manuscripts	Trinity College, Cambridge.
Jowett Papers,	Balliol College, Oxford.
Lawrence Letters,	India Office Library.
Shaftesbury Diaries,	Broadlands Mss, National Register of Archives.

The two indispensable guides to Florence Nightingale's vast output are:

Goldie, Sue, *A Calendar Of The Letters Of Florence Nightingale* (London, 1980).

Bishop, W.J. and Sue Goldie, *A Bio-Bibliography of Florence Nightingale* (London, 1962).

Other printed sources and authorities include:
'Report upon the State of the Hospitals of the British Army in the Crimea and Scutari', *HC, 1854-55,* vol. XXXIII.
'Report of the Board of General Officers appointed to inquire into . . . the reports of Sir John McNeill and Colonel Tulloch . . .', *PP*, 1856, vol. XXI.

Allen, Donald R., 'Florence Nightingale: Toward a Psychohistorical Interpretation', *Journal of Interdisciplinary History* vol. VI, Number I, Summer 1975
Andrews, Mary Raymond Shipman, *A Lost Commander: Florence Nightingale* (Garden City, NY 1929).
Anon., *Addresses presented to Sir John McNeill . . . and Col. Tulloch* (Edinburgh, 1857)
Anon., *Proceedings of an ordinary meeting of the municipal corporation of Calcutta* (Calcutta, 1864)
Baylen, J.O., 'The Florence Nightingale/Mary Stanley Controversy: Some Unpublished Letters', *Medical History*, vol. 18, (1974)
Beddoe, John, *Memories of Eighty Years* (Bristol, 1910)
Bell, E. Moberly, *Octavia Hill* (London, 1942)
Bellis, H., *Florence Nightingale* (London, 1953)
Blackwood, Alicia, *Narrative of personal experiences . . . During a Residence on the Bosphorus throughout the Crimean War* (London, 1881)
Bolster, Evelyn, *The Sisters Of Mercy In The Crimean War* (Cork, 1964)
Bowd, D.G., *Lucy Osburn c.1836-1891; . . .* (Windsor, NSW, 1968)
Bryce, Charles, *England And France before Sepastopol, looked at From A Medical Point Of View* (London, 1857)
Carpenter, J. Estlin, *The Life And Work of Mary Carpenter*, 2nd edn. (1881), reprinted Montclair, New Jersey 1974.
Carpenter, Mary, *Six Months In India* (2 vols., London, 1868)
Carter, Henry Bonham, *Suggestions for Improving The Management of the Nursing Department in Large Hospitals* (London, 1867)
——, *Is A General Register for Nurses Desirable?* (London, 1888)
Carter, Victor Bonham, *In A Liberal Tradition* (London, 1960)
Chadwick, Edwin, *The Precautions To Be Taken Against Cholera, (Principles of Central Action)* (London, 1871)
——, *"Circulation or Stagnation"* (London, 1889)

Concannon, Helena, *The Irish Sisters of Mercy in the Crimean War* (Dublin, 1950)

Cook, Sir Edward, *The Life of Florence Nightingale* (2 vols., London, 1913)

Cope, Zachary, *Florence Nightingale and the Doctors* (London, 1958)

Davies, Celia (ed.), *Rewriting Nursing History* (London, 1980)

Davis, Elizabeth, *The Autobiography of . . ., a Crimean Nurse*, Jane Williams (ed.) (2 vols., London, 1857)

Davis, John, *Florence Nightingale, or the heroine of the east* (London, 1856)

Donnison, Jean, *Midwives And Medical Men* (London, 1977)

[Doyle] Sister Mary Aloysius, *Memories of the Crimea* (London, 1904)

Edwards, Edward James, *Nursing Association For The Diocese Of Lichfield, etc.* (London, 1865)

Eyler, John M., *Victorian Social Medicine* (Baltimore, 1979)

Faber, Geoffrey, *Jowett* (London, 1957)

Ffrench, Yvonne, *Florence Nightingale, 1820-1910* (London, 1954)

Finer, S.E., *The Life And Times Of Sir Edwin Chadwick* (London, 1952)

Fink, Leo Gregory, *Catholic Influences In The Life of Florence Nightingale* (St. Louis, Mo., 1934)

Fleming, Donald, review of C. Woodham-Smith's *Florence Nightingale*, *American Historical Review*, vol. 57 (1951-2)

Galton, Douglas, *Healthy Hospitals* (Oxford, 1893)

Garrett, Elizabeth, 'Hospital Nursing', *Transactions of the National Association for the Promotion of Social Science* (London, 1866)

Gaskell, Elizabeth, *The Letters . . .*, J.A.V. Chapple and Arthur Pollard (eds.) (Manchester, 1966)

Goldsmith, Margaret Leland, *Florence Nightingale. The woman and the legend* (London, 1937)

Goodman, Margaret, *Experiences of an English Sister Of Mercy* (London, 1862)

Goodman, Margaret, *Sisterhoods in the Church of England*, 3rd edn. (London, 1864)

Greenleaf, W.H., 'Biography and the "Amateur" Historian: Mrs. Woodham-Smith's "Florence Nightingale"', *Victorian Studies*, vol. II (Dec. 1959)

Gurney, Joseph John, *The 'Record' And Miss Nightingale* (London, 1855)

(Hall, Mrs S.C.), 'Something Of What Florence Nightingale Has Done And Is Doing, *St. James's Magazine*, vol. I (April-July 1861), pp.29-40

Hay, Ian (John Hay Beith), *One Hundred Years Of Army Nursing* (London, 1953)

Hennessy, James Pope-, *Monckton Milnes* (2 vols., London, 1949, 1951)

Holloway, S.W.F., 'The All Saints' Sisterhood at University College Hospital 1862-99', *Medical History*, vol. III, (1959)

Howe, Julia Ward, *Reminiscences 1819-1899* (Cambridge, Mass., 1900)

Hubble, Douglas, 'William Ogle of Derby and Florence Nightingale', *Medical History*, vol. 3 (1959)

Hutchinson, George, *Address . . . on the Treatment Of Criminals In The Punjab* (Bristol, 1866)

Huxley, Elspeth, *Florence Nightingale* (London, 1975)

'Hygiene' [Charles Hathaway?], *Calcutta and its Health Officer* (Calcutta, 1863)

Jones, J., *Memorials of Agnes Elizabeth Jones, By her Sister* (London, 1871)

[?Jones, Mary], *The Training Institution For Nurses St. John's House, Norfolk Street* (London, 1863)

Kinglake, A.W., *The Invasion Of The Crimea*, . . . (8 vols., Edinburgh & London 1863-87)

Kirby, Percival R., *Sir Andrew Smith, M.D., K.C.B.* (Capetown, 1965)

Kopf, Edwin W., 'Florence Nightingale as Statistician', *Publications of the American Statistical Association*, vol. XV (1916-17)

Lambert, Royston, *Sir John Simon 1816-1904* (London, 1963)

Lammond, D., *Florence Nightingale* (London, 1935)

(Lawson, George), *Surgeon in the Crimea*, Victor Bonham-Carter (ed.) . . . (London, 1968)

Longmore, Thomas, *The Sanitary Contrasts of the British And French Armies during the Crimean War* (London, 1883)

Lückes, Eva C.E., *What will Trained Nurses gain by joining the British Nurses Association?* (London, 1889)

——, *How Far Should Our Hospitals Be Training Schools For Nurses* (London, [c.1890])

Macalister, Florence, *Memoir of the right hon. Sir John McNeill . . .* (London, 1910)

Mackerness, E.D., 'Frances Parthenope, Lady Verney (1819-1890)', *Journal of Modern History*, vol. XXX, no. 2, June (1958)

MacMunn, George Fletcher, *The Crimea In Perspective*, (London, 1935)

Mahājana Dharmapāla, *The Administration of Sir John Lawrence in India, 1864-1869* (Simla, 1952)

Manton, Jo, *Mary Carpenter And The Children Of The Streets* (London, 1976)

Martineau, Harriet, *England And Her Soldiers* (London, 1859)

Martineau, John, *Life and Correspondence of Sir Bartle Frere* (2 vols., London, 1895)

Mills, John Saxon, *Sir Edward Cook K.B.E. A Biography* (London, 1921)

Mitra, S.M., *The Life and Letters of Sir John Hall* (London, 1911)

Moore, R.J., *Sir Charles Wood's Indian Policy 1853-66* (Manchester, 1966)

Nash, Rosalind (ed.), *Florence Nightingale to her Nurses* (London, 1914)

O'Malley, I.B., *Florence Nightingale, 1820-1856. A Study of her life down to the end of the Crimean War* (London, 1931)

Osborne, Sidney Godolphin, *Scutari and Its Hospitals* (London, 1855)

Panmure Papers, George Douglas and George Dalhousie Ramsay, (eds.) (2 vols., London, 1908)

Pickering, George, *Creative Malady: . . .* (London, 1974)

Pincoffs, Peter, *Experiences of a Civilian in Eastern Military Hospitals, . . .* (London, 1857)

Pitale, Balkrishna Nilaji (ed.), *The Speeches And addresses of Sir H.B.E. Frere* (Bombay, 1870)

Poole, Stanley Lane-, *The Life of . . . Stratford Canning* (2 vols., London, 1888)

Ramsay, Grace, *Thomas Grant, First Bishop of Southwark* (London, 1874)

Rathbone, Eleanor F., *William Rathbone. A Memoir* (London, 1905)

(Reid, Douglas A.), *Soldier-Surgeon; . . .* Joseph O. Baylen and Alan Conway (eds.) (Knoxville, Tenn., 1968)

Rickards, E.C., *Felicia Skene at Oxford* (London, 1902)

Rolt, L.T.C., *Isambard Kingdom Brunel* (London, 1970)

Rosenberg, Charles E., 'Florence Nightingale on Contagion: The Hospital as Moral Universe', in Charles E. Rosenberg (ed.), *Healing and History* (New York, 1979)

Sargant, N.C., 'Mary Carpenter . . . and her Connection with India . . .', *Indian Church History Review*, vol. XII (1978)

Saywell, Ruby Josephine, *Mary Carpenter Of Bristol* (Bristol, 1964)

Scharlieb, Mary, *Reminiscences* (London, 1924)

Seymer, Lucy Ridgely, *Florence Nightingale* (London, 1950)

Shrimpton, Charles, *La Guerre d'Orient. L'Armée Anglaise et Miss Nightingale* (Paris, 1864)

Skelley, Alan Ramsay *The Victorian Army At Home* (London, 1977)

Smith, Brian Abel-, *A History Of The Nursing Profession* (London, 1960)

Smith, Cecil Woodham-, *Florence Nightingale* (London, 1950)

Smith, F.B., *The People's Health* (London, 1979)

Smith, J.L. Clifford-, *A Manual for the Twenty-Fifth Anniversary of the National Association for the Promotion of Social Science* (London, 1882)

Smith, Reginald Bosworth, *Life of Lord Lawrence*, 6th edn. revised (2 vols., London, 1885)

Spiers, Edward M., *The Army and Society 1815-1914* (London, 1980)

Stanley, A.P., *Supplement to the second edition of the memoirs of Edward And Catherine Stanley* [1880?]

(Stanley, Mary) *Hospitals and Sisterhoods* (London, 1854)

Stanmore, Lord, *Sidney Herbert* (2 vols., London, 1906)

Stephen, Lady, 'The Real Florence Nightingale', in *The Woman's Leader*, 15 February 1929.

Sterling, Sir Anthony Coningham, *Letters from The Army In The Crimean*, London [1857?]

Strachey, John and McClelland, John, *Memoir on Cholera* ([Calcutta?], 23 March 1863)

Strachey, John and Strachey, Richard, *The Finances And Public Works Of India From 1869 to 1881* (London, 1882)

Strachey, Lytton, *Eminent Victorians*, first published 1918 (London, 1977)

Tabor, Margaret Emma, *Pioneer Women* (London, 1927)

A Lady Volunteer (Fanny Taylor), *Eastern Hospitals and English Nurses* (2 vols., London, 1856)

(Taylor, Fanny), *Religious Orders* (London, 1862)

——, *The Stoneleighs of Stoneleigh, and other Tales* (London, 1880)

Taylor, James S., *Alexis Soyer A Chivalrous Chef* (Washington, 1921)

Temple, Richard, *The Statistics of The Indian Empire* (London, 1881)

——, *Men And Events of My Time In India*, (London, 1882)

——, *Lord Lawrence* (London, 1889)

Terrot, Sarah Anne, *Reminiscences of Scutari Hospitals in winter 1854-55* (Edinburgh, 1898)

(Terrot, Sarah Anne), *Nurse Sarah Anne With Florence Nightingale at Scutari*, Robert G. Richardson (ed.) (London, 1977)

Trevelyan, Charles Edward, *The British Army in 1868*, (London, 1868)

Tulloch, Alexander Murray, *The Crimean Commission and the Chelsea Board* (London, 1857)

Twining, Elizabeth, *A Few Words on Social Science to Working People*

(London, 1862)

Twining, Louisa *Deaconesses for the Church of England* (London, 1860)

——, *Nurses For The Sick* (London, 1861)

——, *A Letter to the president of the Poor Law Board . . .* (London, 1866)

——, *Recollections of Workhouse Visiting and Management, . . .* (London, 1880)

Verney, Sir Harry, (ed.), *Florence Nightingale At Harley Street* (London, 1970)

(Vicars, Fanny), *Work in Brighton . . . or Woman's Mission to Wormen* (Preface by Florence Nightingale) (London, 1877)

Wedderburn, William, *Agricultural Banks For India*, (Bombay, n.d. [1880?])

——, *Octavian Hume, C.B., Father of the Indian National Congress* (London, 1913)

Whitcombe, Elizabeth, *Agrarian Conditions In Northern India*, vol. I (Berkeley, 1972)

Williams, Thomas Jay, *Priscilla Lydia Sellon* (London, 1965)

Wintle, W.J., *The Story of Florence Nightingale*, ([London ?] 1896)

Wood, Catherine Jane, *Boards Of Guardians and Nurses* (London, 1893)

Wrench, Edward M., 'The Lessons of the Crimean War', *British Medical Journal*, 22 July (1899)

INDEX

Abbott, Evelyn 200
Acland, Prof. H.W. 102, 162-3, 169
Acton, Dr W. 193
Airey, General Sir Richard 84
Airy, Sybil 165
Aitken, Dr W. 95
Albert, Prince 65, 73, 118
Alexander, Dr Thomas 67, 76, 77, 83, 115
Anderson, Dr A.54
anti-compulsory vaccination campaign 191-2
Army Medical Department 25, 76, 96, 102
army medical schools 63, 75, 76, 77, 81, 94-5, 102
Aspden, Richard 87

Baines, Mrs M.A. 157
Baker, W.E. 123
Balfour, Dr T.G. 67, 75, 83, 96, 100, 196
Barracks Improvement Commission 81, 93, 95-7, 104, 114
Barrett, Jerry 85
Barrington, Mrs Russell 190
Beecher, Henry Ward 176
Blackwell, Dr Elizabeth 90, 157, 197
Blackwood, Lady Alicia 43
Blomfield, Bishop C.J. 27-8
Bolster, Sister Evelyn 29, 68n9
Bowman, Dr William 175
Bracebridge, C. Holte 26-7, 33-4, 38, 40, 42, 45, 50, 53, 55, 61, 157
Bracebridge, Selina 26-7, 33, 38-9, 40, 42, 50, 52, 86
Bridgeman, Rev. Mother Mary Francis 29-32, 42-3, 45, 47-9, 56-67, 155, 201
British Nursing Association 168-9
Brodrick, G.C. 171
Brougham, Lord 132
Brunel, I.K. 102
Budd, Dr W. 143
Burgoyne, Sir John 101
Burns, – (Irish soldier) 51
Butler, Josephine 131, 196-8

Cambridge, Duke of 68, 88, 96, 102, 108
Canning, Lady Charlotte 11, 33
Carlyle, Thomas 188
Cardwell, Edward 95-6, 103, 108, 190
Carpenter, Mary 129-37, 139-40, 151n50, 188, 191, 196
Carter, Henry Bonham 135, 163, 169
Cautley, Sir Proby 115
Chadwick, Edwin 88, 90, 91, 97, 98, 99, 114-15, 134, 143, 186, 195
Chisholm, Mrs Caroline 84
cholera 16, 48, 56, 63, 127, 138, 141-3, 184
Christian, Princess 169
Clarendon, Lord 25
Clark, Sir James 76, 92, 157
Clarke, Mrs M. 36, 38-9, 40, 52
Clough, A.H. 157, 185
Clough, Miss 53
Codrington, General Sir William 62, 63, 156
Contagious Diseases Acts 191-8
Cook, Sir Edward xi, 17, 75, 86, 160, 202
Cotton, Sir Arthur 145, 147
Cox, C.L. Army-Surgeon 117
Coyle, Mary Ann 39
Cranborne, Lord (Third Marquess of Salisbury) 127, 128, 130, 146-7
Cranworth, Lady Laura 13, 66
Crimean Hospitals 53-4, 57, 59-61, 63, 65-6
Crowhurst, Donald 201
Cuffe, Rev. Fr Michael 47
Cumming, Dr A.J. 46-7, 79

Dale, Rev. T.P. 162
Daly, Timothy 170-1
Daughters of the Faithful Virgin (Norwood Sisters) 28, 30, 34, 47
Davis, Elizabeth (Nurse) 61, 201
Dean, Miss 57
Deeble, Mrs 94
DeGrey, Earl 118, 126-7, 130, 195
Delane, J.J. 123

Dickens, Charles 52
Disraeli, Benjamin 50
Dufferin, Lord 135
Duffy, Rev. Fr Michael 58, 66
Dunmore, Lady Catherine 106

Ebrington, Viscount 88, 132
Ethelreda, Sister 34
Ewart, Dr Joseph 117

Fagg, Emma 36
Faithful, Emily 133
Farnall, H.B. 170-2
Farr, Dr William 81, 96, 99, 114-15,
    122, 123-4, 126, 132, 166, 184,
    194
Filder, William 73, 82
Fitzgerald, David 63-5, 77
Forester, Lady Maria 25-6, 28
Forster, W.F. 102
Frederick, J.J. 124, 126
Frere, Sir Bartle 118, 127-9

Galton, Douglas 91, 93, 96, 99, 101,
    107, 119-20, 123, 126, 127-30,
    138, 143, 147, 171, 196
Galton, Francis 87, 199
Galton, Marianne 17
Garrett, Dr Elizabeth (Anderson)
    166, 196-7
Gaskell, Mrs Elizabeth 16, 17, 49-50,
    91
Gibson, Dr J.B. 95
Gipps, Miss 39-40
Giraud, Rev. Mr 161
Gladstone, W.E. 91, 104-6, 120,
    147, 194-5
Gleeson, Rev. Fr. Michael 66
Goldsmith, Margaret xi
Goschen, G.J. 177-8
Grant, Bishop Thomas 28
Grant, Sir Alexander 136
Green, Mrs [T.H.?] 190, 200, 201
Greenhow, Dr E. Headlam 98-9, 201
Gregg, Sam 49
Grey, Rear-Admiral F.W. 58-9
Grey, Third Earl 81-2

Hadley, Dr 56
Hall, Dr John 33, 56-67, 75-7, 79,
    82, 84-5, 156, 201
Harding, Jane 46
Hardy, Gathorne, 172-3, 177
Hart, G.H.R. 147
Hastings, G.W. 132-5

Hathaway, Charles 137
Hawes, Sir Benjamin 63-4, 67, 101-3
Herbert, Mrs Sidney (Lizzie) 11,
    25-7, 33, 37, 42, 50-1, 62, 90, 91,
    100, 103-8, 200-1
Herbert, Sidney 23, 26-8, 30-3, 36-7,
    41-5, 49-50, 52, 62-5, 67, 75-6,
    78, 83-5, 86, 87-9, 90, 93-7, 99,
    100-8, 114, 115, 119, 120, 127,
    156-7, 193, 195
Hill, M.D. 132
Hill, Octavia 132, 189
Holyoake, G.J. 185
Hopkins, Ellice 132
Howell, T.G., Army Surgeon 117
Hume, Rev. Mr 25-7
Hunt, Mrs Maria 41

India
    army barracks 121
    army death rates 114-15, 122-6
    prison reform 130, 137-8
    sanitary reform 114-18, 120-1,
        140-5, 148, 192
India Office 115, 117-19, 121, 124,
    128-9, 135, 138
Inglis, Lady 11
Invalid Gentlewomen's Institution,
    1 Harley St 11-17, 25, 35, 40, 46,
    131, 158, 183

Jebb, General Sir Joshua 157
Jervoise, Dr J. Clarke 99
Johnson, Dr Walter 89
Jones, Agnes 173-7, 201
Jones, Dr Henry Bence 103
Jones, Mary 23, 38, 86, 160-2, 173-4,
    199
Jowett, Benjamin 19, 23, 86, 87, 92,
    100, 119, 127, 130, 147-8, 171,
    178, 183, 184-6, 200

Kaiserswerth 21-2, 173
Kellett, Mrs Elizabeth 41
Kidd, Mrs 175
Kinglake, A.W. 52, 78, 82-3
King's College Hospital 16, 157, 160-2,
    164

Lawfield, Mrs 38, 58, 67
Lawrence, Sir John 118, 120-2, 125-
    6, 128, 131, 137-40, 201
Lefroy, J.H. 63, 66, 75-7
Leith, Dr A.H. 124-6, 201
Lewis, Sir George Cornewall 97, 195

Liddell, Sir John 196
Linton, Mrs E. Lynn 190
Liverpool Workhouse Infirmary 174-5
Longmore, Dr T. 95, 196
Louisa, Grand Duchess of Baden 168-9
Lugard, Sir Edward 101

McNeill, Lady 89-90
McNeill, Sir John 53-5, 65-7, 73, 76, 80, 82-5, 89-90, 97, 105-7, 114-15, 117, 157-8, 185-6
Macpherson, Dr Duncan 117
Manning, Rev. Henry Edward 29-32, 42, 47, 61, 65-6, 193, 200-1
Martin, Sir Ranald 91, 95, 115
Martineau, Harriet 92, 103, 119, 123, 170-1, 195-6
Menzies, Dr Duncan 33, 36, 42, 79
Middlesex Hospital 16-17
Mill, John Stuart 20-1, 172, 185-9
Mills, Arthur 171
Milnes, Mrs Annabel Monckton 83, 90
Milnes, Richard Monckton 18, 20, 26-7, 50, 66, 185-6
Mohl, Madame 16, 20
Moore, Rev. Mother Mary Clare 27, 29, 36, 39, 47-8, 92, 155
Mouat, Dr F.J. 138
Murray, Lord 74, 83

Nash, Rosalind 92-3
National Association for the Promotion of Social Science 99, 117, 130, 132-5, 138
Neison, G.P. 99
Netley Hospital 76-7, 93-5, 176
Newcastle, Duke of 26, 35
Newman, Rev. John Henry 30
Newmarch, William 132
Nightingale, Florence
    ambitions 12, 16-17, 19, 68, 72-3, 85, 118-19, 130, 132, 183-4, 199
    and midwives' training 159-63, 201
    and moral welfare of troops 41, 61, 121-2, 193, 195
    and nursing 15-16, 21-2, 27, 35-6, 39-40, 42-4, 50, 155-6, 158-9, 164-70, 178
    and Poor Law 170-3, 177-8
    and women's suffrage 188-90
    army sanitary reform 67-8, 74, 78, 82, 89, 97-8, 117, 122, 140-2
    contagion theories 79, 96-100,
116, 163, 167, 192, 194
    family background 18-20, 22-3, 42, 49-50, 132, 198
    hospital design 93-4, 102, 119, 128, 160, 163
    ill-health 54-6, 78, 89-93, 108, 117, 136, 159, 186
    managerial qualities 14-15, 27, 35-7, 38-40, 42-3, 49, 52-3, 62-3, 66-7, 80, 117-19, 158-9
    manipulative impulse 11-13, 26-7, 37-8, 44-7, 49, 53-4, 64-5, 72-9, 81-3, 88-90, 103-6, 114-15, 119, 123-6, 129, 169, 176-7, 188, 191
    novelist's sense 12, 16-17, 55-6, 64, 176
    political opinions 72, 177-8, 190-1
    private self 85-7, 176, 198-9, 202
    religion 21-2, 23, 48, 183-5, 187-8, 199
    reputation 42, 50-2, 67, 72, 201-2
    statistics 96, 98, 123, 163, 184
    Suggestions for Thought ... 20, 22-3, 156, 183-8
Nightingale, Mrs W. (Fanny, mother of F.N.) 13, 18-20, 22, 49, 91, 198-9
Nightingale, Parthenope (sister of F.N.) 13, 16, 17, 18-19, 22, 25-6, 49-51, 65-6, 86, 198-9, 201
Nightingale, William Edward (father of F.N.) 11-13, 18-19, 51, 185-6, 198
Nightingale Fund 67, 72, 156-62, 164, 167, 170, 178, 198
Nixon, Richard 201
Norman, H.R. 123, 126
Northcote, Sir Stafford 128-30, 138

Osborne, Rev. S.G. 51

Palmerston, Lord 25, 74-5, 93, 96-7
Panmure, Lord 52, 58, 63, 67, 73-8, 81, 83, 87-9, 93, 97, 156
Parkes, Dr E.A. 67, 95
Pickering, Sir George 89
Pincoffs, Dr Peter 74-5, 77
Pirrie, Nurse 198-9
Ponsonby, Sir Henry 168
Poor Law 85, 92, 169-74, 177-8
Potter, Beatrice (Webb) 189
Prendergast, Joseph Samuel 51, 54-5
Pringle, Matron A.L. 86, 198-200

Prostitution 16-17, 192-8

Quarantine 100

Radcliffe Infirmary 168
Raglan, Lord 52-3, 55, 82
Rathbone, William 168, 170, 173-4
Rawlinson, Robert 53, 67, 83
Redpath, Marie C. 169
Rendle, Dr William 86
Roberts, Mrs 54, 155
Robinson, Robert 54
Robinson, Sarah 132
Roebuck, J.A. 52, 72
Ronan, Rev. Fr William 31, 46
Rose, Sir Hugh 124
Russell, W.H. 25, 51-2

St John's House Nurses 27-8, 33-4, 36, 38-40, 52-3, 56, 157, 159, 160-1
St Thomas's Hospital 86-7, 94, 98, 155-9, 165, 167, 169, 173, 175-6
Scutari Hospitals 35-8, 43, 47, 54, 56, 58, 79-80, 85
Sellon, Lydia Priscilla 27
Sen, Keshub Chunder 136
Shaftesbury, Lord 96-7, 131-2
Shepherd, Rev. C.P. 27-8, 32, 39
Sheridan (Nurse) 61
Shuttleworth, James Kay 132
Sieveking, Dr E.H. 169
Simon, Dr John 98-100, 132
Skene, Felicia 33
Smith, Brian Abel 169
Smith, Cecil Woodham xi, 17-18
Smith, Dr Andrew 25, 64, 75, 77, 79, 83, 85, 94, 156
Smith, Mai (aunt of F.N.) 11, 40, 42, 87, 89-90, 157
Smith, Samuel (uncle of F.N.) 26, 65-6, 90, 115, 155, 157, 185
Somerville, Mary 189
Soyer, Alexis 53-4
Sprey, Sister Mary Winifred 62
Stafford, Augustus 52, 72
Stanley, A.P. 31, 186
Stanley, Lord (15th Earl of Derby) 115, 119-20, 123-7, 132, 138, 201
Stanley, Mary 31-2, 43, 45-7, 73, 94, 100, 156, 201
Stanmore, Lord, *Life of Sidney Herbert* 26, 108, 201
Stansfeld, James 178

Sterling, Sir Anthony 69n40
Stewart, Dr A.P. 166
Stewart, Mrs Jane Shaw 94, 155-6
Storks, General Sir Henry 58-60, 75, 83
Stowe, Harriet Beecher 176
Strachan, Alexander 177
Strachey, Lytton xi, 17, 18, 26, 202
Strachey, Ray 188
Strachey, Sir John 121
Strachey, Sir Richard 138
Stratford de Redcliffe, Lady 27, 37
Stratford de Redcliffe, Lord 25, 37, 46, 58, 59-60
Strzelecki, Count Paul 124
Sutherland, Dr John 20, 53-4, 67, 73, 75-7, 83-4, 86-7, 91, 96, 99, 101, 114-15, 118-20, 124-5, 127-9, 137, 143, 147, 156, 163-4, 170, 174, 177, 188, 195, 197-8, 200

Tait, A.C. (Bishop of London) 161
Taylor, Dr A.H. 65
Taylor, Fanny 54, 201
Temple, Richard 145
Terrot, Sister Sarah Anne 49
Torrance, Matron Elizabeth 199
Truelove, Mrs 186
Tulloch, Alexander 53, 67, 73, 75-7, 83, 97
Twining, Elizabeth 188
Twining, Louisa 162, 173, 176, 188, 191

University College Hospital 162

Verney, Sir Harry 161, 171, 188, 195-6, 199
Victoria, Queen 50, 55, 65, 67, 72, 73-6, 78, 83, 85, 86, 117, 147
Villiers, C.P. 170-2
Vivian, Sir Robert 115

Walker, Dr J.P. 125, 138-41, 175
Walker, Henriett 175
Ward, L. (purveyor) 36
Ward, Lord William 55-6
Ward, Mrs Humphry 190
Wardroper, Mrs S.E. 155, 159, 164-6, 168, 175
War Office 25-6, 29-30, 32, 53, 58-60, 63-4, 67, 72, 75, 77-8, 80-2, 88, 91, 93, 95-7, 101-5, 107-8, 114-15, 118, 121-4, 129,

135, 193, 195
Wear, Mary 53-4, 57-61
Wells, H.G. 37
Whitfield, R.G. 158, 200
Williams, Dr C.B. 106
Williams, Miss Rachel 199
Winkworth, Catherine 16

Wood, Sir Charles 115, 119, 123-6, 130, 138
Woollett, Rev. Fr J.S. 57
Wyatt, Matthew Digby 119
Wynter, Dr Andrew 114-15

Youl, Rev. Dr 29

Critical Praise for *Marry a Mennonite Boy and M*

"*Marry a Mennonite Boy and Make Pie* is a funny, r
memoir about early adulthood and the struggle to r
identity with one's encounters with the World. '   of
narrative shared by so many Mennonites in the   _arly
twenty-first centuries, told honestly and unas'
                              —Danie*   College

"There comes a time when each of us need to de_   .ow close or
how distant we need to be from the world of our chila..od to become
what feels true for our adult selves. This book perfectly captures that
time."

                              —Sherri Klassen, University of Toronto

"Diana Zimmerman exposes the emotions that accompany the com-
ing-of-age struggles of a Mennonite woman who eagerly seeks to learn
about the diverse and multicultural world that becomes her new reality. That struggle eventually finds a peaceful haven in connections with
others who are on the same journey as they face, together, a future filled
with new discoveries."

                              —Lauren Friesen, PhD, University of Michigan

"Diana writes an entertaining, honest, coming to age memoir of a
young woman who struggles to honor her TRUTH in the midst of
the ever-present Mennonite culture. While some people never chose to
leave the 'safe and certain' Mennonite Culture, Diana earnestly claws
her way through to her own truth."

                              —Victoria L. Creighton, Clinical Director, Pine River Institute

"Diana Zimmerman's literary snapshots bring a lost world to life. Standing on the brink of the Internet era, her youthful characters struggle
with faith, friendship, and the future in ways that are hard to imagine
now, except through a book like this. A consummate act of memory."

                              —Sofia Samatar, author of *A Stranger in Olondria*

Published by Workplay Publishing, 2018.
Newton, KS 67114

workplaypublishing.com

ISBN 0-9905545-8-9
Cover design and interior layout by André Swartley
Photos by Diana R. Zimmerman

PRINTED IN THE UNITED STATES OF AMERICA

Marry a Mennonite Boy and Make Pie

a fictional memoir by

Diana R. Zimmerman

for Marica

Diana R. Zimm

WORKPLAY PUBLISHING

Table of Contents

What Comes After   11

The Carrot Problem   81

Chino's Moon   139

None of the Above   199

Afterword   245

This book is dedicated to everyone it represents in even the smallest way.

Author's Note

This book is the memoir of a summer, a written photo album of a time and a place. The snapshots are colored with splashes of fiction and interspersed with drawings of imaginary tableaus that might have been. This blend of truth and imagination is able to tell a story truer what pure memory can provide. Names and other details have been modified as a gesture of respect and appreciation for those who find their faces in these photographs. The only name that remains unchanged is my own.

What Comes After

I would love to go back there and sneak into that house when no one's home. I'd walk upstairs and scrape little patches of paint from the walls to take a peek at what I know is underneath. I'm sure it's still there because we couldn't get it off. And believe me, we tried. Nina's writhing beast, Beth's spiral suns, Sheila's giant alphabet and the geometric designs I copied from the notebook I hid under my mattress—none of it would budge. We thought Barb the landlady was going to kill us when we told her it wasn't coming off. She didn't. She had a better idea. Those watercolors turned out to be tougher than Pine-Sol and Clorox, but they were no match for Sherwin Williams.

The house must have stood there when 11th Street was a lane through a cornfield, and our somber-suited grandfathers broke ground for the Mennonite college on the other side of town. Everything evolves. The fields sprouted a Winnebago factory, the college built a theatre and a science center, the Mennonite grandfathers passed the torch to unruly girls like us, and the two-story house split into sagging apartments.

That place was heaven and hell wrapped into one burrito. Whoever added the stairway up to our door didn't bother to attach it to the siding, so it wobbled disastrously. Earwigs ran under the spoons when you opened the kitchen drawers and the guys who lived there before us never once cleaned the bathroom. But we paid the deposit, and that made the apartment beautiful. That alone eclipsed the disrepair and the bugs.

In the steaming Indiana summer of 1991, our sophomore year of college was over and were finally on our own. For the first time in our lives no one would tell us what to do. Four girls, one apartment, four months. I could feel my life waiting to leap into my arms. The higher the mercury climbed, the better it measured our fever. I refused to go home to the farm in Pennsylvania where I would have to obey my parents' rules all summer and pretend I still thought our Mennonite church ice cream socials were fun. No way. I was staying right here with my best friend Beth and the other two girls she picked to be our housemates.

Beth had written me the semester before, while I was in Costa Rica, to say that she found the perfect housemates for us. "Nina is so awesome," she wrote. "She's an Art major. She was in our art history class, remember?" I had no idea who she was talking about. "She wants to live with us! Yay! And Sheila Friesen. I don't think you know her that well—she's an Elementary Ed major—but you will love her. Remember the girl who got fined for falling in the fountain in front of the library?" I'd heard about that, but I didn't remember who it was. "That's Sheila. She is SO FUNNY!" Beth was sure I knew them and I was sure I didn't.

It didn't matter. Whoever was good enough for Beth was good enough for me.

As soon as I got settled, I would start feeling like my old self again. Of course. There was nothing wrong with me. Everything would be fine. I would smother my growing knot of sadness under a blanket of silence until it stopped kicking. It would, right? You can forget about something if you don't talk about it. Can't you? If you have a secret and you keep it inside your skin, inside your lips, then it doesn't exist in the world. It's only in your head, which doesn't count. All I needed was a little time. And some tequila wouldn't hurt.

On the day we moved in, I was ready to haul my boxes up the stairs at seven AM, but I didn't have the key. I had to wait around until ten o'clock when Nina's brother Anthony brought everybody else from the campus dorms. Tom dropped me off in the yard on the way to his summer job painting houses, and I piled my stuff under a tree. I got comfy on my pillows and opened my anthology of Thornton Wilder plays. Seemed like optimal early-summer reading material for a Theatre major, and something about *Pullman Car Hiawatha* was bothering me. I needed to read it again. That woman who dies at the end and says she understands everything now—what does she mean? But the gnats got a little out of control, so I had to put a towel over my head. That made it dark and stuffy, which made me sleepy, so I ended up exchanging Thornton for a little nap. At first, I was afraid someone from the apartment downstairs would call the cops about the squatter in the yard, but I soon realized that no one lived there.

I'd packed up my dorm room months ago in the chill of January, then flew south for a cross-cultural semester in Costa Rica. I told my mom that, during the week since my feet landed back on American soil, I'd been staying in the dorm with Beth. That was a lie. Of course I stayed at Tom's house. And I'm not complaining. There are worse things than a whole week of sleep-overs with your boyfriend, but I was dying for my own bed, someplace to unpack my boxes and call home. Being homeless is exhilarating for about two days, and then it's not.

I had this feeling Tom, or everybody, really, could see through me like glass. That feeling freaks me out. It makes me want to hide. Because if Tom could see through me, he would see what I saw. There would be a pair of bottomless brown eyes piercing straight to the day I was born, two steady hands on my face, and a voice pleading, *"No te vayas."* Every time it flashed through me, I had to swallow down a knot that seized in my throat. This can't happen. Nobody else may see it. I'm in love with Tom and I won't ever let him go. Nothing in Costa Rica is my real life. My life is here. I decide.

Anthony's red pick-up finally turned into the alley and pulled up. It was heaped with duffle bags, trash bags, boxes, and the mattresses that no one noticed slipping through the front doors of the dorm. That's what Beth says, anyway. She says in the mayhem of moving, no one even blinked as they picked up their beds and walked. The dorms throw everyone out at the end of the winter semester so, if you've signed yourself up for summer classes in May and June like we did, you have to find somewhere else to live. And where are you supposed to sleep? Flat on the floor? The girls rode in the back of the truck, even though it's illegal, so they wouldn't lose anything going over the railroad tracks. They promised to lie down if they saw a cop.

Beth jumped out of the truck before it even stopped and came leaping over to hug me. We squealed and yelled and jumped up and down while we were still hugging.

I recognized Sheila and Nina immediately. I can't say I remember the thing Beth said about Sheila falling in the fountain, but I can believe it. Sheila's not that graceful. When she tried to jump out of the truck, she lost a sandal and stubbed her toe. Her mom is Indian, so that must be where she got her gorgeous heart-shaped face and brown eyes like a puppy. When we said hi, she was laughing and crying at the same time over her toe.

Nina picked her way out of the truck and came over to say hi, too. She's one of those people that, when you hug her, it's like hugging yourself because she's so small. I'd seen her before.

She hung around the art building and that's about all I knew. I'm afraid of people that small in the same way I'm afraid of newborn babies. A girl like me could accidentally break a thing like that without even dropping it.

❧❧

By the time Anthony honked the horn and drove away, we were drenched in sweat, giddy as a flock of parakeets, and it was lunch time. Our upstairs apartment contained a jumble of coffee-stained t-shirts, mismatched flip-flops, spiral notebooks, overdue library books, incense burners, family photos, copied cassette tapes, and snow boots in search of a summer home. We even had a pet. My ancient goldfish named Methuselah, who missed me terribly while Beth fish-sat him last term, had survived yet another winter and swam merrily around in his ice cream bucket home by my bed. He loved me. He would kiss my finger or my nose when I poked it in the water.

"I'm starving!" I said. I'm always starving.

"Me too," Sheila said, coming out of the room she and Nina were sharing. She lifted the V-neck of her oversized undershirt and disappeared inside it for a moment like a turtle, mopping the sweat from her face.

Beth stood in the doorway of our room, tossed her ponytail and said that she could eat a water buffalo with cheese.

"Gross," Nina said, scrunching her eyes shut at the thought. She stopped pulling folded clothes out of a Samsonite suitcase and gave a shudder.

"You don't like cheese?" I asked.

"I don't like to think about eating animals," Nina said.

I said the only thing I could think of which was, "Oh," and looked at Beth. Beth raised her eyebrows and blinked.

"So. Do we have any food?" Forget eating animals. Just don't make me eat our moving boxes.

Beth opened her mouth to say no, but something occurred to Sheila. "Oh my God!" Sheila said, looking shocked. "Does anyone know how to cook?" Her hand flew to her hair and began twisting. The metal bracelets on her arm made nervous music. "Beth? Do you?"

"Well. Sort of," Beth said.

"Diana?" Sheila asked me. "Because, I don't."

I laughed.

"Oh no!"

"I can make pancakes," Nina said. Her flowered sun-dress and black eye make-up made a confusing combination. "And strawberry syrup out of strawberry jelly. It's so easy. You just—"

"Eggs!" Sheila remembered. "I can make eggs!"

"See?" I said, "We're fine."

"Yeah, but I we don't have anything now."

"Oh no."

"Shit."

Nina giggled a delighted giggle.

"I could go to Seven Eleven," I offered. "And get peanut butter and jelly."

"Wait," Beth said. "Not yet." She marched into the kitchen. The rest of us followed.

Beth ducked into the dark pantry. On the narrow shelves, previous generations of students had abandoned a dusty bag of rice, several boxes of salt, the greasy dregs of a Crisco bottle and a mostly-empty can of coffee. A pile of forgotten onions seemed to believe they were underground and showed notable signs of life.

"A-ha!" Beth held up the grimy bag of grains. "Lunch!"

"Yay!"

"Oh..."

"Gross!"

"There's only one problem," Beth said. She disappeared back into the pantry and mumbled a curse. Then she burst into laughter.

"What?" I said.

Beth stepped into the light holding the rice in one hand

and a decrepit frying pan in the other. "Guys? This is the only thing we have to cook with."

Nina giggled.

Sheila started twisting her hair again, jangling her wristful of bracelets.

"Check the cupboards," I said.

We found a few surprises like a moldy wooden spoon, empty peanut butter jars with no lids and what I recognized to be mouse turds, but nothing a girl can cook in. Sheila saw a spider and screamed. I offered to smash it but then Nina screamed.

"I guess we could eat the onions," Beth said, trying to look sad but her eyes sparkled.

"Ew! Are you serious?"

"No thank you!"

"Can't you make rice in a frying pan?" I said. "A little?"

But Beth's ideas were still coming. "I know! Wait!" She ran into our room and came bouncing back holding her little red hotpot above her head like the Statue of Liberty's torch. "Hotpot rice!"

"Hotpot rice!" Sheila howled like that was hilarious.

Nina squealed and cheered.

"Can you make rice in a hotpot?" I asked.

"Why not?" Beth shrugged. "You can make Ramen."

I couldn't argue with that, so I swallowed my doubts and went back to unpacking.

Maybe I could have saved the hotpot if I had seen Beth's preparations. She filled it half full of rice, then added water to the brim. I didn't know how to cook, but I did score in the 99th percentile on an aptitude test for mechanical reasoning. "Mechanical reasoning" doesn't mean you can fix things—it means you can tell ahead of time something like that is never going to work.

I had to bike to the Seven Eleven to buy peanut butter and jelly after all, and the hotpot couldn't be salvaged. No amount of soaking and scraping could remove the disaster melted into the metal and plastic. We kept it, for a while, on top of the refrigerator as a sentimental tribute to our first meal together. Eventually it went to hotpot heaven with the charred layer of rice still cemented to the bottom.

ঙ৽৵

No matter what we did to those walls, they weren't going to get any worse. The kitchen wore a horrible coat of dark-smudged yellow, and the rest of the rooms were shades of tired grimy white. A decade of grubby college students can wreak havoc on a paint job. The more your Mennonite mom makes you clean the house so that you will know how to live decently when you leave home, the less you do it when that day comes.

Beth said we should draw on the walls. I said we should not. Sheila said we should buy bleach. Nina said she had water-colors. We all looked at each other and hesitated. Water colors? As in water soluble? As in, we can wash this off later like nothing ever happened? A girl cannot be expected to resist that kind of temptation.

We had the sense to call Barb, our eternally-patient landlady, and ask her permission before we started painting. We promised watercolors would not do permanent damage. Barb said she didn't care what we did as long as we cleaned it all up before we moved out. The house wasn't hers anyway—she just managed it for a friend who was a missionary or something.

Nina produced her precious paints and told us to be careful not to get any green in the yellow. This was no Crayola set of paints, and the brushes were so special they practically each had names. We promised not to mix the colors and to never leave the brushes drying upside down. Nina swirled her wet brush around in the purple and set about creating ghostly little waif spirits that wafted mysteriously through the rooms. Beth unleashed colorful exploding suns and lanky brown bodies that resembled her. Sheila said she can't paint to save her soul and she got one of her anxiety attacks when we tried to encourage her.

"No, you guys," she begged, starting to wheeze. "I'm not

artistic like you are. I wish I was, but I'm not, okay? I just don't feel comfortable. I'm not good at things like you guys are." Then she had to rummage around for her inhaler.

I'm no artist either, but I love bright colors, so I painted my heart out. I warmed up with a few lopsided flowers here and there. Then I drew borders around the windows and doors— shaky replicas of the traditional designs that I practiced painting on pottery in Costa Rica. I hoped that if I got used to looking at them, my eyes would stop prickling every time I opened that notebook. The one I kept pushed under my mattress. While I painted, I could see the pursed lips of the potter as he patiently drew on the pages for me. So that I would never forget. Then he spelled his name below. I felt the hot windy shade of the porch and heard the palm leaves rustle beside the kitchen. Under his name, he wrote mine in small, perfect letters and traced a heart around the names—the cheesiest 4th grade thing you ever saw. But so completely sincere. A few days ago. It made a lump pop into my throat that I could hardly breathe around.

There were no rules. You could paint anything you wanted, anytime you wanted. We kept the paints and brushes in a drawer of the giant Desk so everyone could use them. Even Sheila finally got over herself and painted a huge row of ABC's in a circle around the living room. She said it was a practice run for her future kindergarten classroom. Later, she added "PHYS WORLD SUCKS" and a stick figure on crooked gallows because of how much she hated that class.

It didn't have to be pretty, and before long it wasn't. Somebody got black in the Pepto-Bismol pink, for one. Nina was so upset about that she started crying and shut herself in the bathroom. All I can say is it wasn't me because I never used the black. I tried to paint the Dancing Bears, but they looked more like demon-possessed dolls. The more I tried to fix them, the worse they got. Nina's waif-spirits became bigger and more tortured until the only place you could go to get away from them was Beth's and my bedroom. Bad words, tic-tac-toe games, hand smears, foot prints, butt prints. Beth started painting beautiful terrifying masks one after the other, and quotes about oppressors from Bob Marley songs. Sheila began a life-sized self-portrait in the hall beside her door, but we ran out of brown, and she couldn't think what other color to be. So it stood there like half a ghost. The painting stopped being decoration and started degenerated into desecration. A giant red vagina appeared in the bathroom, looking like a larger-than-life Venus Fly Trap. Then Nina pained the crowning glory of horrors in the kitchen with the last that was left of the black and the red.

Remember that story about the woman who goes insane in the upstairs room with yellow wallpaper? Similarities exist. We weren't trapped by a lock like she was, but we were upstairs. Struggling to get out in other ways. The crazier the walls got, the harder we tried.

৩৵৵

Furniture, if you think about it, is a luxury. As long as you have a roof over your head, water in the tap and a reasonable pan to cook your rice in, who cares if you have to sit on the floor?

The only piece of furniture that came with the apartment was The Desk. The living room contained a Desk so immense and so heavy that it must have been assembled in that exact room. No human being could have gotten that thing up the precarious stairs and even God couldn't have gotten it through the door. We could have used it as a table if we had chairs, but we didn't. Not one. So we set Sheila's ancient stereo on it and stashed cassette tapes and phone bills in its drawers.

Between the four of us, we owned one fan, one floor lamp, a Mr. Coffee and the five single mattresses provided by the dorm. We ended up with an extra because Beth stole one for me, and Sheila, afraid that Beth would forget, took another. In the chaos of loading Anthony's red pick-up truck, no one was counting.

Beth and I took two of the mattresses, dropped them onto the floor of our bedroom and pushed them together to make one big bed. Nina and Sheila dragged two into their room and pushed them against opposite walls. They're friends, but not best friends like Beth and me. The extra went into an inexplicable closet, christened The Pit of Sin, which opened off the kitchen.

I guess we could have painted furniture on the walls. Funny we never thought of that.

We soon came up with a couch, but it wasn't so much a piece of furniture as the remains of one. Tony Royal, our friend the cafeteria thief, said we could take it when he graduated and left town. It's hard to say whether or not it was an improvement over sitting on the floor. It was a furry pink thing with offensive springs that would violate you if you weren't careful. But you could lie, sit, or stand on it as long as you avoided the springs. You could lose things under it.

Beth lounged on that couch like Queen Bathsheba while her boyfriend Curtis and his brother Dan carried it all the way across town from Tony's house to ours. She says they thought it was funny. They started out on the college side of town, where our thoughtful forefathers planted a corridor of maple trees along every sidewalk, and hauled it to the Winnebago-factory side of town. No shade, no sidewalks. Curtis and Dan grew up in Africa because their parents are missionaries, so I guess they're used to being hot and walking a long way.

I can't believe Beth had the nerve to lie on the couch all the way home. I would never do that. Then again, I weigh a lot more than she does. That's the effect Beth has on men—they leap at the chance to carry her down the street in the summer sun while she lies on a couch. If that was me, they would expect me to take a corner. Honestly, so would I.

When we had to get the couch out at the end of the summer, we didn't bother to carry it down the perilous stairway to the street. Why? Nobody wanted it. We dragged it to the door and threw it off the porch. It crashed to the ground beside the stairs and then we set it on fire. The neighbor man who hated us called the police, so we had to say it was an accident.

You should have seen Beth working on the cop to get him to believe that, after we accidentally dropped the couch off the porch, it somehow caught on fire. She's an English major and makes up amazing stories.

That was a fantastic idea. It was much easier to throw away after it was all burned up.

⊱✦⊰

Our kitchen was a petri dish for disturbing plant and animal species. The whole south wall was a row of windows, so it was 95 degrees in there for months on end. If you left the milk on the counter, it turned rancid by the time you were done with your cereal. If you forgot the last of the lentils in the refrigerator, they would come back to life in a few days. We constantly had to revise the refrigerator for the source of suspicious smells and whatever we found to be resurrecting from the dead went into the trash. When we found something truly unspeakable, we flushed it down the toilet. I bought a flyswatter to fight off the wildlife.

Household chores were nobody's job. You could do them if you wanted to. If nobody wanted to, then nobody did them and nobody complained. That's the advantage of not having rules—if you'd rather do something later, you can, and if you don't want to do it at all, no one will grumble at you. It gets messy, though.

In the sink, the dishes piled up until one more spoon would cause an avalanche or there was nothing left to eat with. We got used to filling the coffee pot with water in the bathroom because you couldn't get it under the faucet in the kitchen. Theoretically, we were each supposed to wash our own dishes, but I figured out why that never works. Because if I am going to wash my dishes, but first I do something like take a shower or decide to drink more coffee, and then Sheila puts her dishes on top of mine but has to go answer the phone because her Grandma Friesen called, now I can't wash mine because they are under Sheila's. And if Sheila is still on the phone when I have to leave? By the time I get home, there is a mountain in the sink.

I think I washed more than my fair share of dishes in that

cruddy kitchen, but who knows. Beth cooked the most because she was the one who knew how. Thanks to her, we didn't live on only Ramen with hotdogs. I thought, out of gratitude and human decency, that it would be nice if she didn't have to wash the dishes, too. Sheila tried to chip in at the sink sometimes, but the threat of discovering something alive between the festering plates was hard on her nerves. The stress gave her asthma.

Nina never even used the dishes. She only had to eat about twice a week to maintain her stick figure, and she didn't seem hungry all the time like me. Hers were the containers of food that spoiled and had to be thrown away, things I would have sold my soul for, like, left-over Chinese take-out. We would never have thought of eating what belonged to Nina. Although I doubt she would have noticed. She obviously didn't think of it either.

Curtis and Dan brought us a microwave. They found it on one of their dumpster dives and they thought we might like it. Of all the gems they unearthed from the trash, that is one they could just as well have left there. I think it was one of the first models ever sold and it weighed almost as much as me. The cord was frayed, the round dials wouldn't turn and somebody had seen fit to duct tape it in several places. Curtis put a cup of water inside it and plugged it in. I ran out onto the porch, holding my ears, praying to God that it wouldn't explode.

Explode is not quite the word for what happened, but it sounded like an explosion—one that lasted a full minute until a bell rang and Curtis pulled a steaming cup of water from the belly of the beast. The monster worked. I was terrified of it, though. I could feel it cooking my brain and my future children, even through the walls, as it somehow produced its terrible thunder. I bolted from the room anytime anyone turned it on. How can a duct taped microwave not be an agent of death? I'll save my risky behavior for somewhere besides kitchen.

❧❧

When the house was built, The Pit of Sin must have been intended for storage. I doubt it was intended for sin, although you never know. Lucky for us, it was big enough for both. The Pit of Sin was hotter than the kitchen, stuffy, and smelled of the need for a shower. The defining feature of The Pit, the one which determined its destiny, was the presence of a door we could close. We piled our mountain of snow boots and empty boxes in such a way as to leave a narrow passage from the door to the single mattress in the back corner. It was a guest room, you might say, that guests were not expected to use alone.

Strictly speaking, I don't know that any of The Ten Commandments were broken in that little room, but I know a lot of our Sunday School teachers' hopes for us were dashed against that ratty mattress. It belonged to all of us, and we all tumbled into its windowless refuge—all of us except for Sheila. Sheila's the only one who missed out on The Pit of Sin, but it wasn't for lack of trying. She had a fling with Rajesh, the gorgeous Indian guy who broke her heart, but that was at his house. He would never have deigned to put his elegant leather-wearing foot on our rickety stairs. She got over him because of Neil, which was a romance destined to end in the tragedy of him getting engaged to someone else. Nina and Dan had their nights in the Pit of Sin before Dan got stir-crazy and hitchhiked west. Nina was happy like a little bird in those early weeks. Beth and Curtis took their turns too, until Curtis and Tony Royal got on a plane with their passports and Beth began to realize that she would never find anyone she loved more.

Mostly, The Pit of Sin belonged to Tom and me. We could shut the door and make everything else in the world stay on the other side. My confused emotions vanished the second the latch clicked at my back and the palms of my hands slid over his smooth skin. Everything but Tom melted away like ice cream in Los Rios.

As soon as the rest of the house was quiet, we opened the door a crack so we wouldn't suffocate. It was almost as hot in there as the eternal toaster oven we knew we were risking, so our sticky adventures were punctuated by trips to the refrigerator for water. We climbed out the kitchen window onto the porch roof then, with our cups in our hands, and sat in our underwear basking in the cool air of a midnight too humid for stars. It's a good thing the mosquitoes kept us slapping or we would have fallen asleep out there and rolled right into the yard.

❧

"You know that almost-bald patch on Sheila's head?" Beth asked me. We were pedaling our bikes toward the shady end of 8th Street and our first summer class.

"Yeah."

"You know why it's almost bald?"

"No. I thought it just grows that way."

"No."

"What?"

"She pulls her hair out."

"What!"

"Yes. Nina told me."

"She pulls her own hair out?"

"Can you imagine? She twists it and twists it until it comes out."

"I've seen her do that but I didn't know she pulls that hard."

"She does."

"Doesn't that hurt?"

"It has to."

"My God."

"I know."

"Why?"

"She just does. Her nerves."

"She's that nervous?"

"I guess so."

"But why?"

"She just is. She's supposed to take medication but she doesn't like it."

"For her hair or her nerves?"

"Her nerves, dummy."

"Right."

"But I guess it would help her hair, too."

Sheila is not exactly crazy, but she's the first person I ever met with "anxiety" as a permanent condition. It isn't her fault. It's genetic. Her mom is as bipolar as the day is long and won't take her medicine, either. The whole family moved from Mumbai to Indianapolis when Sheila's mom was a teenager—not a wonder she has troubles. Sheila spent a lot of time at Grandma Friesen's house when she was a kid, while her dad was in med school and her mom was having a hard time being a mom. She gets panic attacks that spark asthma attacks and she can never ever forget her inhaler.

❧❧

Barb, the landlady, offered to take ten dollars per week off our rent if we mowed the yard ourselves. We didn't make her say it twice. Mennonites are famous for being industrious even when we aren't hungry—imagine when we are. If we'd seen the mower she expected us to use, we might not have been so eager, but by that time it was too late. We tackled the job in pairs because it could have killed any one of us.

Things were going along well enough until Nina went nuts and wrecked our plan. She and Sheila were supposed to alternate weeks with Beth and me, but when it was their turn, Nina had to go and get herself hospitalized. That could be the straw that broke the camel's back—the threat of having to mow on top of so much inner misery. The yard is huge by anyone's definition, with several annoying pear trees to circle around, and the rattletrap mower weighed a ton. It used to be self-propelled, but it could barely crawl anymore. We pushed it around the house, sweating, swearing, stopping every five minutes to tighten the handle which vibrated loose, and to beat the grass out of the dull blade. It was an awful ordeal.

Yard work, in case you didn't notice, does not obey the same rules as housework. Housework piles up at a uniform speed. Every day that you don't wash the dishes, the pile grows a little higher. The mound of unmentionables in the laundry basket gets another layer each time you change your clothes. It's a war of attrition that nobody wins—you address the most important things first, like the coffee cups and underwear, and the battles rage on. But you never have to wash all the dishes in the kitchen or do all the laundry in the closet the way you have to mow the entire yard at once. There's a critical point, when it comes to grass, after which an already horrible job becomes infinitely worse, because while you are cutting the lawn around your house, you are also making hay. We learned that the hard way. You have to rake the hay up right away because if you don't, the grass underneath dies and your eternally patient landlady gets very pissed. What is it about people over 30 and grass? Good grief.

I took some extra responsibility because I'm the biggest, and therefore the best match for that mower and the challenge of filling the tank with gas. It was my job to walk to Barb's house and drag the beast from her garage to our yard. Then I rode the gas can to Seven Eleven on my bike and wobbled back with it perched on the bar. Nobody else thought they could do it, and it's not even hard as long as you don't have to stop. In Costa Rica I saw entire families cruising down the road on 10-speed bicycles—I think one girl should be able to manage one gas can. And, no, they did not have a baby seat.

The weeks clicked along. Mixing the mental exertion of summer classes with the physical struggle against that mower created a little balance. Even Nina learned to beat the beast into submission. Then she turned herself in to the mental facility and our pairs were ruined. No more doing the happy dance because it's someone else's turn.

She only stayed for two weeks in Pine View, but she didn't mow much after that. She worked forty hours a week, and on Saturdays she went to therapy. None of us had the nerve to ask her to take her turn. Sheila would never have suggested a thing like that—she would have pulled out the rest of her hair first. Beth thought about it but she chickened out. She didn't want Nina to think she was insensitive. I didn't care what Nina thought of me, but I felt sorry for her and I didn't want to make her tell me she would try.

Meanwhile, all around the house, the grass kept growing.

When Troy and Brenda moved in downstairs, Troy offered to help. They worked at the Winnebago factory and had matching mullets. I never imagined anybody who wore such terrifying Metallica t-shirts could be so kind. I told Troy it was okay, not to worry about mowing. I know he pitied us as we struggled with that mower, but we didn't want him to tell Barb he was helping and take away part of our discount.

The Little Red Hen was right. Sometimes you just have to do things yourself.

Sooner or later, I'm going to have to spit it out: that summer I had a problem I didn't know what to do about. I didn't get to go to Pine View, though, like Nina.

There's a category of people in the world who aren't supposed to have problems, and I embody it. Not because I try. I'm one of those chronically happy people—an extrovert. I've been called "bubbly," which I think is an overstatement, and people are always saying what a positive attitude I have even when I think I'm being crabby. Can you imagine how annoying that is? Happy people like me are allowed to have little problems like bee stings and bad-hair-days—but no big ones. No existential misery allowed. No sulking. No lying in your room with the lights off because you can't bear to come out. You are the one who will always get off your butt and do something about it, whatever it is. It's like some unwritten law. If you're a tomboy with a healthy tan and a hearty appetite, you work it out yourself. Period. No one takes you seriously when you're down. They can't. They don't believe you.

If you're small and skinny like Nina, with big black eyes and a talent for painting convincing human figures in tortured positions, it's alright to be fraught with problems. It's a plus— like a tasteful accessory. Artists are supposed to be somewhat miserable, from what I gather. Nina grew up in a typical-looking American family with a picket fence and parents who, on Sunday mornings, dressed everyone in matching colors and then came home from church to have fights that ended with broken plates. She says that's why she's an atheist. It's not that I envied her pain—I envied how expertly she managed it.

I didn't ask to be born a robust ball of energy and pragmatism. With sincere Mennonite parents who dutifully raised their daughters to be good, right, and to be nice no matter what. They never shouted, threw plates, made empty threats or broke any rules. No traumas. No excuses. No exceptions. If you're happy and you know it, clap your hands.

Every student goes abroad for a cross-cultural study semester—it's not even a unique experience at our school. I did not expect to come unglued over it when it was my turn. In a tiny town called Los Rios, nestled between the mountains of a tropical dry forest, I practiced Spanish and learned to make indigenous pottery. I'm not the first student to go there, nor the last.

You're supposed to like it well enough; you're not supposed to love it. You're supposed to discover how wonderful your life in Indiana really is. You're supposed to find friends there, not find yourself. It is not supposed to break your heart to get on the bus and ride away three months later, looking out the window at the beautiful waving hands. And you are for sure not supposed to get someone stuck in your heart that you are never going to see again. You're supposed to be delighted to come home.

I told myself I would be happy when my term in Costa Rica was over. I faithfully anticipated my breathtaking reunion with Tom at the airport. A mighty orchestra would play in the background, and he would lift me off my feet. He was tall enough to, and strong like that. Everything knotted in my belly would unwind like a scarf, slip from my shoulders and blow away in the wind. I couldn't picture what would happen next but of course it didn't matter.

I did not want to leave Los Rios.

Inside of me something wailed with the howl of wolves. For the yellow afternoon light on blowing palms, the hourly ruckus of roosters, the belt of the Milky Way stretching from horizon to horizon where moonless nights are black. And for the sweet *guayaba* taste of the boy with the sharp quiet eyes of a hunting bird, who rolled rr's like a purr. But I did what was expected of me: I walked away. I did as I was told.

What's wrong with me?

Why am I so broken?

Everyone babbles on about listening to your heart, but what if your heart tells you to do something ridiculous? Something that makes no sense whatsoever? Then what? And what if you're doing your best to explain to your heart that it's ideas are ill-advised and impossible, but it won't shut up?

The questions echoed back to me, shaking the bedrock below me. I climbed the mountains and valleys of my inner landscape, searched under rocks and in the tops of the trees for answers. It's embarrassing to be overwhelmed by something that sounds that trite when you try to explain it, so I didn't try.

There was Tom at the airport when we landed, the new boyfriend I left for three long months, waiting with hugs and kisses to welcome me home. I clutched him like I was drowning, hoping his arms would make the pain in my chest go away, hoping they would make me back into who I used to be.

I never told him about the rainforest boy. Although, somehow, he knew.

❦

There is no refrigerator in the kitchen. Nothing here requires electricity except the bulb. The kitchen is not even a room in the house; it is a wooden addition with a brushed earth floor connected to the back of the house made of cinderblock. It is neat as a pin. It is virtually empty.

Beside the back door is a woodstove. Is that what I will call it? It does not have a name in my language. They call it the oven but it isn't that either. On top of a roughhewn wooden base, two open-ended clay ovals are placed, and, inside of them, sticks smolder. There is no stovepipe. Thin white smoke escapes through the spaces that are purposefully left between the boards that form the walls, the space below the roof.

The kitchen sink is a sectioned cement tub. It is set through the wall so that the drain runs into the scorched yard where chickens dash around clucking. Cool water comes from a faucet with a round metal knob like the one outside the farmhouse where my mother hooked up the garden hose on dry August evenings. The sink is also the washer, where every morning Hilda, who asks me to call her Mamá, scrubs the clothes of the day before into spotless submission and drapes them over the barbed wire fence at the back of the yard to dry.

In the shallow section of the sink sets a clay pot, its opening covered by a lid. Inside the pot, the half shell of a round nut called a jiícaro *floats on water. When we are thirsty, we reach into the pot, scoop water into the jiícaro and lift it to our lips, cool water running down our chins in the smoke-blackened kitchen. Curling mango leaves skitter and sun stripes slip across the floor.*

In this kitchen, more than anywhere else, I am a foreigner. Here, I not only have no words, I am helpless. I do not know how to wash my own clothes. I cannot fry an egg. We do not have cereal or apples or bread. We have rice, beans, tortillas made of corn that my papá, called Tito, grinds. We have canned tuna, sometimes a tomato, a strange sweet custard made of purple corn, stewed chicken for a birthday. When Diego, who says he is my brother, goes fishing and brings home little bagre, *mamá Hilda fries them in boiling vegetable lard, eyeballs and all, and we devour them down to the brains in their heads, driven by a need for nutrients for which we have no names.*

❧❧

Tom says he used to watch me in the library. That's impossible, because I used to watch him in the library, berating myself for being so Mennonite and ordinary. He sat across from me in the lounge, absorbed in whatever book lay in his lap, looking unattainable with his batik shirt and Eskimo moccasins, a bandana tied around that ring of curls. Sometimes he fell asleep, and then I could stare at him as long as I wanted. I convinced myself that he came from somewhere exotic, that he wasn't even a Mennonite—or not one with a boring pedigree like me. His hair was too long and curly. His skin was too olive. And he did not buy those beaded mukluks at Payless. His grandfather was Native American? His mother is Mexican? Was he born and raised in Czechoslovakia? The first half of my sophomore year passed and I didn't even know his name, just that I wanted a boyfriend like him someday. I swear he never once glanced up at me. He says it's the other way around.

We met during finals week, as if, in spite of everything that was right about us, destiny had other ideas. He walked, with my friend Matthew, into the dorm lounge where I sat slouched over my Theatre Set Design project, slaving with glue and an exact-o knife, sometime between midnight and sunrise. There I was, far beyond the reach of any human emotion and most coherent speech, my eyes plastered open by pure caffeine, in a horrible coffee-stained sweatshirt and let's not talk about my hair. Matthew introduced us, incredulous that we hadn't already met. At that point, I couldn't even care. After meeting me in my bleary, catatonic state, there was no way he would ever like me. There went that possibility.

Or not. We found each other at the Christmas dance on Saturday night and it was clear that my red eyes and coffee stains hadn't repulsed him the way I expected they would. That had never happened to me before—the delirious synchronicity of being crazy about someone who is simultaneously crazy about me. He told me I was the most beautiful girl in the school, which was completely ridiculous. Me: the most average white American girl in the fifty states. I don't think so. Monica is more beautiful. She's skinny as a supermodel and grew up in Belize. Camila is more beautiful, with her fearsome blonde hair, combat boots and self-confidence. And Beth. Hello? Beth is twenty times more beautiful than I am. She's slim and brown and I would give my left leg for her curly hair. Lucky for me, Tom saw no comparison.

Everything was right except the timing. Two weeks into our newborn romance, Christmas break split us apart, and then I left for the winter term in Costa Rica that I couldn't find my way back from.

I thought it would go away. That's how it works, right? I was sure those nights in The Pit of Sin would speed the day.

The only naked man I'd ever seen before that summer was the guy in the biology textbooks with arrows and labels along the sides. This gave me the basic idea of what to expect, but the possibility of being confronted by a living example scared the devil out of me. I tried to be calm. I told myself to be brave. Tom must not sense my naiveté or for sure he would get up and leave in his whitey-tighties.

Tom, as it turns out, came from the same kind of upright Mennonite family as I do, in spite of his intriguing footwear, and was every bit as virginal and uncertain.

It takes a long time to learn to hear beyond the zealous youth pastor in your head, but you can do it if you don't give up. In the Pit among the boxes and snow boots, we worked out a new set of rules, messing up the sheets, falling off the bed, giggling and shushing each other until the early summer dawn.

వ

In May and June, the college offered intensive courses with the full twelve-week curriculum crammed into three, a merciless and unproductive method for learning anything whatsoever. It was a miserable experience for both professors and students during a time of year when nobody with any sense wants to spend their days inside.

The Theatre department didn't offer any summer classes, so I signed up for two English classes with Beth: Literature of Transgression and Pardon, then Twentieth Century Thought in Literature. Those classes marked the beginning and the end of my ill-fated English minor. Sheila took Phys World, billed as "basic physics for non-science majors." It was terrible—I took it the next summer. Science majors weren't required to take remedial Theatre classes, so how was this fair? Nina had her job in the Admissions office and her personal problems.

In the first literature class, we were subjected to a relic of an Irish history fanatic who could draw a parallel between Ireland and anything you could name. Poor Professor Williams lost his trains of thought or missed them completely, confused book titles, confused class schedules, confused us, fell asleep, put us to sleep, and inspired me with a profound desire to flee academia while I still had the spark of life in me. I had thought I wanted to minor in English, but this was not at all what I had in mind. What an unnerving experience to hate the first class you take in your own minor. But, I reasoned, it can only get better. I'll make sure never to have Professor Williams again—if he somehow lives to see another school year.

Professor Mary Perry, who taught our second class, was one of those brilliant eccentrics. She gave the first impression of being crazy, but only because she had zero concern for what people think of her. She believed in ghosts and fairies, for example, and amused her literature students with bizarre digressions on subjects like the digestive systems of cows. I don't know what that had to do with anything. One minute we were discussing Rilke and the next she was expounding on how cows chew the grass, barf it up into their own mouths, and chew it again. I missed the connection.

The fact that she became my lifelong friend did not prevent me, I'm sorry to say, from hating her class almost as much as I hated Professor Williams'. This was not a good time for me to meet up with existentialism, Nietzsche, *Death in Venice* and *Mrs. Dalloway.*

When the Registrar's office opened in the fall, I walked in and dropped my English minor like a hot rock.

Beth says that *Mrs. Dalloway* is a fabulous book and that I should give it another try. Then again, Beth loves all books categorically. I gave *Mrs. Dalloway* my best shot, but I couldn't keep track of what was happening. Nothing made any sense. Clarissa was too much like me, maybe—everything moving at different speeds, times and places refusing to stand still, things escaping from their contexts.

Sometimes in the middle of class I had to hold my breath so I wouldn't start crying for no apparent reason. Not about *Mrs. Dalloway.* About everything. I had stepped off the plane from Costa Rica a week before summer classes started and flopped back into academia like a fish not worth frying. I tried my hardest to be okay, but somewhere inside me I couldn't get my balance. Like when you put on someone else's glasses and all of the sudden you're dizzy. I tried to concentrate on inanimate objects, hoping to make the world stop spinning, but it didn't work.

This was the wrong time for me to contemplate questions of existence. It was the wrong time for me to read the literature of fracture and confusion. I sat in those classes and wondered things, but not the kind of things my hopeful professors would have wanted.

I wondered about Abraham. When God called him to leave his people and go to a strange land, did he think he was going crazy?

What would have happened if I hadn't left Los Rios?

How long until I am happy again?

Am I doing something wrong?

What is the matter with me?

I wondered about my deserted rainforest boy. He spread his blanket on the dry stubble near the middle of the plaza and we lay there in the dark underneath everything that ever was. I asked him what he wanted to do in his life. He said *trabajar* like I had asked him a silly question. Then he asked me the same thing. I said *escribir*. He said *escribir que?* I said *cosas.* He said *aquí puede escribir cosas.* Which is perfectly true.

I wondered if I was losing my mind.

I wondered if you could go ahead and lose your mind without anyone noticing. Or would it be like the guy we read about who turned into a cockroach? Would it be obvious?

I hate that story.

Something about him reminded me of a bird—as if he could lift, circle, and disappear into the tamarindo trees along the quebrada. There was an eagle in his face—in the set of his eyes and the curve of his lip. Something fierce and delicate, at home in high, quiet places.

He bowed his head, intently drawing on raw clay vases with a nail driven through a piece of wood. The winged serpents that live in his ancestral memory crept through the sharp point into daylight. When he looked up into my face, I knew things I had no words for. Things that live in my bones.

When words are absent, everything else speaks: slim brown fingers holding the rough tool, a shiny black ceramic surface, wind, the dog scratching her flees in the shade, a hen scolding her chicks, a neighbor laughing, parakeets, breath that goes in and out of everything and fills the quiet world.

How will I say in words what I understand in silence? If I trap it in syllables, how can it be true?

My life called to me from the dust gathered on my feet, and I heard it but I didn't know who it was that spoke.

❦

Beth is my best friend and she has been since we were fifteen. We met on the first day of our second year of high school, both of us cursed with having to start the day in gym class. Do not underestimate the gravity of this for fifteen-year-old girls who spend the wee hours of school mornings in the clutches of curling irons. All that work, just to have Mr. Snavely smile at us, roll his eyes, and tell us to go get our gym shorts on. He was young and kind of cute, and he never questioned the way we all needed to sit out because of our periods with astonishing frequency.

Our school didn't have that many black girls. Beth isn't exactly black, she's more like brown, and there weren't that many brown girls either. Anyway, believe me when I say the eye-catching thing about Beth that morning wasn't her skin tone or her curls, it was her outfit. She wore a bright yellow blouse under a scarlet red jumper—or was it the other way around? And she had enormous pink-tinted glasses, like the ones I wanted but my mom said mine were fine.

It's not that my fashion choices were any less dubious. What does a Mennonite girl who loves school more than life itself do in anticipation of starting 10th grade? She makes herself a new skirt. Oh yes. A lovely calf-length, red, white, and teal striped thing, with an extra-wide waistband and box pleats. This demonstration of my domestic ability made me feel so capable. I tied a matching teal ribbon around the neck of my white button-down blouse. The dress code at the Mennonite high school forbade pants for female students from time immemorial until the year after Beth and I graduated. Seriously. The year after.

I smiled at her because she didn't seem to know anyone.

"Hi. I'm Beth," she said, like it was the best news of my life.

It was.

Beth was the friendliest, funniest girl I ever met. Mr. Snavely made us warm up by running around the soccer field while he studied his stopwatch. Beth and I always ran together—if you can call it running. We giggled, gossiped, and tried to trot as slowly as we could without walking. She told me that her mom grew up Mennonite in Kansas, and that her dad is from Kenya. He was a student at the university when her mom arrived in a group of missionaries charged with teaching English and Sunday School to the children of nomads. He already spoke English, and he didn't care about Sunday School, but he liked to invent reasons to visit this certain American teacher.

Beth's family lived in some part of New York City now, and Beth was staying here in the dorm. Beth's mom came to this school, too, and lived in the dorm—all the way from Kansas. I didn't know anyone from any of those places, not even the dorm. It explained to me how she got her cinnamon tan and uncontrollable hair, why she sang all the words to rock songs we weren't allowed to listen to, and why she couldn't believe our mall was closed on Sundays. I envied everything about her. She ate whatever she wanted and never put on a pound of pudge. I felt like a rosy pink pig next to her long, dark, exquisite sort of beauty.

Beth is pretty resilient. She doesn't pull her own hair out or lock herself in the bedroom and refuse to speak to anyone. The whole time we were in high school, I never thought once about how having an African dad might matter to a person. Parents were parents in my estimation, a necessary evil and worthy of as little attention as possible. A talent for mechanical reasoning doesn't prohibit me from being painfully dumb.

Now I know she was mortified. Now I know she would have given anything to look like me—like nobody, like everybody, like all the other fifteen-year-old girls with two hundred years of Mennonite lineage in Pennsylvania. Now I understand that she was confused and frightened by this Mennonite high school built on the somber principles of our German ancestors, where the girls still had to wear skirts and no rock music was allowed—or lipstick, or jewelry, or dancing, and every school day began with church. Now I get that she felt like she landed on another planet. I'm sure she tried to tell me then, too, but I couldn't understand. She landed on the only planet I knew.

❦

"Can I ask you a question?"

"Yes."

"What is it that you liked so much about Los Rios?"

I took a deep breath and watched the steam from Beth's first cup of morning coffee curl around her with her hair. We were sitting on the porch with our bare feet on the top stair. She hadn't asked me much about Los Rios yet and I hadn't volunteered. I didn't know how to bring it up.

"I don't know."

"I mean, besides warm weather and all. Because I don't think it's just the weather you fell in love with."

"Right. It's not just the weather." I took a deep breath. How am I supposed to explain something I can't get my head around? "I'm trying to figure it out too."

"Is it the boy?"

"No," I said, staring past my coffee at the grass below us. "I mean yes, but no. Not just him. Yeah, everybody was nice and everything was all gorgeous. But. It has something to do with me."

"What do you mean?"

"About how I was."

"How were you?"

"I was—just me. Nobody there knew me. At all. I was just myself. And it's okay to be a little weird when you're a foreigner. You know?"

She coughed a laugh and raised her mug for a coffee toast. "Good point."

"Nobody expected me to be any certain way. I could just be."

"Were you different?"

"No. Not really. That's why it doesn't make any sense."

"Who says it has to make sense? You can love anything you want."

"Yeah, I guess."

"You can."

"I know. I..."

I'd wanted so much to try to tell her everything about it—every minute. Now she was asking, and where were the words?

"There were no parents. Or somebody who goes to their church. Or might know somebody who goes to their church. Y'know? No professors. Nobody who knows anybody that knows me. Nobody who ever even heard of a Mennonite. They think *Menonitas* are the same as Mormons."

Beth gulped her mouthful of coffee so she wouldn't spit it out when she laughed.

"I never had that," I said. "I'm used to people taking one look at me and asking if I'm from Pennsylvania. In Pennsylvania, old ladies I've never seen before walk up to me and ask me if I'm a Zimmerman."

Beth nodded and blew into her mug. She has problems in life but that's not one of them.

"People there kept asking me if I'm related to Madonna."

Beth wasn't prepared for an explosion of laughter and this time she spat hot black coffee all over the stairs. That made me laugh too, and I spat my coffee off the side of the porch, down onto where our waiting bikes were parked.

"Madonna?!"

"I'm serious!"

"Did you spit that all over my bike?"

"You spit on my feet!"

We had to set our mugs down or the rest would have been on our feet and our bikes as well.

"I'm so sorry!"

"It's okay."

"What did you say? Did you tell them she's your cousin?"

"No!"

"Why not? I would have."

It's true. She would have. Beth thinks of everything. To be honest, it didn't even occur to me. I could have been Madonna's cousin.

Hell, I could have been her sister.

❧

Somebody who lived in the apartment before us forgot their red lightbulb in a drawer of The Desk. They probably thought a colored light in the living room would be cool, which is what we thought when we found it. It didn't take long, though, for us to figure out how something as awesome as an actual red lightbulb ended up forgotten in the drawer of a desk. Although you could see enough by its glow to avoid falling headlong down the obsolete interior stairway to the first-floor apartment, you couldn't read by it, and what were we doing here if we couldn't read? We had to put the regular bulb back if we were going to pass our summer classes, and the red one went into the drawer where it came from.

Until the weekend. The red lightbulb was perfect for parties. We called them Red Light parties in honor of the bulb that set the room on fire, the sultry color suggesting indecencies that each and every one of us would have been far too mortified to commit. The living room didn't even look like ours with the red light on. Our faded pink couch became a beautiful burgundy. The splotches on our filthy carpet faded away, and even the friends we saw every day in class appeared different and somehow surprising.

Being underage and being as it was summer, we had two main problems to solve every time we went for the red bulb. One: How to get alcohol? And two: Who to invite? I was almost 21, but almost isn't good enough so Tom had to buy our wine. That is so lame. I tried going into Reynolds Liquors myself, once, but of course the guy at the cash register asked to see my ID when I set the big jug of wine on the counter. I had to say I forgot it and act like I couldn't believe I had been that dumb. The Carlo Rossi family size cost $7.00 at Reynolds. It tastes like sugared vinegar, but we all liked the "blush" well enough, and $7.00 split by four is $1.75 each. It's a better deal than Boone's Farm.

Solving the second problem was trickier, especially after the summer term ended and everyone who had someplace more interesting to go went there. Curtis and Tony Royal came to our Red Light parties before they left to backpack through Europe. Dan came while he was around. Of course Tom was always there. Dan's best friend Colin came up until the night he kissed Beth and she was so repulsed she wouldn't let us invite him anymore. That was us.

Sometimes Sheila's Elementary Ed friends came. They were nice enough. A pack of future second grade teachers doesn't exactly bring the house down, though. Sometimes Beth's new International Student Union friends came, but they never stayed around long because Beth said at their parties they always have piles of food, and we never had any. Sometimes my hippy theatre friends came smelling of patchouli. Sometimes Nina's artist friends came with their long bangs lopped over one eye. And sometimes pretty much no one came at all. You never knew what to expect. We always tried to get Nina's brother Anthony to come, but I think he was afraid of us.

I climbed up on The Desk to exchange the lightbulbs, Beth popped a Bob Marley tape into the stereo, Nina poured our wine into coffee mugs, and we were ready. We danced and gulped sour wine, laughed, pretended to argue and invented silly drinking games. Beth smoked cigarettes on the porch with Curtis. I tried to teach Tom how to salsa. He hated that. Colin and Dan told us stories about the missionary school they went to in Kenya—like how they got sent home from 3rd grade for putting a tarantula on the teacher's chair. Nina, who forgot to eat again, threw up in the bathroom. That's pretty much it.

The only thing I hated was when "No Woman, No Cry" came on. When I listen to that tape on my own I can fast-forward through it, but I can't do that in a room full of dancing people. Everyone else loves that song. They would've all stopped dancing and yelled, "Hey! What are you doing?! I love this song!" and then I would've have to explain. Not an option. I had to hold my breath through almost the entire thing, and if I'd already drank a lot—if my toes tingled and my lips felt numb—it was better for me to go lock myself in the bathroom. That way I wouldn't faint from trying not to cry.

He loved that song—the boy in Los Rios. The potter who I was going to forget. We put *Legend* and some C batteries in the tape player and sat under the tamarindo tree in the merciful night that falls early at the equator. He didn't know of Bob Marley or reggae music. He asked me to play it again and again.

I didn't know how to translate it. "*No Mujer—No Llore,*" asking a woman not to cry, or "*No Mujer, No Llanto,*" like women cause you to cry, and none of one equals none of the other. I couldn't even explain my confusion. I just said "*No Mujer No Llorar*" and he reached his dark fingers to touch my face and said, "*No llore, mujer.*" Then he teased me and asked me, "*Vas a llorar?*" I said, "*No.*" He said, "*Yo sí.*"

I didn't, either.

Then.

Now, my stomach and my heart kept doing something where they made me feel like I was choking. Not trying to push air in and out helped. Cold water helped too. Sometimes I had to stay there on the bathroom floor crumbled like I'm praying toward Mecca until half way through "Could You Be Loved."

After we drank all our wine, smoked all our cigarettes, and danced to songs that said things like "Legalize it" and "we share the shelter of my single bed," we couldn't think of any more rules to break. Nobody wanted the party to be over, though, so we dragged pillows and blankets from the bedrooms to the living room floor, and giant gab sessions ensued.

I'm the sleepyhead. For all the enthusiasm I can have about a party at 10 PM—and I can have a lot—I'm the first one down. Beth and Sheila could discuss politics and religion until the sky paled from black to gray, but I always fell asleep while it was still black. Even Tom could stay up arguing that everyone should just live and let live. It's not that I don't care or didn't want to be cool. I tried. But I would float away by accident while the words spun around me.

Morning found us all sound asleep in a giant tangle, the door standing wide open letting in the early chill, the red light burning, pale now, above us.

The parents of normal American college students would be thrilled to discover that that their kids, on weekends, were dancing in their own living room, drinking cheap wine and falling asleep with their clothes on. Right? Not ours. Oh no. Ours would have gone into cardiac arrest. They pictured us playing Rook and drinking Pepsi. But our parents are not normal Americans and neither are we. Our parents are Mennonites and we are what comes after.

We have to figure out how to live in the world they tried so hard to shelter us from, with all of the martyrs they gave us. And the rules. Maybe I've got an extra bad case of this vertigo because my parents still lived on a farm, and I'm kind of trying to make a two-generation leap, here. Everybody else's *grandparents* lived on farms. Their parents got day jobs and lived in houses with elaborate flower beds and even though they sang four-part harmony like nobody's business, their moms wore lipstick and their dads went to things like baseball games. Not mine. It wouldn't cross their minds. On both sides of my family, my generation was the first to unpin the coverings from our heads and go to college. Some of us, anyway.

I dreamed someone was frying bacon. As I started to awaken I could still smell it, and I tried to stay asleep. I knew it was a dream. It was impossible that there could be bacon in this house because we couldn't afford bacon, and no one would be cooking it as I slept, because I always woke up first. Then I was awake, lying on the living room floor between Tom and Beth. My head hurt. Hot late-morning sun poured in the window over a pile of people with sheets and legs sticking out. I was so thirsty I thought I might die. And somebody was definitely in my kitchen frying bacon.

I untangled myself and went to see. Colin and Dan were standing over the stove fixing our motley family a home-style hangover breakfast of pancakes with syrup, eggs with bacon, orange juice, coffee, and toast. They said they were trying to be quiet but they were doing a pretty terrible job of it. Colin said he woke up because he was hot. Dan said he woke up because he was hungry. Colin said he got paid on Friday and let's make breakfast. Dan said yeah dude.

Colin was so generous I will never get my head around it. That was his paycheck. Who does that?

After a feast in which we stuffed our hangovers with foods forgotten to our impoverished diet, we had "church." Why not? It was Sunday morning. We sang every Bob Dylan song Colin could play on his guitar, Nina read a Sylvia Plath poem and then I read from *The Prophet*: "Think you that the spirit is a still pool which you can trouble with a staff?"

Then we had to get back to our homework.

Here's some Mennonite history according to me. I had to study it in high school—and I got an A—so I used to know a lot more about it. This is what I've managed to remember: The Catholic Church had its panties in a twist, having lost a limb to the Reformation. The Protestant Church, all zealous and new, was on a roll stamping out heresy wherever they smelled it. Nobody had a shred of patience for the blasphemy coming from a batch of rabble-rousers in Zurich. These trouble-makers called themselves Anabaptists before their sect got named after Menno Simons, and their primary offense was the new ideas they preached about baptism. You might not think that's something to lose your head over, but Menno Simons and Conrad Grebel did. Whereas everybody else was baptizing infants, the Anabaptists said that baptism should be a symbol of adult choice to follow Christ. They required a lifestyle of simplicity and rejected all forms of violence. Even violence in self-defense.

It seems innocuous to me. How dangerous is a group of people whose hallmark is that they won't defend themselves? I guess you had to be there.

It was a dreadful time to present a new idea—about anything. The feuding Catholics and Protestants found one thing to agree on: get rid of these Mennonites. They arrested the Mennonite thinkers and hung them above the city in cages to die in public for being heretics. For generations, Mennonites were pursued. Their tongues were torn from their throats. They were hunted, threatened, chased, captured, tortured, burned at the stake, stretched to pieces, decapitated, drowned, or dragged to death behind horses. How's that for a children's story?

The survivors scattered throughout northern Europe where foreign governments tolerated them but let's not confuse that with hospitality. The opportunity to settle on another continent called "The New World" was the best news they ever heard.

In the days when Pennsylvania was still a colony, a Mennonite man named Hans Brubaker purchased 1,000 acres of land from William Penn. He came to America on a ship with 300 other Swiss and German Mennonite immigrants, praying to find peace and a homeland.

Hans cleared woodlands to create fields for planting. He married a woman named Anna. He built a house, a barn, a mill on the river for grinding grain. He fathered children, who fathered children, who lived in his house and farmed his land, passing it on to their sons and to their grandsons. The last one was my grandpa.

I played on the stairs of his rambling farmhouse and took naps on the bed in my mother's childhood bedroom for eight years, until Grandpa sold the farm at a public auction. The city that was barely a town when Hans felled the first tree opened its jaws on all sides and swallowed the farm whole. The mayor's office declared the house and the barn to be historical monuments and wrote into law that nobody may change their exterior structure, ever.

This is where I come from. This is who I am.

Or who I was.
Or who I thought I was.
Or who I started out as?

For sure, it's who I was supposed to be.

❦

Mennonites don't do alcohol, at least not the kind of Mennonites I come from. We learn that the "wine" in the Bible was really grape juice; they just called it "wine" back then. It's interesting. On communion Sunday we eat real bread, and at some churches they actually kneel down to wash each other's feet. But of course Jesus didn't mean for us to drink *wine*. Drinking alcohol of any kind is a sin like lying, stealing, and committing adultery. I never questioned this for a minute.

Until I got to college.

Several Mennonite colleges exist, and my parents said I could pick whichever one I wanted to obtain what I expected would be my psychology degree. I tossed out the Canadian ones because that seemed unnecessary, those in dull and distant places like Kansas, and anything that ended in "Bible College." That left me with two finalists: the "good" one to the south, and the "bad" one to the west. Almost everybody from my school who didn't get married and start having babies right away went to one of the two. The virtuous kids who wanted to be nurses and youth pastors went south. The troublemakers who did things like wear "Question Authority" t-shirts went west.

I surprised everybody and picked the bad one. It's not that I thought I was bad or aspired to become bad—I'm just curious. If I go to the *good* Mennonite college, I reasoned, I know what will happen to me. I could already envision my life described in one paragraph like the summary on the back cover of a book. I'll go to college, get married to a Mennonite boy, have a lovely Mennonite family, make lots of pies, get old and die. Or something like that. But if I go to the *bad* Mennonite college? Who knows? If I go to the bad Mennonite college, all bets are off. Anything could happen. Maybe I'll marry a Mennonite boy and make pie. Maybe not.

I heard that some students who graduated from our pious high school in the womb of the Mennonite motherland and went to the bad Mennonite college decided it was alright to drink. They felt fine about it, and not at all in danger of hellfire. I even knew a girl who became a feminist and stopped shaving her legs. There were male students at that college, somebody said, that sometimes wore skirts. Because they felt like it. Could that be true? The daughter of our substitute math teacher started sleeping with her boyfriend after she went to the bad Mennonite college. She didn't lie about or apologize for it, either. I couldn't begin to imagine how you stop thinking that's a sin, because it says right in the Bible that it is. But I had to know. How? It wasn't that I wanted to do all the bad things. I wanted to figure out how you decide they aren't bad anymore. That's all. Really.

I stopped shaving my legs almost right away. Only the dorky girls who should have gone to the good Mennonite college shaved. The cool girls said it's sexist to define female beauty as the skinny, hairless, pre-pubescent body of a little girl. Some of them didn't wear bras. They said that being ashamed of your breasts is assimilating patriarchal oppression. I tried that, too, but it was an unpleasant experience, and I strapped my oppression back on at the first available opportunity.

I quit going to church. Who was watching over me? Who was going to scold? We had to attend a certain number of the daily campus Chapel services, or they wouldn't let us graduate—that should be more than enough. "Chapel" is church on a weekday.

I got invited to parties where people were drinking alcohol right in front of me, and had a riotous time with drunk people who, I discovered, instead of being scary, are incredibly friendly. But I still wasn't interested in trying it, myself. I heard about somebody's roommate who got drunk for the first time at one of those parties. She peed her pants on the way home. And her shoes. No way in hell was I about to risk that. Make a drunken freshman fool out of myself? Nope. I had no idea what that fire-water might do to me, and this fear overpowered my usual curiosity.

Besides, not only is drinking frowned upon by my genes and forbidden by the college, but when you're still eighteen it is also illegal. Just the thought of getting busted by the cops—and I heard of this happening weekend after weekend—petrified me into complete sobriety. For my whole first year of college.

Then the theatre students packed up and followed our professor to London for the three-week History of Theatre course in the heart of a city where the drinking age is eighteen. There, in a pub called The Zetland Arms, in the presence of the friends who fruitlessly offered me every drink you can imagine for months on end, I ordered a rum and coke.

I thought they were going to faint. Some of them clapped. I smiled and shrugged.

It was strange—sweet and somehow piquant, with an end that made me shiver. I sipped it slowly and ordered another. The crisp edges in the room softened, and Mean Tabitha, who I never really liked, became friendly as a sister. My toes tingled and my lips became slightly numb.

"How do you feel?" Mean Tabitha asked me, and in the friendliest gesture she ever made, laid her long red curls against my shoulder.

"Good," I said. "My lips feel kind of weird."

Shrieks of laughter burst from her wide red mouth, and she hugged me, nearly knocking us both off our chairs, squealing, "You're drunk! You're drunk!" in unreasonable delight.

I wasn't drunk, but I was somewhere I'd never been before, that much is true. And my fear of this mysterious liquid that could rob you of your senses evaporated like dawn mist in the morning sun. This is what all that fuss is about? This is the terrible soul-stealing sin? This is the devil brew? I giggled all the way back up the street arm-in-arm with Mean Tabitha thinking, "This is the last time I am letting somebody else tell me what to be afraid of."

It pretty much was.

I wanted to be a psychologist ever since I outgrew my elementary-school ambition to be an acrobat or an astronomer. People interest me. Emotions interest me, and I have a lot of them. I've been recording them in rambling diaries ever since I was nine years old, kind of as if I were my own case study. During high school summers, I read psychology textbooks and Carl Jung because I wanted to get a head start.

My English teachers always said I should be an English teacher because of how much I love to read and write. I thought about it. But here's the thing: I'm going to read and write whether I'm an English teacher or not, and at least if I'm something else, I can read and write whatever I want. The thing I most love to write is poetry and if you think I was going to go to college so people could tell me how to write my own poems, you have to be crazy. And then grow up to tell other people how to write their poems? I don't think so. I compromised. Psychology major, English minor.

I declared my major and minor when I registered for college, but before my brand-new linens lost their crunchy crinkle, I ditched psychology and changed my major to Theatre. The good Mennonite college didn't even offer a Theatre major. They had "Communications" which is a fancy name for the media, which is not the same.

Part of the reason I switched majors was math. On my last day of high school, I kicked my calculus textbook across the room, and would have been suspended if there'd been another day to miss. That isn't like me. I'm usually better at self-restraint. But for twelve years I hated math with the pure blue flame of loathing, and for twelve years I did it anyway. I never imagined that psychology required the study of statistics. I missed that in the story about Pavlov's salivating dogs. My hatred for, and inability concerning, math is so profound that nothing was going to draw me back into its clutches, not even psychology. I was not taking any more math. Period. The end.

The other thing is that Theatre is fun. I got a student job as a stage hand for campus events, and the theatre people seemed to like me. They invited me to their parties and tried to convince me to drink beer, which I would have none of. They let me help build the set for the fall play and told me I was a natural. They told me about their exciting classes like Acting, Theatre Set Design, and the History of Theatre class that went to London every other year. This year they were all going, and I could go too if I was a Theatre major. All I had to do was talk to the Registrar and for four years my work would be like play. Did I really want to spend my life sitting in an office listening to people's problems, anyway? Statistics I and II, or History of Theatre in London? Could it be more obvious?

The day I changed my major I hit my head so hard that I fell flat on the floor, but that was afterward. I went to the Registrar's office and filled out the paper she passed me. She smiled, congratulated me, and it was done. Then I bounced back to my dorm room to write a letter to my parents, telling them the happy news which I did not expect to make them happy at all. Our family didn't go to the theatre, except for high school plays. We didn't go to movies, either, except for ones like Mountain Family Robinson, and travelogues where somebody shows films they spliced together of national parks they visited on vacation. Theatre, like all art and music of non-religious verbiage, was overtly gratuitous. It suggested sins that began with vanity and ended with God-only-knows what.

But I had the card to trump it all: this was a Mennonite college, therefore my parents had to approve. If the Psychology program was acceptable, then the Theatre program was too.

Right?

I planted myself on a stack of pillows under my side of the hinged loft-beds that Dad and I built in the garage and then assembled in the room. Four pages of giddy delight poured from my pen.

My parents and I weren't in the habit of calling each other—we did our chatting through the mail. Mennonites are frugal like that. Long distance phone calls are expensive, and postage stamps were 29 cents. Waste not, want not. More with less. Anyway, the mail works fine unless you're having an emergency. And it makes things like this easier. My parents called the phone in my dorm room to say things like "Happy Birthday," but I couldn't dial outside the area code. If I needed to ask whether or not my fever was dangerous or when my last tetanus shot was, I could call them collect on the pay phone in the basement beside the washers.

I did my earnest best to tell my parents something they wouldn't want to hear in such a way that they couldn't say much more than, "How nice." Then I was ready to toss the envelope in campus mail. I folded the letter and leapt from my seat on the floor, forgetting that the loft bed was lowered into the perpendicular sleeping position. My head slammed into the plywood that held my mattress, and I landed on the floor on my back beside my own good news.

I didn't know whether to laugh or cry, so I did some of both before I tried again, slower this time. I hoped it wasn't an omen. I could always assert that I don't believe in omens, if anyone suggested it was.

❦

I'd never even heard of the Grateful Dead until I arrived at college. If my life had a soundtrack, it would begin with hymns in four-part harmony, ladies singing Bible songs to autoharps, and my dad's gospel bluegrass. I ventured onto the slippery slope of Christian Rock at about fourteen because, as the song says, "Why should the devil have all the good music?" You don't go straight from Bill Gaither to *Steal Your Face*. Sting seemed harmless, then U2, then REM, and then one day my mom busted me with a Cure tape. I should have known better than to leave it lying beside my stereo. The picture of giant red lips on the outside of the lyric sheet was bad enough, but the words on the underside made her cheeks burn and earned me a lecture on Christian values. After that, I borrowed only dubs.

The name "The Grateful Dead" doesn't sound like my kind of music and the idea of groupies called Deadheads freaked me out a little. Then this weird guy who tried college but dropped out a few weeks later told me that Deadheads were actually dead people, and when he said it he was dead serious. His eyes went large and round, and he wasn't trying to be funny. He said it was all satanic.

When I heard the Grateful Dead for the first time, I fell in love before I even realized who I was hearing. I didn't know that the Grateful Dead was hippy music, or that the guy driving the VW bus with the tie-dyed curtains at the windows would obviously not be playing anything else. He offered me a ride from the grocery store back to campus, and I recognized him as the roommate of some of my theatre friends. As I climbed into the incense and cigarette saturated bus, music with a keyboard trickling like the morning sunshine caught me off guard.

"Who is this?" I asked.

"The Dead," he replied, perplexed. He clearly thought I would know that. *Wake of the Flood.*

"Oh," I said trying not to sound confused. "It's great."

"Yeah, it's a good one."

This didn't sound like the satanic music you'd expect zombies to listen to.

The shaggy-headed tie-dyed friends I was making were so brave. They questioned the rules. They were the theatre students and the music students and the ones who had by far the best parties. They did things that I thought might be morally wrong like smoking pot and sleeping with their girlfriends but they were so nice. They didn't seem dangerous to me or to each other, and they were definitely not already dead.

I understood I'd found the perfect guy when I learned that Tom liked the Grateful Dead too. I discovered that on the night we smuggled tequila into the library and I kissed him because he was too shy to kiss me first. I knew we were meant to be. This is The One I prayed, all my boyfriendless life, that God would send me. I was in love with his broad shoulders. And his long hair. And patchouli oil, too? You see? Jesus does love me.

Beth wasn't wild about the Grateful Dead, although she did attempt to like them, at least at first, out of friendly solidarity. She failed. Nina and Sheila thought it was old-people music, which left only Tom on my side.

I didn't mean to take sides with Tom about something; it just kind of happened. It's a serious misdemeanor to side with your boyfriend—against your girlfriends—about anything. That is a breach of The Unwritten Rules of True Feminism. And no it doesn't matter if it is something as inconsequential as liking a rock band full of old white guys. Boyfriends are men in disguise, like wolves in sheep's clothing. You start off down that road; you have no idea where it will take you. The next thing you know you could find yourself letting them open doors for you and make suggestions about your hair or clothes.

The more weeks that ticked past, the more it seemed to matter—not the music itself, but our beads and our wavy dancing and the way Tom and I and our other friends could blow off anything with the slightest whiff of "politics" as being "bullshit." Nina, Sheila, and Beth were concerned about what we brushed away. Desert Storm. Something called a Balkan War. Winnie Mandela sentenced to jail. At first it was all about which tape to put in the stereo. I played the Dead. Nina played the Eurythmics. Sheila played C+C Music Factory. Beth played Arrested Development.

Later, it was about everything.

❧❧

I do not know how to eat the soup.

An enormous bowl sets on the table in front of me with floating fist-sized potatoes, gristly chunks of meat, yucca, whole carrots, halved ears of corn. And a spoon.

My mamá *Hilda smiles at me because she is pleased to have made me something special.* "Coma," *she says.* "¿No le gusta la sopa?"

I like soup and I am hungry, but I don't know what to do. The soups that I am familiar with consist of small-cut meat and vegetables, not these ingredients boiled whole. I look again, but she has not given me a knife. She stands smiling at me in confused expectation as I blink helplessly at my plate.

I must find some words I can use in this language, and I have so few.

"No entiendo," *I say.* "¿Cómo?"

"Ay mamita," *she says, through an accidental giggle, and asks me if I've never eaten soup before.* "Así," *she says, and taking my spoon, she slices off a piece of potato and offers it to me as if I were a giant 20-year-old baby.*

"Ah," *I say.* "Gracias." *I take the spoon.*

Mamá Hilda disappears into the kitchen and then joins me with a steaming bowl for herself. The delicious broth is scalding hot, and I spill it on the table as I chop at the carrot and then at the corn with my dull utensil.

"No no," *she interrupts me.* "El maíz, no. Ay mamita. No sabe comer la sopa," *and she giggles again.* "Mire," *she commands. She dips her fingers into the boiling broth, fishes out the ear of corn and bites the kernels from it in the way of every summer.*

"¿Ya?" *she asks me, meaning do I need more help or do I get it now.*

"Sí," *I say.* "Ya."

"Provecho."

"Gracias. Igual."

I know nothing. Not how to eat, not how to speak. All my life, I have heard people talk of being born again and although this is not what they meant, I see that this is its truer meaning.

When we are finished, our faces shine with sweat and soup.

❦

Before we even ran out of clean underwear or decided something had to be done about the bedding, the kitchen towels presented a problem. At least to me they did. How do you clean up a mess with something that's dirty? Believe me, I tried. It's hopeless because no matter how careful you are, you only make the mess bigger. We had three towels at first, but were already down to two since Sheila set one on fire. They had to double as hot pads for removing boiling pots from the flames of our gas stove—an excellent way to set their little fringes ablaze, burn yourself, nearly set the house on fire, and destroy a perfectly good kitchen towel.

A coffee spill or two, cooking oil that missed the pan and has to be mopped from the stovetop, milk that landed outside the bowl, then a quick rinse in the sink, and soon the dish towels were crusty, molded, greasy rags, unrecognizable as anything intended for use near food. The classic trip through the washer and dryer wasn't an option. We didn't have a washer, nor had we received the revelation that we were living practically beside a laundromat. And yet something had to be done.

A thought pecked at the back of my brain. Would that work? Why not? Nothing I could do was going to make those kitchen towels worse. Who cares if everyone laughs at me?

In Los Rios, where I had woken up on sunny mornings a few weeks ago, my mamá Hilda didn't have a washer. She had soap, water, and a cement wash sink against which she scrubbed our clothes to a fierce cleanliness never produced by an agitating tub of suds. I clicked off the list in my head: I didn't have laundry soap, but I had various other kinds of soaps. I had water. No cement wash sinks anywhere, but there's a cement slab at the base of our wobbly steps. Why wouldn't that work? I filled a bucket with water and grabbed a small plastic bowl to use as a scoop. I never did this in Los Rios; my mamá did it for me. But I watched, and how hard could it be?

"What are you doing, *loca?*" Beth asked when she saw me heading toward the door with my bucket of water and supplies.

"An experiment."

"What kind of experiment?"

"A laundry experiment."

"I hope it works!"

"Me too. These towels are disgusting."

"Can I watch?" Sheila asked.

"Sure. Don't laugh. I never tried this before."

"Did you learn it in Costa Rica?"

"Sort of."

I had to fetch the broom and sweep the dirt from the cement before anything had hope of getting clean on it. I dumped a scoop of water on it to wet it, then spread the immoral dish towels out and poured water over them too. I squirted them with a generous amount of dish soap. Then I commenced scrubbing them back and forth against the rough cement, which—of course—produced more mud, even though a minute ago, it appeared clean. I rubbed and scrubbed, slopped and scraped, dumped more water, squirted more soap.

"Cool!" Sheila admired.

Not terribly. Two of my knuckles were bleeding. Mamá's knuckles never bled, whether because they were so toughened by the constant necessity of repeating this task, or because she had learned to do it without scraping them on the cement, I can't say. I had to keep washing the blood away so that I wouldn't make the towels worse instead of better.

Getting the soap out was the hardest part. I had to send Sheila up to the kitchen for another bucket of water and I was making an enormous mess. I somehow managed to soak my shirt, and a puddle of mud had formed around my bare feet.

I wrung and rinsed, twirled and twisted, beating the suffering towels up and down against the cement with one hand while attempting to pour water over them with the other. Mamá made it look a lot easier than this. If I had to wash bath towels and work jeans this way like she did, I think I would cry.

The kitchen towels turned out a heck of a lot better than I dared to imagine. They weren't exactly white, but they were a lot less brown. Sheila had to get me another bucket of water to wash my feet, and then I walked up the steps and draped the dripping towels over the banister in the sun.

"There," I said, when I walked back inside.

Beth looked up at me over top of the book she was reading.

I shrugged my shoulders and went into the bathroom to check if our medicine cabinet by some chance contained Band-Aids.

Curtis and Dan, with their fearless dumpster diving, fed us like dime store royalty while they were in town. Their midnight expeditions yielded such harvests as donuts, bread, pancake syrup, orange juice, wilted vegetables, expired canned goods, hotdogs that still smelled okay, and, of course, the microwave. They would hit the dumpsters behind Kroger's, the one behind the Seven Eleven and the ones in the fancy housing development on the other side of campus.

I always meant to go along and try it myself, but somehow I never did. For one, you have to go at three o'clock in the morning, at which hour I am never in the mood to do anything. The other thing is, it's risky. Dumpster diving is illegal for some reason, a law that defies all logic. Just because someone doesn't want something should not mean that no one else is allowed to have it. You can be fined several hundred dollars for dumpster diving in the state of Indiana. In some places, the police have better things to do than chase people stealing each other's trash, but not in this town.

There's one other reason that I never went along. I'm embarrassed to say this, but there is one thing about dumpster diving that scares the crap out of me, and it's not cops or the inconvenient hour. It's rats. I don't know if you see rats when you dig through the garbage at 3 in the morning or not. But you could. You're at the right place at the right time. Even though I rarely flinch over worms, spiders or little mice, I think that if I came face to face with a real live rat in a dark dumpster, I would scream my bloody head off. Something about their beady eyes and snaky tails puts me straight over the edge. Then the cops would get us for sure.

The other way to get free food is to steal it before it hits the trash. One of Tom's housemate stole flocks of frozen chickens from Kroger's, shoving them inside his out-of-season coat, and trying to keep his teeth from chattering as he paid for a pack of cigarettes.

But the hands-down best place to steal food was from the college cafeteria. No question. Security alarms on doors were slow in arriving to northern Indiana church colleges, and Tony Royal knew how to get in since he had been the trusted student manager for four years. He never told us how he did it—he wasn't a complete crook—but he could get in without a sound, without a key, without a trace, and open the door from the inside to let in the rest: Curtis, Dan, Colin and whoever wanted to join them. First, they feasted. Then they hauled out pounds of meat, blocks of cheese, dozens of eggs, buckets of ice cream. I never did that, either. I kept thinking of how mortified my parents would be if I got caught stealing food from the cafeteria and I lost my nerve. Plus, what if I got kicked out of school? Then what? I would have to go home.

Beth is gutsier than I am. She went along like Maid Marion a few times, including the last time when the security guard busted them, and they had to run for their educations.

Charlie, the senior citizen security guard, must have seen movements through the shadowy cafeteria windows and come to investigate. The thieves were in the kitchen giggling in hushed hysterics, scooping chocolate peanut butter ice cream into their mouths faster than they could swallow it, their loot of food piled beside them, when the lights flipped on. I'll bet they almost gave old Charlie a heart attack as they burst out of the kitchen at a dead run, breaking for the emergency exit on the other side of the dining hall. They were closer to the door than he, and much more agile, but had the disadvantage of having to run with their shirts pulled up over their heads so he wouldn't recognize them. Charlie took off after them yelling, "Hey! You kids! Get back here!"

They hit the crash-bar on the door seconds ahead of him and burst into the sweet black night where they could abandon the precaution of hiding their faces. They made it off the campus ahead of old Charlie and lost him in the alleys and shadows of 8th Street.

The only things they scored that time were the pair of somebody's forgotten sunglasses that Dan had stuffed into his back pocket and the ice cream scoop that Beth found still in her hand.

❦

Girls loved Dan. It wasn't only Nina. He had a sort of muddled mystique about him that comes from having grown up in Kenya. He never saw *M*A*S*H*, for example, which caused intense puzzlement and fascination. He had these awesome sandals that were made from an actual tire and will never wear out. Ever. When he was pissed off, or if you startled him, he would swear in Swahili. It was adorable.

There were moments when I could see what all the fuss was about, but mostly he was too gangly for me. And I hate mustaches no matter where their owner grew up. I never saw *M*A*S*H* either, and that doesn't make me cool or mysterious. I never saw it because we were only allowed to watch *Little House on the Prairie,* and we had to turn even that off if something scary happened like a house fire or a wagon wreck. Where's my mystique?

He was Nina's torment.

Poor Dan. He tried. He liked Nina. They went out on a few actual dates—like to dinner and the movies. Nobody else I knew went on real dates like that. They went for walks and then found a room where they could close the door. Dan slept over in our Pit of Sin with her a few times. But he had an incurable case of wanderlust, so when his one summer class ended, he stuffed a backpack full of t-shirts and hit the road. He wanted to hitchhike to California and back. He'd be here again by September, he promised. We all told him he was crazy, but Dan never cared on a day in his life what anyone else thought of him. That's part of what made him irresistible.

Nina seemed to be alright when he left. She was gloomy and lovesick, but as stable as any of us. She said she was sure that this time apart would benefit their relationship. She said she needed time to think. She said that this way, during the summer, they could both see other people. Then she painted a life-sized replica of him, wearing nothing but grapes, on the wall by her bed.

The Carrot Problem

Nina planted a garden. Or let's say: Nina meant to plant a garden, but she lost her grip before she got any seeds in the ground. I know that sounds terrible, but it's true. Clearly, her problems were real, I just couldn't conceive of them, and I rolled my eyes at her.

The joke was on the rest of us. We all covered our mouths with our hands and giggled, "Nina is insane!" not intending to be right. Nina, the girl who never had a dirty fingernail, who would die at the thought of injuring a worm, not only announced that she was going to plant a vegetable garden but that she was going to excavate it herself. She found an old rusted rototiller in the shed and hauled it out. The rototiller was such a dinosaur that it didn't use gasoline and could presumably till the earth with the bare force of human muscle behind it. Nina had precious little of that. It weighed more than she did, and her chosen garden plot beside the shed had a thick mat of grass.

She must have felt her grip loosening, and found a need to push hard against something. I grumbled at her under my breath for thinking of backbreaking labor as fun. I remember summers on the farm where "gardening" meant being obligated to haul offensive rocks out of the potato patch and to hoe rows of vegetables that struggled in pure shale. There's nothing charming or entertaining about it. God knows that at her home Nina never had to do anything she didn't want to—she said so herself. Her parents are Mennonites, but not the kind that populates Pennsylvania. They're the kind that don't have to wear out-of-fashion clothes or grow their own green beans. That's why I laughed at Nina out in the "garden."

Ha," I smirked to myself. "She's trying to make up for nineteen years of being spoiled by killing herself in the dirt."

Turns out I was right.

"Hey, Nina. Let me help you," I offered. At least I weigh more than the rototiller. Just because I thought she was full of shit doesn't mean I didn't feel sorry for her.

"No," she sang out, "I'm fine."

She wouldn't let any of us help her—not me, not Sheila, not Beth. This went on for a couple of days, and we started to believe her. A rich stripe of earth emerged beside the shed. It grew in width until a row of tomatoes could conceivably be planted there. Sheila caught the garden fever, and Beth too. They talked about the carrots and corn and cucumbers we would harvest, all natural and homegrown. I didn't want to be a wet blanket so I tried to say supportive things, but I know a lot more about the travails that gardens face than these girls from suburbia. For one, they don't weed and water themselves. Plus, there are several million species of bugs in the world that like veggies every bit as much as we do and don't mind eating them green.

That night Beth and Sheila and I lay sprawled on our furnitureless living room floor. I was supposed to be doing what they were doing—reading for class tomorrow—but I wasn't. I had given up hours ago on Seamus and the Bog People, and commenced making little colored beads out of bakeable clay. Colors always cheer me up.

It was far too hot to learn anything but of course professors don't consider that when they compile their reading lists. Nina was in her room where she spent a lot of time taking naps at absurd hours and then wandering around the house when the rest of us were sleeping.

Sheila sat up from her reading and said in a voice so loud we all jumped, "Hey you guys!"

"Damn, Sheila!"

"Sorry."

"What's up?"

"Can we get ice cream?"

"You are the devil…"

"Do we have any money left?"

"No."

"How much is it?"

And then, before we could even calculate the consequences of this misdemeanor, the door to Sheila and Nina's room opened, and Nina emerged. She looked normal to me.

"Hey Nina! Wanna get ice cream?"

"You guys," Nina said, ignoring or missing the question, "I think I need to go to Pine View."

We all shut up and the ice cream melted right out of our minds.

"Pine View?" Beth asked, to be sure.

"Right now?" I asked, wondering how.

"Why?" asked Sheila, without hesitation.

But Nina answered her. "I've been having some problems

and I need to get help. I'm afraid I could be dangerous to myself."

She was as calm as if she were announcing that she wanted to go to Seven Eleven for a Coke. This was the last thing any of us anticipated. Pine View is a mental hospital. I knew Nina wasn't a glowing ray of sunshine, but I guess I thought she was acting the part of the tormented artist. Who knew she'd been sitting alone her dark room feeling suicidal? She just walked out of her room and asked to be taken away.

It was a bit of a problem because we didn't have a car.

I went from my general mild annoyance with her to feeling sorry for her in fifteen seconds. How much would you hate to have to ask your housemates to drive you to the mental hospital? She seemed tinier than ever, like a sad child.

I told her not to worry—I would be right back with Tom's car. I went out into the night, unlocked my bicycle and flew down the dark streets, not even pausing for stop signs, praying that Tom would be home. He and his housemates were watching some TV murder mystery and drinking Labatt's Blue.

"Hi, Di," he beamed when he saw me through the screen door. "Come in. Want a beer?"

"Actually, no. Can you come here a sec? I have to ask you something."

"Sure. What's up?" Tom stepped outside with me.

"Can I borrow your car?"

"Yeah. What's the matter?"

"Nina says she needs to go to Pine View." I mumbled the last part so that no one else would hear me.

"Oh! Oh my God. Is she alright?"

"Well..." I shrugged my shoulders. It was a dumb question.

So I drove Nina to Pine View in Tom's car. I can't imagine what we talked about on the way. I doubt we said much. I never had any idea what to say to her unless we were having a disagreement.

I stayed close beside her while she talked to the sleepy-eyed night receptionist. I put my arm around her. I held her hand. How weird to feel yourself love a person you thought you didn't even like.

The receptionist wrote things on papers and paged the night nurse over the intercom.

The night nurse peered over her glasses at us and told us to go home.

Nina didn't budge. "No," she said. "I will hurt myself."

I stood by her, pressing back into her clenched palm. My heard pounded and I felt faint. She will, I wanted to say. You should see what she did to the yard with the rototiller.

Holy God. What if they won't take her?

A lot of people had to talk to a lot of other people about letting someone self-admit without a doctor's signature. But we weren't going to find a doctor with office hours at this time of night, and I wasn't taking Nina back home just to have to sit on her until morning so she wouldn't slit her wrists. We could spend the night in the waiting room for all I cared.

The night nurse called her away to another room where a doctor could talk in private with her. I stood at the reception window in the common area where patients were watching animal documentaries on TV, and answered questions about Nina.

"She's nineteen. Yes, she's a student. No, her parents don't know she's here. I don't think she's on any medication."

I waited for a while on a flowered couch that was itself almost enough to drive you mad, until the receptionist came to tell me that Nina would be staying. She must have convinced them that she was ill because she didn't come back from the room, and I drove away alone in the car.

Having to pay bills is a wonderful misery. It's the price tag on no one being able to tell you what to do. We suffered it joyfully, like martyrs singing hymns as flames lapped our toes. The $88.00 we each had to pay for rent took us ages to earn with part-time student wages and odd jobs. And then there were the utilities on top of that. To spend the afternoon on required reading, or earning a 20 dollar bill—that is the question. Our laments rose to heaven as the flames moved closer, but we would not recant. No price is too much for your freedom. Our singed eyebrows were living proof that we could take care of ourselves.

The good thing about the rent payment is that you always know how much it's going to be. It's the biggest bill, and therefore the worst, but at least there's never a surprise. The other ones, like the phone bill and the water, depend on who you call and how long you stay in the shower. You might think you're being careful, but when the bill comes you find out for real.

Our gas, electric, and water bills went to the office of Barb the landlady instead of coming to the house where careless renters might lose them or do something harebrained like let the water get cut off. Each month when I took Barb the rent money, I brought the utility payments too, and she gave me the next set of bills to divide.

The phone bill came to the house. I set up the line myself because somewhere in the back of my mind I already suspected that I would not move back to the dorms on campus, ever. When the phone bill came, we took turns pouring over its pages, circling our long-distance calls with different-colored pens, and then adding up how much we owed. Landlords don't care if you get your phone cut off, so you can take care of that one yourself. It's not like the water, which, if it got cut off, would cause your house to be more disgusting than it already is, or the gas. In the summer the gas bill isn't a big deal but in the winter it is, and if you didn't pay it, you would freeze to death among the exploding pipes.

On the first of each month, I put $88.00 each, plus utilities, into an envelope and rode my bike across town to Barb's office at Century 21. I pedaled up 9th Street and along the railroad tracks, past the Winnebago factory, across the overpass above the highway—far away from the familiar safety of the college campus and out onto Lincoln Avenue.

I arrived soaked with sweat, and tried my best to project serene adult confidence as I pushed against the heavy glass door. The blast of icy office air made me shiver. I handed over the precious envelope and waited for the signed receipts with our next bills, anxious to burst into the muggy sunshine again and pedal as fast as I could back to the familiar safety of our own private chaos.

Sheila's grandma Friesen must have thought we were one uncivilized set of girls. She's almost more like a mom to Sheila than a grandma. She lives at the retirement community near the college and, being as we were Sheila's friends, she wanted to get to know us. At least, she thought she did. I'm sure Grandma Friesen never saw anyone eat the way we ate the night she took us to Ponderosa Steakhouse—especially not girls. She must have thought we were pigs. Nina missed the feast because she was in Pine View, but I'm sure they feed you well there. Unbalanced people must need a balanced diet even more than the rest of us. We tried to mind our manners but Beth kept making us laugh with our mouths full, then Sheila choked on her diet Coke and some came out her nose.

At Ponderosa, you can eat all you want at the buffet for one price, plus you get a slab of steak, a baked potato and bottomless Coke. We were so hungry—not only in our gurgling stomachs, but in our minds where empty pockets and empty pantries haunted our dreams, and then we woke up to them. We were hungry in our blood cells, where a diet of rice and ramen is not good enough. Tossed salad, fruit salad, potato salad, chicken wings, fish sticks, tacos with meat and cheese and salsa, spaghetti and meatballs, mushroom soup, vegetable soup, macaroni and cheese, egg rolls, tuna salad, green beans, sweet corn, sauerkraut, baked beans, sweet and sour pork, fried shrimp, carrot sticks, and an ice cream sundae for dessert: didn't Mother always say you must at least try a little bit of everything?

Again and again we got up to fill our plates, chattering with Grandma Friesen about our house, our summer classes, and how none of us really knew how to cook. No matter how much we ate, there was always more.

In the car, I thought I was going to throw up. I felt like I was suffocating because I couldn't get a deep breath. Sheila sat still as a corpse. Beth was pale green. I slipped my hand out the open window and let go of the complementary lollipop I was licking. No way. Not even.

When Grandma Friesen dropped us off, we thanked her, trying not to gag, and lumbered up our rickety stairs. I guess she satisfied her curiosity about us that day, because we never saw her again. She often invited Sheila to her house for meals, but I'm sure she was scared to try to feed the rest of us.

I wish people were like camels that can store their food and water for months. Even to be like one of Professor Perry's cows that passes it all around a few times. But we were girls, and in the morning we were starving again. They don't give you doggie bags at all-you-can-eat buffets. The next day you're on your own.

❧❧

Curtis and Tony Royal grew scruffy beards and lifted a *Let's Go Europe* from the public library. They made lists of cities and flipped a coin to decide if they would stop there or not. Then at the beginning of June they packed bags of granola bars and extra socks, and took a bus to Chicago O'Hare with every intention of flying standby to Europe. It must have worked, because they didn't come back.

I hate to say this, but I barely remember them leaving. I should have been paying more attention since Beth is my best friend and Curtis was her boyfriend. What kind of terrible friend doesn't attend to you with tequila and tissues when your love walks out the door?

I imagine we threw a party the night before, with the red lightbulb, to say good-bye. We must have danced and drank wine. The rest of us slept in a pile in the living room while Curtis and Beth filled the Pit of Sin with wickedness until morning. They must have hugged and kissed at the bottom of the stairs before he walked away. They promised to write, that much I know, because they wrote to each other for years—epic accounts of their adventures, inspirations and other loves.

None of us imagined they would get married. None of us imagined marriage, period. We called it bullshit, and a stupid convention to which we would never bow. Boyfriends? Yes. Lovers? Absolutely. Husbands? Hell no.

I thought he was just some guy she liked. I expected that she would forget about him or begin to find him somewhat gross, the way you do when you stop liking someone. If I had known then that Curtis was the love of her life, I would have tried to be nicer to him all along. I would have paid attention to him instead of tolerating him. He always complemented my poems, so I said I liked his sculptures. That's about it. I did like them. I didn't understand them very well but they were beautiful in a confusing sort of way.

To be honest, lost as I was in my own labyrinth, I wanted Beth all to myself. Good for me if her stupid boyfriend left. I didn't say that, but I thought it. So, yes, later when I was crying through boxes of tissues, berating myself for being a terrible friend, I deserved it.

Beth is better than I am at masking her sorrows. After Curtis was gone, she danced around the house with her cigarettes, and on the wall she painted an enormous cupid taking aim at the door. She and cupid were on the hunt. Almost right away, she started going out with a guy named Johan and pretended to get over Curtis so fast that I assumed she never missed him.

❧✦❧

The last thing I expected is that while I was in Costa Rica, Beth would become such close friends with Mean Tabitha. Turns out Mean Tabitha wasn't mean to Beth. She glowed on her like the afternoon sunshine, radiant and warm. Mean Tabitha was only mean to people she considered below her, people who did things like grow up on chicken farms in Pennsylvania and don't know the meanings of words like tahini and sashimi, who hadn't watched all the right movies and didn't speak proper slang. Mean Tabitha, like Beth, was from the city, where people are not nearly as clueless. Mean Tabitha was from Chicago. She henna-ed her hair and drank gin and tonics and made it very clear that she had slept with both men and women.

Beth loved her, this was evident. She would drop anything if Mean Tabitha called, and she always came back from their adventures draping her hair over one shoulder like Mean Tabitha, holding her head sideways and sighing in painful boredom at the ordinariness of the rest of her life.

"I invited Tabitha over to dinner."
"Oh. Okay."
"She's bringing wine."
"Cool."
"What's the matter?"
"I've never really—felt comfortable around her."
"Why not?!"
"I don't know. She makes me all self-conscious."
"Tabitha?!"
"Yeah."
"About what?"
"I don't know. I get the feeling she thinks I'm stupid."

"She does not," Beth contradicted me. "That's just her sense of humor."

"She was nice to me in London," I conceded, instead of saying mean isn't funny, which is what I was thinking.

"See?" Beth said.

"Yeah."

"Oh, hi!" Mean Tabitha squealed at me when she came in the door. "You're back." She said it like I was a stray or something.

"Yes I am," I said. I placed a brave smile on my face.

She stretched out her arms and gave her lips a big pucker, which warned me I was about to get a loveless hug and some urban air-kisses.

"So, where were you again?"

"Costa Rica."

"Costa Rrrica!" she repeated, rolling the R long and loud, and giving her hips a shake. "Did you fall in love?"

"No," I lied.

"Good job," she said, patting me on the butt like we were on a football team, and going toward the kitchen to find Beth. "It's so lame to go off and think you fell in love just because you finally left home."

"Right," I said.

I've been in the room with her for 60 seconds, I thought, and how miserable am I?

Dinner was a hooting, squealing, guffawing affair consumed in a circle on our living room floor where everyone except me talked all at once. I'd never been to Chicago, which is where they'd all been on spring break. Together. I didn't know any of the people they were talking about. I didn't get what was so funny.

They decided to go see *Jungle Fever* in Riverside over the

weekend. I wanted to go too, but I was trying to save money for the Grateful Dead show.

"That following the Grateful Dead shit is so fucked up!" Mean Tabitha said. She rolled her eyes and shook her head.

See? I told you she was mean. She could have said she hoped I had fun or something decent.

"I'm not following them. I'm just going to a show."

"Whatever," she said tossing her hair over her other shoulder. "I don't think getting all stoned and peaced out is an appropriate way of dealing with life."

Beth didn't say anything, but she was watching her intently. And nodding. "Anyway. Sorry for you," Mean Tabitha said. "It's a FABULOUS MOVIE!"

"Annabella Sciorra's in it right?" Nina asked. "She's so hot."

"So hot!" Mean Tabitha said with her mouth full.

"Spike Lee rocks!" Beth said.

I didn't know who Annabella Sciorra was. I didn't know who Spike Lee was, either, until I saw that movie. I'm terrible with names. I'm terrible with movies. And I was trying to be a Theatre major?

Mean Tabitha was right about me. I'm a nerd.

I have never been so anxious to finish swallowing my food so I can go to the kitchen and wash the dishes as I was during that meal. I washed them all, and I made it take as long as I could. That wasn't the only meal Mean Tabitha came to at our house, but it was the only one I stayed through. If I ever invited anyone to dinner who was that mean to Beth over her plate of rice, I would say I was sorry and never invite her again.

෨ඍ

The hands, the voices, the brush of coco palm leaves across the hot tin of the open workshop roof keep the same steady rhythm. The abuela, Doña Delfina, forms a giant tinaja from the same clay her bones are made of. Her arms move steadily, doing this earthen art practiced by her mother and her grandmothers ever since the time when jaguars lurked in this forest. Her son called Chino is leaning against the door frame of the house. The other son, my host papá, who is called Tito because he is the youngest, sits on a small wooden stool by his wife, Hilda. She bathes a finished pot in red slip by dipping a strip of cloth, and dragging it in wide circles. This work is as indispensable as it is unhurried.

Pedro, the son of the woman next door, will come back today from the capital city in a box to be buried here with the old people. Something went wrong on a wet mountain road far away, and the motorcycle he bought with the lottery money came to rest under the bus.

"Pobrecita, la señora," Doña Delfina laments, without looking up.

"Dejó tres chiquillos," Chino says. He shakes his head and scuffs his sandal against the dirt floor of the workshop.

"¿Será que andaba borracho?" asks Tito.

"Quién sabe," says Hilda, dipping. "Tal vez."

The old woman Doña Delfina pronounces the city to be a dangerous place. One by one, they agree.

"Sí."

"Sí."

"Sí."

Then they wait, and she will continue. "Mucha gente se muere en la ciudad," she muses.

"Sí."

"Sí."

"Sí."

"Muy peligroso," *cautions* la abuela *as her hands press and stroke the cool earth.* "Se muere mucha gente, allí."

"Es cierto."

"Aquí no."

"Aquí, se mueren solo los viejos."

"Se muere mucha gente en la ciudad," *the old woman chants to herself and her children. I think of the hen tied by her leg to the jocote tree and how she calms her chicks.*

"Quién sabe por qué," *Chino wonders, staring out across the dry yard where the sun is pounding like thunder.*

"Quién sabe," *agrees Tito, aiming a lazy slap at a mosquito that tickles his shin.*

"Quién sabe," *repeats Hilda, pulling the paint cloth around.*

❧❧

The carrot problem reared its ugly head soon after Nina came home from Pine View. It wasn't even a carrot problem; it was a general vegetable problem, but carrots became the case in point. Sheila missed it because she was at Grandma Friesen's house, safe from the monotony of our rice and lentils. The rest of us were sitting on the living room floor scarfing exactly that.

"You guys," Nina said to Beth and me, "I think we should start buying our food at the Co-op. They have such fresh vegetables, and they're all grown organically. I think it's important to support farmers who don't put chemicals into the earth."

"That's great," I said, pretending to consider this while I chewed. "The only trouble is that everything at the Co-op is so expensive."

"Mmm-hmm," Beth agreed.

"But, think about it. Where would you rather have your money go? Who would you rather support?"

Money? What money? My five dollars a week, on which I was perpetually hungry? Beth could see the storm clouds gathering right there in the living room, as the hot and the cold air of Nina and me began to collide. "I think shopping at the Co-op is great," she said, clawing for middle ground, "but it's true that it's more expensive than Kroger's."

"But, don't you think it's worth it?" Nina asked. "Pesticides are killing our rivers. They kill fish and animals and hurt our Mother Earth. Also, it's healthier for us to eat organic food. Think about the chemicals."

Is this supposed to be some kind of newsflash? Because I thought it was common knowledge.

The problem is that we had a kind of commune among the four of us. We each put five dollars a week into a kitty. This yielded a total of twenty dollars with which to buy staple foods like rice, ramen noodles, coffee, eggs, and other necessities like dish soap and toilet paper. Any luxuries, like canned tuna, apples or cheese, were the additional expense of the individual. The kitty was "our" money, and no one person had the authority to use it on anything we hadn't all agreed on. Five dollars isn't much, but it was the best we could do if we wanted electricity and a phone. Nina's full time job in the Admissions office paid two dollars more per hour than the rest of us made, so of course she could afford more. And she barely ate.

"I think the Co-op is cool," I said. "And I hope someday I have enough money to buy everything there. But right now I don't. We need to get as much food as we can for as little money as possible. How many organic carrots can you buy at the Co-op for a dollar? Three? That's fine. People should do that. But if it's my last dollar we're talking about, I'm taking it to Kroger's where you can get a whole bag. You know? If we buy our food at the Co-op, we'll go hungry."

I was serious. And I was pissed. Just because she still gets an allowance from her parents, she's going to preach to me about vegetables? Hold me back.

Nina cracked out her extra-quiet angry voice. "Well I would rather eat one carrot from the Co-op than a whole bag from Kroger."

"I'm not trying to be a bitch." I said. "I'm trying to say we can't afford it. We won't have enough food. If you want to buy yours there and be separate, it's okay. It's up to you. I just can't. I'll starve."

So she did. She seceded from the commune. Nina supported politically correct produce while the rest of us proceeded to poison the planet. She still had to chip in, though, for dish soap and toilet paper.

Every single time I see a carrot, I think of Nina. To this day. I don't know if we ever completely forgave each other for our respective insensitivities, and the dumb thing is: we couldn't afford vegetables anyway, that summer. We didn't buy carrots at all, even from Kroger's. Nina never once brought them home from the Co-op. She brought dried beans which she never cooked, small tomatoes that sprouted fuzz in our warm refrigerator, and suspicious-smelling tofu that she daintily picked out of the box with chopsticks.

Nina taught me the joy of cleaning. She did it accidentally, like all the other things she taught me. Cleaning is the closest thing to starting over that a person can do, most times, and I learned this from Nina on that day.

The day we had the carrot problem, I couldn't read a word of the four million pages assigned for the next morning. Instead, I marched into Beth's and my bedroom and put it into Spartan order. It's not that I wanted to clean; it's that I was so mad I didn't know what else to do with myself. I snatched the broom from the porch and swept our bedroom floor, but I was still furious. So I crawled around pulling a bucket of hot soapy water behind me, and washed it with a rag—the whole disgusting wooden floor. I'd bet my liver it had been ten years since someone did that. The grime I removed was shocking. After that, I wiped down the windows with vinegar.

Then I stormed into the kitchen and washed the dishes. I swept the kitchen floor, washed it on my hands and knees, cleaned the bathroom and scrubbed the toilet. The process took hours.

And then, after all that, I wasn't mad at Nina anymore for being a waify, snotty little twit. I was too tired.

I couldn't resist the temptation, though, of painting a fat orange carrot on the wall. I painted it in my room so it wouldn't start another fight.

Sheila's voice woke me up when she got home from work.

"Wow! The kitchen looks awesome! What the...? Oh my God! The bathroom!"

"Thanks."

Exhaustion still glowed in my limbs.

"You did all this?"

"Uh-huh."

"Wow, Diana... Are you okay?"

"Yeah. I just got in the mood to clean."

The mood to clean. That's a good one.

"I'll say you did!"

When Beth and Nina got home, they both told me how awesome the house looked, too. If I'd have been any madder I'd have rubbed holes in the windows, but I didn't say that.

Poor Nina. Somehow, with all that soapy water, I managed to put out the fire. I sweated the poison out of my blood and felt all right again. Nothing like cleaning to wipe away the feeling of helplessness and create the illusion, at least for a few hours, that you are in control of something. And, of course, you also get the self-righteous pleasure of everyone else having to recognize that you cleaned up their mess without being asked, and for no apparent reason.

❧❧

My friend John who drives the bus with curtains inherited Harriet from somebody who graduated, and the mean kitty next door to him was trying to murder her. He asked me if we would take her before she lost a leg. I said yes without hesitating, and then had to go home and announce that I had sort of agreed to get a cat. Sheila worried about Barb, but Beth and I convinced her that Barb wouldn't care. To prove it, Beth painted an extra-large cat on the wall behind the couch. Nina, with her cautious new optimism and a freshly-shaved head, set about creating the ideal kitty-home for our feline family member among the clutter in the Pit of Sin.

The first problem we had with Harriet was how to get her home, and there were plenty to follow. I should have taken a box to John's house, not a string. I swear I knew this, but I didn't remember until it was too late. As Beth and I walked up to the back door, we called "kitty-kitty-kitty," and Harriet materialized before us. We looked at each other, both hoping this wasn't going to be our cat, that this was some stray out trolling for treats.

Harriet was not exactly your dream cat. On the day we met, she was a lean, mean year-old alley cat that somebody named after Harriet Tubman. Ironically, this Harriet was white. She had random orange and black patches, but they made her look more mismatched than pretty. And she had a deformed tail. It took a permanent U-turn to the right just above her butt, so it always pointed sideways. I asked John what happened to her, and he said, "Nothing." She was born that way.

We envisioned the kind of kitty that would let you hold it in your arms and carry it around with you, but that was not Harriet—especially not strangers with suspicious intentions.

She let her stiff body be petted, but when she felt her four feet being lifted from solid ground, she twisted like a snake, sunk her back claws into the flesh of my arm, and was free. That's why I brought the string.

What a terrible idea. What was I thinking? You cannot lead a cat, no matter how hard you try, by means of a string on its neck. I knew this. She was not my first cat.

"You want to try?" I asked Beth, when it became clear that Harriet did not like me, nor did she want me to hold her.

"Hell no! You're crazy!"

"She might let you."

"I don't think so."

"She thinks I'm a monster."

"Shut up."

"Just try."

Beth tried, but it didn't go any better for her. Plus she screamed when Harriet scratched her, and then Harriet was more scared than ever.

It took us an hour to get her home, and John's house is six blocks from ours. We developed a procedure that worked like this: carry Harriet three steps, let her jump down and run ahead until the string caught around her neck, catch up to her, pull her six inches, pity her, pick her up, repeat. It would have been easier if she had always run in the right direction when we let her down, but she didn't. The journey was excruciating. By the time we got her home we didn't even want her anymore.

The last steps of the trek proved to be the hardest—the ones where I lifted Harriet, pinned her terrified clawing body against my precious chest and climbed the stairs to our apartment. Nina opened the door, cooing like a new mother.

"Awww! Hello, Harriet." She reached out to touch the bristling neck. "What took you guys so long?"

Inside the door, I released my death-grip on the spring-tight body, and Harriet leapt from my clutches in a desperate race for she-had-no-idea-where. Nina screamed and withdrew a trembling hand. Sheila, who was running from the kitchen to the living room to see the new arrival, collided with her in the hallway, screamed even louder than Nina, and sent the poor kitty fleeing into Beth's and my bedroom.

She hid in our closet all day and, like a turtle in her shell, she would not come out. No amount of milk, no amount of tuna, no amount of falsetto sweetness convinced her to show her face. She didn't budge until all of us had gone to sleep and she could explore her new digs on her own terms.

In the morning, cat food lay scattered all over the kitchen floor, and the precious loaf of bread that we kept on a shelf in the pantry was on the floor too, gashed open in several places, huge chunks of it missing. Once a scavenger, always a scavenger. John didn't warn us Harriet was a thief, but she was. That cat would have stolen candy from a baby. We learned to lock her food in the cupboard under the sink and we had to keep our bread in the refrigerator. She chewed through a pizza box, once, to get at the left over crusts inside, and it wasn't because we didn't feed her. We did. It's that she was a lot like us—always hungry.

❧

Professor Williams' voice wavered on about human re-mains petrified in mud, hour after interminable hour. I tried to focus, but it was a losing battle. A critical situation, brewing in the depths of our closets, kept sneaking into the spotlight of my attention, eclipsing the mysteries of The Bog People. We had a laundry problem—a serious one. Our dirty clothes piled higher every day, and the stack of acceptable t-shirts on my shelf was almost gone. The questions consumed me as Professor Williams rambled. How are we going to get our clothes all the way from our house to the laundromat on campus? A mile is too far to walk with your laundry. How do you carry a laundry basket on a bicycle? I measured the space between the seat and the handlebar. It wouldn't fit.

Of course, there was one obvious solution: borrow Tom's car. But no way were we about to do that. Depend on a man for something necessary like laundry? We would rather gash open our veins. Jugs of wine are one thing; clean underwear is something else.

When the idea hit me, I sat bolt upright in my chair. Had Professor Williams noticed, he might have thought that at last I understood the beauty of The Bog People. But he was gazing past us at something only he could see.

The plan was simple and the only thing we needed to buy is string. Using four equal pieces of twine, we could tie the corners of my pink Rubbermaid laundry basket between my bicycle and Beth's. Why not? I saw it done all the time in Los Rios—when the object is heavy, carry it between two. Ladies carried buckets of steaming tamales for sale suspended from a broomstick passed through the handle. They walked the streets each holding an end, the bucket swinging between. My sister Estefani and I each took a handle of the sack of dirty dishes and lugged it from our house to the home of the neighbors who had a well on the days when the tap produced no water.

Beth laughed when I told her. She rolled her eyes. She called me *loca* and she said if you say so.

Tom got mad at me for some reason, probably insulted that we wouldn't accept his offer of the car and embarrassed in advance for the awful bloody mess he imagined we would make. He stood on our porch as we prepared for take-off, scolding down at us like a magpie. "Guys, you can take my car you know. Guys! Take my car! Diana, I hope you realize you could hurt yourself!"

Yes, I was aware of that. Like anyone ever died of a scraped knee. And there's no way we were going to ride fast enough to break our necks.

Sheila came out to watch too, amazed at our complete willingness to make fools of ourselves. I could hear her wondering, if the system worked, how in the world she was going to repeat this operation with Nina. Beth was the one who had the sense to put the clothes into a trash bag to avoid leaving a trail of socks and underwear down the street. We tossed the bag into the basket and mounted our bikes.

"One. Two. Three. GO!"

It was not as easy as I thought. Beth wobbled a lot. I wobbled a lot. You had to lean your bike against the weight of the basket, but not too much or you would lose it the other way. You had to ride far enough apart to keep the basket off the ground, but not so far as to rip a string or yank the other person off balance. And always at the same speed. We left the house shrieking and wobbling, laughing until tears blinded us.

Corners were the worst, because the outside girl had to hurry up, the inside girl had to slow down, and you must stay the exact same distance apart. On the first of three I went too fast, got ahead of Beth, and we crashed. On the second, howling with laughter and gripping the handle bars with white knuckles, we calculated better and made it. The third and last turn presented us with a dilemma: a bus was coming, opposite us, into the intersection. Is it more important to obey the traffic signs or to keep our rhythm? We both had stop signs, after which the bus had the right of way.

"Oh my God! Oh my God!" we screamed.

"There's a bus!"

"What should we do?" I asked, because we had to both do the same thing.

"It has a stop sign."

"So do we!"

"Yeah, but we're not stopping!" Beth decided.

Who would run over two innocent girls who were willing to risk their lives to do their laundry? In a perfect parallel, we swooped out onto 9th Street in front of the bus that sat idling at the stop sign. The driver yielded the right of way, staring in open-mouthed disbelief.

The moment the bus pulled onto 9th Street behind us, something went wrong. Beth screamed. I screamed. The basket bounced and swung wildly. Beth held steady but for some reason I braked and sent us down in a pile of wheels, legs and string. The bus driver blew the horn and passed us in the other lane.

"Are you okay?"

"Ow, my leg," Beth said through gritted teeth. She showed me the pink rope burn blooming on her calf.

"What happened?"

"The string."

"Are you okay?" I asked. Because we were kind of in this together.

"Yeah."

"I thought we were going to make it," I said, helping her up.

"Me too," she said.

"Don't tell Tom."

We got ourselves together and pointed our bikes toward campus. We managed a synchronized grand entrance into the college parking lot where our friends and people we don't know turned to look, and then look again. We even took our last corner without falling, although we hooted and squealed a lot.

Our friend Camila came over to where we landed, her leather boots and bag squeaking sophisticatedly as if she were riding a horse with a fine English saddle.

"What are you guys doing?" she asked, with one eyebrow raised.

"Laundry."

"You're crazy. Why don't you go to King Arthur's? It's right behind your house."

"King Arthur's? You mean that video arcade place?"

That's where all the town juvenile delinquents went to smoke cigarettes and write bad words in the bathrooms.

"Yeah. The other half is a laundromat," she said.

"What?"

Well how were we supposed to know? We don't play video games, and we write bad words on our own walls.

So after that we did our laundry at King Arthur's, which turned out to be four blocks away. We put our clothes in trash bags and slung them over our shoulders like Santa Clause bringing a nasty surprise to naughty children. I could even ride my bike with mine, driving with one hand. It was considerably easier than the tandem method, and much safer.

୨◈୰

Harriet didn't get much friendlier as timed passed. She did appear to remain with us voluntarily, however, probably because of the absence of terrifying toms and because we gave her the one thing she loves: food. In exchange for these favors, she endured our attempts to give her affection. She did not love any of us in the least, and we, to our immense disappointment, did not love her. Cats are supposed to purr themselves to sleep in your lap, but Harriet never purred. She did not like us or our laps. When she wanted to sleep, she hid somewhere.

"I think Harriet is emotionally abused," Nina said, with that knowing tone she picked up at Pine View.

We were all lying in front of the fan in the late afternoon heat. It was our only fan, otherwise I would not have been in such close proximity to Nina. Since she'd gotten back from Pine View, she was driving me crazy. Everybody was either "co-dependent," or "passive-aggressive," or one of her other new diagnostic words. Then there was the carrot thing. Now our cat was emotionally abused? Please.

"I think she's a bitch," I said.

Sheila giggled.

Beth coughed so the noise she made wouldn't sound like a laugh. "Why do you say that, Nina?" she asked. This was her way of telling me to shut the hell up.

"Because. She seems to ask for affection, but then when you approach her, she rejects you. I think she has negative as-sociations with touch."

"Maybe she wasn't petted enough as a kitten," Sheila specu-lated at the ceiling, dead serious. "Maybe she was taken away from her mother too young."

"But I think she has been abused by people," Nina insisted.

That fake voice made me want to sit up and say, "Talk right!" But I didn't.

"I can see that," Beth said. "I don't think she likes us."

Sheila snorted.

"Bitch-cat," I mumbled. I tried not to, but it popped out before I could stop it.

"See, like that," Nina said to me. "You always say negative things about her, Diana. And animals have spirits like people do. I mean, it's not just you—it's all of us. We laugh and say she's ugly. And we make fun of her tail. I think it hurts her feelings."

"Do you think so?" Beth asked. I know she was trying to stay in the middle of the conversation in order to keep me out. I can tell you Beth doesn't believe there's a cat in the world that cares what you say about its tail.

"Yes, I do."

"I don't know. I don't think she can understand language that well."

"It's not the language. It's the vibes."

Vibes. But of course.

"If I offend her when I say she's ugly," I said, "I hope she re-members I'm the one who rescued her ass from John's house."

"Oh, I'm sure she does!" Nina assured me. "But I think we should speak more kindly to her. About her."

That night in our room Beth and I did to Nina what she accused us of doing to Harriet. It was one of the good nights, just like old times, when Beth and I were best friends and there was no one else to complicate things.

"Can you believe Nina?"

"Oh my God!"

"Can you believe her?"

"No!"

"I thought I was going to laugh right out loud when she said that about Harriet. It was awful! Did you catch how I coughed?" Beth asked.

"No. I was too busy trying to keep my eyes from rolling out of my head!"

We burst into whispered hysterics.

"I can't believe you said she's a bitch!"

"I know," I gasped. "I can't either! I just couldn't help it. That girl is too crazy."

"She is, Diana. I think she came out of Pine View crazier than she went in."

"I know! So do I! And that voice!"

Beth touched my arm, widened her eyes, cocked her head to a concerned angle and did a perfect impression of Nina: "I really think you should speak more kindly to Harriet. She understands English, you know."

Beth is a brilliant impersonator. It's one of her most amazing abilities, of which she has a lot. We laughed until we were wiping away tears.

❧

Sheila burst in the door with a cardboard box under her arm, breathless after pedaling all the way from the campus mail room at top speed. When she plopped it down on The Desk, it rattled.

"Omygod!" she gasped in one breath.

"You got a box!" I said. I closed my diary, interrupting the treatise on my adventures with Tom in The Pit of Sin, and tossed it to the floor beside my feet.

"Omygod!" Another gasp.

"Breathe, Sheila."

"Omygod."

"Do you need me to get your inhaler?" Nina offered.

"No. I'm okay."

"Yeah?"

"Yeah."

"What is it?"

"My mom."

We knew her mom wasn't in the box but we had to wait to find out what was until Sheila had gone to the kitchen, drank several glasses of water, and washed her face in the bathroom. Then she sat down on the floor and gashed at the packing tape with her keys. Getting a box in the mail is the best, especially when it isn't even your birthday. Nina knelt behind her, watching over her shoulder. Even Harriet sidled over for a sniff.

Beth missed it because she was off with Johan someplace. I worried a little about letting her out of my sight with him because something about him made me nervous. But he was so ridiculously hot that what can you do?

When she pulled back the cardboard flaps, Sheila groaned, Nina gasped and Harriet walked away. She tipped the box over, and out onto the floor tumbled bottles and bottles of vitamins.

"What is that?"

"My mom."

"Are those vitamins?"

"Yes. You guys, I'm sorry about my mom."

"Don't be sorry, silly."

"Why is she sending you vitamins?"

Sheila was reading the folded sheet of notebook paper that appeared among the supplements. "She's on a health kick, now," Sheila said. "She says the right vitamins can prevent cancer and aging, so she wants me to take these. Every day."

"What?!"

"You'll kill yourself!"

"She says she went to a homeopathic doctor who told her about it." Sheila slapped the paper down and rolled her eyes. "Oh, you guys."

"Homeopathic medicine is the best," Nina nodded.

There was vitamin C, vitamin E, vitamin B complex, calcium with vitamin D, fish oil capsules, garlic oil capsules, iron supplements, selenium, magnesium and an enormous container of protein powder with a little scoop. It must have cost her a fortune. Plus postage. Sheila was already stuffing them back into the box, red with embarrassment that there was nothing "good" like cookies or chocolate or a loaf of homemade bread. That's what my mom sometimes sent.

"I'm sorry there's nothing good."

"What do you mean there's nothing good?"

"My mom is so weird. She's always does this."

"Vitamins are good. We probably need them."

"Well..." Sheila stopped stuffing and looked up with a question on her face.

"Think about it," I said. "When's the last time we ate fruit?"

"Um..."

"Besides bananas."

"Gina brought strawberries to the office yesterday," Nina said.

Nice. Like Nina's strawberries helped any of the rest of us.

"That's true." Sheila perked up a bit.

"I think you should take them," I told her. "Not all at once, though."

That sent Sheila into a little storm of incapacitating giggles.

"We can all take them," she brightened. "Here!" and she deposited the box of compressed nutrients on The Desk beside the stereo.

We could have eaten for the rest of the summer with the money Sheila's mom spent on that box of remedies for things that weren't wrong with us. But we took them, and perhaps they saved us from complete malnutrition. They didn't make us feel any better or any less hungry, though. Isn't it ironic how a plate of pure starch can fill your belly for hours on end and costs almost nothing, while a belly full of vitamins costs a fortune and makes you feel like you might puke, yet you could still swear you are starving? Although, I have to say, no one became wrinkly that summer or developed cancer.

◆◆◆

I cried my eyes out the day I had to sit down and write to my parents for money. I tried my best to figure another way out of my predicament, but nothing worked. Our second summer class was just beginning, and who were we kidding? There was no part-time job that would allow me the time I needed to study and still pay the bills—at least not one I was qualified for. I thought about becoming the world's first Mennonite prostitute but the truth is I didn't exactly qualify for that, either.

I ran the lights for weekend events in the campus theatre. Professor Williams hired me to mow his yard every week and mulch around his beloved bushes. Professor Perry heard about my green thumb and offered me her yard work as well. For the rest of the summer, she managed to find a never-ending list of tasks for both Beth and me, involving pruning, clipping, snipping, spraying, weeding and watering. She also paid us to dig up all 400 of her iris bulbs, soak them in bleach water, and plant them again because she was convinced they had slugs. Which, they didn't.

It still wasn't enough.

I tried so hard to get by on my own. I gave up everything I could think of except food. And wine. I washed my clothes without soap and winced through the sunburn I got without sunscreen. Tom said I could eat at his house so sometimes I did, but that didn't solve anything. June was about to begin. What kind of adult writes to her mom and dad asking for money to pay the rent the first month it comes due? A false one, that's what kind. One who is trying to be something she's not. I was sure I could do this if I tried hard enough. But I was trying my best, and even somebody with my remedial math skills could see the numbers were not going to work out.

I didn't expect to be trampled by a stampede of sobs when I opened my notebook to a clean page and wrote, "Dear Mom and Dad," on the first line. It blindsided me. I knew I was poor; I didn't realize I was angry. Turns out I was furious—with everyone.

I was mad at Mary Perry for talking about existentialism while I'm trying to figure out how to exist. I was mad at Nina for managing to be miserable in spite of having everything. I was pissed at Beth for acting like having to write your parents for money is no big deal. And at Tom for trying to help me solve my problems when I wanted him to hug me and shut up. And at Harriet for needing cat food which is way more expensive than dog food. And at my mom and dad. None of this was their fault, but I was angry at them too. For frowning at me and folding up their wallets, which they never did, but I always feared. So I was angry just in case.

I was angry at my mailbox for never holding the letter I waited for, the one written by delicate fingers that destroyed me without meaning to. I gave him my left-over airmail envelopes. He promised. I believed him. Did he forget me already? I was mad at myself for waking up again from dreams of Los Rios. I was mad at myself for getting on the bus. I was mad at myself for being wrong about everything.

My mom is better at math than I am, so she must have expected that letter sooner or later. When you're twenty, you can't imagine that other people have swashbuckled through these jungles before you, and you refuse to believe it no matter who tells you, or how. My parents sent me the money in a card with a kitten and a Bible verse. They even said I didn't have to pay them back, which made me feel both better and worse.

When you're a kid, you obey your parents' rules, they feed you, and everything makes perfect sense. Eventually, I guess, you grow up, you have to find your own food and you get to make your own rules. But what about the awful place between the two where you have to obey your own rules or you'll go crazy, and you have to obey your parents' rules or you'll starve? Nobody warns you about this. Nobody warned me.

When my parents called on the phone one night during my senior year to ask if the rumors that floated east across 600 miles were true—that I was sleeping with my boyfriend—I froze. It was midnight in Pennsylvania when they called, and they are never up so late. I thought they were going to say somebody died. And then they asked me that.

My face burned and my heart pounded. I could tell, through the silence on the phone, that there was only one answer that would get me to graduation, even if it sent me to the special level of hell for girls who lie to their parents. It was the perfect trap.

I cried my eyes out that day, too. If we didn't love each other so much in spite of our irreconcilable differences, all of this would be so much easier. It would be nice to have fights like normal people once in a while, but we can't. We're Mennonites. We don't know how to fight. Besides, when every question in the world boils down to What The Bible Says versus Anything You Could Possibly Say, what's the point?

A few weeks after Harriet moved in, she disappeared.

We kept her trapped inside at first so she would understand that we were her new mothers and that she didn't live at John's house anymore. When we decided to let her out, I thought we might never see her again, but all we had to do is rattle the cat food bag from the porch and she appeared like a genie. Sometimes she wanted to be inside; sometimes she wanted to be outside. Personally, I can relate.

Then one night she didn't come back at all. I called kitty kitty and shook the bag of food until the whole thing was reduced to crumbs. She did not appear, yowling at the screen, at any point during the night, and she wasn't on the porch, pissed at us for locking her out, in the morning.

Nina said she ran away because we were mean to her. Sheila was sure she went back to John's house. Beth thought she got hit by a car. I had another theory that I didn't want to think about. I called John, instead, who said he hadn't seen her. We weren't heartbroken, but we were a little insulted that our cat ditched us. On the third day, however, like a resurrection, she returned.

"I'll bet you fifty bucks she's pregnant," I said.

"Pregnant?" Beth burst into laughter.

It was an amusing thought. A creature that skinny and unappealing?

"Oh no!" Nina clapped her hand over her mouth. I knew she was thinking rape. Her face said it plain and clear.

"Why do you think that?"

"Because," I shrugged. "That's what cats do. When they go in heat, they disappear. Then they come back. Pregnant. Anyway, we'll see."

I was right. We had a whole barn full of cats when I was a kid in Pennsylvania.

Harriet's scrawny body slowly filled out and she became kind of pretty. Except for her crooked tail, she looked like a normal cat. But she kept on growing until she was as ridiculously fat as she had been thin, until she resembled a football with a head. All she could do was lie around.

Strangely, she seemed to enjoy her prenatal pudge. She would squint at us and purr with something like love in her eyes. She ate more cat food than you'd think possible, and we gave her special treats like dishes of milk and scrambled eggs. She stopped jumping up and running away if we sat too close to her or if a door slammed—whether because she liked us more or because she decided it wasn't worth the effort, who's to say?

I don't know much about cat gestation, but those kittens seemed to be in there an awfully long time. Either she was carrying a dozen, or they were going to be born grown up. I had a dream that she exploded. It wasn't as gory as it sounds, but that dream gave me a bad feeling.

❧❧

I was lying in bed trying to get through *No Exit,* when Beth walked in and told me what Nina said. *No Exit* is a book about being miserable, which I didn't need any help with, and we were supposed to finish it by tomorrow. Beth and Nina spent the entire evening outside on the steps having some private conversation they did not want anyone else to overhear. At first I tried not to sulk, but it didn't go well. Finally, I gave up and sunk into bed with Sartre.

"Is that a good book?" Beth asked me, closing our door behind her. She had a funny expression on her face.

"If you like hell."

"Good. Because I have to interrupt you."

"Thank you!" Relief seeped into my bloodstream.

"But you have to promise not to laugh, Diana. You CAN-NOT LAUGH."

"I'll try."

When you say it like that, I start laughing before I even know what's funny.

"Well." Beth plopped down on the bed next to me, making everything in the world alright again. "You won't believe what Nina just told me."

"Oh no. I'm sure I won't."

"We were sitting out on the steps and I asked her if her time in Pine View was, you know, helpful to her."

"Yeah?"

"And she started talking about how their concentration on spirituality made her realize that her spirituality is neglected."

"Uh-huh?"

"And then she said suddenly it all clicked with things she read about The Goddess in her Women's Spirituality class."

"She's a witch!" I guessed. I couldn't resist.

"Shut up. You don't even know. And she says she felt the Goddess calling her."

"Wait. I thought she was an atheist."

"Shut up!"

"Sorry."

"So now she's super into Goddesses and women's spirituality."

"Okay?" I asked. Beth was trying not to laugh, but I hadn't heard anything funny.

"Which is great. But she said she thinks she might be a lesbian."

"Oh my God."

"Can you believe her?"

"Yes. What about Dan?" It wasn't that I cared whether Nina liked men or women, it's that last I heard, she was in love with a man.

"That's what I said! And she said that wasn't love. She said it was a desire for affection. Because before, she couldn't accept her attraction to women."

"Oh," I said. "Maybe that's true."

Beth started giggling. I was glad to have thrown Sartre on the floor, but I don't really think being gay is something to laugh about.

"I think it's great if she's a lesbian," Beth said. "Good for her. But then she said she realized she's in love with ME!"

"Oh shit."

Laugh? Why did Beth think that would make me laugh?

"Oh shit, is right! She wants me to go sleep with her in The Pit tonight!"

"What?"

"Shhh!"

"Are you going to?"

"No! Just because she's a lesbian doesn't mean I am!"

"What did you say?"

"Ugh. God. It was awful. I didn't know what to say. I was so shocked. Not the lesbian part, but that she said she's in love with me. And she wants to go get in The Pit with me!"

No kidding. What's wrong with her? Beth is *my friend.*

"She's one of my best friends and I love her. And I mean, she's beautiful but...she's too unstable! For one second, I almost said yes. For the hell of it. But then she would latch onto me like a leach and drive me crazy. Look at Dan."

"I know."

"Anyway, I told her I love her but I'm not in love with her, and we should just be friends."

"Ugh. I would throw up," I confessed. If I was ever going to get busy with a girl, something I couldn't quite imagine, it would have to be a different one.

"You should have seen her. The way she looked at me with her huge eyes. You know what she reminded me of?"

"What?"

"Harriet, when we first got her."

We stuffed our faces into our pillows to smother hoots of laughter.

"Shhh!!"

"This is definitely better than *No Exit.*"

"What am I going to do?"

"I don't know! What can you do?"

"Why couldn't she be in love with Sheila?" Beth begged the fat orange carrot on the wall. "That would be perfect!"

"Oh please. Do you think she's really a lesbian? Or she decided it would be cool to be one?"

"I don't know. Maybe she is. Maybe that's why she was so unhappy."

"Well, for her sake I hope so. I hope she figures out how to feel better. I guess we'll find out when Dan gets back from California."

We turned the lights off, and I lay listening to Beth breathe as we fell asleep. I always expected she would have boyfriends—boys love her—and I tried my best to like them. I endured them. I shared her with them. But a girlfriend? Why is that different?

I lay there a long time wondering how I would survive if Beth and Nina became lovers. I didn't care if Nina liked girls. But please not Beth. I don't know how you share a girl with a girl.

༉༂

I'm dead asleep when I sense the movement in my bed and at first I think it's Tom. Then I'm awake. I'm in Los Rios, Tom is not in my bed and the whole house is moving. I hear my sister, Estefani, in the bed bedside me, start to scream, "¡Mami! ¡Mami!"

The bed is shaking, and the floor and the walls and the roof. Someone screams in the neighbor's house next door.

The wall, I think. O God, the cement wall. Please don't let it fall on me. Please don't let me be crushed here under the rubble in this place where no one will ever find me.

"¡Está temblando!" squeals Mamá Hilda from her bed. In our house where the inner walls do not meet the roof, we are all in one room.

Then it stops.

For one unforgettable second, a complete stillness descends over the world. Until that silent second I haven't noticed the noise in the grumbling belly of the earth.

Then the tiny town bursts to life. Petrified dogs bark warnings from every porch. Confused roosters commence madly crowing an hour of their imagining. Disturbed hens cackle from their perches in the jocotes. Mamá Hilda and Papá Tito, in their bedroom, have turned on the light, and a yellow beam streams over the wall to where Estefani and I lay in our beds.

"¡Qué temblor! ¡Qué miedo! ¡Muy malo!" Estefani exclaims to me over and over, as if I have missed what happened. "¿No tiene miedo?"

Mothers and sisters call to each other from windows and porches. Doors slam. Somebody kick-starts a motorcycle. Everybody is up and dashing around calling out to neighbors to be sure everybody is okay. I do not move from the cocoon of my bed draped with its mosquito net.

Radios and televisions come on up and down the street. My

brother Diego, in his room on the other side of the house, turns his radio on loud and over the ruckus of the awakened town comes a voice saying words that penetrate the fog in my brain:

"...la calma. La cosa más importante es mantener la calma. La calma. La cosa más importante es mantener la calma."

It's two o'clock in the morning, the radio voice says. I roll over under my mosquito net and thank the wall for standing there beside me. Everything in this flustered little town is alright.

In the town on the other side of the hill, we will learn tomorrow, clocks leapt from their nails on the walls. Houses twisted away from their front porches, but no one is injured. No homes are lost.

The only casualty of this quake is my notion of the earth as something definite and unmovable.

Tom and I bought tickets to see the Grateful Dead. Okay, to be honest, Tom had to buy them and I paid him back. We invited everybody else too, but neither Sheila nor Beth nor Nina wanted to spend their hard-earned money tagging along with the hippies, even for 48 hours. I was kind of relieved. You know how it is when you have different kinds of friends that don't go together well? And you don't want to push them apart, but having them all together at the same place at the same time gives you a stomach ache? Right. I wished more than life itself that we could all be one smiling happy family of Deadheads, but seeing as we weren't, I didn't want a bellyache at the show.

I threw my backpack into the bus with the tie-dyed curtains and a squirming bunch of braided, beaded kindred spirits. The two and a half hour drive to Deer Creek is long enough to merit an overnight camping trip where we could practice being Deadheads and see if anyone would guess we were really wayward Mennonites in disguise. The campground buzzed with tunes drifting from VW buses and long-haired barefoot girls selling hummus on pita bread. We pitched our tents among hundreds of other pilgrims, feeling at home in the throng of stoned peace lovers. We could wear our beads, forget our shoes, share our beer with the neighbors, and not take showers. Give peace a chance.

Menno Simons would be so proud.

Laura, who was two years older than me and had been to lots of Dead shows, told me I should bring my homemade bead necklaces to sell.

"Are you serious?" I asked, skeptical of what genuine hippies would think of my efforts.

"Oh yeah. People will love them!"

"But they're not that..."

"Shut up." She gave me a little slap. "They're gorgeous."

Then it clicked—she smokes a lot of weed and she'd already bought three.

"Okay. I will."

"I bet you'll sell all of them. Bring a blanket or something and if you see the cops coming, quick roll it up and act like you're just sitting there. That's what everyone does. You'll see."

Subversively selling necklaces under the noses of cops? That sounded way too exciting to miss. The worst they could do is take away my necklaces—you can't get thrown in jail for that. Can you?

"You mean, during the show?"

"No, no! Outside. During the day. Just bring them. You'll see what I mean."

It wasn't hard to figure out, once you got there. And I wasn't nervous about the cops, either, after about ten seconds. A benevolent microcosm sprung up on the grounds surrounding the amphitheater: people in costumes with their dogs, their lovers, their friends, their children—milling about, mulling it over, sunbathing, napping, doing tricks, playing instruments, dancing to the music, passing by, staying a while, and lined along the thoroughfare selling cold water, clandestine beer, t-shirts, swirly skirts, sandwiches, concert bootlegs, books, bumper stickers and of course every imaginable variety of jewelry. It was like dreaming and being awake at the same time.

I found an open spot beside the busy lane between a guy with huge dreadlocks selling colorful hair wraps and two girls who appeared to be sound asleep. I knelt and spread out the quilt my mom made me, and then arranged my flower necklaces in a semi-circle around my knees. I pretended I was sitting in a garden. I smiled up at each admiring glance and did my best hippy-girl glow, asking, "Flower necklace? Five dollars."

Laura was right. I sold almost all of them, and traded one to the guy beside me for a hair wrap that lasted two years before it fell off—the one and only dreadlock I ever owned. I paid Tom for my ticket and bought flowy rainbow skirts and a bumper sticker that said "My Goddess gave birth to your God" even though I had nothing to stick it on.

Sure enough, the cops came by, but it was all a part of the circus going on around me. Their somber stroll down the lane provoked a wave effect that ran ahead. When the guy with the hair wraps suddenly whisked his wares into his tie-dyed sheet and rolled everything into an innocent-looking ball, I flipped my quilt in half and stretched out, pretending to bask in the lovely summer sun. The cops strolled by, scowling in their uniforms behind their dark glasses.

A guy with long dreads and a big Rasta hat was leaning up against his bicycle smoking some sort of cigarette on the other side of the road. Minding his own business, as far as I could tell. Some more guys with dreadlocks and Rasta hats wandered up to him and started chatting. I couldn't believe my eyes when they grabbed him and threw him on the ground.

I thought he was getting mugged right there in broad daylight.

"They're cops," the hair-wrapper informed me when he heard me gasp and saw the shock on my face.

"Cops?"

"Yeah. Pigs."

I stared in horror as one of the fake Rastas kept the real one pinned, and the other took his backpack. He pulled from it a package of something I couldn't see but I got the idea.

"Poor guy," I said.

"It's a damn shame," the hair-wrapper agreed. "You be careful."

"Yeah," I said, "I will. You too."

"Always, sister."

I guess he couldn't tell by looking at me that I didn't know which of the potential evils had been confiscated from the guy with the bike, or that whatever it was, I had never sampled it. The fake Rastas led their distraught victim away in handcuffs shouting something about his bike.

Even though pot smoke hung heavy in the air everywhere we went, I didn't try any. I could have. Some of the braver renegade Mennonites rolled joints and passed them around, but neither Tom nor I had the nerve for even a puff. We were too scared of getting caught. After I watched the cops jump that guy, even my curiosity about being stoned evaporated. Are you kidding? Risk that in order to be even more muddled? I've never needed any help to lie around giggling at cloud shapes.

The hippy scene gave me something easy to be, something to have in common with somebody. It's kind of like being Mennonite—as long as you're nice, you're at least half way there.

Every day I could think of fewer things I had in common with anybody. Being brokenhearted does that to you. Even in my house, I felt alone. Right before my eyes, I was turning into the straight white girl while everybody else was transforming into lesbians and women of color.

All of us wanted a new world, but mine was different. The world I wanted had a little house with a red floor, and on the back porch in the afternoon shade, a potter with skin like a baby's cheek and the fingers of a pianist pulled vases from clumps of clay. I didn't know what to do besides stare at the geometric designs I painted on the wall. They read Audre Lorde. I read Sam Sheppard.

A sympathetic community of lost souls was a perfect fit for me. And even if the Deadheads were actually dead like that weird guy said, so what? I thought I might be too. If they smile at you, tell you your dorky necklaces are beautiful and offer you a beer, let's not get lost in the details.

❧❧

"Sometimes I'm afraid."

"Of what?" Beth said over her book.

"This is going to sound dumb," I confessed. I figured she would laugh at me, but I didn't care.

"Okay."

"That I'm going to hell."

"You are?"

"Yeah. Aren't you, ever?"

"Well... Sometimes. I guess."

"I know it's stupid. I mean, I don't think I even believe in hell. But sometimes, I'm scared anyway."

"Why?"

"I don't know. I guess because I do so many things you're supposed to go to hell for. You know."

"Yeah. I think it's bullshit, though," she said, and acted like she was going to start reading again.

"Oh, I know!" I hurried. "I do too. I hope so, anyway." I wasn't done and I needed her to keep listening. "But it was so ground into my brain my whole life that drinking is a sin and premarital sex is a sin—even dancing is a sin. Well, dancing I don't worry about."

"But you guys don't actually...'have sex'. Right?"

"We might as well."

"Yeah. True."

"But it's not just that. I mean, like, in general. If my parents saw me—or anybody else from back home—they would say I'm not living a 'Christian life.' That would mean I was going to hell."

"Well, I don't think you are," Beth said.

"I hope not. But sometimes I'm afraid I could. You know? What if they're right? They could be. We don't know."

"Man, I keep forgetting how much your parents made you go to church," Beth marveled, laying down her book to fix her ponytail.

"Yeah. A LOT. But you did too."

"Not like you, girl. My dad wouldn't go, so my mom only took us sometimes. Mostly she made up Sunday School lessons for us at home. And, yeah, she talked about heaven and hell. But... I don't think she believes in hell either."

"Really?"

Beth shrugged.

I never heard of a grown-up Mennonite who didn't believe in hell.

"You're lucky," I said, and I meant it with my whole heart. I wished I could blow off eternal damnation like that, but I was too scared.

"Yeah I guess so."

"It doesn't seem fair that you can say, 'Oh yes I believe in God and heaven, but I don't believe in hell and Satan.' You know? Don't they, like, go together? You should have to believe all of it or none of it."

"Right. I guess I'm not sure I believe any of it," she said.

Had I gotten anywhere? Not really. Did I feel any better? No.

"I like the eastern religions better," Beth said, opening her book again to show me we were done. "Like Buddhism."

"Yeah."

"They don't have heaven and hell—just people and Nirvana."

"That would be great," I said, getting up to make more coffee. "I wish we could have that."

⚱

When I was in sixth grade, I stood up in church during what we called "Revival Meetings." This decision to stand to my feet, while the congregation sang a final hymn of "invitation," meant that Jesus had moved my heart of stone and that I wanted to confess my sins, accept God's forgiveness and now be eligible for heaven and church membership.

The preacher, called an "Evangelist," was George R. Brunk III, and he pasted a paper inside the front cover of my Children's Living Bible—a Bible with color pictures of The Good Shepard carrying a lost lamb back to the fold, and Daniel gazing up to heaven from the lion's den. The paper has my name and the date written on it in George R. Brunk III's handwriting. It says that on this day I decided to follow Jesus and that my sins are forgiven. And he signed it, I guess, as proof.

This little paper, he told me and the other sixth graders who knew that sixth grade is the time you should stand to your feet during Revival Meetings, is in our Bibles for us to look at because sometimes Satan taunts us, telling us that maybe God hasn't truly forgiven us, that our souls really aren't saved. Now, when the devil tells us our salvation isn't real, he smiled, we can open our Bibles to this reminder that the devil is a liar and that we are going to heaven when we die.

I didn't bring my Children's Living Bible to the upstairs apartment on 11th Street. It sat proclaiming my salvation from the bookshelf upstairs in my parents' farmhouse hundreds of miles away in Pennsylvania.

Tell me how a church that once suffered bodily torture for insisting on adult baptism now baptizes sixth graders and calls their decision an "adult decision?" Other decisions I made in 6th grade include putting chewing gum on the seat of Chris Kreider's chair and pretending to throw up chocolate éclairs in Kathy Hershey's front yard.

How is a piece of paper like that supposed to make you feel better if you start to suspect that heaven isn't real—or hell either? I can't imagine that George R. Brunk III's signature will get you through the pearly gates if you decide it's all a crock but then you turn out to be wrong.

ᦄ

The morning Sheila came home from Rajesh's house covered with self-conscious smiles, she went straight to bed and slept half the day. When she woke up, she ate several fried eggs and assured us repeatedly, through mouthfuls, that "nothing" happened—that they talked and made out and slept curled together in his bed, but when he tried to undress her she had to get her inhaler.

Then she waited for him to call. And she waited.

A whole day passed.

Two days passed.

She came home from work and wouldn't leave the house. Every time the phone rang she jumped like a startled rabbit but she would never answer it.

This became so painful to watch that even though I knew, I asked, "What's the matter, Sheila?"

But she couldn't quite say it. She made sounds that didn't equal any words I knew.

"Did Raj ever call?" I prompted.

"No."

"Really?"

"He could've lost my number. Do you think I should call him?"

"No!" Beth commanded.

Nina agreed.

"Well..." I hesitated. I would. I would have caved days ago. Maybe that's why, at 20 years old, I was on my first boyfriend.

"Why?" Sheila begged.

"Because. Men like when a woman plays hard to get."

"Because. You don't want him to think you're desperate."

"But I am desperate!" She was not kidding.

"I think you should call him if you want," I said. "What does it change?"

In the end, she called.

Yes, he said, he'd lost her number. So she gave it to him again, and he said he'd call her as soon as he was a little less busy.

She bounced around the house for the rest of the evening.

But he didn't call. And he didn't call. She almost collided with him coming out of the library the next week, and he said hello, but didn't invite her over. So she invited him. He said he couldn't make it.

I could see how so much hair twisting might produce a bald spot in the middle of a girl's head, and her nails were bitten down to the skin. Beth forbade her to call him again and threatened to disconnect the phone.

"He's not worth it, Sheila," Nina sighed. "Men use women like that. It's accepted by society for a man to use a woman for his pleasure, and then throw her away." I couldn't help but notice how her eyes flickered from Sheila to Beth, to see if this news would cause Beth to reconsider the benefits of loving women.

"Forget him!" Beth scoffed. "He's hot, but he's a jerk. You don't need that shit."

Sheila reached for another Kleenex and blew her nose.

"He doesn't deserve you," Nina said.

Sheila told her to shut up.

"He doesn't," I agreed, and I didn't agree with Nina all that often. "You're beautiful and funny and smart and sweet... What's he? He's all handsome and fancy. So what? You deserve somebody who treats you like a queen."

"Yeah."

"Amen, sister."

"He just...I mean...I never..." Sheila does not have a way with words. "I thought he liked me."

"So, make him jealous," suggested Beth. It always works for her.

"How?"

"Find someone else. Who else do you like?"

"No one."

"Come on."

"I don't."

"Well who could you pretend you like?"

"I don't know."

"Who's on your team at work?"

"Guys?"

"Yes, guys."

"Hey, maybe you could be a lesbian too!"

"I don't think so. I mean no offense, Nina! I mean...I think...I just..."

"It's okay. I'm kidding, silly."

"Oh."

"So?" Beth insisted.

"Sammy," Sheila mumbled. "And Neil. Truman Wise."

"Not Truman."

"No!"

"Gross."

"Sammy?"

"I don't like Sammy."

"Why?"

"He's annoying."

"He looks like a rabbit when he laughs," Nina said.

Sheila giggled a little.

"Neil?"

"Neil's cute," Sheila said.

"Do you like him?"

"Well... I don't know."

"Could you like him?"

"I don't know."

"Doesn't he have a girlfriend?" I asked.

"Who the fuck cares?" Beth practically shouted. "It's not like you have to marry him. Just pay attention to him and let Raj see you having fun with him. Girlfriend shmirlfriend."

I know Neil, and he most definitely had a girlfriend—a boring girl named Katie who wore boring clothes, had boring hair and hung out with boring people. Neil sometimes worked with me as a lighting tech in the campus theatre and he was somewhat boring himself. Sweet, but boring. He didn't come to any of our parties and he frowned at me when I told him I didn't get up for church on Sundays anymore. He wasn't a match I could see for Sheila, but Beth was on a mission that she didn't seem to want my opinion of.

It worked, kind of. It solved the problem with Rajesh, anyway. He never did call, but while Sheila waited for him to feel jilted, she fell hopelessly in love with Neil.

Chino's Moon

There is one last-resort summer job into which the un-
luckiest of the unlucky fall, and I was headed straight toward
it. Corn de-tasseling crews move through endless Indiana fields
pulling tassels from ears of corn, getting cut by sharp leaves,
bitten by mosquitoes, crawled on by beetles, soaked by the
rain, burnt by the sun, screamed at to hurry; hungry, thirsty
having to pee. Desperate high school and college students do
this every year because they pay you well if you survive. The
stories that came to us from the unfortunate souls of other
summers made us shiver and cringe.

Nina was safe in the Admissions office. Beth and Sheila
escaped into the refuge of Campus Maintenance jobs when
classes ended, where they washed windows and painted walls
in the dorms. Due to an absurd stipulation in some financial
aid policy, I was ineligible to earn full-time pay from the school
because my parents own a farm. I don't own a square inch of

it, mind you, and was in danger of having to sell my body for bread, but the school refused to pay me for more than 20 hours of work per week. Period. Forget it. And who, but cornfield bosses, will hire full-time summer help three weeks into June?

Right before my own eyes, I was turning into the prodigal daughter. I could imagine myself, in a matter of days, eating corn silk through my tears as I wrenched it off the ears.

Tina Corning saved me on the eve of the de-tasseling sign-up. She's the peppy young religion prof who hired me to transcribe the hours of boring conferences she attended and interviews she conducted as research for her doctoral dissertation. She'd spoken with every important Mennonite in the fifty states about some giant church merger that may or may not be about to occur—surprisingly stuffy subject matter for someone so lively. I've never typed for more hours about something I found less interesting. But who cares? There were no bugs, and no one shouted at me.

I loved Tina's house. I loved Tina. She had a full refrigerator and sometimes even ordered pizza for which she never allowed me to pay a penny. She never ran out of toilet paper or dish soap or anything, as far as I could tell. I don't like typing at all, but considering the alternative, I uttered not one word of complaint from my comfortable chair.

Each morning I biked to Tina's house and typed until my eyes crossed. I could work as long as I wanted—there was no chance I was going to run out of boring interviews to listen to. The recordings of presentations in large rooms took me forever to get through. The voices sounded like they were coming from the bottom of a swimming pool and I had to listen to the same garbled segments ten times, trying to make sense of the bubbles.

In the afternoons, or when I couldn't sit for one more minute, I did yard work for the professors who so recently released me from the clutches of their dismal reading assignments. It seems that, having failed to convert me to their cult of over-analysis, these professors decided to take advantage of my stubbornness by pitting it against their lawns. In the end, they who had worried that I was witless, and I who had diagnosed them as almost-dead, ended up laughing over iced tea together, eating cookies and telling stories. How can you not love quirky old people who worry about their irises and the bald spots in their yards? And how can you not give cookies to the girl who appears to enjoy the muddy jobs in your garden? Even if she didn't pay a speck of attention in your class.

❧❧

Beth said smoking pot looks boring. All it does is make you stupid. Look how stupid stoned people are.

I can't say I thought it looked boring. I thought it looked fun. Everybody at the Dead show was smoking pot and I guarantee you nobody there was bored. The hair-wrapping guy beside my illegal necklace display didn't look bored. He was happy as a clam. Sometimes I wished I hadn't chickened out.

Nina said Anthony and his friends used to smoke pot when their parents were gone, and the horrible smell gave her headaches. Then she went outside to smoke a cigarette with Beth. Whatever. Sheila said she would never smoke pot because she's sure she would get caught. That's probably a good idea. Poor Sheila suffers from enough paranoia without doing anything that could risk making it worse.

But curiosity nagged. What would it do to me? Would it be scary? Would I see weird things that weren't there? What if I went completely crazy and ran naked through the streets? What if I loved it so much that I couldn't stop, and ended up a drug addict shooting heroin in back alleys? They say that can happen. It all starts with the first time. What if I started crying? What if I accidentally told Tom all about the boy in Los Rios? What if I called my parents on the phone and they could tell I was on something?

Finally I couldn't stand it. I had to know. I hadn't become an alcoholic when I tried alcohol. Why would I become a drug addict if I tried drugs? Everyone else tries pot when they're a rebellious teenager, but when I was a rebellious teenager, I sneaked a Talking Heads tape to a church youth group retreat. How embarrassing to be twenty years old and never to have smoked a joint. Tom hadn't either, but he was pretty sure marijuana would provide him with new enlightenment. He started calling it "herb" like Bob Marley. We decided to try it together the way we were trying everything else.

As the last summer classes ended, Beth had a marvelous idea: we could throw a party downstairs in the empty apartment. All we had to do was go down the interior stairway between the apartments, walk over to the front door, and open it wide. That, and pray that Barb the landlady didn't bust us. Beth had the inspiration just in time too, because soon afterward Troy and Brenda moved in with their Megadeath posters and almost nobody except us was left in town.

Tom had the joint stuffed in his pocket, and after enough cheap wine to embolden us, we went out onto the porch to light up. I already knew what to do—you hold your breath for as long as you can after you suck the smoke in. I guess it's easier for smokers than for non-smokers like me. And it probably helps to have decent weed.

I coughed so hard that Tom had to get me water. Each time my pink lungs met the sketchy smoke, they had an ipecac reaction and it came spewing back out. I had to concentrate with all my might to hold down the tiniest wisp for two seconds. But I made up for my lack of duration with my diligence. I smoked and smoked, hacked and gulped. I hadn't expected this to be difficult.

I could tell Tom wanted somewhere to hide. "You feel anything?" he prompted, rubbing my back.

"My throat is killing me," I rasped. "No. You?"

"Yeah. I feel kinda...nice."

That's Tom for you. He wasn't any higher than I was, and we both knew it. He always acts like being positive helps everything. It doesn't.

When we were burning our fingers on the roach, we went inside to see the movie on the TV that Colin brought over from his parents' basement. The movie was one of those trippy films that are supposed to be funny to high people, with no recognizable storyline or plot. I added my body to the clump of warm wiggly friends on the floor and waited to see what would happen.

Maybe I'm having a delayed reaction. Did I not do it right? Wait. Is that it? Is it starting? I kept asking myself if I felt like doing or saying anything weird. I kept waiting to think everything was funny. I kept checking to see if the movie was getting interesting.

After a while I gave up trying to follow the movie. It was too stupid to be worth the film wasted on it. My eyes were dry, my throat burned and my head felt like a pumpkin. Tom was being an imbecile, trying to act the way he thought a stoned person should, giggling and saying "yeah, man" between every sentence.

What an anti-climax. I coughed my lungs out for nothing. I heard some people don't get high the first time. I don't know why. You can get drunk the first time. You can get pregnant the first time. Why can't you get high? The only unusual thing that happened is a sleepiness as gummy and thick as bread dough pushed me flat onto the floor, from which I don't remember getting up and going to bed.

ഇൟ

Nina's brother Anthony is three years older than she is, and seemed to be completely normal. We thought he was the coolest, and worshiped him with the starry-eyed adoration that only your friend's inaccessible older brother can evoke. He could get into the liquor store too, which only deepened our devotion. He thought we were a pack of silly girls with no taste in wine. We didn't care a bit what he thought as long as he got it for us and brought it over himself, pressing the change back into our eager hands with his scratchy fingers.

He raised one eyebrow and cocked his head sideways at us the night Beth and I hit him up for a fifth of Jose Cuervo Especial. We decided to splurge. The end of Twentieth Century Thought in Lit deserved proper celebration, and there was no use trying to throw another party—everyone left town like an evacuation as they wrote their final exams.

He'd come over to pick up Nina and take her out to dinner, not to do our illegal shopping, but if you smiled and twisted your hair when you ask him, he never said no. He nodded his admiring approval at our sudden improvement in beverage choice and sped off to Reynolds' while Nina finished accenting the dark circles around her eyes with black eye makeup. Whew. That was close. Otherwise we would have had to ask Tom to go pick Jose up for us, and if we'd asked Tom, then we would have to invite him to drink it with us. Don't get me wrong, there were advantages to drinking with Tom, but this was between us and Twentieth Century Literature.

With Nina out to dinner, and since Sheila only drank pink wine, it was just Beth and me—like back in old times except we didn't drink then. We filled up our bedroom with candles in spite of what Smokey the Bear would say, and from the start we sat on the floor so we wouldn't have anywhere to fall. We opened the bottle and passed it back and forth, making up a toast for each round. Beth started.

"To us. For being done with classes."
"To us."
"Cheers."
"Cheers."

"To us again. For getting summer jobs that are not in the cornfield."
"Amen!"
"You can't say amen with tequila, dumbass."
"Okay sorry. Cheers!"
"Cheers."

"To Harriet and her unborn kittens."
"To Harriet. God bless her vagina."
"To Harriet's vagina."
"Gross!"
"You said it first."
"But I was blessing it."
"Okay. God bless Harriet's vagina.
"Hallelujah."
"Amen."
We had to stop and laugh for a little while.

"To Professor Williams. For still being alive."
"And to Camus and Sartre for being dead!"
"Oh my God! Cheers!!"
"Cheers!"
"And may they never return."
"They won't."
"How old do you think he is?"

"Who?"

"Williams."

"Oh. I thought you meant Sartre."

"No! Williams."

"Don't know. The same as Sartre?"

"To Mary Perry for living her whole life with a name that rhymes."

"And for being crazy."

"And for being crazy."

"Cheers."

"Cheers."

"Hey wait! And to the cows! For having a lot of stomachs."

"Oh my God! Why did she say that?"

"I have no idea."

"She is so weird."

"But she's very smart."

"Do you think she's senile or do you think she's always been that way?

"I think she's always been that way."

"So do I."

"Can you imagine when she's senile too?"

Then we had to fall over on the floor and laugh hysterically.

"Okay. I got one."

"What?"

"To Nina and the carrots in the Co-op."

Beth fell over laughing again. "Be nice!"

"I am nice!"

"Oh my God. The carrots!"

"And to the garden." I was trying to pour our shots but the bottle wouldn't stay over the shot glasses.

"What are you doing?"

"Making a mess."

"Poor garden."

"That garden was never going to work."

"And those fucking pear trees!"

"Wait? Why are you fucking the pear trees?"

We both fell over and Beth was trying to say she wasn't fucking the pear trees, she just wanted a few damn pears from those trees that were taking forever, but she was laughing too hard to talk.

I knew what she meant.

We were on, "To Sheila for being our first friend to go bald," lying on our backs kicking like Kafka's cockroaches and screaming with laughter when Nina and Anthony came home.

"Whoa," he drawled, nodding at us as we coughed and sputtered and tried to regain control. "You are two tequila mamas."

That we were.

"Y'wanna a shot?" we asked him.

"Naah. You girls look like you're doin' fine."

Right again.

"To our moms. For having us."

"To the Mexicans. For inventing tequila."

"And big sombreros."

"Salud!"

"Salud!"

"To being roommates in the nursing home when we're 95."

❧❧

It was driving me crazy that Methuselah still had to live in an ice cream bucket. I had cracked his fishbowl last year trying to scrub the algae out of it in the dorm sink, and it was high time for him to have a decent home that he could see out of like other fish. But how? The glass aquariums at Wal-Mart cost $10.99, which equals two weeks of food for me. Unless I came up with a better idea, he wasn't going to get a glimpse of the wide world until Christmas.

I spied the solution on top of our overflowing trash: the jug of Carlo Rossi rosé that we had emptied on Saturday night. Of course a fish could live in that. It was big enough, transparent, and free—or already paid for. The bottleneck presented the only problem, but there has to be a way to get that off. I scoured the premises and came up with a Neanderthal repertoire of tools comprised of rocks, sticks, and a hammer.

I was outside in the yard kneeling on the wine jug with one knee, trying to knock the top part of it off with the hammer, when Troy came out of the downstairs apartment. He said he wondered what that weird and dangerous-sounding noise was.

The idea didn't seem so bad until I started trying to explain it. I mean, maybe I would be lucky enough to break the top off without bashing the thing to shards and slitting my veins. You don't know until you try.

"Are you trying to break that?"

"Well. I'm trying to get this off," I said, pointing to the spout with the cute round handle.

The way he chewed on his lip made it clear that he wasn't a believer.

"What for?"

"I want to put my fish in it. My goldfish."

I think he was speechless, which made me start talking fast.

"It's because his fishbowl broke a long time ago and he's in this plastic bucket he can't see out of. And I feel bad for him."

I felt stupid, now. Just go mind your own business, Troy-With-A-Mullet.

"I got something you could use," he offered.

"Yeah?"

"Yeah. It used to be my hamster cage, but he died. So you could have it. It's plastic, but it'll hold water."

"Oh. Cool."

That was even better. What was I thinking, anyway?

"That way you won't cut yourself," he said, and went inside to get it.

Talk about nice neighbors. Troy isn't the world's smartest guy. He bolts things onto Winnebago's all day, if that tells you anything, but he had me and my half-baked college degree on that one. Mechanical reasoning and all.

ৡৣৣ

If I were the child of my host parents, the man called Chino would be my uncle. All day he sits outside his little store where the men and children congregate, selling soda pop, single cigarettes and mint candies. He laboriously reads the sports and human interest stories in the newspaper he pays for every day from his till. At night he sleeps on a fold-up cot in the back of the store to discourage thieves and ambitious coons from helping themselves to his wares.

He has an impish grin on his face when he says to me, "Quiero hacerle una pregunta."

"Okay," I agree.

"¿Usted cree que un hombre fue a la luna?"

"¿Cómo?"

He repeats the question, asking if I believe that a real man went to the moon, and then adds, "Un americano."

"Sí," I say, perplexed, thinking, doesn't everybody know that?

Then Chino does something I have not imagined. He throws back his head and laughs a deep belly laugh, not of mockery, but of genuine mirth, as if I have performed an amusing and clever trick. It's one of those contagious laughs that make you giggle even when you don't know what's funny.

"¿Usted no lo cree?" *I ask. I have never heard of anyone who flatly disbelieves what we all know to be true.*

"No, no, no," *Chino shakes his head.* "Yo, no."

"¿No?" *I ask, a burst of laughter escaping me, too.*

"¿Cómo puede ir un hombre a la luna?" *he asks, looking at me as if I have told him I am certain elephants can fly.*

But didn't you see the pictures? I start to say. Then I stop. But they showed it on TV, flashes through my mind. Sweet Lord. Listen to me. These are the stupidest reasons on earth to believe anything.

"Pero ellos trajeron rocas," *I try.*

"¡Rocas!" *Chino scoffs.* "¿Quién dice que en la luna hay rocas?"

Now I am the one who cannot stop the laughter. He has left me speechless.

Delighted to have such a cheerful audience for his musings, Chino continues. "¡Son mentiras! Puras mentiras. No se puede ir a la luna."

The more I think about it, the more I can't stop laughing. Because who even cares? One of us is right and one of us is wrong, and in the end, down here in the shade of Chino's front porch a hundred miles from nowhere, what's the difference?

When the moon climbs round above the trees, glowing its milky light over the houses that circle the plaza, I imagine Chino's moon in place of the one I have always known. I tell myself that the news clips and photos shown to me as truth are Hollywood productions, entertainment. I summon the virgin moon, the one untouched by men, the one Chino says tells them when to plant the seeds so they will grow, when to prune trees and set fences, the one who brings babies into the world and tells the old people when to die.

I stare at the silent white orb until I see it born. My skin prickles in the warm night, and a something flutters in my chest. Chino's moon smiles roundly down, mysterious and new.

꩜

Life improved a bit after we discovered split peas. It wasn't that we liked them so much; it's that they were cheap—even cheaper than lentils, which we thought were the cheapest. I spied them in Kroger's in the bean section, lying on the bottom shelf looking forlorn and a little yucky. The name sounds like something your grandma would make you eat, but at that price, who cares? This is why God made curry powder. I held them up and asked Beth if she thought we should try them. She said she remembers hating them as kid. But not to worry. Kids hate everything that isn't candy.

Split peas look like lentils, so that's how we cooked them. We scooped them into a pot to boil with salt and spices, onion and garlic, until they yielded up a scalding green broth. We piled them beside the rice on our plates, and dug in. What a sorry disappointment! No wonder Beth hated them when she was small. We hated them now, but lacked the courage to admit our enthusiasm had been blind. They weren't yummy and soft like lentils. They were coarse and crunchy and tasted like straw. Why does cheap food always have to turn out to be disgusting?

But hungry girls will do what they must. Beth worked to perfect the flavor of this nasty-textured dish and make it palatable. When you have no cookbook, you make things up as you go along. Any spice was a step in the right direction. Soy sauce worked wonders. Circuit-shorting amounts of cayenne pepper at least masked the gristly taste behind a different sort of pain. I put Velveeta cheese on top and named the dish Aunt Diana's Cheese Peas. They were slightly less horrible that way than they were plain.

Much later, after gnashing through pounds of them and giving up hope, I found out the truth about split peas. They aren't like lentils at all. They cook to a succulent softness, but they take three hours like other dried beans. No wonder they crunched in our teeth and didn't taste as good as we pretended. We were eating them raw. I'm sure our moms or Grandma Friesen would have been glad to share this little secret with us when we needed it, but we never thought to ask. We suffered and chomped in our self-inflicted misery of independence.

We didn't really ask our moms things. We told them things. Or more likely, we talked about the cat.

❧

Thank God for the porch roof. If you prop the kitchen window open with a stick, you can climb out and sit on the blazing shingles. We ate out there when it was too hot to eat inside, drank there on cool evenings while we waited for the stars, talked, shouted, told secrets and sang. We also found the porch roof to be a great spot for sunbathing—much better than the yard with its tickling bugs. We couldn't afford bikinis, so we basked on the porch roof in our underwear. What's the difference? No one could see us anyway because we were lying down. And if they did, we didn't care. Up there, they couldn't get us.

The underwear sunbathing ended after the night of the bicycle episode.

Beth heard it first. She and I were in our room sloppily folding laundry in our shorts and our bras. The night was too hot for shirts. And besides, bras are clothes.

"Is that a bike?"

"What?"

"That. That sound."

I stood still and listened. There was the spinning sound of a 10-speed bicycle coasting along the dark street in front of the house.

"Yes," I said, and dropped to the ground where no one outside could see me in my ratty old undergarment.

"Turn off the light," Beth said, jamming a shirt over her head.

"Why?" I asked. I thought putting on shirts covered it, so to speak.

Beth turned the light off, herself. First we heard silence, but then it came again—the sound of a slow bicycle coasting in the opposite direction.

"Somebody's out there. That's the fourth time that bike has gone by."

I went to the open window and pulled the curtain across, then fumbled around for a shirt.

"Shit," I said. What dumb-asses we are, I was thinking. We never pull these curtains. Ever. "I'm locking the door."

I went into the living room to shut the door that stood open to the porch and the steps which connected us with the dangerous world. As I turned to walk back to Beth in the dark bedroom, I heard it through the living room window above the alley by our steps: the sound of a bicycle coasting. My hand reached before I knew what it was doing and smacked the light switch, plunging the living room into shadow.

"Turn off your light," I said to Nina, who was kneeling on her bed with a bouquet of paintbrushes, turning Dan with Grapes into a one-breasted Amazon.

"Why?"

"There's somebody outside."

"A stranger?" she whispered, reaching for her lamp.

"Yeah," I said.

Now the only light in the apartment came down the hall from the kitchen.

Beth walked into the living room and sat on the floor with her back against the couch.

"Shouldn't we call the police?" Nina asked.

"I don't think so," I said, lying on the floor under the window from where I could listen in hiding.

There it went again: the sound of a bicycle coasting by below us, first one direction, then the other.

"I think we should," she disagreed. "Someone is stalking us."

A creep, maybe, or a curious kid captivated by girls in bras. But a real rapist or murderer on a bicycle? I had a hard time summoning that kind of terror. Would the police even come if we reported somebody riding a bicycle up and down a public street?

"I think we should keep our curtains shut," Beth said.

"Yeah," I said. "Me too."

Up until that moment, we believed ourselves to be invincible in our perch on the second floor, the sole point of access over which we imagined that we exercised complete control. Amazing how quickly those illusions crumble the minute you suspect something unpleasant might walk up the steps and stand on the other side of your one way out.

"It's hot in here! Why do you guys have all the curtains shut?" Sheila asked when she got back from the surprise birthday party Neil's girlfriend threw for him. Thank God she missed the spooky sound of that bike. She would have locked herself in the bathroom for four days if she'd heard that, even though it went away almost as soon as the house was dark.

"We decided to shut them," I said. "We heard somebody outside on a bicycle."

"Doing what?"

"Just riding back and forth."

"Who was it?"

"A strange man," Nina answered.

"Oh my God."

"It's okay," Beth said. "We shut the curtains and he went away."

"Oh my God...!"

"It's okay, Sheila."

"Did you call the police?"

"No."

"It's alright."

"Were you scared?"

"Not really," I lied. "More like annoyed."

We were a lot more careful about our curtains from then on, especially after dark. And we didn't sunbathe on the porch in our underwear ever again. We didn't make a rule or anything, it's just that no one felt like doing it anymore.

༄

Tom was a sociology major, which is ironic considering how much he bitched about society. Governments disgusted him, religions annoyed him, and he was suspicious of every kind of "ism" there is except Communism. We thought Communism was a fabulous idea, even though we secretly realized it would never work. He wanted to run a homeless shelter someday, or something like that, to help the people our evil society chews up and spits out. Part of me wanted to point out that to run a homeless shelter he was going to have to have rules and cooperate with things like the state. But I'm not big on arguing over hypothetical situations. In the meantime, he had a full time summer job helping his uncle paint houses.

He was almost always in a crappy mood after work because he hated spending summer days inside. He liked the checks that the painting company cut him, but suffocating in the smell of paint gave him headaches. In my opinion, he gave himself the headaches by thinking too much in all those fumes.

My favorite thing was when he went home to shower first and came over when he felt better about life, exuding sandalwood instead of turpentine. I kind of wished he wouldn't come over when he was grumpy and morose because of course it was my job to cheer him up. Sometimes I got my wish, sometimes I didn't.

We climbed out the kitchen window and sat on the porch roof in a patch of shade from a lazy pear tree. Work clothes and turpentine. No shower. No good mood.

"Are you okay?" I asked him.

"I don't know. I guess I'm feeling depressed."

"You are? Why?" I didn't see what Tom had to be depressed

about. He had a real job, a car, and housemates who aren't crazy. And what was I? Chopped liver?

"'Cuz. I don't know."

Fear shot through the middle of my chest like an arrow. He wants to tell me something he doesn't want to tell me.

"Try."

"Well... I don't know. I'm just confused."

"About what?"

"Everything."

"You want a beer?" I almost never have beer, but that day I did.

"Yeah. That would be great."

I climbed into the kitchen again, forcing myself to breathe. Was he going to dump me? Could he somehow sense what I said in the last letter I mailed to Costa Rica? I got two beers from the fridge and climbed out to sit beside him on the roof again. The hot breeze felt like dragon breath.

"Cheers."

"Cheers."

He was going to have to talk, since I'd produced beer, and he knew it. He wiggled a little, squirming with an inner discomfort that spilled over into his back and legs.

"I just don't know anymore. I mean, I'm just not sure about anything."

I couldn't look at him. I thought I might faint.

"I mean like Christianity and all. Sometimes when I'm with you, I think about the church and everything they say. Like my stupid Sunday School teacher when I was a kid. I don't know what I believe anymore."

A tidal wave of relief swept over me. Suddenly, I loved him a hundred times more. I promised myself never to write any more letters like that.

"I hear you," I said, trying not to sound delighted. "Me neither."

"I'm so confused."

"Mm-hm."

"Everything used to make sense, and I knew what I believed. Now I don't know anything. It's scary. And depressing."

"I know what you mean. I feel the same way. But it first hit me last year, so I guess I'm getting kind of used to it."

He took an enormous draw on his beer and tried to make the burp quiet.

"I don't know what I believe. About anything. Like this," he said waving his beer in the air in front of us, as an example. "I don't know if we're going to hell. I don't even know if I'm a Christian—if I want to be one."

"I don't know anything, either," I said. "But that's why I like it here—at college. Back at home, every question has only one right answer. Everything else is wrong. And 'I don't know' is not an answer. Here, questions can just be questions. Y'know?"

But not for Tom. Not then.

"But a question has to have an answer," he smirked at my silliness. "Right?"

"Why?"

"Oh, so then nothing is true, and nothing matters, and the whole universe is random, and we can all go around doing what we want? What if I want to kill someone?"

"Okay," I said, backing down.

"You can't say that." He glared at me, needing the answer to his question not to be another question.

"I'm just trying to say I agree with you," I said, smacking an ambitious mosquito. "I don't know anything either."

Tom has a paper-thin line between being for him and being against him. The smallest step can land you on the wrong side of it by accident.

"Something has to be true," he insisted, and there was agony in his voice.

"Yeah," I said, thinking about Chino's moon, not one bit convinced anymore.

❧❧

August broke over us like a freshly poached egg, thick and scalding. Matthew, who we adored for having introduced us, called Tom from his parents' house in Iowa. He and his girl-friend Skye were done following the Grateful Dead now, and the VW bus where they live was parked until September in his parents' driveway. Obviously, Matthew's parents are way cooler than mine, or any other parents I knew of. They didn't claim to like that he lived in a bus with his girlfriend, but they were ready not to make a big deal about it. He asked if we wanted to come out for a visit and said we could sleep in his old bedroom in the house. No one else was.

A road trip sounded like the perfect solution to my stir-craziness, so the minute Tom delivered the invitation, I began cramming things into my backpack. Beth asked me what was going on, and I told her Matthew and Skye invited us to Iowa.

"You want to come?" I asked, knowing she would rather be dragged behind wild horses than stuck in a car with Tom, me, and the Grateful Dead all the way to Iowa and back.

"Well..." she said, raising her eyebrows, and staring past the profanities on the wall, "Can I?"

"Of course!" I could have kissed her, I was so happy. With Beth, you never know. But when she glows on you like the sun, everything in the world is right.

I almost wrecked the car on the way there, and I got stopped for drunk driving on the way back. The near-wreck happened because I drifted to the left while fiddling with the cassette player, and when I realized it, I panicked and overcompensated to the right. Then I had to swerve left again to stay on the road, and right again in a terrifying zig-zag, wider each time. Speeding around Chicago on the freeway, all I could do was brake, and pray not to be rear-ended.

I wasn't drunk when the cop stopped us on the way home. I was trying to open a stick of gum, the only weapon I found with which to fight the horrible sleepiness that claimed first Beth in the back seat, then Tom beside me. I guess I was weaving. The two o'clock sun hammered down on us like a punishment and there was no air conditioner to temper it. At 60 miles per hour with the windows half way down, the pressure of warm air on my face felt like a feather pillow, lethal and inviting. The cop didn't even make me take a breath test or get out of the car—I guess my sleepy, cherub face was convincing enough.

After my first pull-over by a cop, I stayed wide awake for a long time and Tom stayed awake with me in case I needed someone to open another stick of gum for me. It was the day after the night we went skinny dipping so we weren't exactly functioning on a full night's sleep.

The five of us were sprawled in Matthew's back yard under a suffocating blanket of night speculating about the new school year when Skye had an idea.

"Hey. Let's go swimming!"

"But we don't have swimsuits," I stupidly said.

"Swimsuits?!"

"Who needs swimsuits?" Matthew asked.

"I hate swimming with clothes on." Skye made a face to show how much she hated it.

"Right on," Tom said. "Where?"

"My dad's friend has a pond we can go to," Matthew said. "If no one's home."

I was a little worried, but I wasn't going to say so. Beth and I had gone skinny dipping in my parents' farm pond once after everyone was asleep, but that's different. It's a familiar pond. The idea of swimming in an unfamiliar place with nothing at all between, well, me and whatever else lives there is somewhat terrifying. I didn't care about being seen naked. Half of us had already seen me naked anyway. I did, however, care about the risk of getting arrested for trespassing with no clothes on. Do they let you get dressed before they handcuff you?

"I think we need some tequila," Skye added.

Excuse me? Drunken naked trespassing? Oh well. They aren't my parents' friends.

Tom went into the liquor store, then we zoomed off down the road singing "Friend of the Devil" at the top of our lungs while Beth unscrewed Jose Cuervo's cap.

Matthew cut the lights and shushed us when we got to the gravel farm lane. We crept along, trying to be unobtrusive in our bus, until the farm buildings came into view and we saw that the house was dark.

"Score! They're not home!"

"Yes!"

"Or they could be sleeping."

"True."

"Do they have dogs?" I asked.

"No dogs."

"Perfect."

The lane curved away from the buildings and into the endless Iowa cornfield. All evidence of danger passed, Matthew turned the lights back on to avoid driving the van into the pond.

It was gorgeous. The water waited, a primordial black in the opaque and breathless night. A wooden dock equipped with a diving board and rope swing beckoned hot, sticky people who spent their last dime on gasoline and tequila to come find free relief. Matthew let the van door open and the *American Beauty* tape playing.

Poor Beth. But weird music is a small price to pay for something to do. Desperate means call for desperate measures.

We piled out of the van with the tequila bottle and stripped on the dock. I tried to leave my clothes in a pile so I could find them later, and in the order I would want them back: underwear on the top, then bra, shirt, and shorts on the bottom. Matthew dove off the dock and came up in the middle of the pond. The rest of us followed, throwing ourselves into the cool milky water and surfacing to catch our breath from the sudden chill. It took us ten seconds to forget that we were naked in front of God and everybody in a stranger's pond.

Those bottles of tequila look gigantic when you take the first shot, but it's amazing how fast they disappear when you share them between five thirsty mouths. The night got warmer and brighter, and our self-consciousness evaporated. We decided to play "Jump or Dive."

We were stifling hoots of laughter at the belly-flopper exectued by Tom, who jumped as Beth called "Dive," when the dusty lane leading to the pond became illuminated by bouncing lights.

"Somebody's coming!" I hissed.

"Shit!" said Beth.

Matthew and Skye both said what the fuck.

I struggled to my feet as fast as my clumsy limbs would move, watching for Tom's head to surface. The lights were getting closer, shooting terrifying yellow beams at the open bus and toward our four wet bodies as we scrambled to dress in a bumbling frenzy. I hoped, for a moment, that the lights might turn and drive toward the house. They didn't.

I grabbed my shirt, jumbling the order of things I carefully placed an hour ago when I was sober, and jammed it over my head. Everything stuck to everything, and only one arm hole presented itself. Beth was giggling uncontrollably, mumbling,

"OmyGod. OmyGod."

Skye tried to kill two birds with one stone. She found her flowy tie-dye skirt and pulled it over her head in attempt to wear it like a dress, but became caught like a fly in a web. She thrashed around, trying to get her arms through the top while keeping the bottom down, but it stuck to her wet skin in all the wrong places. Matthew stood behind her, fighting to find the leg holes in his shorts. Tom surfaced, saw the lights, and swam to the dock where he remained motionless in its merciful shadow.

I stuffed my underwear into the pocket of my shorts and was dancing a strange two-step, trying to coax denim up wet legs, when the vehicle rounded the corner and blasted us with light. There we stood, plain as day on the dock, half naked and frantic, not sure if we should laugh but how could we help it?

The car stopped. I waited for the flashing lights to ignite, but whoever it was, it wasn't the cops. Maybe they were disappointed lovers in search of a place for a romantic encounter. Maybe some other bored students hoping for a swim. Night fishing? I guess it's possible. Somebody else who goes to Matthew's parents' church? That's when I remembered the tequila bottle sitting at the edge of the dock, almost empty, the dregs reflecting a lovely yellow light.

"Shit! The bottle!" I said as I closed my shorts and stuffed my bra in the other pocket.

"Whatever," said Skye, who now had her entire skirt wrapped around her neck.

Maybe it was the farmer, who, having heard a noise or sensed that something was amiss, came to check out what was going on at the pond. Whoever it was, they didn't try to join us, and they didn't roll down the window to yell at us.

The car executed a three point turn in the dusty lane and the yellow beams were replaced by two red eyes that vanished into the corn. We sighed, gasped, giggled, cursed. Tom came up out of the water and polished off the tequila in one gulp.

"Who do you think that was?" Tom asked.

"How would I know?"

"Not the cops."

"What if they call the cops?" I said.

"Why would they call the cops?"

"I don't know."

"Maybe we should leave," Matthew said to Skye.

"What?"

"Yeah, we probably should," Tom agreed.

"Come on!!"

I thought leaving was an excellent idea. It was all fun and games until we didn't know who that had been, or what would happen next. And four of us were drunk twenty year olds.

"Do you think they saw the tequila?" I asked.

"I don't know, but they saw my ass!" Matthew answered.

"I bet they're laughing their asses off," Beth said, wringing out her hair.

"I hope so."

"Yeah, let's get outa here while we can.".

"Okay. Whatever."

We climbed into the van and headed out the lane. We drove all the way to the road with the lights off, bursting to shout out our relief as our tires hit the pavement of public property.

And so, to complete the spree of criminal activities, we finished off the evening of trespassing, indecent exposure, public intoxication, and underage drinking with the crime of driving under the influence. I don't remember a thing about the ride home, but I do remember how hard we tried to act sober when Matthew's mom came down to the kitchen at 3:00 in the morning to see what in the world was going on as we clumsily scrambled her carton of eggs.

❧❧

Poor Colin met an awful fate. I don't mean he died or got maimed or anything—I mean we had to stop hanging out with him. And he got a smudge on his reputation that nobody in their right mind would want. His single moment of bravery didn't go at all the way he must have hoped.

This was no real loss to me. It's not that I disliked him, I just thought he was about as interesting as a cardboard box. He wasn't ugly or obnoxious—in fact, he was smart, unreasonably generous and occasionally funny. He was the last person in the world who you would expect your roommate to make you stop inviting to parties. We kind of needed him. With so many people gone, our Red Light parties had become rather disappointing and we needed bodies, especially males ones, to fill our house and make us feel like we were irresistible, grown up, and a little bad.

Colin did not make me feel irresistible, but he worked pretty well on Nina, being as he was Dan's best friend. And Beth said she thought he was kind of cute—at least until he made his fatal mistake. Colin's allure, which he shares with Curtis and Dan, was that he grew up in Africa. They all went to the same English school together in Kenya, a missionary school at which their parents taught. That's how you know your town has a lot of missionaries: you have to start up a school for all their kids. Beth didn't grow up in Africa but she did live in Nairobi when she was four, so she had things in common with Colin that were lost on the rest of us.

At the last Red Light party he came to, I saw him laugh until he couldn't breathe—that one time. We were playing a drinking game we made up as we went along, and I'm going to venture he was losing. The game involved trying to guess what word somebody else was thinking, and having to drink a big slug of wine when you got it wrong.

After the wine ran out, the discussions began—the part that made me start yawning and nestle up against Tom. Before I could open my mouth and display my infinite ignorance, Tom and I slunk off to the Pit of Sin. Everybody else must have wandered home or to bed, leaving Colin and Beth on the couch under the red lightbulb reminiscing about the Africa of their childhoods.

Beth informed us the next day that Colin was, without exception, uninvited from our future parties. She could not bear to see him anymore.

"Why?" Nina asked, her eyes widening. Then a terrible thought occurred to her. "Did he do something to you?"

Beth set her coffee on the floor beside her, covered her face with her hands, and started giggling. "No."

"Uh-oh," I said. "What?"

"Did he say something?" Sheila tried.

"No."

"So?"

"Okay, you guys," she said, looking up. "You can't tell anyone."

We swore ourselves to secrecy. Cross our hearts, hope to die.

"Well. Everybody else went to sleep or went home. We were sitting there," she said, pointing at the couch, "talking about Africa. When we were little. Then all of the sudden he—um. Started telling me how beautiful I am."

"Oooo," I hooted.

"Go Colin!"

"Shut up, guys. Wait. And then he said he wanted to kiss me."

"So, did you?" Nina asked.

"Of course," Beth answered like it was obvious. "Johan is an ass and Curtis is gone. Why not?" Then she collapsed into giggles again, and pulled the neck of her t-shirt up to cover her face.

"What?!"

"What's so funny?"

"So?"

"It was disgusting!" she gagged, coming out of her t-shirt with a face like Mr. Yuck. "Aaagh! He just poked his tongue out all squishy and gushy! Bleagh!" She almost wretched through her laughter.

"Gross!" we all howled, making more faces like Mr. Yuck.

"I'm sorry Nina. I'm sorry guys. But I don't think I can look at him again."

"But isn't he in your major?" Nina asked.

"Oh no!" Beth wailed. She covered her face again and curled on the floor in a fetal position. "Yes!"

There wasn't much to be done about that, but indeed we didn't invite him to our house anymore. I felt a sorry for him. I wonder if he heard we were having parties and not inviting him. I wonder if he ever suspected the reason.

Poor Colin, the boy who couldn't kiss. That's one of those things you'd better do right the first time, or you may never get to do it again.

❧

My Papá Tito tells me we're going to the neighbor's house where we will have vino de coyol. *I don't know what this is, but the beginning word is wine, and I am interested. He knows that I'm not supposed to have wine, that alcohol is forbidden by my college, and that as my host father he is to forbid it for me, too. He does, to the best of his ability.*

There are people gathered around a felled tree. It is a palm, long as the arm of God. I would not have suspected that, outside of the pages of a story book, wine could come from a tree. Don Lazaro and his sons have lopped off the enormous leaves with their machetes and carried them away so that the neighbors will not be stung by scorpions, and they have propped up the tree's bald crown, slanting its length slightly downward toward the severed trunk. Dusty children in mismatched clothes clamber up onto the long tree and leap off, shrieking. Careful mothers sit along it clucking like hens. Don Lazaro stands proudly by with a tin lid in his hand, covering and uncovering the square hollow he has cut in the lowest end. He dips into it with his tin ladle and pours a thin white liquid into a glass, which he hands me. He dips in again, and hands another dripping glass to my Papá Tito.

My face must well reflect my incredulity, because Don Lazaro laughs, and my Papá Tito says, "¡Tome! ¡Tome!" reminding me of what I am going to do. He takes a long draw.

I can feel dozens of eyes on me as I lift the tepid liquid to my lips and taste it. Sugary palm tree sunshine brewed in the dark of a thousand starry nights slides into my belly, and I come up for air laughing. Who would have guessed? It isn't wine at all. It is sweet milky sap from veins of wood.

Don Lazaro lifts the lid again, so I can see how the liquid pools in the cut he has hollowed. He points behind him to the capped bottles sitting on a little table under a mango tree and ex-

*plains that the milk, if left to ferment, does indeed turn to wine—
a strong, devastating liquor that will make you dizzy like this, he
says, and laughing, shows me a stagger.*

I try the wine as well. Not then. Later.

*Not with my Papá Tito, but with the boy and some of his
cousins and some of our friends. We walk up the scalding dusty
road one wind-still afternoon, to the next town where no neighbors
will be spying. Or if they are, the news will arrive too late to my
vigilant hosts.*

*The shocking taste of strong palm liquor is solid as the trunk
of a towering tree, forceful and untamed. We laugh through bottle
after bottle at the little table with uncomfortable benches in the
shade of next year's wine.*

*I forget the clock, the calendar, the suitcase under my bed. I
forget that I am speaking another language, that I was not born
here, that I will not die here, that everything about this moment
will disappear like a dream.*

*A blinding headache splits my skull by the time I arrive home
late to dinner, happier in spite of the pain than on any other day
before or since.*

I knew that letters were going to come but wasn't prepared for what happened when I found one lying in my campus mail box. I flashed hot, then cold, then nauseous, and I had to go somewhere to read it—somewhere that is not home. No one must look at me.

Across campus on the other side of the railroad tracks that run behind the theatre, there is a tree I sometimes climbed. It's a scruffy old pine with branches that are naked near the trunk—a hiding place I discovered last spring before I met Tom, when the guy I'd been in love with all year started going out with somebody who wasn't me.

I rode my bike to my tree with the letter in my pocket and climbed up to the seat where I mourned that other heartbreak.

Don't cry. Whatever you do, don't cry.

I didn't want to go home with red eyes and snot on my shirt.

Don't cry.

The problem wasn't my housemates. It was Tom I was hiding from. Obviously, at our house you could cry if you wanted and you didn't owe anybody an explanation. But Tom would expect one. One I didn't have. When he said he loved me, I said it back. And I meant it. I did.

I didn't cry.

I read the letter, and read the letter, and read the letter. I held it to my face. I pressed it to my arms, to my cheek, to my heart. All I could do was think about breathing. All he asked was for me to come back, but I couldn't move from that tree.

Can you love two people? If you love two people, is one fake and one real? Which one? Or are they both lies?

Can you fracture into a thousand pieces on the inside, and outside no one will know? Can you die and still appear alive? Can you live without understanding anything?

What is happening to me? Why can I not let go? Why does it matter more than air? How will I live my life?

Can you ever be alright again, ever, after you are absolutely broken? How can so much pain fit into a heart the size of your fist?

It was like the day in Los Rios that I reached from the shower for my towel and was stung on my pinky finger by the scorpion hiding there. I stared in dumb disbelief at my hand, as a blinding pain surged through my tiny finger and exploded into the entire room. It charged the air around my body like electricity and shook the walls of concrete. All the while, my smallest finger looked exactly the same.

Sometimes Grandma Friesen lent Sheila her car. It was a pickle-green monster from the 1960s, wide enough to fit the four of us across the front seat. Sheila would tell her that we need the car to go to the grocery store or that she had to return a book to the library in Riverside, and Grandma Friesen almost always said yes. Whatever Sheila said was always true. She would not have lied to Grandma Friesen for all the rice in China, although Grandma Friesen never would have known the difference.

We loved having our own set of wheels because when we did, we were free and independent women. We could go anywhere we wanted and do whatever we felt like, as long as it didn't cost any money and wasn't illegal—like drinking—because Sheila was petrified of getting caught.

The car was parked outside on the sweltering Saturday night that we congregated in Sheila and Nina's room, while Beth tried on Nina's clothes. There wasn't anything else to do. We didn't feel like throwing another lame-ass party. We didn't have a television. There were no on-campus activities.

Beth pretended to be a mean, haughty model, teetering around in a pair of heels that were two sizes too small for her. Nina has sexy little dresses that are even sexier on Beth, because Beth's legs are twice as long. One after the other, Beth pulled them on and wrenched them off, probably tearing Nina's heart out by prancing around in her underwear. Sheila and I pretended to be judges, giving her outfits numbers like "9" or "7.5," and we had to say why. The only things of Nina's that would ever have fit me or Sheila are her socks.

The worst thing about being poor is that it's boring. You can have a heart of gold and be as smart as Albert Einstein, but if you have no money, you have no choices. You get to stay home and watch the grass grow. You get to brew another pot of coffee and tell Beth the blue top is a "5" because she got the buttons crooked. Pretty soon, it gets old.

"You guys, we never do anything," Nina complained, and flopped down on her bed. The parade of her cute clothing in disuse depressed her.

"I know," I said. "I'm so bored."

"Yeah," Sheila said. She was laying on her back with her feet up the wall, like a worm trying to go up backwards. "I hate being poor."

"I wish we could go out dancing."

"Me to," Beth said, posing in Nina's little red dress. "I feel like getting dressed up and doing something fun. I haven't put on makeup in like a month."

"Me neither," lamented Nina.

"Me neither," I said hoping someone would laugh. I never wear makeup.

"Ten," I said to the dress. Beth tossed her hair and turned to Sheila.

"You guys are so lucky you're skinny!" Sheila burst out, tumbled by a wave of negative self-esteem. "You look great in everything! I could never wear a dress like that. I'd look like a cow!" She sat up to sulk properly.

Things like that are bogus, because what can you say back? That's true, Sheila, you would. Or try to lie? No, you'd look great. Really!

"Yeah, but you have boobs," Beth said. Beth is so quick it's amazing. "Look at me. I look like a boy."

"Shut up," Sheila said, but a giggle escaped her.

"It's true! You look hot in everything because you have boobs."

Sheila told her to shut up again, but you could tell she'd never thought about it that way.

I have plenty of complaints about my body too, but at that moment the miserable inadequacy of my wardrobe eclipsed them all. I can't help having all these hefty German genes, but there is no excuse for me not to own some decent clothes. Everything in my closet is ugly and dumb. That's nothing to cry over, but suddenly I thought I might.

"Hey you guys, let's go somewhere!" Nina was serious.

"Like where?" Beth asked, now that her modeling career had ended.

"I don't know. Like... Riverside!"

"Yeah!"

"What do you want to do?" Sheila asked, worried that Beth would say something she didn't like, or that Grandma Friesen wouldn't approve of.

Riverside isn't big enough to be a real city, but it's a big town. It has a movie theatre, restaurants, bars, a museum and other things we couldn't afford.

"I don't know. I just want to dress up and go somewhere. Can we? Do you think your grandma would mind?"

"But like what are we going to do?"

"Let's drive around and see what happens," Beth suggested. "Maybe there's something free in the park, or we might see someone we know or something. Anyway, it's better than sitting here. We can all dress up. It'll be fun."

Sheila was convinced. She jumped up and headed for the closet.

The only one not convinced was me. I wanted to go somewhere, but does it have to be a fashion show? I had nothing to wear. Nina and Beth wanted us all to be sexy, and I know that I'm about as sexy as a sheepdog. I'd rather stay home and watch Harriet gestate. I'd rather stay home and wash our mountain of putrid dishes.

"I think I'll pass," I said.

"Why?" Beth made her voice sound horrified.

"I'm not really in the mood to go out."

"Why not?"

Everybody stopped and stared, like now I was ruining the party.

"I don't know." They all just looked at me like I had gone completely crazy. "I don't feel like it right now, guys. Plus, I have nothing to wear."

My special clothes were flowy Grateful Dead skirts. Tom thought they were sexy, but I knew perfectly well they weren't. But it was that or cut-offs. I almost choked on a sob that tried to come out of nowhere.

Did you know that it's already dark in Los Rios? I wanted to say. My Mamá Hilda is in the kitchen straining hot black coffee into a glass. My Papá Tito is telling her something about the cows and he makes her laugh. Do you know they call the owls *solococos* because that's what they say into the night?

"Diana you hafta come."

It's hopeless. I don't know what I want. I just know I don't want to be here.

"Come on, Di. It's a house thing."

That's not true. I do know what I want. I know what I want more than air. I want to be in Los Rios. Help me.

"You'll find something. Anyway, who cares what you wear?"

What if I do it? I could. I could get on a plane tomorrow. I would be happy, then. Laugh. I don't care. I know it.

In the end I gave in and went with them, not because I wanted to, but because it was easier than making them let me stay home. Music blasted and girls ran everywhere: trying on, grabbing this, dropping that, sharing mirror space. Hairspray and perfume filled the air. I was in the bathroom brushing my teeth when I heard Beth's scream and the sound of crunching plastic.

"Oh! No! Methuselah! I'm so sorry! Diana!"

I ran to the bedroom holding my toothbrush. I love Methuselah, my little fish. He loves me.

There was Beth, bubbling apologies so fast I couldn't understand a word. There was Methuselah, my precious fish, flopping in the half-inch of water that remained after Beth accidentally stepped on his new home and broke the side off. I ran to the kitchen breathing curses at my stupid idiot friend, filled the old ice cream bucket with water, and hurried back to save Methuselah.

Poor fish. That must have been terrifying. How could she do that? Methuselah has always been in the same spot. Tonight she forgets where he is and steps on him? I was too mad to even look at her. All I could do was stare at my beautiful little fish swimming in the horrible old bucket again, and thank Jesus she hadn't smashed him flat. Beth got towels and cleaned up all the water and I didn't say, *Oh that's okay.*

We drove around Riverside a few times with the music turned up and the windows rolled down. It was by far the stupidest evening of my life, even more stupid than staying home with Harriet. I sat cross-legged in the back seat beside Sheila, singing along with UB40, thinking about what my parents would say if it quit school.

No free activities, or paid ones, were taking place in the Riverside park. Of course we didn't see anyone we knew. What? Driving down the street? In Riverside? Even if we did see someone, what were we supposed to do? Slam on the breaks, leap out of the car and say hello? Too young for bars and too poor for restaurants, we settled for the drive-through at TCBY.

We should have gone to Walmart. At least then, we'd have gotten to walk around and show off the outfits we went to so much trouble to pick out. All that fuss and we never even got out of the car.

❧❧

Mary Perry invited Beth and me inside for orange juice and cookies after we finished watering her flowers. She and Beth got to talking about books, which can take a long time, so Mary had to keep getting us more orange juice and more cookies. I don't have as much to say about books as Beth does, but I can nod while I chew. We weren't going anywhere as long as the free food kept coming, so by the time we got on our bikes to ride home, it was almost dark.

As we crossed the alley and approached our house, we could see that something was amiss. The whole apartment was lit up like Christmas, every available bulb burning brightly in the deepening dusk. Sheila sat outside at the top of the stairway snapping off what remained of the bitten nails on her fingers and toes. When she saw us she jumped up so fast she almost fell down the stairs, her overloaded nerves sizzling like stir-fry.

"Oh you guys! Oh you guys! Something happened to Nina!"

"What?" Beth asked.

We couldn't help but imagine the worst. Was there blood? Is she alive? Was that the ambulance siren we heard as we left Mary's?

"I don't know! You have to come see this," Sheila sputtered, hurtling herself back up the stairs.

"Where is she?"

"In here," Sheila answered, and stopped with her hand on the door.

Oh. That confused me. If Nina was safe inside with Sheila and her nail clippers guarding the door, then nothing too awful had happened.

We hurried up the stairs behind Sheila, mumbling curses.

I had a feeling I was going to need Tom's car again to take her to one kind of hospital or another.

Sheila, shaking and pale, lead us straight to the kitchen where we stopped short and sucked in our breath with horror.

The wall. The whole grimy yellow wall was transformed into a crimson and black mural of agony and death. Some ghostly being, larger than life, writhed there in blood and smoke, dying a death unidentifiable and unimaginable.

"She's in our room with the lights off and she won't talk to me," Sheila wheezed.

Without another word, Beth disappeared into the dark room which I would not have entered to save my mortal soul. There I stood, speechless, in the kitchen with Sheila who was losing it herself and the ghoul on the wall.

"Let's go out on the porch," I said. I almost turned the light off so we wouldn't be able to see that thing in its aguish, but the thought of it hiding in the dark was a thousand times more terrifying. We climbed out the window and sat with our backs against the house in the shadow where it couldn't see us.

We left it on the wall. We couldn't paint over it, seeing as it was Nina's creative work and the rule was there are no rules. We cooked while it watched over our shoulders. We washed dishes while it suffered beside us. Our lucky lack of a kitchen table saved us from having to eat our cereal with it. We got so used to it that we barely noticed it anymore, except when we brought visitors into the house and heard them catch their breath. I even tried not to smudge it as I wiped the wall when Harriet got diarrhea and shit all over its foot.

If Dan would have loved Nina even a little, maybe she wouldn't have had to take that little Pine View detour and then spend the summer insisting she was done with men. She might have spared us the horrible thing on the kitchen wall.

I know all about unrequited love and how miserable it is, so don't call me unsympathetic. I've just never been quite so public about it. I guess that's the difference between a painter and a writer: one scribbles morose metaphors in her notebook, self-conscious about how much they suck, and the other depicts her pain in living color beside the refrigerator.

Why would you paint a horrible monster like that in your kitchen? Because you don't want it in your bedroom? And the living room walls are too full for a life-sized likeness? And because you need to look at the face of the beast in your mind? I thought about the cave people, and how they supposedly painted portraits of their prey on their walls.

In my next life, I'm going into anthropology. I have a new theory. If you take Nina's artistic impulse and stretch it back a zillion years, you could propose that they painted the shapes, not of the beasts they hunted, but of the beasts that hunted them.

❧❧

The most important difference between Nina and me is that I never had the desire to hurt myself like she said she did. Her hell, kindled by whatever it was, looked velvety and luxurious to me. At least she could scream for help. I opened my mouth, but no sound came out.

I was desperately jealous of the permission she gave herself to let go, to fall apart. I wanted to crumble too but I couldn't. I didn't know how. My eyes felt like marbles in my head, retrieving information which kept me from falling down the stairs or barreling through stop signs, but which was devoid of all coherency. Nothing made any sense.

The last thing I remember, I got on a bus to leave Los Rios. I was sad, but I was all right.

Now, I am nowhere. I am not in Los Rios. I am not on a bus. But I am not in my body, either. My body is hollow. Where am I?

I climbed the tree where I read the letters and waited to feel myself crack but all I did was get terribly hungry, after a while, and crawled on by a caravan of ants.

What can be done for me? Who could help someone like me? No one can give me the answers. No one can give me the questions. The past and the future don't belong to each other and I don't know where I am.

What good would it do me to crack, scream, shave off my hair? How do you solve a riddle with no words?

❧

Beth went for a walk with me because there was nothing else to do. The whole time, I kept searching for words to ask her if we were alright, but everything I thought of sounded clingy like Nina. We stopped at the park and sat on the worn-out kiddie toys in the afternoon shade. Beth picked the faded pink elephant and I got a galloping greenish horse. She lit a cigarette.

"Can I have one?"

"You don't smoke."

"So?"

"Are you serious?"

"Yeah."

Beth raised her eyebrows and handed me one.

"If I breathe in mostly air and just a little smoke, I can do it."

"Ooo," Beth said, mocking my feeble attempt to be bad, "Go girl," and lit my cigarette.

"Cheers."

"I hate this town," she said, exhaling a cloud at the pink elephant.

"So do I."

"There's nothing to do."

"I wish we had a car."

"I wish we were in a real city."

"Same here."

"Like Chicago."

"Yeah. Let's don't stay here next summer."

"Where should we go?" Beth brightened.

I smiled because she said we. "Montana."

"I knew you were going to say that."

"It's so beautiful there. You have to see it to believe it."

"Yeah."

There was no way Beth would ever go to Montana, but it was fun to imagine. And to talk about something different. My parents took us west when we were kids, and I fell in love with the mountains the minute I saw them lifting from the plains.

"We could get summer jobs."

"In Montana?"

"Sure."

"Where would we live?"

"I don't know. We could get an apartment."

"Are there jobs there?"

"We could follow the wheat harvest."

"What?!"

"The wheat harvest. Didn't you ever hear of that?"

"Of wheat?"

"No, silly! Following the wheat harvest. You sign up, and then you spend the summer harvesting wheat from south to north. And you get to go everywhere."

"But what would we do?"

"I don't know. Learn to drive combines?"

Beth burst into laughter.

"We'll kill ourselves! Or someone else!"

"You're right. We would," I said. The cigarette was making me dizzy in a good way.

"But there might be a lot of hot guys," I tried.

"Harvesting wheat?!"

"Well, maybe."

"What if we went to Montana and got regular jobs?"

"What if we didn't want to come back?"

"Well, we have to graduate."

"Yeah."

"How will we get there?" She was pretending to be interested, so I pretended she was serious.

"Bus. Train. We could hitchhike, but we might have too much stuff."

Beth laughed again. "Two girls by the road with twelve suitcases!"

"The train would be fun."

"The train would be fun," she agreed. "Do you know anybody there?"

"My parents do. There's this nice old couple they know. We stayed at their house. And they have an extra room."

"Would they let us live in it?"

"I don't know. They might."

"You want to go all the way to Montana to live with old people?"

"Well..."

The coach turned into a pumpkin right there, and the white horses turned into mice.

"You're crazy." Beth rolled her eyes and crushed the butt of her cigarette on the pink elephant's head.

"Yeah. Probably."

"I'm going to go to Chicago," she pronounced, leaving me all alone by the road with my suitcases on the way to Montana. "My cousin Kyle lives there. I can sleep on his couch. And waitress or something."

She didn't say we.

"That would be sweet," I said.

"Fuck yeah."

I thought we loved this town. I thought we loved our apartment together. Now, she hated it here so I said I did too, but really, I didn't. I only hated that she didn't love it after all.

"Let's go home." Beth got up. "I have to pee."

I stamped my cigarette on the green horse, and looked up at the humid white sky.

❧❧

"Bájese de allí," my Papá Tito says to me on my perch in the tamarindo tree beside Chino's little store. "Se va a convertir en una mujer mona."

I think he is joking, so I throw my head back and laugh my best carefree laugh. He is teasing me as if I were his little girl. In my country, we tell children they'll break their necks if they aren't careful. Turn into a bad monkey woman! How cute.

"Bájese de allí." He says it again. "Es malo subirse los árboles en Semana Santa. Se le puede salir la cola de mono."

"¿Yo?" I ask. Is he serious? This grown man thinks climbing a tree in Holy Week could turn me into a monkey? Oh my. I smile my most reassuring smile. No chance.

"Sí. Bájese de allí. Ya."

Do I have to obey him? I'm not a baby. And I'm not going to grow a tail.

"Vamos," *he says.*

His eyes are shifting, and they won't look at me. His voice has gone cold, and his face is turning dark as night. Everyone has grown quiet. Everyone is looking away. Only the radio continues to blurt out tinny salsa music.

Suddenly, I sense the fear.

I try to swallow my disgust as I swing down out of the tamarindo, embarrassed. How in God's name was I supposed to know that climbing a tree in Holy Week puts you in danger of becoming a monkey here? How?

And don't tell me they really think that.

"Vamos a la casa," *he says, and it isn't a suggestion. It is a command. We start back to the house. His face is dark and fearful.*

Tears of humiliation begin to prick my eyes and nose like pins. I am being escorted home like a disobedient child.

I didn't know. I'm sorry. I can't say any words or I will cry.

"No se puede subir los árboles en Semana Santa," *he explains.* "Es malo. Se cree que se puede convertir en una mujer mona."

"Lo siento," *I say, my lip quivering out of control, as if I were the child I feel I am being treated as.* "Yo no sabía."

"Yo lo sé," *he says.* "No llore." *He pats me on the arm and laughs nervously because he doesn't want me to cry.* "No llore."

"Okay," *I say, wiping my nose with the back of my hand and feeling the start of a flood. I want to turn into a bug and crawl away.*

When we get to the house, I go into my room and try to muffle the storm of frustrated tears. I don't want to be a bad monkey woman. I want to be happy and good. I try, but I don't know how.

On one hand, his believing I could turn into a monkey and my crying about it are equally ridiculous, but he can't help it, and neither can I. Thinking about how funny it is makes me cry harder.

༺∽∾༻

I'm one of those unlucky people whose face turns into a potato when I cry. My nose gets red and thick, and my eyes swell shut like little pig eyes. It's pathetic. No glamorous, beautiful movie tears for me. The day Beth yelled at me for making fun of her, I couldn't stop crying. I thought our friendship was over, that I'd murdered it with one stroke and for no apparent reason. I was sure that on top of being white, I had accidentally aligned myself against her growing black identity. Or she thought I had. I'd now proven how ignorant I really am.

I wished I could die of remorse right there on the couch. It was even worse than the time I tripped that guy in the cafeteria when we were freshmen. I was goofing around like an eight year old trying to get him to notice me, and I tripped him flat on his face in the aisle in front of everyone. Which did not lead to a friendship or get me a date. I wanted to die then, too. What do you say? Sorry sounds so stupid. I didn't mean it? Well then why did you do it? That's how I felt on the day I told Beth she would end up like Kelly. It was another terrible thing I did by accident.

Kelly is my sister. She's a year younger than I am, and my complete opposite. She was always the perfect daughter, the perfect sister, and the perfect student. She's the kind of girl who loves kittens and babies and teaches Sunday School. She got straight A's in every subject every time, went on church mission projects in the summers, and wrote me letters about her "walk with The Lord." Yeah. My actual blood sister. For her birthday she wanted a subscription to *Newsweek*. See what I mean? A whole magazine about nothing but politics—and a new one each week. Gross. Her boyfriend was a farm boy who studied agriculture and did not have long hair like Tom. Kelly embodied the opposite of everything I believed to be good and right. I thought she was a total nightmare. So did Beth.

Every day the house shrunk smaller and smaller as we broiled under the roof. Restlessness festered. Sheila took to sitting on the porch, humming absentmindedly in loud monotone and filing her destroyed nails. Beth would fly into rages that I couldn't understand and rarely saw coming. She painted FUCK THAT SHIT in huge letters right in the middle of the living room and I don't even know why. When I asked her, she said she didn't know either. Nina decided we all needed a lesson from the Kama Sutra, so she got it from the public library and set about painting stick figures in unmentionable positions on every available inch of wall space. I was just hungry. I kept opening the refrigerator, but there was never anything to eat. It was like being trapped on stage in Sheppard's play, "Curse of the Starving Class." Sam Sheppard is a genius. I decided to marry him.

The riotous walls closed in us. Our colorful flowers choked in a jumble of profanity and pictures. Now, when you walked in the door, you felt like you were stepping into a pen inhabited by wild animals. And everything was dirty. Beyond dirty. As in, it had been piling up since I got pissed about the carrots.

Beth, Sheila and Nina were sitting on our floor painting their toenails fire-engine red, talking about the movie *Do the Right Thing*. We'd all gone to Tom's house the night before to watch it for the fouth time—no lie. It's a great movie and all, but I pretty much got the idea the first time around. In fact, since Tom's housemates were all in the living room watching the move, we went upstairs and tore each other's clothes off. When we came back down, the movie was over and everyone was arguing about whether or not Spike Lee is saying that *violence* is the right thing.

It was as hot in real life as it was in the movie. Everything that drives you crazy is worse when it's hot. I sat in a corner of the couch with my bead-making project spread out beside me. It was almost too hot even for beads. The red and yellow flowers kept turning into orange blobs.

Beth was saying that the media always blames racial violence on black people and never on anybody white, and she wasn't looking at me—only at Sheila and Nina. I guess my demonstration of disinterest last night had consequences. I watched her and she wouldn't look at me. I tried saying "mm-hmm" and "wow" sometimes, to show I was listening and that I did care. I shook my head sadly about all the bad things in the world. Nothing. I was in plain sight on the couch with piles of colorful of clay, but I might as well have been in Costa Rica.

I decided to try to be invisible. Maybe if they forgot I was there, I could forget I was there.

I hated when we had to talk about racism. It made me want to crawl in a hole, especially when Beth started flipping her ponytail and wagging her finger and wouldn't meet my eyes. She was mad. She had every reason to be. I just wished I wasn't one of the people she was mad at. What am I supposed to do about being white? I wished we could talk about something else and I knew it was wrong of me to think that, so I felt twice as bad. Sheila is every bit as brown as Beth, but she didn't look away when I tried to say something. When she got mad, I didn't get the feeling she was mad at me. Nina is white. But she was a lesbian now, which somehow redeemed her a little. She suffered her own types of discrimination. Or if she hadn't yet, she would as soon as her parents found out. The house brimmed with their righteous anger.

If only I had kept my mouth shut. After trying so hard to become invisible, I almost had it. Then I shot it all to hell.

"So what do you think will happen in South Africa now that Apartheid is over?" Sheila was asking. Speaking of racial disasters. "Do you think they will make Mandela president?"

"I hope so," Nina said.

"Hell yeah," Beth said. "You know he will get elected. If he doesn't get assassinated or something. Everything is changing so fast now in South Africa. And the American news networks SUCK. You never find out anything unless you read *Newsweek*."

I should have kept my smart-alek comments to myself. But no. I didn't.

"If you start reading that," I said, clawing for something that might spark, in the new Beth, a flicker of my old Beth, "you'll get like Kelly."

It was stupid thing to say. Stupid. Ridiculous. Dumb. I'm such an idiot.

"That's not funny, Diana!" she snapped at me like a complete stranger. "I am NOT going to get like Kelly. Just because someone reads *Newsweek* does not make them like HER."

I realize that. Sorry for trying to be funny.

She forgot that I was her best friend.

"If you don't care what's going on in the world, that's your problem—but some of us do. You can go off with Tom and be a hippy, if you want. But these are my people I and care about them. Okay? So do NOT make fun of me!"

She forgot I was the one who yanked her arm to set her jammed elbow back in place the summer we worked at camp. She forgot she was the one who taught me to swear without flinching. She tried, anyway. She forgot about being nursing home roommates, and the time we went to the Halloween party as Siamese twins with all our hair braided into one big braid.

She kept on not-looking at me the rest of the day, and she wouldn't talk to me. Then she went to hang out at Mean Tabitha's and didn't come home. All night, I kept waking up and she wasn't there. I blew my nose so many times that I used up a whole roll of toilet paper and in the morning I looked like

I'd been stung by bees.

It was supposed to be a joke. I though you would laugh and roll your eyes, and do one of your awesome impersonations or something. You could never be like Kelly, even if you wanted to. I take it back, okay? I take my whole self back. I wish I could erase myself and leave a clean, blank spot in the world. Don't worry—I hate me way more than you ever could.

❧❧

Back in the beginning, Beth was like my twin, my other half. She escaped from the dorm to spend as many weekends at my house as my parents would allow. In the extra bedroom upstairs, we zipped two sleeping bags together to make our own cocoon, where we giggled louder and louder until mom woke up to scold us and hiss that it was three in the morning.

We wrote silly songs and tape recorded ourselves singing them. We did homework together and stayed up all night trying to study for tests. We went to the mall and tried on something in every store. We went on church youth retreat weekends and pretended to come home sick so we could skip school on Monday. In warm weather, we pitched the pup tent by our farm pond and went skinny-dipping while blank windows stared at us like eyes from the house. I suffered with her the nervous anticipation of her first date. She suffered with me through my first heartbreak, writing me mean, funny poems about the heartless boy. Strangers, for reasons I cannot comprehend, asked if we were sisters, although we don't look the slightest bit alike. We wrote a silly song about that, too.

She taught me to dance. I taught her to dive. She taught me to put on makeup. I taught her to shoot soup cans with a BB gun. She showed me how to flirt. I took her fishing. I let her, against all the rules, drive the car around the parking lot of K-Mart one night, and she told me all about how it was when Dylan kissed her. She even showed me, with a sweet little peck on the lips. We proclaimed that we came in two flavors like Life cereal: Plain and Cinnamon.

She picked the bad Mennonite college too, but at the last minute, she told me she didn't want to be my roommate. She wanted to keep Gabi, the same roommate she had in the high school dorm. Gabi was coming too.

Oh.

I couldn't breathe at first. I turned to stare through the window even though nothing was interesting so she wouldn't see the water in my eyes or how mad I was. I thought she was only roommates with Gabi because she couldn't be roommates with me. I guess not.

So Beth kept Gabi, and I had to take whatever random girl the college decided to assign me. Then, I knew I loved Beth more than she loved me. I would never have picked somebody else and let the college give her first a girl from Malaysia, who didn't show up, and then a nursing major who had to study so hard she never left the room.

In the end, it didn't matter because our rooms were right next door. Beth and Gabi's room turned into the meeting place for all the girls on the hall, and we piled onto their beds like a pack of puppies to gossip, study, make extra-strength instant coffee, argue about feminism vs. post-feminism, and paint each other's nails.

Now, finally—halfway to graduation—Beth and I had a real apartment together for the summer, and were roommates like I'd always dreamed.

But some sort of deluge or earthquake changed the map I thought I knew. Beth was black, now, and I was white. She was the same Beth, but she was also different, with prickly edges in places where they hadn't been before. I was dumbfounded, lost in a familiar country. She had new music. She had new friends. She had a bright new anger in her walk. She didn't think our old jokes were funny anymore and she scowled at me for saying the Plain and Cinnamon thing.

My dear and only Beth. I would have cut off my hands to keep from hurting her. I would have done whatever she asked. Now I had injured her with my big, ignorant mouth. She told me to go off and be a hippy with Tom, and called somebody else "her people"—not me. I didn't know what to do. It had never mattered to me what color she was.

That was exactly the problem.

How do you start over in the middle?

None of the Above

Dan came back sooner than anyone expected. He called Colin from Colorado at the beginning of August to say he'd never reached the coast. He had a change of plans along the way and ended up at a commune in Boulder. It was alright at first, but he was ready to thumb it home. The friendly hippies were getting too friendly, and his personal things were becoming communal property every time he turned around.

Nina collapsed into sexual confusion when she heard the news. In spite of her supposed distaste for male affection, you should have seen her while we waited for Dan to show up. She smiled and walked with a bounce, chattered nervously, giggled, and made jokes that she found very amusing. Watching her made me happy and sad at the same time.

Undaunted by Beth's vehement rejection, Colin threw Dan a welcome-home party the night he arrived. He invited everyone to his parents' house to eat, drink, and camp on the lawn. Of course we went, because we love Dan. Even Beth swallowed her pride, lured by the promise of free food. Colin's mother prepared a Kenyan feast for us, which we devoured like lion cubs, and endless bottles of soda pop that we spiked with smuggled rum the minute the parents went to bed. Dan regaled us with tales of Ukrainian truck drivers, the night he spent by a freeway in Wyoming, and the hippy chick who took him to the Colorado commune instead of the coast. After that, it wasn't much different from all the others in the summer's long string of hot nights, cheap drink and discourse about the capitalist, racist, sexist evils of North America.

Rumbling air and flickering in the sky convinced us to ditch the tent for the safety of the basement sometime around midnight. We marched down the stairs in a boisterous caravan and arranged our blanket beds in a row on the floor. The last I remember, it was 2 AM and my headache was already beginning.

During the night, I had a disturbing dream in which I heard someone weeping quietly and inconsolably. I awakened in the blackness of the basement and realized I still heard it. I wasn't dreaming. Over the steady tide of sleepers' breath floated the sound of muffled crying. A sliver of yellow light came from under the bathroom door. I slipped away from Tom and stumbled toward the light. Why would someone be in the bathroom crying?

I tapped on the door.

"Hey," I said.

"Who is it?" choked a little voice.

Nina. Who else?

"It's Diana," I said.

For some reason, I was scared. As she opened the door, I braced myself for something awful. But she was all in one piece.

"Nina!" I wrapped both my arms around her. "What's the matter?"

Her tiny body shook with sobs.

"I—I was—talking to...Dan and—"

She couldn't speak.

"Shhhhh." I stroked her spiny hair and patted her back like a baby. "It's okay. You're going to be okay."

She dropped her head on my shoulder and collapsed on me, soaking my t-shirt with her wet face and snotty nose, but I didn't care. I didn't even notice until later. I held her to keep her from falling and rocked her carefully and told her things I never would have thought I'd hear myself say to her.

"You're going to be okay, Nina. You're a strong, beautiful woman. Yes you are. We love you, Nina. It's going to be okay. We love you and we're proud of you. I know this is hard. We all love you and we want you to be happy. You're going to be okay. Yes you are. You can do this. You can. You can, because you're strong and beautiful. And we love you. Shhhhh."

Beth heard us, and came in.

Nina hiccupped to us an account of her conversation with Dan, who snored softly in sweet oblivion. They'd had a talk after everyone else fell asleep. He hugged her and kissed her on the cheek. She told him she missed him, and explained about her Pine View visit. He said he'd missed her too and he was glad to see her again. She told him she'd thought she might be gay after he left, but that now she recognized there was at least one man on earth who she was attracted to. He said he liked her, but he didn't want to get involved right now. He met somebody in Colorado that he couldn't get off his mind, even though he knew he would never see her again. He said he needed time.

He didn't love her the way she loved him, and her whole being overflowed with sorrow. We listened and talked, sitting on the bathroom floor, until Nina was mopping her eyes and blowing her nose. She consented to lie down and rest a while beside Beth.

I went back to bed and shook Tom to wake him up. I whispered to him, in one big sentence, how Nina was in the bathroom crying her head off and how she said she feels so horrible and ugly that sometimes she wants to kill herself because Dan says he likes her but he isn't in love with her. I had to tell someone.

Dan hasn't got a mean bone in his body. He didn't want to play with Nina's feelings or break her heart. He wanted to be a friend. Poor Dan had no idea what to do about her.

I shut my eyes to sleep, but the sound of sobbing haunted me—a sound so hopeless, so lost—the sound of one lone survivor. It was the kind of sound that could have come from the ghost on our kitchen wall.

I thought about how you can love someone you don't really like, just as you can like someone you don't really love.

And how you can hurt someone you love and not even realize it.

And how, if you hurt someone you love and they don't tell you, they may start to resent you for it and you won't know why.

And how you can love someone and also love someone else.

And how, when you've been dishonest with someone you love and they've believed you, you love them a little less for it even though it's your own fault.

And how you can love someone and not even realize how much until it is too late.

And how loving someone doesn't always mean having happy feelings about them; it means not caring if they get snot on your shirt when they're crying.

❧

"Beth."

"What?"

"Are you mad at me?"

"No. Why?"

Don't you hate when people do that? She knew perfectly well why.

"I just feel weird since the other day. I'm sorry—"

"Oh. Yeah." And then she didn't say anything.

"I wondered—are we okay?"

"Yeah. I mean I think so."

"I'm sorry I said that." Then, like an idiot, I started crying again. Why do I always do that? It ruins everything. I'm such a baby.

"Well. Diana, you're my friend and I love you. But sometimes I don't think you get it. You act like I'm just like you—I mean, you always have. And I'm not."

She was trying to be nice, but a hard edge flashed in her voice like a knife. I've heard her angry a million times, but I don't know what to do when she's angry at me.

I wanted to say what do you mean, but I didn't want to seem stupider than I already seemed, so I tried, "I know."

"Sometimes I don't think you do."

I didn't say anything.

"I'm as much black as I am white, in case you didn't notice. And I care about things you don't seem to care about."

"Like what?"

"Like everything! You and Tom—it's like you're in your own little world. I mean, I like Tom and all. He's a nice guy. But I'm not really cool with all the hippy stuff and peace and love and all."

"I know."

"I have other friends too, you know. And you don't seem to care about them."

"What do you mean?"

"Don't pretend to be all surprised."

I blew my nose.

"You don't like Tabitha, and every time she comes over you run away. When I invited the people from the International Students club to our party, you left as soon as they started showing up. Every time we talk about anything I care about, you roll your eyes. Like you think it's stupid."

"I do not."

"Oh please."

"I'm sorry. I didn't mean it like that."

She raised her eyebrows at me.

"I don't know. I mean..."

I could tell that the more I talked, the less chance I had of saying what I meant.

"Your life is perfect and your family is normal. I'm glad for you, but that's not me. I am not like you. When I was a kid everybody used to ask me if I was adopted. Because they would see my mom, and she's white. You don't know what it's like. My grandfather in Kenya? I don't even know him."

I blew my nose again, because what was I supposed to say? Is it my fault for not knowing what she never told me? If my life was perfect, I would not be sitting here bawling. Hello.

"I'm just saying," she went on. "It's not because I'm mad or something. But I'm different than you. I want to spend time around different people. I want us to be friends, but I'm sick of pretending we're the same. And I'm sick of you pretending we're the same."

She had me there. I wasn't pretending we were the same. I thought we were Plain and Cinnamon. What were we really, then? Apples and oranges?

"It's confusing for me," I tried to explain, but I was crying and my lips wouldn't cooperate. "Because when I left for Costa Rica, everything was—" I caught myself. "It seemed like everything was fine. And now I come back and...I'm all confused about everything. There's Tom who always wants to be around me. And you're...different, now. Nothing makes any sense. I'm having a hard time."

"Okay. Well, me too."

"I know. I'm sorry."

"Okay. Stop saying that."

I almost said it again.

"It's not that I don't care. I just. I don't know. You might not believe this, but I love you, and I want to be your friend. That's all."

"I love you too. You are my friend."

That made me cry more. I nodded.

"You have to give me some space."

I nodded again.

Please hit me on the head with something and wake me up when my life says it's ready to make sense.

I made myself wrap my mind around what she said. It took some practice, but eventually I got it. Beth was right. I had always assumed she was like me, although, even in obvious ways, she wasn't. I saw what she meant about how this boxed her in, made our friendship unfair. But I loved her. All I could do was love her. My heart exploded into a thousand self-loathing fragments.

She said we would be friends, and we were friends. When you love someone and they break your heart, nothing is ever quite the same, though. Even if you deserved it. Even if you both pretend to forget. Even if you live to be ninety five.

❧❧

I know my Papá Tito doesn't understand why I cried so much the day he scolded me about climbing the tree; he only knows that I did. Even I can't quite explain the flood of tears that wouldn't stop. But he believes he caused it, which he didn't, and now he wants to make it up to me.

"¿Le gustan los mangos?" he asks.

I love mangos.

"Vamos," he says. "Vamos a los mangos."

"Okay," I say. I would rather be left alone right now, but I know I can't say that.

"Vamos en moto," he says. "Tome. Téngalo," and hands me a burlap bag.

Wow. He wasn't joking.

He kick starts the ancient dirt bike, lays a machete across his lap, and says, "Súbese."

I swing onto the seat behind him and in a moment a cool breeze is blowing my hair back into impossible knots. We drive away from the town on a dirt road that goes through fields and dry creek beds. Then he leaves the road and we bounce into a grove where mango trees billow up like thunderheads, gathered.

"Llegamos," he says, grinning as we get off the bike. "Mire cuantos mangos. ¿Está lista?"

"Sí," I say. I lean over to pick up a soft yellow fruit from the ground.

"No, no," he says. He points up at the tree and explains something that I can't understand, but I can tell he means that we are not getting our mangos from the ground.

He sees the surprise on my face and guesses that I think he means we are both going to climb the giants, and he laughs and says, "Espérese." He scuffles around in the dry leaves until he finds a fallen branch which, with two swift slaps of the machete, he cuts in half.

"Dame la bolsa," he instructs. He opens the bag I hand him, puts the two long sticks inside it, and holds them apart, stretching the bag tight between.

I wait to understand. I thought we brought the bag for the mangos. What is he doing?

It occurs to me that maybe I am foolish. I am lost somewhere in a mango grove with a man I barely know. He has a machete and a burlap bag. I have nothing. If he means to do me harm, there is no use even if I scream.

But he smiles his wide boyish grin, now, and holds the bag out flat by the handles he has made, looking up and acting out the catching of things that are falling from the sky.

My face must be funny, because he laughs. Then I laugh. The more I learn, the more I see there is to know.

Then, as Semana Santa is over and he is safe from ancient curses, he scurries up the enormous mango like an ant, like the monkey which so recently terrified him, and disappears into deep shadows of green.

I discover I am smiling. It's cool in the breezy mango shade that smells of sweet fruit. I listen to the wind ruffle the leaves of the grove and think of how the sound is like water. How did he find this place? Could hands have planted it? Or was it born like the dry creek bed?

I hear him call my name.

"¿Lista?" he asks me from above.

"Sí," I say hoping it is true.

The fat yellow mango drops fast, and smacks into the bag with a force that causes me to stumble. Tito laughs in the tree and says something that must mean to be careful or to be strong.

I roll the fruit onto the ground, and from up in the branches he calls, "Otra." This time I am ready for how fast it falls. I step to the left. I step to the right. Back behind you.

Giggles begin to bubble from my belly at this awkward mango dance. Everything around me is generous: the sun, the mangos, my papá Tito in the tree. They have all so freely forgiven my failures, that I am the only one who remembers them.

❦

For twenty years I heard that I must listen for the call of God in my life; nobody suggested I listen for my life to call me. God was supposed to speak from some exterior place and ask me to do something that would be to some degree self-sacrificial, and I would feel undeniably compelled to do it in spite of the trepidation I would experience. Jonah and the Whale is a prime example: God tells Jonah to go someplace he doesn't want to go, so Jonah tries to run away, but God sends along a giant storm to practically sink his boat and a whale to swallow him when his buddies throw him overboard. Or Moses, having to lead his tribe to wander around in the desert for 40 years. Or The Virgin Mary, having a baby with an angel and getting to explain that to her mom and dad. I would know this call when I heard it. It would be an unmistakable compunction to do something noble but unpleasant.

When my life called to me in Costa Rica, I didn't know who was talking. It wasn't a call to help anyone, so I didn't recognize it. I expected a call to speak, to teach, to improve something that needed to be better. The last thing I anticipated was a call to listen, to learn, to discover what is already right. I'd never heard of a burning desire that wasn't suspicious.

I figured it out. I got the message, eventually, but not that summer on 11th Street. That summer, I wrestled with the angels and nobody made any headway.

Two years later, I finally lay down on the little bed back in Los Rios, and into the dark filled with frog songs came this simple question: "What does it profit a girl if she gains the world and loses her soul?" From that moment on I knew who was talking. Even though, kind of like getting pregnant with an angel, it didn't make a shred of sense.

၄၀၄၇

Mary Perry announced that she wanted to visit her brother in Ohio before the start of the new school year, so she asked me if I would stay overnight at her house. Her dog, Luther, doesn't do well in the car, and she couldn't bear to leave him alone. I couldn't bear him at all, but she was going to pay me so of course I said yes. It was only two nights. She told me to help myself to whatever I found in the kitchen. Free food sounds exciting, but all I found was skim milk and canned soup. I had to walk Luther three times a day so he wouldn't shit on her rug, so even though I could go home in between, it was kind of like living nowhere for the weekend.

The house had lots of bedrooms upstairs, which used to be filled with Mary's brothers and parents. I would stay in her room, she said, because that's where Luther was used to sleeping, and she didn't want him to feel lonely or confused. I'm pretty sure he was both. I'm not the terrier kind of girl. I like a dog I can wrestle with in the yard without being afraid I'm going to squash it. Luther was alright for a small dog, but the dignity of cats is hard to reconcile with the lack of dignity of cat-sized dogs. And he snored.

On Friday morning before she left, I stopped by to receive my last-minute dog-sitting instructions

"Come. Let me show you my room where you'll be staying," she invited, and turned toward the stairway in the living room.

It would have been fine with me if she said, "The room at the top of the stairs," and let me get on my way, but never mind. Old people have their own timetable which is run by its own set of gears. I followed her up the flight of somber stairs to a landing which must have resembled our own living room in its respectable former life. She walked straight across the polished wood floor and into a small, immaculate room. Then she turned and beamed at me. "The queen's chamber!"

I smiled back and even managed an airy-sounding chuckle, as a stiffening kind of horror crept over me.

Oh Mary. Mother of God.

In the center of the room stood a tall, slim, meticulously-made single bed with a pale yellow bedspread—the kind covered with little balls, like the one on the bed I used to sleep in at grandma's house. An enormous crocheted doily hung over the sides of the 3-leafed table that stood beside her bed. On the table sat a loudly ticking wind-up clock, a Bible and a radio that was old enough to get into bars. From the mirrored dresser smiled a photograph of a young, radiant Mary wearing cats-eye glasses. Beside it, stood another older photo of a somber-faced couple surrounded by several young boys and a little girl. The room was almost identical to my own bedroom in the Pennsylvania farmhouse: the tall windows, the single bed, the shade tree outside, the cross-stitched bureau scarf on the dresser. Only, Mary had never left.

"Now you be a good boy, and don't keep poor Diana awake with your snoring," Mary lovingly instructed Luther, who wagged his tail at her in non-comprehension. "Be a good boy."

I lay on the hard little bed that night staring at the ceiling. Where am I? Is this my life? No, this is Mary's life. I had to take the clock downstairs and stuff it under the couch pillows so I wouldn't hear every single second individually. Luther fell asleep and started snoring.

I thought about Tom. Up until right that minute, I would have sworn I never wanted to get married. But was this the alternative? No, it couldn't be. Just because a woman isn't married doesn't mean she has to sleep in the stern single bed of her childhood with yellow family photographs on the dresser.

Does it? Mary is a college professor. She could buy herself a king-sized bed with feather pillows if she wanted to. Although, is that any less depressing if you have the whole thing to yourself? Forever?

The idea of having a shared bedroom with his and hers sides of the closet like my parents mortified me beyond words. How predictable. How boring. But this was a different kind of awful—the disappointed kind. I lay there listening to Luther snore, trying to decide which one was worse.

I was never in my life so happy to see Mary Perry as when she got back from Ohio. I couldn't wait to curl up on my mattress on the floor of my dirty disheveled house with mayhem on its walls and impatience in its heart. I couldn't wait to pull the door shut behind me and Tom in The Pit of Sin, where a single bed is plenty big for two.

What happens if you don't know anyone you want to be like when you grow up?

What if you want to pick "Both A and B?"

What if you want to pick "None of the above?"

❦

The picture is crystal clear in my mind. I was something like seven years old, sitting on a brown folding chair in the basement of Erbs Mennonite church. Scotty and I had on the same new shoes, which means either he picked girl shoes or I picked boy shoes. I think it was him and he thinks it was me.

We were in "Children's Church." Usually, after Sunday School, we had to go upstairs to sit with our parents through the boring sermon that never ends, but on Children's Church days, we got to stay in the basement. Each Sunday School class sat in a row with our teachers. We sang kids' songs like "Jesus Loves the Little Children," and, "Running Over," and then Alma Bomberger told us a Bible story. I loved Children's Church because Alma always used the felt board for her stories. The felt board was an easel covered with felt, and she could make pictures on it by sticking felt figures to it. She made Abraham and Sarah going across the desert with their camel. They passed things like pyramids on the way. When they got to the Promised Land, she put up palm trees that came in two pieces—the brown trunk and the green top.

I remember sitting there between Sharon and Scotty. The rows were arranged according to age, so there were little kids in front of me and big kids in the back. I was thinking about my life, as Abraham and Sarah laughed at God, and baby Isaac appeared in a blue felt blanket. Next year I would be eight, and then I would be in second grade. I counted up to figure out that by the time I got to sit in the back row with the big kids, I would be twelve.

And then?

After that I would be a teenager. When you're a teenager, you go to high school. I couldn't imagine being that big, but I guessed if I was lucky enough not to get terribly sick or die in an accident, I would. And then after that, I would be big enough to get married.

I knew that after you're done going to school, there are two things you can do—one is go to college, if you're smart, and the other one is get married. I was pretty sure I was smart enough for college and of course I was going to get married. I didn't really know how it works about going to college and getting married—like, which one you should do first—but people, I already knew, got married when they were twenty. Yes, that sounded about right. I would get married when I was twenty. God would send me a husband, and we would get married. Later, when I was twenty-two or twenty-three, I would have children.

And then, well, that's all. That's what you do when you grow up.

Then Children's Church was over, so we said a prayer and we got to stand up and sing "Father Abraham" because that's what the story was about.

❦

We walk hand in hand down the middle of the dusty road.

"¡Camine! ¿Por qué corre?" *he says, and pulls on my hand to make me walk slower.*

"No estoy corriendo," *I say. Running is something else.*

The palms make moonlight puddles that ripple over our toes in the night wind. Neighbors call out hello. He pulls my hand again.

"Despacito."

Even slower? You call this walking?

I am thinking about how this is ridiculous. He said let's walk, and we are walking, sort of. I asked him where we would go and he looked at me strangely and shrugged. Like he wanted to say what do you mean, but instead he just said it again: a caminar.

Past Dona Delfina's house. Past Chino's little store. Along a live jocote fence hanging with small purple fruit. Past a dark house where no one lives, and he says we could get married and live there.

I laugh.

"¿Adónde va?" *He asks me, pulling me back again.*

"No sé," *I tell him. You walk because you're going somewhere, right? You walk fast to get where you're going.*

"Aquí solo caminamos," *he says. He puts my arm around his waist with one hand and pulls my head onto his shoulder with the other so that we are walking hip to hip.*

I feel it. It's like a dance. The slowest dance. Stepping forward to a rhythm that is like breathing.

We aren't going anywhere. We're walking. Cicadas shrill in the trees. An owl asks a riddle.

I learn to walk. How to go nowhere.

In my country, going nowhere is bad. Tonight, going nowhere is being where you are.

Don't wait for me to tell you any more about the boy. In case you're wondering, I'm not going to. I don't want to talk about it. I couldn't then, because I had no words, and I won't now, because the particulars aren't important. Anything I could say will sound trite, and nothing was trite. Everything was elemental. From the first kiss that seared my conscience to the last one of disbelief, and how he fell asleep in my lap like a baby on the way home from the beach and I wished that one hour would take the rest of my life.

Does it matter? He taught me to walk. What else do you need to know?

I'll tell you what you need to know: I didn't know I loved him until it was too late. I believed it was impossible, therefore it was. And even so it shaped me in its burning crucible, taking away what I was and making me into what I previously was not. That is all you need to know. You get the picture.

Imagine the story, if you like. Make up how it happened, what we said, where we walked. Make sure we laugh, and then we cry. Some of it will be right and some of it will be wrong. It doesn't really matter. The details are beside the point.

୨ৡ

When I moved out of the dorm to go to Costa Rica, I had no intention of moving back to campus, ever. I wouldn't have to—I was going to turn twenty-one in the fall. The college had a rule that said all full-time students had to live on campus during normal semesters until they were twenty-one. This was so we wouldn't drink—a faulty strategy which was a complete and spectacular failure. But if you want to finish your education, you have to obey the rules no matter how dumb they are. I liked the dorm well enough, but living off-campus in your own apartment with no Resident Advisors (meaning spies) and no Open Hours (meaning no boys in your room after 10 PM) was way more awesome.

Beth, Nina, and Sheila would have to go back to the dorms before September and there was nothing they could do about it. They wouldn't be twenty-one until next semester or next year. I was practically six by the time I went to kindergarten, which was a huge bummer then but was working out well for me now. I called Barb at her office to ask if I could stay. I kind of loved that dirty, rickety place. She said yes, but we still had to clean up the walls at the end of the summer. And she warned me that in the winter, the electric bill would be a lot higher.

It wasn't hard so sell my parents on the plan because the apartment cost less than the dorm, provided that I found at least two new people to live with. Also, I would have a kitchen, so I didn't need the full meal plan at the cafeteria. And nobody loves a bargain like a Mennonite does.

What can I say? The thought of new housemates brought delicious relief. Which did I want more: for Beth to leave, or for her to never go away? I didn't care either way about losing Sheila, and couldn't wait to lose Nina—I'd been dreaming of that day since she came back from Pine View. New housemates bring new problems, but sometimes new problems are more appealing than old ones. New problems sounded fantastic.

I thought even my new problems were solved when Matthew's sister Claudia said she would move in with me, and then Tom's friend Jason needed a place, too. But Claudia balked when she heard about Jason taking the other room. She said she wasn't sharing a bedroom; she needed her own. The rent was too expensive for Claudia and me by ourselves, and I didn't want to throw Jason out. The thought of a male housemate at the top of the stairs on the outskirts of town made me feel safer. I couldn't quite see sharing a room with him, though.

I toyed with the idea. Of course, we would sleep in our own beds...But, no matter how I arranged it in my mind, it was just too weird. Tom would have a conniption. That, and my schooling would be done. At a whiff of something they disapprove of, my parents stuff their wallets back into their pockets, and sleeping near boys was the top taboo. Not an option.

Claudia caved when she saw I wasn't going to. She agreed to share the big room with me, as long as we put up an enormous black dividing wall that weighed a bloody ton and would have crushed the life out of us if it had fallen. It's not that she didn't like me. She wanted privacy for when her boyfriend came over. To that end, the wall was entirely useless, let me tell you. We might as well have all three been in one bed, none of us getting any sleep.

My parents still pitched a fit about Jason. They said they were not going to pay for me to live together with a man outside of holy matrimony. I had to beg and even cry, and perform all sorts of excruciating mental contortions to make them see how desperately ridiculous they were being. Even though Jason had his own room. Even though I was sharing my room with Claudia. Even though I had my own boyfriend—a different boyfriend—who couldn't care less if a man lives in the house.

Even though having a big strapping guy in the house made it safer.

Safer. Ah, yes. This, they couldn't deny. Thank goodness I thought to say that before it was too late. Due to safety concerns, and without any lightness that could be mistaken for approval, they agreed to pay the rent for me to live under the same roof as a man I wasn't married to.

Under one condition: Do not tell Grandma. Or any cousins who might tell Aunt Judy, who would for sure tell Grandma.

So you see? Selective truth telling is not something I invented myself. Perfected, maybe, but who's going to throw the first stone?

◈

I don't know whether Neil realized that Sheila was crazy about him, or if he assumed he'd found an unusually devoted friend. He probably figured it out on the Monday morning he told her the big news: over the weekend he popped the question, and Katie said yes. Sheila suffered a sudden wave of nausea and said she had to go home. If he didn't get it then, he must have the next day when Sheila came back to work and couldn't look at him anymore. She would have quit her job to avoid him if Beth hadn't stayed up all night talking her out of it.

Sheila has the heart of an angel but she sometimes reminded me of a balloon with the air pouring out of it—so much enthusiasm, so little coordination. What she wanted more than anything else in the world was to be a mommy. Sheila had baby fever from the time she was eight. She loved children to the point of distraction, to the point of wanting to teach kindergarten five days a week, nine months out of the year.

I would shoot myself. I'm serious. I like kids and all, but large collections of small children in enclosed spaces make me as crazy as Sheila already was. I could not imagine how this would work when she graduated. I couldn't imagine how anything would work when we graduated.

She didn't want to have babies immediately, but she wanted to find their daddy. Each possibility that slipped from her radar into the abyss beyond produced floods of tragic tears. She was right about Neil. For as boring as he was, he would be a great dad. And let's not even digress among the beautiful babies that Rajesh would someday make. The ghost of childlessness laughed at her from inside the closet and behind the bed.

I couldn't really relate. I'd never been sure if I even wanted to have kids. Why was that so hard for me to imagine? But I couldn't imagine being one of those people with no kids, either. Which seemed more preposterous: me with a diaper bag and a stroller, or me as one of those dried up old ladies who nobody visits? Heads or tails?

Beth said she definitely wanted to have kids someday. Nina expected she would adopt, especially if she decided to be with a woman. Harriet was about to have babies whether she wanted them or not. She couldn't wash her own back anymore. She couldn't even move.

I was rolling onto our mattress bed where Beth lay reading *The Color Purple* one late-summer night when Harriet came waddling over to us. This was peculiar. Harriet sometimes decided to accept small amounts of affection, but she never offered it herself. Purring loudly, she stepped up on the bed and insisted on lying snuggled up against me.

Beth's book sank to her lap, and her mouth dropped open.

"She's going to have her babies," I said.

"There?!"

"Eww! No!" I removed Harriet to the rug on the floor.

She lumbered back onto the bed.

I pushed her down to the rug again, but it was useless. Harriet had made up her mind: she was getting in bed with me. I imagined she must be scared, seeing as these were her first kittens, so I let her stay. I would be petrified if I was her. That whole thing about labor and birth? That is the single most terrifying thought in the universe, if you ask me. It shouldn't be possible and it isn't fair.

A few hours later, I woke up to something fuzzy and wet poking my face. Harriet had maneuvered half of her giant self onto my pillow and was butting me with her wet, whiskery nose. She was purring even louder than before. By the streetlight through the window, I could see there were no kittens yet, but that's when I noticed the bubble. A ping-pong-ball-sized bubble stuck out of Harriet's back end. She remained perfectly calm, even as her giant vibrating belly seized with convulsions. I sat up and petted her.

"Hey. Harriet," I murmured. "You okay?"

She meowed back.

Then I saw the giant wet spot—yes, in the bed—right beside my pillow.

"Cat-water! Gross!" I meant to be quiet, but Beth rolled over and opened her eyes. She sat up.

"Is she okay?"

"Well. Her water broke in our bed."

"Ugh!" Beth scooted as far away from us as she could.

"Look at this. She has a bubble."

"Oh. Is that bad?"

"I don't know."

"Gross."

"Yeah. But she seems okay."

She did. She acted like she thought she was Queen Elizabeth.

I remembered the other time I saw a cat give birth. My mom and sisters and I were sitting on lawn chairs in the yard husking a mountain of sweet corn when Cinnamon walked up to us and laid down under Michelle's chair.

"Hey girls," Mom said, "watch that cat."

We all looked at Cinnamon. She wiggled and writhed for a moment, meowed once, and out slipped a tiny gooey kitten.

Cinnamon never had a bubble.

What if Harriet was in trouble? Was she in terrible pain? What if she died? What if her babies were dying inside her at this very moment? It's not that we wanted kittens—half the time we weren't even sure we wanted Harriet. But to die in childbirth? How can one woman let that happen to another?

"Harriet? Are you alright?" I asked, petting her.

She purred up at me with half-shut loving eyes.

I turned on the light and found the phone book. There are a lot of vets in the yellow pages, and even some serious animal-lovers with 24-hour phone numbers. I woke one of them up at 2:30 AM to tell him my laboring cat had a bubble.

"She should be okay," he said. "If she hasn't had kittens by morning, call me back."

We put Harriet into a giant cardboard box out of which

she was too fat to jump, put a towel over the wet spot in the bed, and went back to sleep.

I opened my eyes to the watery light of early summer dawn. The clock said 5:07. I stumbled to the living room to check the box. Harriet gazed up at me and began to purr again. Her belly bulged big as ever. I waited, holding my breath, but there were no more contractions.

"Shit. Oh shit."

I woke Beth who said the same thing and I dialed the vet again.

"Well," he said, "you have two choices. We can give her an injection to re-initiate labor, or she can have a cesarean section."

"How much does that cost?"

"The injection is twenty dollars and the cesarean is fifty. The danger with the shot is that her uterus is tired. If it tears, then we have to do a cesarean too."

I said we would call him back in a few minutes.

"That damn cat."

"What?"

I repeated the bad news.

"Shit," Beth said.

"Why don't we just tell him to put her to sleep? It has to be cheaper. I mean, we don't even want these kittens."

"Diana, we can't. Nina will die."

"Shit."

She was right. Nina didn't necessarily want kittens either, or love Harriet more than the rest of us, but that would have put her over the edge.

"If we kill Harriet, Nina will kill herself."

"You're right," I had to admit. "She will."

"She'll go completely crazy."

"I know. I know," said. "But *I* will go crazy if we have to pay seventy dollars for a cat to have kittens! God!"

"Well, what should we do?"

"Wake up Sheila and Nina. They have to help decide. Because if they aren't going to pay, I am going to have her put to sleep. And if I have to take Nina and drop her off at Pine View on the way, I will."

We decided to try the injection.

I biked to Tom's house, woke him up, and made him understand that I needed his car keys now, that Harriet was having her babies and her contractions stopped and I hadn't slept all night and Nina was going to lose it again and we had to take her—Harriet—to the vet right *now*. So, *HURRY!*

The vet called us back at 7:30 AM to tell us we could pick up our cat. The shot worked, and Harriet was nursing six healthy kittens.

Six. Healthy.

Dr. White told us that Harriet has a "very small pelvis" and an "unusually tiny birth canal." It cost forty dollars when he rang it up—twenty for the shot and twenty for the emergency visit at 5:30 in the morning. We divided the bill and each paid twice our weekly food allowance for our cat and her six squeaking babies. They were born huge, with their eyes already opening. All six of them were indeed healthy as horses and not one of them died.

From then on, Harriet became my cat and we loved each other. She chose me and I helped her in her moment of need. At least that's what she thought. It was Nina who saved her life, but I let her believe what she wanted. I am the one, though, who scratched together the money to have her fixed so that her "small pelvis" and "unusually tiny birth canal" would not cost us immense amounts of money and suffering three times a year for the rest of her amazingly long life.

❧◊❧

I decided to cut off my hair. Not for the Sinead look like Nina, but because I always suspected I would be crazy-cute with an Amish-boy bowl cut. This might be a fine place to digress and ask if anyone except Amish boys should even attempt an Amish-boy bowl cut, but here's the problem: I was curious. I can't stand being curious. Eventually, I cave. Always.

"I'm going to give myself a haircut," I announced to the household in general.

"You're so brave," Sheila said.

"If I need help, will you help me?" I asked.

"Me! Oh no! I, um— You should ask Beth!"

Beth was painting mean-looking birds above the couch with her Walkman on so she didn't hear me.

I went over and tapped her on the shoulder.

"Yeah?"

"I'm going to give myself a haircut. If I get stuck, will you help me?"

"Sure," she said, and turned back to the wall. I was starting to worry about how we would get all that mess off, and there she was, still painting.

I opened a drawer of The Desk and took out our scissors.

Everyone who had left for the summer was trickling back into town and I needed to look different. I couldn't stand the idea of seeming like the same girl I'd been last year, because I didn't feel like the same one. So what if I couldn't explain what had changed? I just needed to be new, somehow, and that's all. Since I couldn't lose twenty pounds by the weekend or afford a new wardrobe, I went into the kitchen to fish around for the right bowl.

It might be called a "bowl cut," but I can tell you it is not produced by tracing an actual bowl. No matter how I placed the bowl, if it covered the back of my head, it didn't leave me any bangs at all. I stood giggling at myself in front of the bathroom mirror wearing the biggest bowl I found, but I could see this was not going to produce a look that was remotely cute. So I ditched the literal bowl and kept the bowl idea, cutting around my face, across my ears, and hacking off a foot of light brown locks in the back.

The front wasn't that hard to get straight but the sides didn't want to be the same. I worked and worked to make them even, but every time I got it right, I shook my head and they were wrong again. There was hair everywhere, and I could not see at all what I was doing to the back of my head. Cutting blind made me nervous because the long colorful hair wrap from the Grateful Dead show was back there and I did not want to amputate it.

I learned something new about myself that day: my hair is curly when it's short. I'd gotten my hair cut before, but not like this. My parents would never have permitted a girl to have a boy's haircut. The Apostle Paul nixed that possibility about 2,000 years ago in a letter that my kind of Mennonites take as a fashion mandate. I couldn't believe my eyes as boisterous brown curls flipped every which way around my ears. Cutting your own hair is hard enough even if it doesn't turn out to be curly. If it turns out curly, it's impossible.

I stuck my hacked-up head out of the bathroom and called for Beth.

She let out a hoot of laughter when she saw me, said something like, "Oh honey," and snatched the scissors.

I was right. I am kind of cute with an Amish-boy bowl cut. Anyway, I looked different, alright. Tom tried to smile supportively, but the best he could do was raise his eyebrows and mumble, "I liked your long hair."

Right. So did I. But I always wanted an Amish-boy bowl cut, and you don't know until you try.

❧

We waited all summer for those pears. The first time we mowed the yard, I noticed little green balls hanging from the trees as I circled around them. I assumed they must be apples. They looked a little like mutants though, and for a while I worried they might be crab apples. I bit into a crab apple once when I was about ten years old. It's one of those things, like bowl cuts, that very curious people do. I thought the little crab apple couldn't be all that bad—but it was all that bad and worse. I hoped to God we didn't have two giant crab apple trees. Imagine the irony—four hungry girls with two trees of inedible fruit. All we needed was a talking snake.

Fortunately as the summer matured, the crab apples turned into pears. We waited forever for them to yellow. Beth painted a tree with giant yellow fruit on the wall facing the window, hoping the lazy trees would peek in and get the idea. Nina went into the yard to put her hands on them and bless them. Beth saved our coffee grounds and carried full cans outside to dump over their roots. I made each one a bead necklace for her trunk.

I knew pears ripen in August because I remembered how my mother would "do pears" right before the misery of summer ended and I was released back into the joy of school. "Doing pears" meant canning them: coring, peeling and cutting them, then boiling them in glass Mason jars full of sugar syrup so we could eat them during the rest of the year when pears weren't in season. As a child, I didn't realize that "canned fruit" meant it could come in an actual can.

When the pears finally came, they came at once—two trees hanging with ripe juicy yellow pears on the tail end of a summer devoid of fruit. We couldn't reach them where they grew high up in the branches, so we had to wait until they dropped to the ground like sweet, fat rain. Then we had to figure out what to do about the bees.

❦

"Oh my God! Bees!" Sheila screamed, and ran away waving her arms. "I'm allergic to bees!"

Beth turned tail and ran, too. So did I.

These were not lazy honey bees, either. By the time the ripe pears hit the ground, they were riddled with little holes made by hungry birds and commandeered by furious yellow jackets. But we were every bit as hungry as the birds and just as furious as the yellow jackets that were filling up the yard. We couldn't even mow the grass for all the mushy, buzzing, rotting fruit.

"I know what we can do," I told Beth.

"What?"

"Let's wake up early tomorrow."

"Why?"

"Because yellow jackets can't fly around when it's cold."

"They can't?"

"No."

"Why?"

"I don't know. No bees can. And it's wet. Their wings stick to them."

That made her laugh.

"Want to?"

"Sure. Like how early?"

"I don't know. Five thirty?"

"Damn, girl." But the way she said it meant, yes.

I woke up in the chilly dawn that didn't feel like summer anymore, and reached over to shake Beth. She mumbled, scowled at me, remembered the pears, and sat up.

The wet grass was cold on our bare feet, and as I predicted, only the bravest and most desperate yellow jackets were hopping sluggishly around. First we gorged ourselves, standing there giggling in the hazy slanted sunlight, pear juice dripping from our lips, our fists, our elbows. We devoured pear after pear, still cool from the fresh night, free and ridiculously sweet. Then Beth collected the best ones into plastic bags to take inside for later. I picked up the broken ones, the rotten ones, the ones full of holes, and lobbed them into Nina's abandoned garden where the yellow jackets could feast without posing any serious risk to Sheila.

If I could have canned them like my mom, we would have had pears until Christmas. Instead, we ate them as fast as they fell, racing the spreading brown spots that threatened to devour them first. We didn't stop until not a pear was left anywhere and the refrigerator hummed empty again.

❧

Nina and Beth went out for a Talk—the kind with a capital T—about Dan and everything, leaving Sheila and me in an unusually quiet house. I took my notebook and climbed out the kitchen window onto the porch roof to write a letter in Spanish. In my mind, I was so far away that I didn't see Sheila stick her head out the window beside me.

"Hey," she said.

It scared me so bad I almost screamed. I jumped and dropped my pen, which rolled down the roof into the rain gutter. I know Sheila doesn't understand Spanish, but I have a paranoia about people looking over my shoulder when I write. It freaks me out. Even when I'm not writing something secret, like I was at that moment.

"Oh! I'm sorry!" she said.

"You scared me," I tried to laugh, and hoped I looked casual about flipping my notebook shut.

"I'm so sorry, Diana!"

"No, it's okay. What?"

"You lost your pen."

"It doesn't matter. I have a hundred."

"Um. Never mind."

"What?"

"I didn't know you were busy."

"I'm not! Plus I lost my pen."

"Oh, okay. Well, um. Want me to teach you to belly dance?"

I couldn't believe my ears. "You know how?!"

"Well, no. I mean, kind of. I mean like, I know how you're supposed to do it, but I'm not very good."

"I have the belly, but I'm not very coordinated," I said squinting up at her in the window."

"Shut up."

"But, yeah! Show me."

I climbed back through the window into the house with Sheila and put the letter under my mattress for later.

"Okay," Sheila began, after we closed the curtains to avoid entertaining the neighbors. "Put your hands like this." She poked her elbows out to the sides and put one hand on top of, and the other under, her bust.

We were standing in front of Nina's full-length mirror in our underwear. Sheila insisted that's how you have to start. In this pose, we looked more like two naked nuns than belly dancers. She says her mom used to practice with her when she was little, but the instructions stopped when her mom went on a Christianity kick. Sheila's mom's kicks added a lot of variety to her life.

"You move everything below your arms—like your legs and your hips—while you keep everything above your arms still. Like this."

She began stepping her feet and twitching her hips to some silent, magical rhythm that made her pink panty-clad belly swing and tremble. Above it, her head and shoulders were almost perfectly still.

"No way!" I marveled. "Sheila!" She's the last person on earth I suspected of having so much control.

As soon as she remembered herself, the music stopped and she collapsed into giggles.

"Shut up! I'm not very good! I'm so embarrassed."

Belly dancing didn't go so well for me. Try moving the lower half of your body while the upper half stays stock still. I'd say it couldn't be done if Sheila hadn't just demonstrated.

Not only is dividing yourself in half nearly impossible, this was the first attention I'd ever paid to my hips. I'd noticed their usefulness for carrying things like heavy books or baby cousins, but I had never considered them as separate from the trunk of my body like you do with a leg or an arm. It's not in my genes. In my four hundred years of somber Mennonite ancestry, there has been as little hip-swaying as possible.

"This is hard!" I gasped. We were both sweating and my abs hurt.

"I know. You have to concentrate."

"But it looks easy when you do it."

"Loosen your hips. Try to—"

"I'm trying. I can't—"

"Bend your knees a little more, and... Yeah! See? That's better!"

My blue-clad belly wasn't cooperating as well as her pink one, and my shoulders kept tilting back and forth.

"Aaggh!" I crumbled to the floor clutching my ribs. "No more! Sheila, you're killing me!"

My instructor dropped down beside me. Lying on the floor was an adventure in nastiness after an entire summer of not having a vacuum cleaner. But at least we had a shower.

"Thanks."

"Oh. Yeah. You're welcome," Sheila said, remembering to be self-conscious.

"Man. I should have learned this before I went to Costa Rica. You have to dance that Spanish music with your hips, too."

"Can you teach me that?"

"Ha! No! I can't even do it myself."

We lay there in the grime, tingly and tired.

"Have you ever been to India?" I asked her.

"No."

"Do you think you'll ever go?"

"I hope. Sometime. My mom wants to go. Maybe I'll go with her. I don't want to go by myself."

"Why?"

"Because. I don't know anybody. I have all these uncles and aunts and cousins that I don't know. I can't even talk to them. I don't know where they live or anything. If I go by myself, I'll be totally lost."

"Oh."

"Do you think you'll ever go back to Costa Rica?"

I thought for a minute. "I don't know."

"Why not? You seem like you loved it there. You should."

"Yeah. I know. Maybe I will."

Then I told her something that even I didn't know until I heard myself say it. "But if I go there again, I'm never coming back."

"What do you mean?"

"I mean if I ever go there again, I'm not coming back. I left once. I don't think I could do it again."

"Oh. Wow."

"Yeah."

I couldn't believe I'd said that. This giddy feeling bubbled through my whole body and I knew I'd tripped over something true.

❧

I vomit on the bus. I stumble forward, grab the trash can, and vomit. The mango comes tumbling out of me, the disgusted bus driver eyeing me in his rear view mirror.

I make myself breathe.

I stepped onto the bus in the perfect sun of this suffocating April morning. The door closed behind me. Chicharras screamed from the trees.

Every minute, I am getting farther and farther away. Everything is done. Everything that was going to happen has happened. Nothing is left now. Nothing. But pictures in my notebook and stories with no words.

I am on the bus. I am nowhere.

We enter the cold dark capital city where my life is waiting to take me back. I am split wide open, broken like the mango I tore with my teeth. All that is left is the seed.

❧

There is no reason why that shower couldn't actually have been brown. The toilet and the sink were white porcelain from a previous historical period, so it's no surprise the fiberglass shower wedged into the corner didn't match. Brown isn't quite the right word. It was more like tan—a graded shade of tan that started as eggshell white at the top and darkened to a rich earth tone on the floor. I appreciated how forward-thinking it was of the owners to choose a brown shower for a rental apartment.

I wasn't even mad on the day I decided to clean the bathroom—it just seemed like the decent thing to do before my new housemates arrived. Obviously, either I would do it, or nobody would. I was the one who was staying, so that kind of thing was my problem.

I dumped some bleach into the toilet bowl and swished the water around with the flyswatter since we didn't have a toilet brush. I'm sure the flyswatter benefited from that as much as the potty. Then I poured bleach into the sink and wiped it with a rag. It wasn't a bad job at all, once you get started. I should have done this months ago.

I turned the shower on for a moment to wet it and slung a generous splash of bleach onto the floor. With my brand new scrub brush in hand, I knelt down and stuck my head into the fumes that the bottle so grimly cautioned against inhaling. I was not at all prepared for what happened when the water, the bleach and my stiff new brush met with the tan of that shower floor. A pale smudge began to emerge.

"Crap," I said out loud. I knew I shouldn't have used bleach on something brown. Way to go.

Then it dawned on me. A multicolored fiberglass shower? In shades of tan? White at the top, brown at the bottom? White around the outside, brown on the inside? Holy God, you have got to be kidding me.

I scrubbed some more, and watched another patch of eggshell white emerge.

No. Way. I swear I felt bugs crawling on me.

I stood up and tried scrubbing at shoulder height where the white began its fade to tan. To say it came right off would be untrue, but when I pushed hard, the tan layer yielded to my brush.

Now I had a choice to make between two dreadful options: either I spend the rest of the afternoon scrubbing the horrible brown shower to whiteness, or I screw the lid back onto the bleach and see if I could convince everyone else of my original thought—that I had ruined a tan fiberglass finish with bleach. I might be able to pull it off. Who would really care, anyway?

I never thought I'd see the day when I heard myself say this, but I did: I cared. For all the crud in the kitchen, all the filth on the floor, the lack of sanitary measures in The Pit of Sin and the chaos on the walls, the idea of standing buck naked that close to the grime and dead skin cells of everybody else who had ever stood naked in there? I couldn't do it. Not now, anyway. I guess I had a little dignity after all. I thought of Mamá Hilda in Los Rios, tossing bleach at the rough cement of the shower and scraping it with her broom. I thought that shower was mildly gross because of the damp smell and the cobwebs in the corners. But it was a thousand times cleaner than this.

Beth walked in because she had to pee. "Are you crazy?" she asked me. There was sweat dripping from my nose, and bleach water everywhere.

"Probably," I said. "But look."

"Oh my God!"

"I know."

"It's white!"

"Can you believe this?"

"Ewww!" she yowled in disgust. "Gross!"

Nina appeared in the doorway to see what was so nasty.

"I cannot believe you're touching that," Beth grimaced.

Nina put her hand to her mouth and didn't say anything.

"It's too awful," I said. "I wish I didn't care. But I do."

The brown shower crossed the line. I didn't even know I had a line regarding how much dirt is ok, but I guess I do. You don't always anticipate, ahead of time, what is going to be too much, but never fear—when it stares you in the face, you recognize it.

৩৯৫

I'm not kidding. I went straight to the Registrar's office to unload my English minor as soon as the CLOSED sign flipped to OPEN. I swapped it out for Women's Studies. With a Theatre major and Women's Studies minor, I would graduate fully prepared for absolutely nothing that I could think of and I didn't care. Life is short. I hadn't come to college to read books I hated.

In classes like Liberation Theology, and Women in Text and Image I would be safe from Camus, Sartre and the dripping Bog People. Give me Erika Jong, or give me death. No more drawing symbolism from sludge. Forget picking apart the seven levels of hell. Stop the contrived comparisons.

I wanted to read books that kept me up at night, not that put me to sleep. I wanted to write stories that are so true, they frighten me. And poems that grab you and shake you and speak to your internal organs. Maybe I'd try writing a play. Ever since I read *The Night of the Iguana,* I'd been thinking about it. If I could just get enough quiet around me to hear myself think, maybe I could figure out what I was trying to say. I don't think there's a minor for that, although Women's Studies has to be a step in the right direction.

Since we used water colors on the walls, we all assumed that soap and water would clean everything off. Wrong. Not water, not soapy water, not soapy water with bleach. Not Ajax, not Heavy Duty Mr. Clean, and Drain-O took off the paint underneath as well. I called Barb to let her know we hit a glitch, praying she wouldn't come over to see.

She didn't. Barb, still patient, agreed to buy multiple gallons of white paint and use our free labor to do some home improvement. I felt sadder than I expected about covering up the craziness like that. I mean, it was awful, but it was ours. It told a story, if you knew how to read it—like a totem pole, but flat and without the chronology of vertical design.

Everybody had to paint one room. I took the living room, Beth painted our bedroom, Sheila painted hers, and Nina had to do the kitchen. I, for one, was not about to paint over that creature and neither were Beth nor Sheila. We all volunteered so quickly to paint a different room that she got the kitchen by default. The kitchen was a big job for little Nina, but she didn't make us try to explain.

We left the whole apartment looking lots better than we found it, especially the puke-yellow kitchen. The place felt as strange as a foreign country when we finished, all white and innocent. I swear it was quieter. The air seemed easier to breathe without that living mural growing on its walls like moss.

"Lucky you. I wish I was staying too," Sheila said.

"Come visit any time," I told her. But I knew she wouldn't.

I wrote down Beth's new dorm room number and the phone extension so I could stop by when I went to campus. She volunteered to take the extra-tiny room at the end of the hall because in that one, you didn't have to have a roommate if you didn't want one. She didn't. Even I was still going to have a roommate.

❦

"It smells like paint in here," is what Jason said when he walked in with his gaggle of backpacks and his guitar.

"Yeah," I told him. "We painted all over the walls and then we couldn't get it off. So we had to redo everything."

"You should have left it," he said.

"Naaah," I answered. "It was kind of a lot."

Both Jason and Claudia had been to Costa Rica too, so finally I could talk about it without having to say everything. I played my Juan Luis Guerra tape until it was threadbare and nobody begged for Paula Abdul. They'd both been to more Grateful Dead shows than I had, so no one rolled their eyes at me or made comments about people who deal with issues by not dealing with them. I could be lost sometimes, and they didn't accuse me of not caring.

Classes started again. Harriet weaned her giant babies. I put an empty Tampax box in my closet to hide the letters that kept coming.

From outside in the night sky, Chino's silent moon looked through the window at me under the quilts in my chilly bed like it was trying to tell me something. I had a feeling that when I figured out what it was saying, I would know how to be okay.

৽৽৽

Years passed before I saw that 11th Street house again. I don't get to travel a lot. Living in Costa Rica, you have to consider that half your income is the fact that you're never cold. And that is not the half you can put toward plane tickets.

Beth went to grad school a few states away, so she made a few weddings and reunions. She told me she went by that crumbling house we shared, and that our stairway is gone. The two floors are reunited and the house is just a regular house again; it isn't apartments anymore. She said a family lives there, now. Not our kind of family—the kind with parents and children. Maybe the owners got tired of the constant coming and going of penniless students who never clean. Maybe the complaining neighbors wore them down. I guess our kitchen isn't a kitchen now, either. The living room isn't a living room. Somebody's husband's Sunday sportcoats are probably hanging above a row of shoes in The Pit of Sin.

I wonder if the kids don't ever lie on their beds when the evening sun is at a slant and pretend to see pictures on the walls.

"I see a flower."

"I see a cow."

"I see a whole bunch of triangles going like this..."

"Over there it says shit."

"I'm telling mom you said a bad word!"

I wonder if the mother didn't buy a big mirrored dresser to place in front of that unnerving expanse of wall in the sunny south-facing bedroom, because somehow it seemed to be staring at her.

The year I turned 40 I was finally in the States for the summer, so I took a little road trip and swung through my alma mater. I had tea with Mary Perry at the retirement home, and we laughed about the crazy iris combinations that bloomed after Beth and I dug them all up and replanted them randomly. I walked into the campus theatre, stood on the empty stage, and breathed a while with the familiar spirits there. Then I went to see the house. Down shady 8th street, across the railroad tracks, past some sort of industrial monstrosity that didn't used to be there, and then—sure enough. There's it was. I didn't make it up.

If you scraped away the paint upstairs, you would see everything I've told you about. It's just there like something archeological from another age. They put new siding on the house, thank God, which makes the edges crisper, otherwise it looks the same. Except that our door has turned back into a window and the little porch is gone, along with all sign of our precious, wobbly steps.

Afterword

Before we graduated, Tom and I decided to get married. We didn't know when—maybe in a year? That sounded about right. He didn't drop to one knee and produce a ring, or anything ridiculous; it's more like we decided it one morning. One morning through hangovers, with biscuits and gravy.

Okay, it was my idea.

We'd both gotten internships in Indianapolis, because what were we supposed to do? Break up because we graduated? That didn't make any sense. For the first year, we could live in a shared apartment with other interned graduates, but eventually you have to get married or set up two households. Which also makes zero sense. By now you know that our only hope of sharing expenses without destroying our families was to get married. So we kind of gave in. People have gotten married to please their families for centuries—what's the big deal? That's why they invented marriage in the first place. For some reason,

I didn't want to make an announcement. I didn't like when people congratulated me, which is not how I expected to feel after I went to so much work making Tom understand what the choices were.

There was one thing I needed to do before we went off into the world to start our internships, get married and begin our Bohemian Mennonite future: I had to go to Costa Rica.

Everything that happened there, had happened two years ago. Two and a half, to be exact. And this was my last chance to go back, ever. Figure it out: From here on, Tom and I would do everything together. I wouldn't be happy about my husband taking vacations without me, so obviously I wouldn't be taking them without him. And I knew I could never take Tom to Los Rios. Not that he wouldn't want to go. Not that he wouldn't be welcome. The problem was me. I couldn't.

I needed a two-week visit, that's all. Of course your memory idealizes things, and two and a half years later, there was no way I would find everything as delightful and picturesque as I remember it. What about the cockroaches? Don't you remember how awful? What about the scorpions? Don't you remember how terrifying? What about earthquakes and how miserable you are when you wake up in the morning to discover no water comes from the tap? The family toilet becomes unspeakable. Yes, yes. You forget about these things. Just because all I could remember were blissful afternoons and starlit strolls doesn't mean that I would therefore be happy if I went completely crazy and tried to live there. Hello. Smell the coffee. How would I support myself? Plus, it's easy think you're in love with someone who writes you heart-breaking letters, someone you never have to put up with in person, who effectively exists in your imagination. I know that.

I swear my intention was to close a chapter. And that's what happened. A chapter closed, just not the one I intended.

❧❧

Rain falls in sheets from the near black heavens onto the tin roof above the open corridor where we rest on a thin blanket. The immensity of infinite water, deep night, primordial sound. Speech drowns in our mouths.

I lie with my head on the belly of the potter who is not imaginary. These are the fingers that carve the letters onto the pages that fly to me like precious birds. Everywhere all around, deafening dark rain more tremendous than mountains.

I could say that a voice speaks to me, saying not to be afraid, but there is no sound other than water coming down.

I see. I understand everything now.

❧❧

On my second return from Los Rios I was more undone than on the first, but this time I could make out the writing on the wall. It said that I'd found my place, and it wasn't with Tom. It wasn't in the dark wings of the theatre where I'd landed a coveted internship. It was far away in the middle of nowhere in the mud and the dust with more questions than answers and a sweet if inexplicable peace in my gut that only stopped twisting there.

I told Tom I couldn't marry him. Yes, it was my idea. Yes, I changed my mind if you must say it that way. It was as horrible as you might think. We both cried ourselves sick—he because I destroyed him for no reason at all, I in a confused catharsis of terror and relief.

The third time I opened my passport for the entry stamp at San Jose's Juan Santamaria International Airport, I had no intention of taking the return flight.

I don't know where Sheila is, but I heard she married Tony Royal, the cafeteria thief. I can only assume they've taken to more honorable means of procuring food for their family. And Nina, I don't know. She's not nineteen anymore, so most things must be easier. She's a survivor with the sense to ask for help when she needs it which is not something all of us can do.

Beth and I never stopped being friends. Maybe for a moment we did, but if I hadn't gone and immortalized the bad days, we would both have forgotten them. You do that. You forget the bad days. I know, because I have decades of diaries in boxes—diaries overflowing, mostly, with frustrations I don't remember. We probably won't be roommates in a nursing home because there's no way I am going to have the money for that type of luxury.

But then again, we aren't 95 yet.

About the Author

Diana Zimmerman was born in the traditional Mennonite community of Lancaster County, Pennsylvania. She received a B.A. in Theatre from Goshen College, Goshen, Indiana, in 1993. Her poetry has been published by Goshen College's *Pinchpenny Press, Rust+Moth, When Women Waken,* and *Rhubarb Magazine.* In 2014, her poem "A Perfectly Good Woman/El Tren" was nominated for a Pushcart Prize. Diana's first work of prose, an early-childhood memoir called *When the Roll Is Called a Pyonder,* was released in 2014 by Electio Publishing. Diana publishes poetry and personal ponderings on her blog www.dianarenee.com. Since 1995, Diana has resided almost exclusively in the Guanacaste province of Costa Rica. She is currently accompanied by her three surf boards and two cats.